NEW YORK CALLING

NEW YORK CALLING

FROM BLACKOUT TO BLOOMBERG

edited by Marshall Berman and Brian Berger

REAKTION BOOKS

Published by
REAKTION BOOKS LTD
33 Great Sutton Street
London EC1V 0DX, UK
www.reaktionbooks.co.uk

First published 2007

Printed and bound in China by C&C Offset Printing Co. Ltd

British Library Cataloguing in Publication Data
New York calling: from blackout to Bloomberg
   1. New York (N.Y.) – Social conditions – 20th century
   2. New York (N.Y.) – Social conditions – 21st century
   3. New York (N.Y.) – Social life and customs – 20th century
   4. New York (N.Y.) – Social life and customs – 21st century
   5. New York (N.Y.) – Economic conditions – 20th century
   6. New York (N.Y.) – Economic conditions – 21st century
   7. New York (N.Y.) – Intellectual life – 20th century
   8. New York (N.Y.) – Intellectual life – 21st century
   I. Berman, Marshall, 1940– II. Berger, Brian
   974.7'1043

ISBN-10: 1 86189 338 8
ISBN-13: 978 1 86189 338 3

Permissions: 'At Least it's Not New York', © Richard Meltzer, reprinted by permission of the author.
'The Homeless', portions of which have appeared in different form in Margaret Morton, *Fragile Dwelling*
(New York, 2000), © Aperture, New York, reprinted with permission.

Contents

THE THINGS WE DO 239

Introduction

Marshall Berman

Spirit is a power only by looking the negative in the face and living with it.
Living with it is the magic power that converts the negative into being.
—Hegel, *The Phenomenology of Spirit* (1807)

London is drowning, I live by the river.
—The Clash, "London Calling" (1979)

You know that nice park in the South Bronx? . . .
the block is burning down on one side of the street,
and the kids are trying to build something on the other.
—Grace Paley, "Somewhere Else" (1985)

When I was a child in the Bronx more than half a century ago, New York's publicly owned radio station WNYC used to make this announcement every hour on the hour, all through the day and night: "This is Station WNYC, New York City, where seven million people"—at some point in the early 1960s it became eight million—"live in peace and harmony, and enjoy the benefits of democracy." I was thrilled by this language. Later on I learned that it was a gift of the New Deal and the Popular Front. By the time I arrived, historians seem to think, these movements were exhausted, worn out. But their language sounded fresh and alive to me.

What did those big ideas mean? They meant that New York was full of grand material structures—the Harbor (still thriving all through my childhood), the Statue of Liberty, great buildings, Times Square, Penn and Grand Central Stations, Central Park, the Brooklyn Bridge, and many more; we should learn to love them but also to understand their human costs. Our family weekends often featured structures. From the deck of a ferry or a skyscraper, we would exclaim, "Wow!" (I'm still happy to exclaim it.) Then my mother would say something like, "Isn't it beautiful? And don't forget, you can

get here on the subway." And my father would say something like, "And don't forget who built this." "Who?" I would ask. Before long I caught on and knew the answer: "People we never heard of, who worked themselves to death." It was only later on that I realized they meant people *like them* who worked themselves to death. (My mother was valedictorian of her high school but never had a chance to go to college. When I went, and learned about "alienated labor," she was delighted, and used the phrase for the rest of her life.) But they were proud of the city that anonymous, exploited, alienated people like them had built. The bad deals they had got in their lives were mitigated by their pride in being part of what they loved to say was "the greatest city in the world." The message on the air was a melody they could dance to. The New York they hoped to pass on to us was a real community, a place where the sadness of individual lives—and there was plenty—could be overcome by the glory and harmony of the whole.

When I left New York at the start of the 1960s to go to graduate school in England, I could hear the message till my ship, the SS *United States*, was well out on the sea. When I came back at the end of the '60s to teach at City College, part of the City University of New York, the message was gone. No one could remember when it went, or why. (I wrote to WNYC, and its Public Affairs Department said it would get back to me, but it never did.) I asked people, and many people told me, "Don't ask!" It took me awhile to read their melancholy. What they meant was that New York as an idealized beloved community was gone with the wind, and nothing could bring it back.

I wouldn't accept this. I had come back here for New York's very special form of peace, harmony, and democracy, and I was determined to enjoy them. Forty years later, I'm still determined. But honestly, I had no idea then how far my city of dreams had unraveled, and how much more it was still going to come apart.

Yet New Yorkers have a wonderful capacity to *live through* disintegration, to build up even while they are burning down. And in fact, day after day, year after year, all through the latter part of the twentieth century, we were bombarded by visions of our city coming apart and falling down. "The disintegration of New York" became a media cliché, but it was rooted in something real. The terrorist attacks on 9/11 were the climax of a long wave—that's what historians call these things, "long waves"—that had been breaking and crashing against us for years. A year or so later, Bruce Springsteen released a beautiful album, *The Rising*. The album begins with a heartrending dirge, "My City of Ruins." "The Rising" says about cities what Springsteen has always said about men and women: the trauma of falling into ruins offers us a post-traumatic chance to rise, to rebuild ourselves in a better way. We didn't ask for the trauma, and we don't want it, yet if we look it in the face and live with it, we can become more than we are.

Before my story starts, I need to make a point about New York's story. It is a story as rich in ironies as it is in skyscrapers. One of the things that made the late twentieth century so bitter here is one of the things that has always made New York so sweet: its intense and vibrant street life. Our nineteenth-century street system, built for pedestrians to walk around in, and our early-twentieth-

century mass-transit system, built to move streets full of people en bloc, constitute public space of a breadth and depth undreamt of in the rest of the US (and possibly unmatched in the rest of the world). A random walk in the street or ride on the train can give us a splendid view of the abundance, diversity, and color of New York life. All of our people's energy and beauty are there to see, hear, feel in the street. But this means that our strains and rages are out in the street as well. Openness of being is one thing that makes New York a thrill. But openness may lead our tensions and struggles—between classes, between races and ethnic groups, between men and women, between generations—to boil over openly, in front of everybody. The New York street strips us naked, sometimes in the midst of people we may not want to be naked with. But it strips them naked, too.

One of the first changes that struck me when I came back was the *violence.* When I was growing up, urban violence was pretty scary (I was a victim more than once), yet it was limited, ritualized, mediated by established gangs, and it consisted mostly of acts that teenagers did to each other. The Fordham Baldies and the Savage Skulls had no interest in adults and pretty much left them alone. (This is why adults often described the 1950s as safe; they weren't so safe for kids.) Starting in the 1960s, a new kind of violence broke out, propelled by a hard-drug epidemic that brought millions of new people, mostly amateurs, into the cast. I can't explain why it broke out. The endless American "war on drugs" and its enormous police apparatus made it worse. Still, there really were dangerous drugs out there, and the craving for them, and for the danger, were not created by the police. The violence of the late '60s was driven by addiction and its desperate, anarchic, insatiable needs. Gangs could and did make truces, but if you were supporting a habit, you were in a state of war with everybody, including the people nearest and dearest to you, and the war could never end. Drug addiction can help explain why, after thirty years of remarkable stability in homicides, from the early 1930s to the late 1950s, in the span of barely a decade, from 1959 to 1971, the number of killings more than *quadrupled*. (In many other American cities, increases were even worse.) Humphrey Bogart in *Casablanca* (1942) warns the Nazis, "There are certain sections of New York, Major, that I wouldn't advise you to try to invade." The drug epidemic that started in the 1960s collapsed the distance between those neighborhoods and all the rest.

I was a lifelong New Yorker happy to be home, and I was pretty blasé; I couldn't believe there was anything significant about city life that I didn't know. I found out I was wrong. My first spring back, in my shabby but solidly middle-

class apartment house on the Upper West Side, someone left their keys in the front door. Within five minutes a junkie had seen and seized them, broken into the building, beaten up two women, and grabbed all the goods he could hold. Police stopped him a block away; he was carrying too much stuff and foaming at the mouth. Some people remembered him from the appliance shop around the corner, where he had worked for years. The cops said the same thing could happen again tomorrow. *You folks can't leave anything unlocked anymore; the city's full of people running around out of control.* I recall I gave them quite an argument: "Oh, come on, surely you exaggerate," I said. Was I really so clueless? I had a lot to learn.

I learned plenty at CCNY. When I arrived there in the fall of 1967, I instantly felt at home in the South Campus Cafeteria. It was the most brilliant, hilarious conversational environment I've ever been part of. (Woody Allen joked about it in *Bananas* in 1971, and right away I could see why.) I was happy to smoke marijuana there; it was a fine accompaniment, and sometimes a stimulant, to the fabulous symposium that went on till they shut the building down at night, and it went on even then. The late-'60s spirit moved people to share it all—not only drugs but books ("Here, you'll love this"), clothes ("Here, you'll look great in this"), confessions—of thefts, betrayals, abortions, bad trips, suicide attempts—always with a smile. But the late-'60s counterculture, so delightful for me and other people who were already grown up, was a lot more toxic for people who weren't grown up yet. Among kids I knew, drug use escalated faster than the Vietnam War. As the '60s turned into the '70s, the great Cafeteria conversation seemed to slacken off. Now more of the kids at the tables were totally faded out; whatever planets they were on, they were lonely ones (cf. "Lonely Planet Boy" of 1972 by the New York Dolls). I came to feel that the kids who were doing drugs most were least equipped to handle them; their ego identities (thank you, Erik Erikson) were most like frail reeds. I saw kids who were sweet acid-heads in 1969 drop out and come back as angry, snarling junkies panhandling on St Mark's Place in 1971. One year I lost two students who died of drug ODs. I talked with a drug counselor, and he said, "Are you sure they were the only ones?" But how could I be sure? I started telling my kids they "weren't ready" for the stuff they were doing, they were "too young"—and in the instant I said it, I felt myself *geworfen* into middle age. I was barely thirty, just a little older than many of them. Overnight I became prematurely mature, a kind of hippie square, saying things I never dreamed I'd say: *Stop! Don't do it! Get out! Get in a program! Get clean! Go home!*

It took the city years to learn how to defend against the next great collective catastrophe: *fires.* Starting late in the '60s, they burst out mainly in poor minority neighborhoods all over town but also in ethnically and economically mixed neighborhoods like my own Upper West Side. For years, midnight fires ate up not only buildings but whole blocks, often block after block. Then we found out that even while large sections of the city were burning down, most massively in the South Bronx, their firehouses were being closed and the size of their crews was being reduced—on the grounds that they were losing population. This was done according to a formula created by the urban division of the RAND Corporation (the Pentagon's R&D subsidiary) to give '70s politicians all over America an "objective," "impartial," and supposedly non-racist basis for slashing social services. Dozens of ordinary nice neighborhoods, like the one where I grew up, were being deprived of fire protection exactly when they were burning down. They morphed into gigantic, twisted, grotesque ruins—"recent ruins", in choreographer and composer Meredith Monk's apt phrase.

In the 1980s, trying to convey the horrific process New York was going through, I called it *Urbicide*. It went a long way back. My school, CCNY, the place I've been for forty years, is set on Harlem Heights, roughly between 130th and 140th Streets. In the late 1960s, on nice days I liked to walk home along the side streets in the 130s, between Amsterdam Avenue and Broadway. When I first arrived, those streets were jammed with boys playing ball, girls jumping rope, mothers feeding babies, old folks playing cards. But from one school year to the next, or even from fall to spring, I could see them thin out. Kids I had met as part of stickball teams became solitaries throwing Spaldeens against walls—and now suddenly there were lots of walls, an abundance of play space just when the players had disappeared. I would come back in September, and densely packed rows of houses would be gone, streets that had lacked sunlight were suddenly flooded with it. It was ghastly. Some of the same people were there, but the kids, even as they grew, seemed to grow paler. Were they less nourished or just more

worried? Sometimes I'd ask people what had happened. They would point all around, say, "The fires, the fires," and shake their heads to signify the whole thing was uncanny and they didn't get it. Sometimes they would clasp my arm or shoulder and look into my eyes with dread.

New Yorkers have always loved baseball, not just as a marvelous game but as a metaphor for existence. In the late twentieth century, the metaphor took on a melancholy spin. If the heroin epidemic was Strike One, people said—people on television but also people on the street—and the explosion of violence was Strike Two, the rain of fire felt like Strike Three. A very wide range of New Yorkers came to feel that history had thrown our city an array of pitches that were hopelessly beyond our reach, and we were about to be called—or we already had been called—*Out.*

In the mid-1970s, political economists invented a word to explain the nightmarish world-historical process in which our city was caught: they called it *Deindustrialization.* Starting in the late '60s, Deindustrial progress destroyed millions of manufacturing jobs in the US. In fact, Chicago and Detroit, world capitals of heavy industry in a region they started to call "the rust belt," were afflicted a lot worse than we were. But hundreds of thousands of jobs, mostly connected with the waterfront and the garment industry, were lost in and around New York. We had a great class of people who had spent their lives working themselves to death; suddenly they became a class of people who were dying for work, and that turned out to be even worse.

Some of the Deindustrialization literature derived from Political Economy, and many of the pundits in the 1970s mass media spoke as if these losses were

inevitable, inexorably determined by the operation of free markets and technological progress. In fact, though, two of the changes most disastrous for New York stemmed from political decisions made by particular men. The Port Authority of New York and New Jersey decided to close most of the docks and terminals around Manhattan, to move the great bulk of waterfront trade to New Jersey, and to reorganize its immense New York investments around one enormous speculative real-estate enterprise: the World Trade Center. Around the same time, the Defense Department decided to close the Brooklyn Navy Yard, New York's biggest industrial facility, which had employed a hundred thousand people at its peak, and had nourished a whole complex of satellite industries just outside. (The Yard is the place where *On The Town*, 1949, one of the all-time-great New York movies, begins and ends.) The Navy moved most of those thousands of jobs and billions of dollars in infrastructure to the South— ironically, at exactly the moment when thousands of blacks and Latins were migrating north in search of precisely those entry-level industrial jobs that were either disappearing or moving the other way. A generation of blacks and Latins were conscientiously following the American immigrant model—the model that had worked for Irish, Germans, Italians, Slavs, Jews—just when the American immigrant-industrial city was crumbling. Who were the men behind those dreadful Port and Navy Yard decisions? I don't know. But one reason we have a history profession is to find out. Whoever they were, I'm sure they had their reasons— just as Robert Moses had his reasons for crashing the Cross-Bronx Expressway through the heart of the Bronx, and Walter O'Malley had his reasons for moving the team with the biggest and most devoted fan base in baseball out of Brooklyn. It's crucial to identify these guys and call them to account. They should be put in place alongside Moses and O'Malley in New York's Hall of Shame.

Even after Deindustrialization, the cloud-capped office towers downtown still offered plenty of work for *other* people, hypothetical people with impressive educational credentials and up-to-date computer skills. But the ground was cut out from under a great many of the real people who were here. For years this was called "The Mismatch." It became the ideological basis for a massive exodus of corporate headquarters from New York in the 1970s. The claim was that young New Yorkers were too illiterate, too lazy, to uppity, to be lower-level employees in modern corporations. I felt that there was a lot of racism and a lot of bullshit in these claims. Still, I knew that American business was totally dependent on computers for its communications, and as a teacher I could see that kids who grew up in poor homes and poorly financed schools were locked out of the computer world. If the mostly minority kids who went to urban public schools (this means *state* schools in the us) were ever going to become part of the white-collar workforce, they and their schools were going to need massive Federal help. They were more desperately in need of help in the 1970s than at any time since the Great Depression. But at just this Nixonian moment, Federal help for urban populations disappeared. (The early-'70s Federal government, controlled by the GOP, spent plenty on new suburban infrastructures, even as old urban infrastructures collapsed.)

In the 1970s and '80s, New York's ruins were its greatest spectacles. It gradually emerged how they had come to be. All around the town, landlords of old buildings were having more trouble than ever with tenants who were ever more unemployed.

As many old, shabby buildings began to crumble, they were being redlined by banks—*redlined*, a crucial word in the 1970s—so that landlords on the wrong side of the line, as most were, couldn't get bank loans to fix their buildings up. As a result, buildings deteriorated faster, and landlords lost hope. Many came to feel that their buildings were worth more dead than alive. The result was a tremendous, protracted boom in arson, with many people—especially kids and old people—killed in the crossfire. All through the 1970s it happened simultaneously in dozens of neighborhoods. But the biggest firestorm was in the South Bronx, not far from where I grew up. At the start of the 1980s, I was finishing a book on what it means to be modern. But I came to feel I couldn't finish till I had gone back to where I'd started. So I went back—the house I grew up in was still there and still lived in, but the whole block across the street had burned and crumbled into ruins, and then had started to sink into the swamp that the whole neighborhood was built on. I spent many lonely afternoons wandering through the Bronx's ruins. What was I looking for? I picked up a broken speaker and a broken slab of

marble; they kept me company for thirty years, on the window sill just a few feet away from where I wrote, till just a couple of years ago. I met fellow wanderers (and camera crews) from countries that not so long ago had had formidable ruins of their own—Germany, Japan, Poland, the USSR—along with brilliant American artists, photographers and filmmakers as obsessed as myself; over thirty years I've seen their work and felt proud that I knew them when. I met a German art critic who told me that when her friends came to visit, they were totally indifferent to the grand structures she loved, but they implored her: "Where is the South Bronx? Take me to the burning buildings! I want a lover from the ruins." (The German painter Anselm Kiefer has created a great array of enormous landscapes of ruin, inspired by World War II but also—and this is their genius—remarkable facsimiles of the desolated Bronx. Another remarkably Bronx-like landscape was created in the 2002 film *The Pianist* by Roman Polanski (a European, an American, and a Jew—a survivor of the Holocaust and a man whose life has been wrecked several times): his vision of the ruins of Warsaw at the end of World War II. It is as if the Bronx, in its depths of disintegration, came to symbolize the twentieth-century world.

It was hard to believe the enormity of these ruins. They went on and on, block after block, mile after mile, year after year. Some blocks seemed almost intact, with live people—but then look around the corner, and there was no corner. It was uncanny! The fire years created a whole new vocabulary and iconography. As witnesses of 9/11 know, urban fires make great visuals. There were years of tabloid headlines, magazine covers, documentary films (in many languages) with titles like *The Bronx Is Burning!* A new urban picturesque emerged out of horizons lit by lurid flames, montages of buildings in different stages of disintegration, shards of beds, tables, TV sets, fragments of clothes (especially children's clothes), the rubble and debris of people's lives. For several years the *Times* carried a box that contained addresses of buildings destroyed the previous day or night. (I and many people I knew always turned to the Building Box first, even before the box scores: would our own old homes be there?) Sometimes these images helped generate empathy and solidarity: these shattered fragments of people's lives could have been *ours*. Sometimes they were used to support one of the great media clichés of the 1970s: that the poor people of New York were inflicting this destruction on themselves. Many elected officials insisted that the victims of the fires were also their perpetrators; hence they deserved no sympathy or emergency aid. A typical metaphor: the victims of fires were "fouling their own nests." During the 1977 World Series, the camera in the Goodyear Blimp showed a night panorama of Yankee Stadium and, maybe half a mile away, an anonymous building on fire. Head announcer Howard Cosell started shouting, "What's wrong with those people? Why are they doing this to themselves?" Cosell, who grew up in poverty in the Bronx and Newark, should have known better. But his tirade hardened into a "Blame the Victim" cliché. The saddest part was that so many victims—including many of my students and their parents—blamed themselves. (A typical '70s shot on the local news featured a family standing in front of the smoking building, clutching their last few possessions. Only yesterday this burned ruin was their home. The children are in tears. The man of the family, in anguish, appeals into the camera: "What did we do wrong?" The newscaster replies, gravely, "We don't know, Mr Vargas, we just don't know.")

After seeing life in New York unravel for years and years, I wasn't surprised by the fiscal crisis of 1975–6, which brought the city to the verge of bankruptcy. But the fact that I had felt it coming didn't make it any easier to be a hostage to people who prided themselves on their hostility to New York: Gerald Ford in the White House and a legion of "Southern Man" types who dominated Congress—and indeed who have dominated American politics since the 1770s. For the first time since the Vietnam War's heyday, I started watching the national news. One standard news clip then was a Congressman going back to his home district and asking his constituents what should be done about New York. There was a standard tirade, and the news people were able to find plenty of people to deliver it, often while shaking their fists and grimacing for the camera: New York is a parasite, it contributes nothing to America, it is noisy and dirty, it is full of foreigners and disgusting sex, every kind of sinfulness, hippies and homosexuals and Commie degenerates, a blot upon America, and now God has given America the chance to rise up and destroy New York forever, wash it down the drain! One clip featured a Congressman from a Gulf state, in a district that lived totally on Federal money, with a naval base and a shipyard. (Its building and repairing capacities may even have been moved there from Brooklyn.) He asked his constituents, "Should New York live or die?" They jumped to their feet, grinned obscenely at each other like the people in a classic lynch-mob photo, and screamed, "Die! Die! Die! Die!"

I can still hear those screams; thirty years on, they still cut through me. Their primal power makes me wonder: Did this really happen, or did I imagine or dream it? Maybe both. Southerners I've asked who are old enough to remember the 1970s can testify to scenes not far from the one in my head. An art teacher I met in North Carolina in 1990 told me how she had been booed and shouted down at her church meeting when she said that if Jesus could love Mary Magdalene, they could learn to love New York. The *Times* in those years was printing letters from all over the country, some of them pathologically sadistic, looking forward to New York's destruction. One letter, from an MD in Washington who had grown up in New York, said something like "New York had better learn to be humble before its betters. If we want, we can crush you." And this was the year when President Ford gave his famous "NEW YORK DROP DEAD" speech. He didn't actually say anything as honest as "Drop dead!" He merely said he would veto any Congressional plan to bail New York out, because the fate of New York was of no concern to "the American people." "DROP DEAD"

was the excellent paraphrase in the next day's *Daily News.* The front page showed Mayor Abe Beame reading the headline on the steps of City Hall. Beame displayed the page, looking both wounded and defiant. Whatever the Federal government may do to us, he was telling the world, we won't go quietly. It was Beame's moment of glory: for just an instant he looked like John Garfield at the end of *Body and Soul* (1947)—or like Garfield might have looked, had he lived—surrounded by creeps poised to crush him, blowing them off: "What are you gonna do, kill me? *Everybody dies.*"

Another thing that made it hard to be a New Yorker then was that many of the élites whose power was supposed to protect us against predators identified with the predators. They polarized the city into *us* and *them.* Addressing New York's enemies in Washington and around the country, they said: You are perfectly right in your rage and hate, only it should be directed not against the city as a whole but only against *them. They* are the cause of the fiscal crisis; *they* take our resources and give nothing; *they* deserve suffering, malice, punishment; you can trust *us* to create a selection process that will flush them out. A right-wing think tank, the Manhattan Institute, became a clearing-house for polarizations. The most notorious was Roger Starr's "Planned Shrinkage."

Starr (1918–2001) had a profile something like Robert Moses's: a German-Jewish patrician intellectual with a Yale education and a lifelong dedication to public service in New York. At different times he served as the city Housing Commissioner, as an officer of several foundations, and as Urban Affairs Editor of the *Times.* Starr's idea for dealing with the fiscal crisis was to divide the city's population into a "productive" majority that deserved to be saved and an "unproductive" minority that should be driven out. Starr would take advantage of already existing patterns of race and class segregation, and strive to eliminate not bad individuals but bad *neighborhoods.* Once a neighborhood was targeted for extinction, state power could assault it in a structured and coordinated way:

close schools and health facilities, suspend police protection, turn off water mains, disconnect electric-power lines, end garbage collection, do everything that can make a neighborhood humanly uninhabitable. Through coordinated administrative action in many neighborhoods (Starr didn't say which), the city could eliminate an "unproductive" *two million people.* It wasn't specified where they would go, but the great thing for the city, as he and his friends saw it, was that once they were "out of here," the city wouldn't have to care: "We should . . . stop the rural Puerto Ricans and blacks from living in the city [and] reverse the role of the city . . . It can no longer be the place of opportunity . . . Our urban system is based on the theory of taking the peasant and turning him into an industrial worker. Now there are no industrial jobs. Why not keep him a peasant?'

If this was meant as analysis rather than abuse, it had big problems. Never mind Starr's political economy, which imagined a world full of stable peasant societies yearning to receive millions of poor emigrants expelled from cities. Never mind his urbanism, which mistook a very local and temporary crisis for the world-historical Death of the City. Let's think about the political changes that would be necessary within any country in order for government officials—Starr's "we"—to have the power to expel millions of people from cities, or to prevent them from moving to cities in the first place. The system known as modern democracy, in which people are free to move around inside a country and live more or less where they want, would have to end. The state would have to gain police control of everyday life. The outstanding modern instance of this is, of course, is Fascism—though I should say Tsarist and Stalinist Russia also offer helpful hints. (The Tsarist expulsion of Jews from Anatevka at the end of *Fiddler on the Roof* might be the sort of move Starr had in mind. But *Fiddler* is a 1960s comedy, its heroes walk off with the dignity and resilence of Chaplin's Tramp. In real twentieth-century life, mass population transfers have been tragic and murderous.) Did Starr really want to bring in Fascism, just to *schlag* the poor? I can't say; I never got near the Manhattan Institute's faulty towers. I sometimes thought "Planned Shrinkage" had been planned as a masterpiece of Swiftian irony, and it had got out of hand. (It reminded me of the project at the start of Kurt Vonnegut's 1963 satirical novel *Cat's Cradle* to get the Marines out of the mud by a system of climate alteration that might bring about the end of the world.) But Starr worked hard to convince the world that he was not guilty of irony. Of course a plan like this was too outrageous for any elected politician to even try to implement it, but it created an aura that hung in the air like a Cheshire Cat's malevolent smile. For years, anytime anything mean was done to blacks or Latins or poor people, somebody would say, "Look, it could be so much worse." It's sad that Roger Starr's long career, based on an honorable ideal of public service, should have reached its climax with a plan to slash the public and smash the city. In this sad trajectory, we can see how New York's political culture devolved, from WNYC vision of community to something much more like a state of war.

"FORD TO CITY: DROP DEAD" is one of the all-time great newspaper headlines. It fulfills the promise of tabloid journalism: to tell the truth like a wise guy. Ironically, it turned out to be not just a great headline but a superb consciousness-raiser. It helped the city get the aid it needed. I figured that would happen: the billionaires in the GOP would get the word to the party's Sunbelt Pharisees that all markets were integrated—the key word today would

be *global*—and that the act of crushing the biggest city in the country, and the biggest economy, could easily recoil against them. Those billionaires owned the GOP as well as the world, and I knew they would get the word to the White House; I knew the White House would cave and sign on to the Federal loans (at extortionate interest, of course) that New York needed to pay off its creditors; I knew the city would get something like what it got from Congress, an Emergency Financial Control Board, and the Board would get it back into the credit markets soon. (In fact the Board turned out better than I thought it would: it was run by Felix Rohaytn, a financier who was also a liberal Democrat and who had the candor to admit that "We have balanced the budget on the backs of the poor.") I knew all of us would go back to something like business as usual. I even knew that Ford's "Drop Dead" speech would hurt him in the 1976 elections: there were plenty of people who shared his overall view of the world yet who thought his nonchalance about wiping out New York showed a dangerous lack of judgment. I did my best to get this across to my students, so they could see the sky wasn't falling and relax a little. Still, it hurt to feel all that hate out there, those mobs shouting "Die!"

Sometimes, in the midst of the 1970s horror show, there were surprise happy endings. Through the decade, New York lost something like 2,000 buildings a year to fires. The fires felt like an inexorable force; year by year, they enveloped more and more respectable neighborhoods. Why would these poor people destroy their world? There was endless speculation, foundation grants, conferences. Nobody could quite get it right. The left's explanation was brutally simple: the landlords did it—i.e. arson—and they did it for the money—i.e., fire insurance. An unusual alliance came into being to get this story out: the Fire Department, the insurance industry, and the New Left. The Mayor's Arson Task Force, established by John Lindsay, was the most radical agency in city government. Its reports dramatized ideas like "fire accelerants" (chemicals which NYFD. chemists found in about 90 percent of tenement fires) and "the ecology of fire" (which limited the damage if somebody came in ten minutes but could wipe out a whole block if nobody came for half an hour); it made arson clear. Meanwhile, some of the giant insurance companies, which had bought up thousands of Bronx insurance "pools" in the pastoral early 1960s, suffered staggering losses. Lloyd's of London, symbol of capitalist solidity for nearly 300 years, lost £60 million on Bronx fires and was deeply shaken. In the early 1980s, the insurance industry decided to bail out: all the major insurers resolved to stop paying claims on tenement fires. They got strong public support, because people in the '70s had a pretty good idea of what was up. And then, instantly, as if by magic, *the fires stopped.* In the last year of fire insurance, the Bronx lost about thirteen hundred buildings; in the first year of no fire insurance, it lost twelve. No money, no fires—the simple, crude explanation was totally right. Amazing! Moreover, the New York left had won something. True, it was a limited, defensive victory, stopping something horrible from happening rather than starting something new. But that was also true of the American left's great victory: stopping the War in Vietnam. And most people who identified with one left identified with both. Both victories were less than the left hoped for. Neither fulfilled the '60s revolutionary hope, "A single spark can start a prairie fire." Instead, both helped to put great fires out. But putting fires out made real differences in many people's lives, and indeed made it possible for their lives to go on.

Meanwhile, in the midst of Roger Starr's archetypal "unproductive" neighborhoods, the kids were starting to produce. "You know," wrote Grace Paley— who had been a South Bronx kid fifty years before—"the block is burning down on one side of the street, and the kids are trying to build something on the other." The South Bronx, at its moment of greatest misery and anguish, and in some sense *because of* its misery and anguish, created the mass culture called hip-hop. Hip-hop today envelops the whole world. I knew of no one in the '70s who imagined that anything like this could happen. The kids of those neighborhoods in those days created because they had to; they couldn't help themselves, they couldn't stop. The Bronx above all became more culturally creative than it had ever been in its life. In the midst of dying, it went through rebirth.

You could say it started on the subways. The subways were probably drearier and scarier in the early 1970s than at any time in their history. The stations were full of broken benches impossible to sit on, unfilled light sockets, long, dark shadows. The cars were old, painted battleship gray, and flaking away;

many had been recalled from deep storage when a shipment of new ones had turned out to be dangerously built and had to be withdrawn immediately. Suddenly, hundreds of trains were drenched with aerosol-sprayed graffiti, saturated with luminous primary colors and exuberantly bold designs. Actually, there were two forms of graffiti, inside and outside the cars. The outside forms were artful and brilliant forms inscribed on dull backgrounds; the inside forms were simply tags, repeated endlessly in claustrophobically dense backgrounds. Their graffitists, who worked mostly in crews, were happy to identify themselves and to be recognized. Most of them were black and Latin teenagers; most were boys, though a few of the best were girls; they came from all over the city (some from my school), but from the South Bronx most of all. They were endlessly denounced by politicians and in the mass media, and repeatedly arrested. The enemies of graffiti couldn't even tell the difference between inside and outside forms. (I used to cite this as evidence of a "collapse of critical standards.") I even heard a neo-conservative sociologist, a lifelong Cold Warrior, say he envied the USSR, where there was "no nonsense about freedom of expression," and where the state could simply arrest kids like these en masse and bury them in labor camps. Still, in the course of the '70s their work developed a vibrant new visual language. They made themselves at home in a drab and disintegrating environment, and infused that environment with youthful exuberance, bold designs, adventurous graphics. Some of them showed exceptional artistic talent. They differed in aesthetics and sensibility, some playful and insouciant, others existentially desperate; some projecting spontaneous overflows of powerful feeling, others elaborate patterns of design; some highlighting pure visuals, others blending images with texts (IF ART IS A CRIME, MAY GOD FORGIVE ME); some conveying instant entertainment, usually through takeoffs on figures from Disney or Warner Brothers cartoons, others more ruminative, abstract, even hieroglyphic; some addressing their audience with respect and deference, others blowing us off with in-your-face punk disdain. My favorite was Lee Quinones, whose murals fused surreal landscapes with provocative texts: WAR IS SELFISH DEATH, MAN IS ALMOST EXTINCT—remember, these were the Cold War years, when the US and the USSR were brandishing nuclear missiles at each other.

Two of the major artists who emerged from this scene died young: the painter Jean-Michel Basquiat (1960–1988), initially known for his street art under the tag SAMO, and the muralist Keith Haring (1956–1990), whose early work was done in the great dark, empty spaces of the Times Square subway station. (When they were alive and well, I thought of Haring as the comic mask and Basquiat as the tragic. But comedy is pretty tragic when you die young of AIDS.) However, the great majority of kids who did this art survived; they're still here. As they grew up, many would succeed as serious painters, animators, and theatrical, fashion, and video designers. Some became solid citizens of SoHo, of Seventh Avenue, of Broadway; some went to Hollywood. Looking at their life stories, we can see their graffiti years as first steps on a ladder upward and admire their resourcefulness in finding markets for themselves. But when the Bronx's graffitists began, they had more than self-marketing in mind: they saw themselves as citizens, and insisted on the civic and public meaning of their work. Indeed, it was a shared desire to get out of their neighborhoods (in which many were already doing well), and to communicate with a larger public, that made public transit so alluring. In the late '70s and early '80s, their civic spirit plunged them

into a brutal, grueling, immensely expensive, materially and humanly destructive conflict with the arrogant and unresponsive bureaucracy of the MTA. "If the MTA only understood graffiti," said Chris Matos, aka Daze, a very talented graffitist and painter, "they would know it's one of the best things subways have going for them . . . We could contribute a lot to the beauty of New York." I remember what I thought: *Don't hold your breath, kids.* Later on, within the private sector, some of these kids did very well. But it's crucial to remember that behind the private success, there was a public failure. And it wasn't the kids who failed.

Alongside the graffitists, and sometimes the same people, was the first generation of rappers. In the poorest Congressional districts in the US, rap was an exemplary *musica povera.* (I remember the first time I saw it. Like so much else I saw, it started in the subway, with a single ragged and scrawny kid, backed by small speakers with a drum track, telling the story of his life.) Some of the early rappers came from musically sophisticated families with strong backgrounds in jazz and R&B. Others had grown up too poor to take music lessons or own their own instruments but had a strong feeling for rhythm, powerful voices, and sharp wits. In the late '70s, at my school, CCNY, during Club Hour every Thursday, somebody would bring out turntables, and a DJ would scratch and collage dozens of records together while kids in the audience took turns playing MC, rapping over an open mike. (Some teachers rapped, too; I would have loved to, but I just couldn't rhyme.) I was delighted. What it meant for me was the power of *the word,* which was what I had been trying to teach all along. By the end of the '70s, rap was busting out all over. But a concentration of great DJ's came from the South Bronx. They vied with each other in dozens of small clubs, parks, high school gyms, and auditoria, with thousands of active and participant young listeners, to create a distinctive rap sound of samples, beats, and rhymes.

The spirit of early raps tended toward dance-hall and party music; it was bawdy and shallow. But the first great rap hit, when it came at last, was heavy, dark, and deep. This was "The Message" by DJ Grandmaster Flash and the Furious Five, released in the Reagan summer of 1982. "The Message" showed that there was not only a national but an international audience for rap:

> Don't push me, 'cause
> I'm close to the edge,
> Trying not to lose my head. Hah!
> It's like a jungle sometimes
> It makes me wonder
> How I keep from going under. (Huhh huh huh Huhh.)

MC Melle Mel then takes us on a tour of his neighborhood: "Broken glass everywhere, people pissing in the streets like they just don't care; I can't stand the pain, can't stand the noise, got no money in my pocket, so I got no choice." Myriad horrors are packed into two minutes: aggressive rats, aggressive junkies, nice girls turned into addicts and whores; kids, burned out before the age of ten, who want to grow up to be drug dealers, because these are the only people they know who command respect; their big brothers, who grow fast from unemployed to hired killers to dead. The rapper addresses a handsome corpse in his coffin: how could he have been so dumb? "You lived so fast and died so young." The rapper's attitudes are complex and hard to keep in any sort of emotional balance. He insists on the self-destructive idiocy of the people in the slum he lives in but also on their human dignity. Like Howard Cosell, asks, "What's wrong with these people?" But he doesn't settle for an easy answer— not even the answer that they are victims, though he makes it clear that they are. His voice alone makes it clear that he sees himself as one of "them", but his story is about "us," not "them." This complex of feelings forces him to walk a thin line. His refrain warns us, "So don't push me 'cause I'm close to the edge / Trying not to lose my head." And, once more, the concrete jungle with police sirens, voices ordering everyone to freeze, cars taking them away. But then, unexpectedly, a burst of wishful thinking. The rapper identifies with two people who are maimed by violence but who get help and manage to survive:

> They pushed a girl in front of a train,
> Took her to the doctor, sewed her arm on again.
> Stabbed a man right through the heart,
> Gave him a transplant and a brand new start.

"The Message" became an instant classic, endlessly quoted, sampled, and parodied. And it was a breakthrough for the whole genre. Suddenly there were people all over the world who wanted to listen to rap music from the Bronx and Brooklyn and Harlem, and who wanted to develop raps of their own. The

Sugarhill album cover by AQ Graphics became a classic in its own right. It portrays the group hanging out on a block of abandoned tenements; it looks like a typical block in the 1970s South Bronx (where the group lived and worked), or in Harlem, or on the Lower East Side, or in many parts of Brooklyn: claustro-phobically dense only yesterday, weirdly empty today. There are the guys, their boom box, a skewered traffic light, and nothing: plenty of nothing.

So what's the message? That social disintegration and existential desperation can be sources of life and creative energy. A whole generation of kids, from neighborhoods that "Planned Shrinkage" would have destroyed forever, broke out of poverty and ghetto isolation and became sophisticated New Yorkers with horizons as wide as the world. They had been through great losses without losing themselves. Not only had their suffering not destroyed their idealism: in some mysterious way, their suffering had *created* idealism. As The Clash affirmed that "London is drowning, I live by the river," these kids from the Bronx could tell the world not only that "We come from ruins, but we are not ruined," but "We come from ruins, but we shall overcome." Their voices became the voice of New York Calling. Their capacity for soul-making in the midst of horror gave the whole city a brand new aura, a weird but marvelous bank of bright lights. They, and all New York with them, succeeded in the task that Hegel defined for modern man just 200 years ago: if we can "look the negative in the face and live with it," then we can achieve a truly "magical power" and "convert the negative into being."

At its best moments, in those years of crisis, the cultures of Uptown and Downtown converged. In Red Grooms' (1937–) brilliant installation, "Ruckus Manhattan," we could hear New York Calling again. "Ruckus" was an enormous environment, constructed out of canvas, plywood and papier-mâché, encom-passing hundreds of pieces of the city: streets, buildings, human figures in all shapes and sizes, painted in Grooms' familiar idiom, the Expressionist cartoon. There was a miniskirted Statue of Liberty, a wildly twisted Brooklyn Bridge, a luminously sleazy Times Square, a Stock Exchange that was sleazy in it own right, a Staten Island Ferry, a carnivalesque Woolworth Building, a luminously sleazy Times Square, a Stock Exchange that displayed its own form of sleaze, a million signs. "Ruckus Manhattan" was assembled collectively by a large crew, which evoked New York's crews of graffitists, except that Grooms' kids got paid. There were further homages to the city's graffitists in Ruckus' demography— aggressively multicultural—in its hot, extravagant carnival colors, and in its overall air of in-your-face wiseguy exuberance. What marked "Ruckus" as a Downtown product was its intellectual power, its wide horizon, its vision of the city as a whole. Grooms conceived the subway as the power that embraced all the city's features and brought them together.

The biggest hit of the show was Grooms' graffiti-laden life-size subway car. Spectators could enter the car, sit on its seats and interact with his plaster-cast

of characters—shoppers, high school kids, businessmen, a red-faced and red-robed baby, a Hasid, a girl of the night, art critic Harold Rosenberg (or his double). These figures not only spilled out of their clothes, but overflowed with vitality. They seemed to entice us to "Please Touch." (When people did touch, they often felt disappointed: Was it only plaster? They looked so *alive*.) Grooms' subway car maintained a permanent rush-hour density. People didn't want to leave, or kept coming back. If they had babies (as I did then), they often sat them next to Grooms' red-robed, red-faced "Ruckus baby" and told stories or sang lullabies to both. Grooms' New York combined a satirical vision of people with a fervent belief in "the people." To enter his junky yet radiant inner space was to feel ourselves as part of a new Popular Front. For a generation of insulted and injured New Yorkers, Grooms' public art helped us imagine that we could really *be* a public: not only a New Deal but a new love.

*

All of this happened more than twenty years ago. At that point, there were still more bad moons yet to rise. The first assault on New York, in the '60s and '70s, had featured a heroin epidemic, an explosion of personal violence, a firestorm of arson, and an almost-bankruptcy. The second round, in the '80s and into the '90s, unveiled a homelessness crisis that put thousands of families out on the streets; a new disease, AIDS, which destroyed thousands more people, especially in the fashion and culture industries, and especially the young and healthy; and a new drug (a product of the Federal "war on drugs"), crack, which ravaged neighborhoods that people had broken their backs to stabilize, generated a whole new array of gangs, and raised the homicide level to twenty-four hundred a year, including many small kids who were killed simply for being there. A generation before, during the great fires, our newspapers constructed Building Boxes. Now they developed a new, up-to-date feature: Killing Boxes. These black-bordered features listed the names and ages of the dead, the sites and manners of their deaths. During the Crack Wars, in the late '80s and early '90s, it was a rare day or night when the killing boxes weren't full. (They were dropped in the '90s, as city life got safer, but they have been revived since 2003 to mark deaths in Iraq.) I scanned them every day, just as I had scanned the Building Boxes every day years before. Every so often I saw a name I recognized. I remember wondering: Now what was he, or she, doing there? But I knew that so often the answer was just that people were *being* there. I thought: So now there's a death penalty for *being*?

Oy! How could we live through this?

It brought me back to my favorite piece of literature in the whole world, *King Lear* (1603–6). There's a moment in Act Four when Edgar says that as long as we have the capacity to say, "This is the worst," we can be pretty sure that things will get even worse. And yet, strangely, this time the worst *didn't* make things worse. Not that there weren't new torrents of misery, but this time, more than last time, people knew how to cope. In Act Five of *Lear,* Shakespeare's cornucopia of horrors has poured out even more horrors, and everybody onstage is under fire. We see the Duke of Gloucester, who has been abused, assaulted, and maliciously blinded, and who now seems ready, even eager, to drop in his tracks. Edgar moves to pull him out of the line of fire. Gloucester sees no point in going on and urges Edgar to let him be—in effect, to let him die: "No further, sir, a man may rot even here." But Edgar will not let go of him:

> What, in ill thoughts again? Men must endure
> Their going hence, even as their coming hither:
> Ripeness is all. Come on.

"Ripeness is all." In the 1970s and '80s, a generation of rappers, writers, and street and subway artists made a cultural breakthrough, and created a verbal and visual language of collective pain, a language that was perfectly attuned to a city in the process of coming apart. Once we knew this language, it could help us survive more elaborate and more grueling permutations of pain to come. Who could have predicted AIDS, or the Crack Wars? But then, who could have predicted the industrial crash, the firestorms, near-bankruptcy, mobs calling for our death? The language could help us "Come on," help us live through the pain, help us overcome. It was a language where ripeness was all.

*

New York City feels like a very different place today. It has gone through spectacular population growth; the Census Department expects it to reach nine million within a couple of years. It is more saturated with immigrants, more ethnically diverse and multicultural, than it has ever been, more like a microcosm of the whole world—and thanks to New York's distinctively configured public space, you can see this whole world right out there on the streets. Its mode of multiculturalism is sexy—and threatening to the ultra-orthodox in every religion. Summer in New York is hot and humid—it is summer as I write—but great for bringing people together, and for looking at them. Look at the colors and complexions of the men and women holding hands on Upper Broadway, say, or at King's Plaza in Brooklyn, and of the children they are pushing in their strollers: colors never known under the sun. (Newspaper photographers and TV local-news crews love these tableaux, and they are right to; what better reason for having cities?) And today's sexiness coexists—as it often has not— with safety. Over the last decade, by the numbers, not only homicide but all violent crimes have significantly dropped. The tremendous increase in violence that started in the 1960s, and that for decades seemed inexorable, has been reversed. We would be foolish not to worry about eruptions of terrorism, but any anxiety we may feel about world politics coexists with a remarkable sense of greater safety in our everyday lives. We are back to 1950s levels of safety today (around 600 homicides a year; about a quarter of what it was in the early '90s)—and tonight. Who knows why this happened, or how long it will last? Really, nobody knows. But something is happening that I never could have imagined: a metropolitan life with a level of dread that is subsiding. Some people say they're worried that a life without dread will lose its savor. I tell my students and people I know not to worry. If they just scrutinize their lives, they will find grounds for more than enough dread to keep them awake. While they're up, they should seize the day and take a midnight walk.

If you come back to the city's poor minority neighborhoods, the ones that "Planned Shrinkage" planned to wipe out—Harlem, the South Bronx, the Lower East Side, Bedford-Stuyvesant, and dozens of others—it is easy to feel you have been in some sort of time travel. Mayor Ed Koch's $5 billion Ten Year Plan for Housing Rehabilitation has been an immense success. (Ironically, since leaving office, Koch has moved so far to the right that he avoids taking deserved credit for using state power to help the poor and for demonstrating the American welfare state at its best.) The City Housing Authority, and

many local Community Development Corporations, have rebuilt hundreds of blocks. They have been financed by local banks, forced by the Federal Community Reinvestment Act of the 1990s to pour money back into the cities where so much of their money came from.

The most amazing thing in all this is that that immense expressionist dreamscape, those jagged, haunting forms of recent ruins, are nearly gone. I love the Bronx Zoo, but for years I didn't go, because I couldn't bear to take the el through miles and miles of ruins. But finally, early in the 2000s, I bit the bullet. My son Danny's class at PS 75 was making a Class Trip, and they desperately needed parents, and I wasn't teaching that spring day, and how

could I say no. As we came into the Bronx, I prepared myself for the worst. The kids would be sitting down, so they wouldn't see much of anything, and they certainly weren't going to hear any of it from me. I stood up, craned my neck, and—*the ruins were gone.* In their place were ordinary buildings, parked cars, kids on bikes, trucks unloading, mothers with babies, people getting on and off buses, old people sitting on beach chairs watching the world go by—the whole *shmeer* of modern city life. I said to the teachers on the train with me, "Look, it looks like an ordinary city!" They said, "Well, *isn't* the Bronx an ordinary city?" I realized they were young, still in their twenties; when the Bronx was burning, they weren't even born. Now, it looked like nothing much—and yet, a miracle.

The genius of New York's recent housing projects is to look far less innovative than they are. Their main innovation is that they do not look like projects at all; they look like colorful, accessible versions of the thousands of vernacular, ordinary apartment houses that served for generations as emblems of New York, till they were burnt down. (They also look like some of the "social housing" in central and northern Europe.) But to look like an ordinary city, only a few years after looking like apocalyptic ruins, is a tremendous urban achievement. No monuments are here to mark this change, but their absence is likely to feel like a relief.

What about the rest of the city? For instance, what about downtown? It's more crowded than it's been in my lifetime, and also more multinational and multicultural, more a real microcosm of the world. The big office buildings are full of workers from India, Russia, China, Japan. Most of them, especially the young ones, seem a lot more fluent in computer technology and language than I am. (But that seems to be true of my sons, my students, and most young Americans as well.) There is also a tremendous overflow of tourists, staying in the dozens of new hotels that have gone up in midtown in the past decade. Many New Yorkers I know resent their presence, but I am delighted: this isn't the prison domain of the Count in Kafka's *Castle* (1922), it isn't a claustrophobic Willa Cather *shtetl* in the middle of the prairie, this is the greatest place in the world, so why shouldn't people want to come here?

For most of my life I've enjoyed getting into conversations with strangers on the streets, especially around Times Square. I ask people where they are going and do they need any help. One thing I've heard from many people recently is that they aren't going anywhere special, they're just walking around the streets—often they say they want to show the streets to their kids—and that they love the New York streets "because they're so real." I agree with them, and I'm glad they can see this and appreciate it. They feel like specimens of all the Americans who after 9/11 expressed such generous feeling and let their Congressmen know they cared. All this appreciation and friendliness are so different from the bad vibes that surrounded us only thirty years ago. Have we changed? I honestly don't think we've changed very much. Have they changed? I think they've changed a lot more. America has been steadily filling up with immigrants for the last forty years (after being closed for the forty years before), and people around the country are far less frightened than they used to be by human diversity: demographically, the rest of America has become more and more like New York. At the same time, environmentally, America has become more and more of a suburban car culture without streets, without places where people can walk around and have random experiences and inter-act with strangers. New York is a different environment: if you look up to the top of the buildings, it is brand new, but at the level of the street, it is a couple of hundred years old, rooted in the Paris and London of the Enlightenment. It keeps alive and nourishes the intensely interactive aura of the Modern street— a place where people checked each other out and brushed up against each other, where a random walk could feel like both a communion and a brothel, and where everybody could be both himself, or herself, and somebody else. Even affluent and powerful Americans today are likely to go through their lives deprived of vital energies that any New Yorker on the street can enjoy. Compared with New York, the environments where most Americans grow up feel *unreal*. In the past generation many more Americans have come to feel this, and to love our city for what it is and what their suburban towns are not. Do New Yorkers know how sweet it is to be loved for what you are?

But the ironies keep on rising with the buildings. *The price of love*—just because the whole world wants to be in New York, New York has become impossibly expensive to be in. This seems to go with being a "global city," along with London, Paris, Madrid, Tokyo, Rio, Los Angeles, Washington, DC, and a few more—it's a small club. For a global city, the word is that New York is cheap. The papers feature articles on the frantic construction of luxury housing in Manhattan: so many churches have generated modern miracles, transforming "air rights" into goldmines. And they highlight the resurgence of corporate headquarters in Manhattan: twice as many as were here in 1990. So many neighborhoods have accelerated from abandonment to gentrification in what feels like ten seconds or less. Not just my own dear Upper West Side, or the Village, or Chelsea, but the Lower East Side and Hell's Kitchen and Harlem and parts of Brooklyn and Queens. People who worked through the dark years to keep these neighborhoods alive are falling victim to their own success. When

they see their neighborhoods on the front page of the Real Estate Section of the Sunday *Times,* they feel both swollen with pride and stabbed with dread.

At the start of this essay, I talked about New York's thickness and richness of street life. A special feature of those streets has been their superabundance of small bookstores, record/CD stores, and (in the last generation) video stores. These little palaces of culture have nourished and enriched the city's sense of place; they have helped New Yorkers feel like both citizens of the street and the world. But in rising real-estate markets like today's, little palaces are in trouble. As market pressures crush the shop around the corner, its ex-customers wonder: When will it happen to us? So, for New Yorkers in the 2000s, life is safer than ever, yet we are forced to face ever new ways of being under fire. You could even say our sense of being under fire defines our sense of being at home.

Two or three years ago I saw the headline, "The Bowery Lives Again", and I knew at once that my favorite Bowery life sign, the punk rock club CBGB, was doomed. CBGB's was one of New York's freest voices in the city's most desperate days. It had nurtured a great generation of rockers and a great audience. It had come proudly through the crash; but could it survive the boom? I read the news one day—on October 16, 2006—and I saw it was gone. The landlord that evicted it was an agency set up to aid the homeless. On its last night, many of its far-flung graduates came back. Patti Smith played its very last late-night set. She told the news, the closing was "a symptom of our city's empty new prosperity". But she also said, "There's new kids with new ideas all over the world. They'll make their own places, here or wherever . . . ." A couple of weeks later, writing about those kids in the New York *Times,* she said, "The Internet is their CBGB." But can Cyberspace be a place, a scene? We'll see.

If I were forty years younger than I am, and trying to come to New York now, high on brains, ambition, and energy but low on capital, could I come

here? Well, yes and no. There would be no way I could afford the Upper West Side. Probably no more than 10 per cent of West Siders could afford the West Side—or indeed *any* Manhattan neighborhood—if we had to pay market prices to be here now. That's the bad news. The good news is that today's younger generation, unable to live in Manhattan, has learned to explore the city as a whole with a zeal and energy and resourcefulness that my generation, obsessed with Manhattan alone, never even dreamed of. I can't blame them if they are mad; I'd be mad in their place. Still, they can get here on the subway (and on the PATH, and on the LIRR), and they do, just as my parents took the D train to Times Square from the Bronx seventy years ago. Meanwhile, they have created a New York that's a lot fuller than ours; their horizon is far wider; in their New York, there's so much more *there* there. Last spring, I read at a Hispanic Cultural Center in the South Bronx, in a small rebuilt brownstone just behind the giant neon "H" sign, plugging the History Channel, that highway drivers can see for miles. The kids have made the city's post-1898 official name, "Greater New York," mean something real.

In the Bible, in Genesis 11, the story of the Tower of Babel, God gets frightened by the powers of humans and undertakes to "confuse their language" so they won't be able to understand each other anymore. Devoid of mutual understanding, they fight, their Tower sinks into ruin, and people "scatter over the face of all the earth." But in the cities of the modern world, it appears that they have come together again—or at least set the stage for coming together again. What

would happen if all the peoples who make up a modern city could really understand each other? Could it be that, as God fears, "nothing will be restrained from them, which they have imagined to do"? What will they build then: maybe a Garden City of Eden? The Urbicidal ruins that enveloped American cities, New York most of all, felt like a savage mockery of that dream. And yet, our city of ruins turned out to be a place where people coming from a hundred different places started to talk together and work together in ways people had never quite done before. It will be a time before they can do all that they can imagine. But the power to imagine, to imagine modern life together afresh, is itself an achievement. That is what this book, *New York Calling*, is about.

PUBLIC SPACES

Whatever you think about New York, there's always more. That is its primary beauty, and also its greatest challenge. While legend has it we begin with a city convulsing, that narrative, of New York's decline from its post-war glory years into the funk and failure of the 1970s, is but one among many. Even at its symbolic nadir—the blackout of July 13–14, 1977—the city still *functioned*, and as historian James Goodman noted, "In no neighborhood were more than a fraction of residents looting. But in New York's neighborhoods, the turnout of even the smallest fraction could make an enormous crowd." An imperfect, often corrupt, city government left gaps all over but it offered opportunities too, for artists, immigrants, small-timers and eccentrics, visionaries and cranks, reformers and crooks. As strained as things felt for those who knew an easier era, New York never wholly lost its allure, nor its imagination.

The feel of '70s New York is effectively limned by three films. First is the subway hijack drama, *The Taking of Pelham 1–2–3* (1974). For cynical wit and as a flattering portrait of the city under pressure, it's yet to be bettered. (Favorite line, shouted by an apoplectic MTA dispatcher: "What do they expect for their lousy 35 cents? To live forever?!") There are no trains in *Annie Hall* (1977)—everyone walks, drives, or takes a cab—but it's still a striking love letter to the city and a reminder of just how different New York lives can be. (Best deadpan Jewish Intellectual joke, said at an academic cocktail party: "Is that Paul Goodman?") Woody Allen's all-white city never existed, of course, but the Thunderbolt rollercoaster sure did, likewise a once-beloved Knicks basketball team. *Dog Day Afternoon* (1975) is remarkable for many reasons, its opening montage included. Here are the Circle Line cruise ships and the Triborough Bridge traffic jams, the skid row bums and the beach lovers. At one point, director Sidney Lumet cuts from a man watering his lawn to another washing down the sidewalk—a perfect juxtaposition.

New York's erstwhile recovery has had its costs. Successive economic booms—Wall Street, Dot.Com, Wall Street again, Real Estate *and* Wall Street—have all conspired to tame previously feral parts of Manhattan: Hell's Kitchen, the Lower East Side, even parts of Harlem. Once a riot of kung fu flicks, discount stores, fake IDs and sex, 42nd Street today is the epicenter of Manhattan Theme Park. The demimonde appeal of the area was celebrated in Josh Alan Friedman's *Tales of Times Square* (1993), and for some New Yorkers, Show World and Peepland tokens are recalled as fondly as those once used for subway and bus fares. That the truest face of New York—hustling, vulgar, lust-driven—could thrive so openly didn't please everyone, but in a city where public space is increasingly monitored for corporate benefit, there was something quaintly democratic about Times

Square which hasn't been replaced. Canal Street and most of Chinatown retain their bazaar-like, ineluctably *other* qualities; 14th Street and Chelsea assuredly do not. Far uptown, Washington Heights and Inwood feel like old times, and include the Spanish tinge that's diminished elsewhere.

Even while the redevelopment of Ground Zero languished, the city witnessed a historic construction spree. In Manhattan, new office and residential buildings have risen at a prodigious pace—banks and chain stores even faster. Downtown, radicalism has been usurped by radical upscaling. Should the death of bohemia there be permanent, at least its tombstones are appropriately jarring—curved glass at Cooper Square, a blue trapezoid on Norfolk Street, "high end lofts" on the Bowery. The Meat Packing District is on its last hooves as a place of industry, and Fulton Fish Market has relocated to Hunt's Point after centuries on the East River. Lest there be any confusion, banners affixed to Park Row lampposts adjacent to City Hall declare New York "The Real Estate Capital of the World."

What's lost with such rhetoric is exactly what it touts: New York. The multi-ethnic Bronx Terminal Market was razed to make way for a big box development called the Gateway Center. If the city seems to be blurring, it's not an illusion: a huge strip mall near Starrett City in Brooklyn has the same name; likewise dozens of facilities around the country. (Silliest: the Gateway Center of Ames, Iowa, formerly a Holiday Inn.) A few blocks north, the Yankees, the wealthiest team in American sports, are building a new stadium on what was parkland, partly at public expense. Coincidentally, nearby Mott Haven is the poorest neighborhood in New York, with 46 percent of its residents living below the poverty line.

Brooklyn has two incipient skylines now, one downtown, the other in Williamsburg. Both are the cause of much furor, and developer Thor Equities wants to build a Vegas-style hotel and indoor mall on the boardwalk at Coney Island— the boardwalk! Many amusements and other small businesses have already been forced to close. In Queens, planners can't decide whether Long Island City is the new Upper East Side or an ersatz Jersey City with greater hip-hop pedigree. The Infamous Mobb go neighborhood pride further than usual in "Killa Queens," repping even their zip code, "Triple One-Oh-One," but don't expect to see *that* on any banners. Staten Island—aka Shaolin—doesn't make the news much, but its a remarkable place of widely varying neighborhoods and topography. Here, instead of Manhattanization, the enemy is suburban sprawl. Indeed, it's telling that, having blasted landscapes nationwide for the sake of McMansions and golf courses, Pennsylvania-based homebuilder Toll Brothers has entered the New York City construction market. Why? Luxury condos, of course.

Subterranean Vaudeville

Jim Knipfel

It took decades to finally establish all the unspoken, subtle rules of NYC subway etiquette. The trains have been around for a century now and carry an average of 4.5 million people every day—it takes awhile for all those people to come to an agreement on anything, let alone the proper rules of behavior when they're all crowded together during the evening rush. Because of this, it can take newcomers to the system years to finally internalize everything they need to know when they pass through the turnstiles.

Here are the rules.

Whenever possible, maintain as much distance as possible between yourself and other commuters. Keep your voice down. Don't make eye contact with anyone. Mind your own damn business. If there's an empty seat on an otherwise packed train, it's probably empty for a very good reason. Hell, it took a month after moving to New York before I learned that it wasn't appropriate to use the heads and arms of other commuters for support on a moving train.

The consequences for not following the rules can be alarming. Once on a morning commute, I was surrounded and very nearly given the bum's rush by a group of perfectly normal citizens because (I learned that morning) I *hadn't* followed the rules.

At various times over the years, the city has tried to legislate subway etiquette—threatening hefty fines if you put your feet on the seats, took up an extra seat with a bag, or drank from an open container—but none of it really took. The people governed themselves. And that's part of what made the New York subways such a unique and self-contained world, quite independent from the world that existed aboveground.

All that changed in the days following the bombings on London's underground in July 2005. After that, the rules, the etiquette, the strange and brutal innocence of the subways vanished, as the World Above invaded the tunnels and platforms.

Prior to that, things were lively. There was in theory a police presence on the subways, but you didn't see them very often. Behavior that would in no way seem appropriate above ground was given free reign in the tunnels, so long as you paid attention to the other rules and no one got hurt. Or at least not hurt very badly.

I ride the trains nearly every day, have for years, and have never grown sick of it. On the platforms and in the cars, I have witnessed nearly every kind of insanity you can imagine, from the simply peculiar to the genuinely frightening. On one of my very first hour-long trips down to Coney Island, I watched as a gentle, gaudy, 300-pound transvestite who'd covered his entire face with lipstick tore the pages out of a TV Guide one by one before stuffing them into his purse. I've also watched a monstrous, shrieking lunatic swing a baseball bat at passengers as the train rolled merrily along.

I've vomited on myself twice while riding the subway, and learned that there's no better way to get a seat, no matter how crowded the train is. I've seen rats the size of dogs waddling down the tracks without a care. I've witnessed strangers beaten by gang members for no reason other than that they were there, and have been beaten by gang members myself for the same reason.

I've shared personal secrets with strangers I knew I would never see again, and dodged people I knew I'd be seeing later in the day. Once, I watched a well-dressed man completely undress on an R train during the morning rush. Nobody seemed really sure why he was doing this, but nobody said a word about it. I spent two hours trapped in a stalled train under the East River and saw lifelong friendships forged. I met an amazing musician who could play Shostakovich on a xylophone constructed from soda bottles filled with water to various levels, and a one-armed man who tooted feebly on a harmonica while trying to collect handouts. I've seen stolen property ranging from newspapers and batteries to complete computer systems sold at bargain-basement prices on the trains. Things happen down there that simply wouldn't happen, and *couldn't* happen, anyplace else.

It's easy to get all poetic about the form and meaning and metaphorical implications of the subways, and that's just fine. Lots of people have done it. But for my money, none of that really matters when you ride the trains every day. More than anything else, at eye level the subway is a self-contained traveling theater with an ever-changing line-up. While most commuters are content to keep quietly to themselves, they can rest assured that some sort of entertainment will be showing up soon. Musicians of every stripe, preachers, hucksters, madmen—all with a captive audience for at least a few minutes. On some days a simple ride from Brooklyn into Manhattan can take the form of a musical comedy, on others an action-adventure film. It can be a medicine show, a Greek tragedy, a love story, a taut thriller, a disaster movie, a police drama, or a savage quickie horror film. (In fact, I've often suggested that the Metropolitan Transportation Authority—the corrupt and ill-managed agency responsible for

keeping the whole system running—should use Walter Hill's 1979 low-budget street-gang fantasy *The Warriors* as a public-relations tool. No other film in recent memory more loudly sings the praises of the near-Germanic efficiency and reliability of the New York subways. Whenever you want a train, the film promises, there'll be one waiting for you.)

Not a day goes by that something doesn't happen on the trains to interrupt the slow monotony of contemporary urban existence. Sometimes you have to look for it, but it's down there. It's always down there. An unexpected act of kindness, a shared roll of the eyes with a stranger, a threat on your life, or a reminder that no matter how bad things sometimes seem, they could be far worse. Sometimes it's an instructive lesson concerning some aspect of human nature that you simply didn't care to know about, and sometimes it's an overheard snippet of conversation that keeps you going for the rest of the day.

Normally I much prefer to remain an invisible observer when I'm in the subway. It's much more entertaining to sit back and watch while other people display their various quirks and psychoses. Far too often, however, and for reasons I cannot fathom, the people I'm watching focus their attentions on me. In some cases this can be quite uncomfortable. More often than not, however, it's merely very, very odd.

Over several years, I began to work out a system. I'd developed an intense aversion to crowded trains, so I made a point of commuting when traffic was the lightest. This meant that I caught the 5:55 every weekday morning (surprisingly, the trains do tend to run on schedule). While many subway platforms can be narrow, shadowed, and filthy, the one at my stop was wide and bright and clean. Better still, it tended to be very quiet at that hour.

One morning during the late autumn of 2004, I arrived at the station a few minutes before the train, and strolled down to my regular spot near a mostly unused flight of stairs. Then, as most every morning, I leaned back and stared at the floor.

I heard footsteps behind me. This was a little odd, since so few people used this particular staircase. Whoever it was, she was muttering to herself in a quiet, sing-song voice. At first I figured it was the crack whore who showed up on the platform every once in awhile, but this woman wasn't that loud. The crack whore tended to scream, her words spilling out of her like automatic-weapon fire aimed at whoever happened to be nearby. Not only was this woman too quiet for that, she also wasn't using "motherfucker" quite as freely. In fact, she didn't sound angry at all.

Maybe she's calming down, I thought, considering the possibility it might yet turn out to be the crack whore. She was, after all, the Angriest Woman in the

World, and there's only so long you can keep that routine going before burning out. Normally I'd try to keep my distance from her, but that morning I stayed where I was. The train would be along in a second anyway.

"Can I have a cigarette?" a small voice next to me asked. I'd been so wrapped up in thinking about the crack whore that I'd stopped paying attention to the woman coming down the stairs.

"Hmm?" I asked, as I turned to find myself facing a tiny, wizened old

black woman. Shorter than I was, she was wearing a stained red coat. A tired scarf was wrapped around her head. She might have been homeless or just a bit off, it was hard to tell. Of course there's nothing to say that she wasn't both.

"Can I have a cigarette?" she repeated. She seemed fairly calm about things. There was no anger there, and she was polite. I reached into my pocket for a smoke.

"Brand?" she asked.

"Hmm?" I replied absently, still reaching into my pocket. It wasn't even quarter to six, I hadn't had any coffee, and so I wasn't all there yet.

"*Brand*," she repeated, a hint more firmly. I finally understood. When I at last freed a cigarette from the pack, I held it out so she could see.

"Thank you," she said as she took it between her brittle fingers. Then she leaned in close and asked me, "Do you sing?"

"No, I'm afraid not," I confessed. "Not in public anyway."

"Come on," she insisted, "sing a little song with me."

I had no idea what sort of song this woman had in mind, but it didn't make any difference. "Oh, no, no, no, ma'am," I told her. "I'm afraid I really don't sing." Even though nothing bad had happened and I didn't expect it to, I was beginning to wish that she'd move along down the platform.

"You sure do *look* like a singer."

"Well, I'm not."

She slowly reached out a hand and gently stroked my hair. "*Nice and clean*," she whispered. For some reason, this didn't bother me as much as it probably should have. If it had been a little later, perhaps, or if I'd had some coffee in me, I might've smacked her hand away. I tend to be more accepting of things in the morning. Besides, we were underground, and things like this, if not exactly par for the course, were still things you came to accept.

"Can I have a light?" she asked.

I noticed that she had stuck the cigarette in her mouth. The way things were going, I kind of figured she would be lighting up eventually, much to the fake-coughing, hand-waving chagrin of all the upstanding citizens around us. Smoking anywhere in the subway system was illegal, but still I reached into my bag and began fumbling around for a pack of matches. I knew I had at least one in there.

"You're afraid of me," she said, with a broad smile.

"Not afraid of you at all, ma'am," I assured her. "Just trying to find a pack of matches for you, is all."

As I continued sifting through all the detritus I had stuffed in my bag, she leaned in very close again, to the point where the collar of my coat met my neck. Then she sniffed. "Yep, nice and clean," she said, still smiling, seeming oddly satisfied as she leaned away from me once more.

"Uh-huh," I said, not knowing how to take that. I wasn't completely freaked out yet, just confused. It'd been many years since I'd been sniffed by a stranger. I finally found the matches and handed them to her.

"You look like you're from the future," she told me, without explaining any further.

"I understand," I replied.

She began whispering again, waving the matches about as she spoke. "You know, there are people living in the future."

"I'm well aware of that, ma'am, yes."

She pulled a match from the book, then dropped it. With a series of grunts and heaves, she bent over, retrieved the match, and began striking it feebly against the sandpaper. I didn't offer to help, feeling I'd already conspired enough in this flagrant act of terrorism. She finally got it lit, brought the flame to the tip of the cigarette, and inhaled while stepping toward the edge of the platform. She shook the match out and dropped it on the tracks.

With that first lungful, she doubled over as she erupted in a series of violent, wracking coughs—their force driving her closer to the edge. I was afraid for a moment that she'd end up on the tracks herself.

"Hey, hey—," I said. "Come back here before you fall or something. Jeepers." Dozens of people were killed every year down there after falling—or, more often than not, jumping—in front of oncoming trains. It was usually pretty messy.

She moved back toward me, smoking more comfortably now. "Know what happened to me today?" she asked.

"No, I . . . I can't say as I do." I wondered if it took place in the future. I had to admit, I sort of liked the idea of being a man from the future. Especially a clean one.

Above us I heard the bell announce the arriving train. That was a relief.

"My back," she began. "My back ... *hamma ... no-ashway keenijk ... polly sogrom* ..." Her voice had shifted in mid-sentence and her eyes had closed. Her hands were palm up before her as she gently rocked back and forth. As the light from the oncoming train drew closer, she continued to speak in tongues, or cast some sort of incantation, or call upon the Old Ones, or whatever the hell she was doing. "... *halet menna peenawory* ..."

The train pulled in and wheezed to a stop. The doors hissed open with their familiar two-tone *ping*. The woman stopped chanting and opened her eyes.

"Well," I said, "here's my train. It was certainly nice talking to you, but I've got to go now."

"You're *leavin'* me?" she asked as I stepped through the doors. There was no anger or hurt in her voice. Just loneliness. At that moment, the train operator leaned out of his cab and snapped, "Hey—lady—you can't get on the train with a cigarette."

"What?" she asked, as I aimed myself for a seat.

"You *can't smoke* on the train!"

The old woman took a step back from the doors. As they were closing, however, she leaned forward once more and shouted after me, "*Can I see you tomorrow?*"

*

After the London Underground bombings, a new set of rules was instituted by the NYPD.

Police not only began riding the trains, they also began searching people before they were allowed to pass through the turnstiles. Commuters who were allowed to enter the system were instructed to spy on other commuters, keeping their eyes open for tell-tale behavioral patterns. If someone was sweating, we were told, they were probably a terrorist (in spite of the fact that New York was in the middle of one of its most miserable and sweltering summers in years). Anyone with clenched fists or strange clothes was probably a terrorist, too. And you could be certain that someone who was muttering to himself was about to blow everyone up.

Things that had once been accepted as proper and normal behavior underground were now the sure signs of a suicide bomber. Not making eye contact with other passengers, for instance, which had been understood as a way of avoiding challenging other people, was now, it turned out, the hallmark of a terrorist.

Therefore it had become extremely important that non-terrorists were painfully conscious of their own behavior in order to avoid being mistaken for terrorists and dragged away. No more staring at the floor, no more clenching your fists in anger or frustration, no more dressing weirdly to assert your individuality. The subway was no longer a low-key and quiet place (apart from occasional entertainments and interruptions) where people minded their own business and remained occupied with their own thoughts. Suddenly, as on airplanes following 9/11, riders became little more than a paranoid mob looking for a target.

I guess I can understand these reactions given the circumstances and the fear, but things were suddenly much less fun.

On the morning after the second attempted London bombing in two weeks, I sat down on my normal morning train and began my normal forty-five-minute commute into work. Three stops after I boarded the train, the doors behind me opened and two Middle Eastern men stepped aboard. I didn't notice them, as I was trying to read (the subways are also the last place remaining to most New Yorkers where they can actually sit and read a book for awhile).

The men began speaking to each other quite loudly—much more loudly than is normally considered acceptable for the trains, especially at that hour. That they were speaking their native language only called more attention to them. If nothing else, it exhibited some remarkably bad timing on their part.

I looked up from my book and scanned the crowd in the car with me.

Whether or not they were aware of it, every single set of hate-filled and fearful eyes were glaring at these two men.

I'd never seen anything like it before. People could ignore the man who took his clothes off. They could ignore the maniac with the baseball bat. But *this*? Two guys talking to each other?

I knew then that the subways had changed. Perhaps not for good. Subway culture is like the ocean—it scrubs itself clean and restabilizes itself after awhile—but it was going to take some time.

Yet despite what it's become, I still love the subway. It doesn't matter where I'm headed or what may be waiting for me on the other side. I look forward to every ride, still feel a tiny flicker of excitement in my heart every time I see that tiny, growing light at the end of a darkened tunnel and know that my train is on the way. Part of that excitement, I'm sure, comes from the simple fact that I have no idea what's going to happen once the train stops and those doors open. Something interesting, no doubt.

From Wise Guys to Woo-Girls

John Strausbaugh

When writer Peter Koper and his wife Gina moved into their raw loft space on Prince Street in Lower Manhattan in 1981, the area was a no-name wasteland of dark streets prowled by Bowery winos, heroin addicts and Mafia block capos. A Desolation Row known for its boarded-up storefronts, empty industrial lofts, and John Gotti's Ravenite Social Club, it wasn't quite Little Italy (to the south) and it wasn't really SoHo (to the west).

"We called it Uhoh," Gina Koper recalls. "As in 'Uh oh, we're out of bread.' There was no place to buy groceries except the bodegas. You could walk to some artist's place and buy a $200,000 painting, but you couldn't buy a quart of milk that wasn't sour."

Legal researcher and photographer Don McLeod moved into his apartment on nearby Elizabeth Street in 1980. "Nobody came here," he says. "There was nothing here. If we had friends over and ran out of beer after nine o'clock, we had to take a cab over to East Fifth Street to buy a six-pack. Nothing was open around here. Now every cab driver knows where Elizabeth Street is," McLeod continues. "Big limos all up and down the street every Friday and Saturday night, bringing them in from all over the place. The neighborhood's been Paris Hiltonized." By "them" he means "woo-girls," so called for their habit of standing outside bars all night smoking and shouting "Woo!"

The shift from wise guys to woo-girls, from desolate Uhoh to trendy "Nolita" ("North of Little Italy," a real-estate brokers' acronym coined in the mid-1990s), followed a classic script in the recent evolution of downtown Manhattan. In the '70s and '80s, arty bohemians quietly infiltrated the small, nameless zone, drawn by its funky charm, its cheap tenements, its raw lofts and storefronts they could use as studios. By the 1990s, these pioneers had attracted a growing influx of moneyed hangers-on and hipsters—rock stars, fashionistas, dotcommers, trustafarians. They in turn brought in the bars, theme restaurants, day spas, and other services that lure woo-girls by the limo-load.

By 2000, the storefront studios and tiny art galleries had all been replaced by fashion boutiques with inscrutable names and improbable wares which opened and closed like flowers in a sped-up nature film. Rents and sale prices for living spaces had soared into the stratosphere, as most of the bohemians and artists sold out or were pushed out. (The Kopers remain because they bought their loft well before the boom; McLeod's rent is stabilized.) The chance to glimpse David Bowie skateboarding on Cleveland Place or Lenny Kravitz dining at the restaurant Ballato drew the scenesters. Weekend tourist-shoppers are now decanted by the hundreds from huge buses, handed guidebooks, and sent off to troll the boutiques. Gina Koper's bread needs are amply overserved by a mammoth Whole Foods store on Houston Street. It's not John Gotti's neighborhood anymore, it's Amy Chan's. There's not even a bronze plaque on the wall to show that Chan's Mulberry Street boutique is the former site of the Ravenite, though the store does vend $35 fitted t-shirts with logos like "Ravenite Social Club," "Gotti Girl," and "In Gotti We Trust."

The photographer Allan Ludwig moved into his Prince Street loft in 1984. With his shiny head, Roman nose, and fireplug build, he looks like a supporting actor from *On the Waterfront*, or like a pretty good Picasso impersonator. In warm weather, he likes to share a public bench with his friend George, an old warhorse with cauliflower ears and a face creased and crumpled like a discarded paper bag. They watch as hundreds of tourists wander the once-deserted streets with their guidebooks and cameras. Often, a tourist will ask permission to take snapshots of the two locals.

"It's like they're visiting an exotic culture," Ludwig says. "They want to get their picture taken with the natives."

Asked about the change the neighborhood has undergone, he shrugs philosophically. "We can't complain about gentrification. We started it. We were the pilot fish."

There is, of course, nothing new in this. Artists and bohemians have been serving as the shock troops for real-estate developers in modern cities at least since Montmartre went hip in the 1880s. They "discover" an affordable neighborhood—an ethnic and/or working-class ghetto (the East Village, the Lower East Side) or an abandoned industrial zone (SoHo, Williamsburg)—and infiltrate. By their very presence they eventually begin to make the neighborhood feel safe and attractive to people with money. The brokers give the area a cute new name—in NYC, usually an acronym that sounds like a brand of home appliance, such as Nolita, Tribeca, SoHo, NoHo, Dumbo, Sobro, or Sofi—because evidently professionals will not move into a neighborhood lacking one of these briskly anodyne monikers. At some point the real-estate and style pages of the New York *Times* make this new name official and seal the neighborhood's fate. The new money "redevelops" the area, which means skyrocketing rents and sale prices that drive out both the bohos and the original ethnic and poorer residents. The bohos find a new, as-yet-unmonickered area to infiltrate, and the whole process begins again. Not much interest is paid to where the poor folks go. In NYC it's often the borough of Queens, which so far in the city's history has remained resolutely unhip and uncolonized.

This is all part of the larger process by which cities change and grow. What's different about Manhattan in the 1990s and 2000s is that the borough is running out of artists and bohemians to serve as its real-estate pilot fish. They've been priced off the island. In 2005, the average sale price of an apartment in Manhattan went above $1 million. Rents have soared commensurately. With very few affordable pockets of real estate left in Manhattan for them to make hip, the artists have fled en masse across the East River into Brooklyn or across the Hudson into New Jersey. But even in those places the trendy money has found them, forcing them out of briefly boho enclaves like Brooklyn's Williamsburg. Since 9/11, a huge flow of investment capital has rapidly rebuilt even the formerly frumpy and crime-ridden waterfront of Jersey City, lining it with yuppie condominium towers. Where do the artists and bohos go when they can't even afford Jersey City? They flee the metropolitan area altogether, abandoning it to the yuppies and moneyed trendsters who forced them out.

Throughout the twentieth century, a Manhattan without its resident artists and bohemians was simply inconceivable. Everyone in the world understood that its Greenwich Village poets and painters, its East Village hippies and punk rockers, its gays and radicals and dope fiends, its cultural outcasts and iconoclasts and ass-pains who had gathered there from all across America and the world, were integral to Manhattan's unique culture and charm. There were other big cities in America, but Manhattan was not America, and proudly so. Boston, Chicago, and LA were not Manhattan. Brooklyn, Queens, and Hoboken were not Manhattan either. Only Manhattan was Manhattan, the only place like it in the world, and its sizeable contingent of arty nonconformists played a large role in that.

Now, as politicians and developers collude to make all of Manhattan accommodating to the middle and upper classes, the island is rapidly being leeched of much of its character. It is becoming just another American city, an Oshkosh-on-the-Hudson, complete with malls, Olive Gardens, and k-marts, and attractive to the type of Americans who found the old Manhattan a frightening anomaly, who show very little interest in (or even awareness of) its aesthetic and intellectual traditions, and who could just as comfortably be living in Atlanta or Dallas or San Diego or Anycity, USA.

In effect, downtown has been uptowned. As late as the early 1990s, there was still a ubiquitously understood cultural divide between uptown and downtown Manhattan. Broadly speaking, uptown was where the middle- and upper-class professionals lived—the yuppies and preppies, the idle rich, the Upper West Side liberals and their families, the Upper East Side *Sex and the City* girls. Below 23rd Street (or 14th Street to purists) was the bohemian zone.

Downtowners rarely went uptown; the cliché was "I get nosebleeds above 14th Street." When uptowners went downtown, it was to sample the funk: take in a rock club, tour the SoHo art galleries, gawk at a table of wise guys in Little Italy, eyeball the roller-blading "Chelsea boys," pick up a tranny hooker in the Meatpacking District, cop some weed in Washington Square Park. Or they passed right through the boho zone to their jobs in the Financial District. Then they went home.

*

Uptown and downtown coexisted with and balanced each other. Downtown gave Manhattan much of the funky-spooky charm that set it apart from all other cities in the world. Uptowners brought their expendable income downtown with them and spread it around. It worked out for both sides.

By 2005, that cultural divide and balance had been obliterated, as the uptowners moved below 23rd Street en masse and drove everyone else out. The terms *uptown* and *downtown* exist mostly as geographic markers now, since little of downtown culture, and few of the people who generated it, are surviving the onslaught.

Locals still argue about when the change started. Some date the Beginning of the End to the opening of the first downtown Starbucks; others prefer to cite the shocking day an Olive Garden opened in Chelsea. But most would choose the day Mayor Rudy Giuliani took office in 1994. The island was certainly ready for some cleaning up and image-polishing at the time. But in his zeal to make all of Manhattan amenable to the quality classes, Manhattan's Savonarola demonstrated a downright pathological aversion to anything remotely funky about the borough's culture. Selecting midtown as the initial showcase for his "quality of life" campaign, Giuliani brokered the breathtakingly quick transformation of Times Square from scummy sin-pit to Disneyfied tourist trap, and in so doing set an agenda for the island's wholesale redevelopment. His successor, billionaire bluenose Michael Bloomberg, did not deviate from this course. Both afforded developers the widest latitude in a madly inflationary real-estate boom, rendering Manhattan's residential market beyond the reach of all but the wealthy or at least the well-salaried.

"I think that the city lived with a kind of unspoken compromise from the New Deal until the 1990s that balanced out many interests," says William Bryk, who writes about local history for the New York *Sun*. "Then the rich realized they really could buy the politicians and, under the cover of civil rights litigation, abolished the Board of Estimate. Land use decisions no longer passed through the Board, which consisted of eight politicians who cut endless deals with one another and sometimes did the right thing. Nor do they pass through the City Council, which might be a good idea, too. Instead, they pass through the Mayor's office, which makes him a very powerful man indeed.

"Ed Koch talked like a Republican sometimes, but governed like a New Dealer. Rudy, on the other hand, really believed in the virtue of the markets, without realizing that the spiritual cannot be quantified in a way that the markets will acknowledge. Certainly he despised the oddballs and ass-pains. But without their presence—and high rents easily remove them, since they usually don't have the social skills to make a decent living—Manhattan indeed becomes Cleveland on the Hudson. Then there's no particular reason to be here, because it's just like everywhere else."

The SoHo art zone went almost overnight. SoHo had been an industrial wasteland when it was colonized by artists and dealers in the mid-'70s, taking advantage of some unique collaborations with an unusually sensitive city government at the time. It remained Manhattan's prime art zone for twenty years, a model copied in many other cities and countries. In the late 1990s, SoHo was suddenly transformed into an upscale open-air shopping mall. In a rush, the artists and galleries fled the soaring prices and milling crowds, some relocating to the new, much less convenient art zone of far west Chelsea. The change was so sudden and total there was a *Twilight Zone* surrealism to it, as though aliens had slipped into SoHo one night and switched everything by dawn.

Also in the late 1990s (one is tempted to type "the latte 1990s"), SoHo was briefly home to Silicon Alley, an infestation of dotcommers riding the internet boom. A monstrous Yahoo! sign planted on Houston Street was the stake driven through the heart of the old SoHo. The dotcommers vanished when the boom went bust in 2000, though the sign remained until it was torn down to make way for one of the new, anonymous-yet-ugly office-and-retail towers that are taking over the area. (Under Bloomberg, zoning restrictions on the height of new buildings were loosened in various sectors, including Chelsea and NoHo, the area just north of SoHo. Downtown, known for a century as the one area of Manhattan where you could look up and actually see the sky, was thus primed to become a cavernous grid of shoulder-to-shoulder high-rises, just like midtown.) Meanwhile, neighboring Uhoh became Nolita.

While far west Chelsea is currently home to a small and tentative pocket of artiness, its more convenient and habitable eastern end, from Sixth to Ninth Avenues, has been uptowned. Huge, featureless, yuppie beehive condominium towers were thrown up and instantly filled. Prices for single-family townhouses in the neighborhood topped $3 million in 2004, and continued to soar. To uptowners, accustomed to seeing homes listed for up to $40 million in their own neighbor-

hoods, this was a steal. The requisite chain stores and theme restaurants bloomed. The same sidewalks where one had recently dodged those roller-blading Chelsea boys were now choked with double-wide baby strollers. The entire tone of the neighborhood shifted radically from only-in-Manhattan to could-be-anywhere.

A cluster of public housing towers on the western fringe has, as of 2005, stymied Chelsea's total yuppification, but the folks who live in them have, both literally and

figuratively, been shoved to the neighborhood's margins. "We're an isolated little island," one of them told the New York *Times* in July 2005. "We have great apartments and great rent, but we can't afford to do anything here . . . There are no restaurants you can afford, no food shops you can afford, no clothing stores you can afford. You're living here, but basically all you can do is sleep here."

Across town, the East Village and what was as recently as a decade ago the forbidden zone of Alphabet City have also been uptowned. Moneyed young professionals who wouldn't have dared venture east of First Avenue in 1995 now own million-dollar-plus condos near Avenue C, and the willowy Paris Hilton clones who troll its trendy boutiques and *boîtes* could not tell you what or where Alphabet City was, even if you could pry them away from their cell phones long enough to ask them. The area has been scoured virtually clean of its hippies, punks, artists, radicals, dope fiends, and weirdos; what's left of East Village culture is a simulacrum, a Potemkin Village, like the strip of tourist-trap restaurants that's now Little Italy. The remaining Hispanic residents clinging to its farthest fringe, Avenue D, are a trifling nuisance and will undoubtedly be cleared out soon.

Just to the south, the Lower East Side was simultaneously being drained of its immigrant and working-class residents as well, to make way for its uptownification. The first toehold in America for wave after wave of immigrant populations—Jewish, Irish, German, Italian, Chinese, and finally Hispanic—it was transformed in the mid-1990s, again almost literally overnight, into a trendy club-and-bistro zone both populated and touristed by young urban professionals. The poor Hispanic families who occupied the crumbling tenements were bought out or forced out—one infamous landlord even resorting to taking contracts out on his tenants' lives so that their tiny apartments could be redeveloped into still more of those million-dollar condos.

As in Chelsea and Alphabet City, the persistence of poor blacks and Hispanics in public housing on the fringes of the Lower East Side has so far retarded its total ethnic cleansing, as well as resulting in some wicked culture clashes that on one highly publicized occasion turned deadly. In January 2005, a quartet of white twenty-something trendies stumbled out of the hipster bar Max Fish at 3:15 in the morning and ran into a group of black teenagers who'd strolled over from the projects. The white youths were looking for a cab; the black youths were looking for trouble and had already bungled a mugging a few blocks away. When one of the black kids showed a handgun and demanded money, Nicole duFresne—a pretty twenty-eight-year-old blonde always described in the press as an aspiring actress and playwright, who'd moved from Minnesota to Seattle and then to the Brooklyn hipster zone of Greenpoint two years earlier—spoke the immortal line, "What are you going to do, shoot us?" Her nineteen-year-old assailant did just that, killing her with one bullet to the chest.

A decade or so earlier, it's highly unlikely that a young white woman who found herself at gunpoint on a Lower East Side street would have uttered such a stupefyingly foolish taunt. As thirty-year LES resident Clayton Patterson put it to me, "The white kids who came down here used to have their antennae up. They had some street sense. Now it feels 'safe' to them. They come out of the ATM at 3 in the morning with twenties spilling out of their pockets and iPods plugged in their ears. They might as well pin targets to their backs. This girl sounds like everything she knew about the streets of New York she learned from watching *Law & Order*."

DuFresne's murder made a huge splash in the local press. Loath to blame the victim, no one in the media pointed out that this "tragic event" had effectively ended two lives—hers and that of her killer, who almost certainly would spend the rest of his life behind bars for having risen to her foolhardy dare. Few noted the enormous discrepancy in the media coverage this white woman's murder received compared to the quarter-inch of police blotter she would surely have earned had she been, say, a young Dominican woman shot to death in those projects just a few blocks away. The subtext was obvious: If only those poor folks were removed—maybe to Queens or the Bronx, where they belonged—the streets of Lower Manhattan would be safe for young white women spilling out of bars at 3:00 in the morning.

The entire historic corridor of the Bowery, running from Chinatown north past CBGB's up to Astor Place, is also in the process of being completely gutted and rebuilt as these words are being written. Whole blocks of hundred-year-old buildings are being razed, replaced by the same shiny new condo towers that are being flung up all over downtown. The one that now uglifies Astor Place is called, with no evident attempt at irony, the "Sculpture For Living," and has a penthouse that originally hit the market at $9 million. By 2010 a zone famous for two hundred years for its funk and punks, its bums and dives, will have been erased not just from the cityscape but from collective memory, replaced by a zillionaires' residential area that might well be called the Lower Upper East Side.

What's left of what was once downtown culture? The only honest answer is not much, and a little less every day. One can't help noticing that so many of the surviving artists, bohemians, and weirdos are middle-aged and older; they've hung on because they bought their spaces back in the day or enjoy rents legally fixed at what are now way-below-market levels, and literally can't afford to move. A generational shift is under way. No young artists can possibly afford to live in Manhattan now; they can hardly afford Brooklyn or Jersey. When the older ones go, they won't be replaced. Once the lingering problem of those dangerous ethnics in their public housing is solved, the uptowning of downtown can be completed.

So what? The character of Manhattan has shifted many times, as it's in the nature of all cities to do. New York's reign as the art capital of the world ended before Giuliani Time; there are old-timers who would claim that downtown hasn't *really* been downtown since 1980. Maybe one should simply concede that the downtown–uptown divide was a temporary arrangement, a twentieth-century thing. Money talks, bohos walk. Things change.

But Manhattan will be a very different place when downtown's unique character has been totally flattened, its culture homogenized, its identity erased, the bohos completely supplanted by the Babbitts. When it becomes just another essentially suburban environment retrofitted into the old city grid, constructed entirely to the bland specifications of anonymous developers, with no color, no edge, no eccentricities, no art, no culture, no distinguishing features at all. That will represent not only the uptowning of downtown but the unManhattaning of Manhattan.

Staten Island: The Forgotten Borough

Steve Maluk

On July 13, 1977 at 9:27 PM, Donna Hindelong was driving home from the funeral of her brother Marty when the lights went out all over Staten Island. With the city already in the throes of a severe financial crisis, the Blackout of 1977 had begun.

As far as Donna and many other Staten Islanders were concerned, the lights had gone out three days earlier. That was the day Marty Celic, a young, athletic NYC firefighter from the Island's New Dorp section, succumbed to injuries he had suffered eight days before during a fire on Manhattan's Lower East Side.

The fire had been set by a seventeen-year-old boy in an abandoned tenement on 8th Street between Avenues C and D, then one of the poorest neighborhoods in the city. When New York's Bravest arrived at the scene, five firefighters charged into the building. Minutes later, a second fire was set below them, sending the men scrambling out a window to the fire escape. Leaping for the safety of a rescue platform rising to catch them, four of the men landed safely. Marty Celic, a record-holder in track and field at Monsignor Farrell High School, did not. Weighed down by his equipment, he fell 60 feet to the pavement, landing at the feet of his Chief. Eight days later, just before the Blackout of '77 would dominate the headlines, Marty Celic died, leaving behind his brothers Steve, Mike, and Tommy, his sister Donna, and his two grief-stricken parents, Inez and Matt.

*

Staten Island, for all its history, has always taken pride in being the backbone of the city's work force—its civil servants, its Wall Street high flyers, its donut-and-coffee commuters, and, more often than not, its heroes. Marty Celic was one more example of the dedication of, and sacrifices made by, members of the "forgotten borough." To natives, his death reaffirmed, this time tragically, the contributions Islanders make to the fabric of New York City.

To nonresidents, Staten Island is known only for its ferry, its Mob figures, and "The Dump" (one of only two man-made objects visible from space). To others, it's known for its population explosion, its over-development, its congested roads, and its relatively tranquil quality of life. But to view the Borough of Richmond in such limiting terms is, to residents, blasphemy.

From Wu Tang to Don Castellano, from Bobby Thomson (the Staten Island Scot) to Giuseppe Garibaldi, from Sailors' Snug Harbor to Historic Richmondtown, from the Staten Island Yankees to the NFL's Stapleton Stapes, from David Johansen to Christina Aguilera, from Sammy "the Bull" Gravano to State Senator John Marchi, from *The Godfather* to *Working Girl*, and from the start of the NYC Marathon to the finish of the Five Boro Bike Tour, this thriving, diverse, crowded suburban community—the southern tip of New York State that is further south than parts of West Virginia—offers much more than meets the eye.

By far the least populated and most remote borough of New York City, the Island is often the object of ridicule by outsiders. It can be enigmatic, easy to overlook, and easily forgotten (at least when it comes to snow removal). Yet its steady rise in population since the opening of the Verrazano Narrows Bridge, its recent importance in the outcome of citywide elections (Rudy Giuliani has acknowledged that he would never have been elected Mayor without the Island's overwhelming support), and its new-found position as a haven for non-native Islanders seeking a better way of life would seem to suggest a change from "forgotten" to "newfound."

Known to the Delaware Lenape tribe as "a place of bad woods"—a misnomer if ever there was one—the Island was first visited by Giovanni da Verrazano in 1524. In 1609, Henry Hudson established Dutch trade in the area and named it Staaten Eylandt after the *Staten-Generaal*, the Dutch parliament. When the Verrazano Narrows Bridge was opened 355 years later—considered the watershed event in the history of the place—it was apparent that the Island's days as a rural paradise were over.

*

In 1980, Staten Island contained fifty-nine hundred residents per square mile; today, that number is seventy-five hundred. In 1960 (a time referred to locally as "before The Bridge"), the Island's population was a little over 220,000. As of the 2000 census, there were almost 450,000 people—156,000 households and 114,125 families—residing there. Moreover, the borough's percentage of residents of Italian ancestry (44.6) represents the largest concentration of Italian-Americans for any county in America.

The issue of Staten Island's congested roads is inextricably bound up with its development. In 2004, there were 254,108 vehicle registrations. Most Island households have at least one car, the highest rate in the city. Yet the borough's road system has barely changed since "The Bridge" opened. Motorists depend on one- and two-lane streets as primary roads. Streets such as Forest Avenue, Victory Boulevard, Richmond Hill, Forest Hill, Richmond, Amboy, and Arthur Kill are all saturated daily, with few prospects for improvement.

A ride south along Hylan Boulevard back in the '60s would have included the sight of herds of cows on the hills of The Mission of Mount Loretto, a home for orphans founded by Father John Christopher Drumgoole in 1870. This Irish immigrant, ordained at the age of fifty-three, was determined to counteract the trend of sending homeless orphans to the Midwest. Fortunately, he lived long enough to see his 524-acre seaside farm evolve into New York City's foremost child-care institution.

Today, that same ride reveals row after row of town houses, condos, and million-dollar mansions whose creation was made possible by the destruction of tens of thousands of beautiful trees. The loss of these forests, combined with the noxious odors from the landfill that served until recently as the repository of waste products from both Staten Island and the other four boroughs, resulted in areas almost unfit for human habitation (although some olfactorily-challenged souls did manage to survive there).

For the least urban of the five boroughs, the scale of human-induced change in the Island's landscape has been nothing short of staggering. While it can be argued that urbanization and suburbanization have been in process there since well before the Civil War, the incredible recent pace of change can surely be attributed to the opening of the Verrazano. Former residents returning to their old haunts after an absence of a decade find the old neighborhoods unrecognizable except, perhaps, for the names of the streets. Natural habitat and views have been replaced by town-house subdivisions, office complexes, strip malls, and a proliferation of paved surfaces. Even streams and creeks have disappeared below ground, contained by pipes and culverts.

Proposals for the "twinning" of the Goethals Bridge, near the still relatively open spaces of the Island's western shores, and for the widening of adjacent roadways to facilitate traffic are indicative of the prevalent political mind-set that growth must always be accommodated on the Island, regardless of the impact on the environment and quality of life.

Staten Island today is like a microcosm of what Manhattan began as—a melting pot of different cultures from a multitude of geographical origins looking for a better life. Many native Islanders, dismayed by the loss of their once-tranquil existence, are fleeing south over the Outerbridge Crossing to New Jersey. Known to few, that bridge was named after the Islander Mary Ewing Outerbridge, who brought the game of lawn tennis to Staten Island (and America) after a winter trip to Bermuda.

Transplanted Brooklynites, perhaps glimpsing Ellis Island as they cross the Verrazano, have come to the Island in droves, finally able to enjoy the open

spaces of "the country." Eastern Europeans are also invading the Island, perhaps as a result of the end of Communism in their homelands. The '90s also saw a jump in the number of other industrious peoples (e.g., Mexicans and Indians) arriving on the North Shore, eager to do any type of work in order to send funds home so their families could join them on their adopted (newfound) island.

*

Fans of *The Sopranos* think they know all about the Mafia, a term against whose use Joe Columbo lobbied unsuccessfully in the early '70s outside the offices of the *Staten Island Advance* in Grasmere. But Staten Islanders know the real deal.

The Island is so well known for its gangsters that Francis Ford Coppola filmed the wedding scene of *The Godfather* up on Longfellow Road on Todt Hill. Mr Coppola showed his celluloid smarts by casting Rosebank native Gianni Russo as Carlo, the husband of Connie Corleone, who later feels the wrath of Sonny Corleone, played by James Caan, in one of the all-time great street-beating scenes. The Teflon Don himself, John Gotti, allegedly made his bones on Staten Island with his first rubout for the Gambino family. Sam Gravano loved the slower pace of the Island so much that he moved his family from Bensonhurst to a house in Graniteville clearly visible from the Staten Island Expressway.

When Paul Castellano and his driver were killed outside Sparks Steak House a week before Christmas in 1985, the story made headlines all over the world. "Big Paulie," who lived in a Todt Hill mansion dubbed the "White House" by Islanders, was portrayed as the "boss of bosses" (which he was not) and as the most feared man in America (which he also was not). Overlooked in almost all accounts was the fact that the Castellano murder was one of the easiest "hits" of a don since Brando got whacked on Mulberry Street in the movie. Neither Castellano nor his driver was armed, and neither had taken the simple precaution of having a backup car for protection. When Carmine Galante was

rubbed out in 1979, he at least had been operating intelligently. He was driven around town and never indicated where he would be next. On the day of his death he was riding in Brooklyn when on the spur of the moment he ordered his driver to stop at a small restaurant to eat. Still, the hit men found him, and the picture of him all shot up but with a cigar in his mouth made front pages across the globe.

*

The Staten Island Ferry, the world's greatest bargain when it was a nickel (today it's free), carries over eighteen million passengers a year. While the ferry hasn't transported vehicles since 9/11, the 6.2-mile voyage, which celebrated its hundred-year anniversary in 2005, is still one of NYC's top tourist attractions. Some, however, may not find it such a pleasurable experience, as two retired ferries currently house inmates at Rikers Island. Perhaps no one ever enjoyed the ride across the Bay more than Bobby Thomson, who, on October 3, 1951, rode the ferry on his way to his home in New Dorp after hitting perhaps the most dramatic home run in baseball history, the "Shot Heard round the World." The three-run walk-off blast at the Polo Grounds sent the Brooklyn Dodgers home in defeat and the New York Giants into the World Series.

The ferry has been a mode of transportation for everyone from the hard-boiled detectives of *Law and Order* to the vixens of *Sex and the City*. But in its film history, two movies rise above the rest. Both deal with the daily twenty-four-minute commute across the Harbor to Manhattan, which some have called the best way to visually approach the Big Apple. In both films, the ferry plays a significant and symbolic role. And both attest to how Staten Islanders, by virtue of their dedication and grit, help constitute the backbone of the city's work force.

Working Girl was the 1988 fictional saga of an Island secretary who capitalized on her chance to make her mark on Wall Street. *Ferry Tales*, released in 2003, is a forty-minute documentary that focuses on the camaraderie among a group of real-life female commuters. The cameras follow the women into the ferry's bathroom, where they put on their faces and, so to speak, let down their hair. Over time, these diverse women forge deep personal relationships. Their topics of conversation, like those of Island commuters over the decades, range from the frustrations of married life to their hopes and dreams for the future.

Martin Scorsese was just starting to learn his craft when he directed *Who's That Knocking at My Door* in 1967. The movie included several scenes shot inside the St George ferry terminal and came six years before his seminal *Mean Streets*. More often than not, however, the ferry provided a modest setting for romantic movies, using the magnificent Manhattan skyline as a backdrop. Such was the case with *That Kind of Woman* (1959), directed by Sidney Lumet and starring Sophia Loren and Tab Hunter, and with *How To Lose A Guy In 10 Days* (2003) with Kate Hudson. The ferry has always been this romantic "postcard" showcase for the best New York City can offer.

*

Oyster-harvesting, a major Island business in the 1800s, was mainly conducted off of Prince's Bay. This was within walking distance of Sandy Ground, named for its inhospitable soil. It is here that men went out to rake oysters from the ocean floor to be sent to Manhattan's finest restaurants. Sandy Ground became a mecca for free blacks from Maryland who had learned of the lucrative oystering, thus becoming one of the first communities for free blacks in America.

*

People all across America know the Island as the site of the Fresh Kills Landfill, the primary destination for garbage from all five boroughs and, at one time, the largest single source of methane pollution in the world. The Landfill was closed in March 2001 but was temporarily reopened later that year to serve as a holding area to receive the ruins of the World Trade Center after 9/11. Located on the Island's western shore, half of the 2,200-acre landfill is composed of four mounds, or sections, which range in height from 90 to 225 feet (Coney Island's Parachute Jump is only 25 feet higher).

These mounds are the result of more than fifty years of land-filling, primarily household waste. Fresh Kills is a highly engineered site, with several systems installed to protect public health and environmental safety. Roughly half the site has never been filled with garbage or was filled more than twenty years ago. These flatter areas and open waterways host everything from landfill infrastructure and roadways to intact wetlands and wildlife habitats. Perhaps most representative of nature's ability to adjust to human presence is the Isle of Meadows. Located at the mouth of the Fresh Kills Estuary, the Isle of Meadows was first harvested for its salt hay. The Isle then served as a repository for spoils from channel-dredging operations. Most importantly, it now serves as the source of ideal materials for herons constructing nests.

The potential value of this site is increased by the fact that the Fresh Kills Estuary lies on the Atlantic Flyway. The Flyway is the path used each spring and fall by countless bird species as they migrate to the north and south. The estuary, designated by New York State as a significant coastal fish and wildlife habitat, is one of the largest tidal wetland ecosystems in the Northeast.

These areas can support broader, more active uses. Hopes abound that the site can be transformed into reclaimed wetlands, recreational facilities, and landscaped public parkland, which would make it the largest expansion of New York City parks since the development of a Bronx chain in the 1890s. Plans have been announced that would open three roads leading out of the former landfill to regular traffic, as part of an effort to ease the Island's notorious road congestion. Further plans were recently made public for Fresh Kills being developed into a park in three stages between now and 2035. The city has already set aside $100 million for the project. Not surprisingly, capitalists have their eyes on the site as well (NASCAR pulled out all the stops while negotiating to have a racetrack built there; an overwhelming outcry of public opposition proved enough to scuttle their plan). Given the Island's current problems, however, it is difficult (but not impossible) to fathom that more beneficial uses of the site will prevail. One thing is for certain, and that is that this is an incredible, once-in-a-lifetime opportunity. With creative thinking, Staten Island can transform this controversial site into an important asset for the borough, city, and region.

*

Amid the congestion of the roads and the population boom—and almost akin to the majesty and brilliance of Central Park strategically placed in the center of Manhattan—lies Clay Pit Ponds Preserve. This 250-acre natural area, near the southwest shore of Staten Island, supports a variety of habitats such as wetlands, open fields, sandy barrens, spring-fed streams, woodlands, and over 150 wild deer. As a visitor enters the preserve, leaving the din of the West Shore Expressway behind, the trails reveal families of deer and other wildlife. Islanders knowledgeable enough to know of its existence, and adventurous enough to explore it, are transported back to a time when wildlife and Native Americans were the Island's only inhabitants.

*

Sailors' Snug Harbor, on Richmond Terrace on the North Shore, was a home for retired seamen, affectionately called "snugs," when it opened in 1833. Life was not always idyllic there, especially relations between the sailors and steamboat men. Occasionally, a chalk line would have to be drawn to divide the room. Discontent between Islanders appears not to be a recent development.

In the late 1970s, when the city's fiscal crisis led to the closing of many institutions and when the Greek Revival structures of Snug Harbor fell into disrepair as the population of retired seamen dwindled, Jackie Onassis made a personal visit to garner national support for keeping it open. As a result, it is known today around the world as a cultural jewel.

*

As a mainly white, suburban, Catholic borough, the Island's politics vary greatly from that of the other boroughs. Although Democrats outnumber Republicans significantly (119,601 to 82,193), voters are generally friendlier toward Republicans than in the other four boroughs. The main political divide (some might say a "chalk" line similar to the one the "snugs" drew) is between the areas north of the Staten Island Expressway, which tend to be more liberal, and those to the south, which tend to be more conservative.

In citywide elections, the Island can be described as a true Republican stronghold. Moreover, two of the only three Republicans of the fifty-one-member City Council are from Staten Island. The current Borough President is Jim Molinaro, the only Republican BP in the five boroughs. Former State Senator John Marchi, who was first elected in 1957, recently retired after his tenure as the longest-serving legislator in the United States.

Why do Republicans keep winning on Staten Island if registered Democrats outnumber them? The massive influx of middle-class Italian-Americans from the other boroughs, mainly Brooklyn, has a lot to do with it. These people, although primarily registered Democrats, tend to vote Republican as they morph into the archetypal Republican elector: suburban, white, middle-income, religious, and married with children. However, they don't bother to change their registration, becoming DINOS ("Democrats in Name Only").

In national elections, the Island is not as much of a Republican stronghold. However, it still is not as Democratic as the rest of the city or surrounding Long Island and the Westchester suburbs. The Island's only Congressional seat, currently held by Vito Fosella, has been in GOP hands since 1981. Fosella's predecessors were Susan Molinari and her father, Guy Molinari, one of the Island's most popular and influential politicians. Perhaps this rise in Republican Congressional domination can be attributed to the last Democrat who held the seat: John Murphy, who met his downfall due to Abscam, the political scandal of 1980 wherein an FBI sting operation led to the arrest of several members of Congress for accepting bribes.

Both Guy Molinari and John Marchi have received the ultimate tribute the borough can bestow—both had newly commissioned ferries named after them while they were alive to enjoy the honor.

*

In the early '90s, Island residents became so frustrated with their perceived status as "second-class citizens" that 65 percent of them voted to "secede" from New York City. Fortunately, Assembly Speaker Sheldon Silver decreed that the secession bill had to be accompanied by a home-rule message from the Democratic-controlled City Council, which had no stomach for breaking up the five boroughs. Clearly, wiser heads in Albany (how often do you hear those words?) understood the enormous contribution Staten Island makes to the city and were unwilling to relinquish it.

✳

In 1993, the direction of hard-core rap took a revolutionary turn from the Park Hill projects in Clifton, an area notorious for its violence. That year, the platinum debut album *Enter the Wu-Tang* struck a genre-expanding blow for America's hip-hop nation.

The group followed a long-line of famous natives. Christina Aguilera, born in 1980 in South Beach, got her big break nine years later on *Star Search*; David Johansen, born in 1950 on the North Shore, was the heart and soul of the legendary New York Dolls, the edgy, drug-fueled, drag queen-inspired proto-punk glam band of the '70s. He later reinvented himself in the pompadoured guise of Buster Poindexter and scored with the party classic "Hot, Hot, Hot." Joan Baez, born in 1941 in Westerleigh, energized the civil rights and anti-Vietnam War movements with her soprano voice and haunting songs. Others

include Marcia Clark (of O. J. Simpson trial fame); Robert Loggia (Oscar nominee and current *Sopranos* cast member); Jeb Stuart Magruder (Watergate witness); Alyssa Milano (*Who's the Boss?*); Rick Schroeder (*Silver Spoons*, NYPD *Blue*), and Amy Vanderbilt (*Complete Book of Etiquette*).

Others who spent significant time living on the Island but were unable to call themselves natives include doo-wop legend Johnny Maestro (of The Crests and Brooklyn Bridge fame); Bobby Darin (the Bronx native who made "Mack the Knife" and "Beyond the Sea" American pop classics); Aaron Burr; Roy Clark; Buffalo Bill Cody; George M. Cohan; Ichabod Crane (a real-life US Army colonel and the inspiration for the scrawny schoolteacher who meets the headless horseman in Washington Irving's "The Legend of Sleepy Hollow"); Ralph Waldo Emerson; Emilio Estevez; Eileen Farrell; Giuseppe Garibaldi; Frank McCourt; Galt MacDermot; Paul Newman; Annie Oakley; Frederick Law Olmsted; Emily Post; Robin Quivers, Pat Robertson; Randy "Macho Man" Savage; Steven Seagal; Martin Sheen; Gene Simmons of KISS; and Henry David Thoreau. Sadly, George Harrison spent the last few weeks of his life seeking cancer treatment at Staten Island University Hospital. During this time, it was alleged that he was taken advantage of by one of his doctors, who managed to purchase some Beatles memorabilia from the Quiet Beatle. George died within sight of the Verrazano Bridge shortly after the attacks on the World Trade Center.

*

In 1776, on September 11 at the Conference House, a colonial home at the southern tip of the Island, a peace conference was held to try to avert the Revolutionary War. Benjamin Franklin, John Adams, Edward Rutledge, and the British admiral Lord Howe attended the meeting but were unsuccessful in their efforts.

Exactly 225 years later, 43-year old Tom Celic glanced at the Statue of Liberty as he sat on the ferry with his beautiful wife Roseanne on a beautiful late summer Tuesday morning, on his commute to work in midtown Manhattan. As the ferry cut its engines near Governor's Island, he thought about a race he had run three days earlier, one held every year on the first Saturday after Labor Day. That day, he had joined hundreds of others in Clove Lakes Park to run in the 26th Annual Marty Celic Running Festival. Like his brother Marty back in 1977, Tommy had been a star track-and-field athlete at Monsignor Farrell High School. In fact, he had been the top Staten Island finisher in the New York City Marathon several times. Also like Marty, Tommy was one of the thousands of Islanders who prided themselves on their contributions to the New York City work force. When the ferry docked in Lower Manhattan, he kissed Roseanne good-bye and, instead of continuing to his office in midtown, walked the mile or so to a breakfast conference his firm was conducting.

At 8:40 AM, Tom Celic got on an express elevator that would bring him to the 97th floor of the World Trade Center. Six minutes later, the first plane hit the North Tower. The Celic family lost another of their boys.

*

On September 11, 2005, after running in the Marty and Tom Celic Running Festival, an Islander drove down to Richmond Terrace. He parked next to the Ballpark in St George, spacious home of the Staten Island Yankees, where "Postcards" overlooks New York Harbor. Designed by the Japanese architect Masayuki Sono, the 9/11 memorial comprises two 40-foot postcards, stretching out like wings to the heavens. Plaques honoring the 271 Islanders killed on 9/11 line the inside of the structures. Standing between them, gazing across the Harbor toward the transformed, forever-naked skyline of the greatest city on earth, he was again reminded of that fateful day, and of how much the beautiful Island of Staten, a "Newfound-land" for thousands, means to the fabric of New York City.

There's Hope for the Bronx

C. J. Sullivan

America became aware of the Bronx in 1927 when one of the first talking movies became a nationwide sensation. In that film, *The Jazz Singer*, Al Jolson got down on his knees and promised his Jewish mother that he would move her out of her cold-water flat in congested Lower Manhattan and up to a spacious new apartment on the Grand Concourse in the Bronx. She could proudly strut around her sunken living-room floor and wave out her window at the friends she had known from the Lower East Side that were now living the good life with her in the Valhalla of New York: the Bronx.

It was like he was promising her green grass and high tides forever. After the 1920s, more than 600,000 Jews heard Al Jolson's clarion call and made their homes in the Bronx. Back then, the borough symbolized the immigrant's progress toward the American Dream. The Bronx was a place where things were better for the little man, the immigrant, the unwanted. It was the suburb of early twentieth-century America.

Jolson knew what he was talking about. Having been born Asa Yoelson in Lithuania and come to America as a young boy, he knew first hand the struggles that immigrants faced. How hard it was to move up and live with the myth of streets paved with gold in front of white picket fences. Supposedly the American way of life was attainable by anyone willing to work hard and play by the rules. So to the Bronx they came, because that part of New York City had always taken in refugees, even from other parts of America.

*

Fifty years later, Al Jolson's song of milk and honey had started to sound like a siren's song. By the 1970s what had once held promise had soured. The Bronx had become a symbol of the dark side of the American Dream. In those dark and dangerous years, those who could get out did so. City officials had no answers for them. Mayor Abe Beame—a short, befuddled man—seemed to write off the whole borough. He was happy to stay in the safe confines of Manhattan.

Beame wasn't alone in his not-so-benign neglect of the Bronx. In the 1970s the perception of many residents was that the NYPD did little to fight crime in their districts. The cops complained of low pay, severe budget cuts, and low morale. A lot of them were doing time until they could get their twenty years in and retire with a decent pension. Some seemed happy to sit on their asses and let muggers freely work their vicious trade on the subways and streets. Back then, few Bronxites even bothered to dial 911 when trouble jumped off. You took care of it on your own. A lot of times that approach backfired, and working stiffs getting gunned down in the Bronx for their paychecks was a common tale. If you weren't young, strong, or crazy, you just didn't go out after dark.

The cops lost even more respect after the 1971 Knapp Commission hearings exposed the widespread corruption of the NYPD, much of which occurred in the Bronx, as the 1973 film *Serpico* portrayed in detail. Quite a few Bronx cops back then treated citizens as animals and were not shy about using that term.

Their ineffectiveness came to light on the night of July 13, 1977 when New York suffered its worst blackout ever.

The power grid failed, and the whole city went dark. This was the night that almost killed the Bronx. In every precinct lawlessness broke out. Fordham Road— the borough's biggest shopping district—was torn apart. Thieves pulled tow trucks up to the gates of locked stores and tore them down with chains so looters could run wild and empty out the inventory. There were reports that cops watched and did nothing in the ensuing mayhem. Scores of business owners lost their life's savings and livelihoods. Many never opened a store in the Bronx again.

There were 3,776 arrests that night, with estimates that over 15,000 looters easily eluded the police. In the city 1,037 fires were set, the majority of them in the Bronx. The low-ball cost of the destruction of the Blackout was over $350 million. Power was back on in Manhattan by 1:45 PM the next day. The Bronx had to wait hours longer, and it was the last borough where power was restored.

The one city agency that tried to help the Bronx survive was the Fire Department, but they were too busy responding to blazes set by landlords looking to collect insurance money to do very much. The decent people of the affected neighborhoods had to arm themselves against the rampant youth gangs set loose by poor schooling and unemployment to take over neighborhoods. It is no accident that the ad-hoc street patrol known as the Guardian Angels was formed in 1979 in the Bronx.

After the Blackout the Bronx became known as America's Third World. A land of the poor, desperate, and lawless. TV showed just how bad it was. During the second game of the 1977 World Series, which pitted the New York Yankees—aka the Bronx Bombers—against the Los Angeles Dodger in the Bronx's fabled Yankee Stadium, millions of viewers watched the skyline being engulfed in flames as sports commentator Howard Cosell wailed, "Ladies and gentlemen, the Bronx is burning."

In those fifty years the Bronx became the harbinger of America's future. Whatever went down there would soon come to your state. From the rise of doo-wop to the ascendancy of hip-hop—from urban destruction to urban renewal—from graffiti and youth gangs to uncontrolled rioting, looting, and arson—from the mass exodus labeled "white flight" to desperate soup lines in churches—and flooded unemployment offices and welfare buildings and crushing poverty, the Bronx was on the cutting edge of America's economic decline.

During the 1970s those who escaped—as in the 2005 New Orleans flood—were mostly well off and, in the majority, white. In 1970 over 1,080,000 whites (some Hispanics were included in this) called the Bronx their home. By 1980 that number had fallen to 550,000. In a single decade over half the white residents had fled the borough. By the 2000 census, that decline was continuing. Over 700,000 whites had left, and the smart money said they were never going to come back. A 2002 census estimated that the Bronx had over 1,300,000 citizens; 14 percent were white (down from 55 percent in 1970), 25 percent were black, 48 percent were Latino (up from 20 percent in 1970), and 3 percent were Asian (they hadn't registered significant numbers in 1970).

In 1981, James Baldwin described what brought blacks to the Bronx:

> The life of the city watching it—I watched—well I grew up in Harlem . . . when we made a little money, enough to put something aside—and do not underestimate that effort . . . it is hard for everyone, but, baby, try it if you're black—we began to move across the river to the Bronx, and all those people who had lately become white fled in terror . . . The Motion of the white people of this country has been—and it is a terrible thing to say, but it is time to face it—a furious attempt to get away from the niggers.

It was not just the movement of the population that made the Bronx what it was and what it became. In New York City the Bronx is an anomaly. It is the only borough attached to mainland America. It is also a land of varying geography. The fresh-water Bronx River runs through the middle of it. The borders are surrounded by water—the Long Island Sound in the east and the East River in the west—and most of that waterfront is little used. There are lakes in Crotona Park and Van Cortland Park. Then there are the soaring hills of various neighborhoods that cut them off from the

rest of the borough. The geography of the Bronx dictated how it would be developed. The hills of the West Bronx kept out the creeping erosion of the East Bronx. A cemetery and a vast park kept the Irish enclave of Woodlawn safe from other parts. But geography could only do so much.

*

For all the mayhem and filth of the 1977 version of the Bronx, quite a few of the neighborhoods have rather lyrical names. Out in the far reaches of the East Bronx there is a neighborhood, Silver Beach, which is a small private community of bungalows set above the shores of Long Island Sound. Due to an odd zoning law, the residents own the buildings but New York City owns the land underneath them. It is an Irish enclave that very few people in New York even know exists.

Then there are Mott Haven, Port Morris, Mount Eden, Bathgate, West Farms, Mount Hope, Claremont, and Melrose—names that seem to offer some kind of sanctuary that belies the poverty and crime of those districts. Among the neighborhoods that remain Bronx gems are Belmont, Pelham Bay, Eastchester, Riverdale, and Woodlawn.

Belmont, an Italian stronghold in the 1970s, was a place where the residents kept the peace, not the cops. In 1978 a friend of mine from Belmont told me that some creep was caught on the roof of a five-storey building on Hoffman Avenue raping a retarded twelve-year-old girl. Three men living in the building heard her screams and ran to her rescue. They pulled him off the poor girl,

smacked him around, and then picked him up and threw him off the roof to the street below. When the police showed up, every witness swore he'd committed suicide.

A few years later I found out that my friend met with his own grisly death in Belmont. His body was found chopped up in the trunk of his Cadillac. It seems that he was a Mafia wannabe and thought the way to the top was to have an affair with a capo's wife. The Mafia death ritual for fooling around with a made man's wife was to chop his body up, thus ensuring that the dead Lothario would have to be waked in a closed casket.

Belmont still has an aging Italian presence with great restaurants and food shops, and the Church of Mount Carmel still holds Italian festivals every summer. Albanians have become the new Italians there and maintain the code of policing the neighborhood themselves.

Orchard Beach, while not a neighborhood, was where everyone in the Bronx went to swim and get some sun. It was known as the Bronx Riviera. The Latinos served 50-cent *bacalaitos*—a slab of mouth-watering fried codfish. The Irish kids sold cold beer for 75 cents, and the blacks had the best weed. The cops turned their backs on this black-market swag because they were too busy check-

ing out all the pretty girls—the Bronx had some fine-looking women. The cops were known as "The Pussy Patrol," a name they earned. As the sun set the Latinos would get out their bongos and the hippies would bring guitars and the rest would sing salsa/rock/soul songs as a Bronx jam session fueled by pot and beer would close the night.

Norwood, Fordham, and Bedford Park were Irish strongholds until the 1970s, but with the rise of arson and crime the Irish started to flee north to neighborhoods like Woodlawn and even into Westchester. Latinos became the major ethnic group of those neighborhoods and kept up the tradition of the scores of Irish bars. One thing both groups had in common was Catholicism and a love of *cerveza*. Some Latino bars still have their Irish names, like the Jolly Tinker on Webster Avenue, and others took on Spanish names, like the Latin Quarter. Immigrants from Ireland still live in Norwood. The bars up there retain their Irish names, and the Latino and Irish patrons seem to get along fine.

In the 1980s, recent Irish immigrants were being mugged in Norwood at an alarming rate. And it wasn't by Hispanics. The Irish-American thugs who lived in Norwood were the culprits. They knew the immigrants worked off-the-book jobs in construction and got paid in cash on Fridays. After work they would stop in for a few drinks at the local pubs and stagger home. The thugs lay in wait and beat them for their hard-earned wages.

Well, neighborhood gossip had it that a few calls were made to the boyos from Belfast, who came to the neighborhood and straightened out the Yank thugs quick and fast. The muggings stopped, and the Belfast men returned home to their own troubles in Northern Ireland.

The social-drinking scene in the Bronx was that the Irish and the Latinos had their bars. The blacks had clubs, and the Jews tended to drink in the small bars in Chinese restaurants. All ethnic groups met up in the various after-hours clubs that opened at 4:00 AM for drinking and gambling. Those twin sins were the one sure thing that could bring all races together.

*

During the 1970s youth gangs created major havoc in the Bronx. The biggest gang was the Black Spades—mainly African-Americans. They would bop around their neighborhood carrying golf clubs. If you stayed off their turf they rarely came after you, but I went on a few bike trips through their neighborhood of Mott Haven where I had to pedal my ass off not to get eight-ironed into oblivion.

Then there were the Savage Skulls and Savage Nomads, mainly Latino, and the Golden Guineas, manned by the Italians. The only surviving gang from the 1970s is the Savage Nomads, who have morphed into a motorcycle club out in Hunts Point. Drugs, prison, and violent deaths took care of most gang members. The Jews and Irish kids had no formal gangs, but once in a while they would go out armed with their ethnic identity and some baseball bats and fight as a tribe for their turf.

The gangs pretended to be some kind of neighborhood saviors who were looking out for their own, but to a youth in the 1970s who cycled around every part of the borough and played basketball in almost every park, those gangs were mainly a pack of drug-dealing thugs who only had courage when they were in a pack.

But unlike the 2005 gangs—the Bloods, the Crips, the Latin Kings—the old-school gangs had some style. They all wore cut-off dungaree jackets called "colors" with ornate art boasting their gang's name on the back. The biggest "get" for a gang member was to beat a rival and take his jacket. That was a shame that was hard to live down.

*

A few good things came out of all the darkness, drugs, and crime. The motto on the Bronx flag is *"Ne Cede Malis"*—"Yield Not to Evil." Some started to take that to heart. One former Black Spade, Afrika Bambaataa, formed two original B-Boys crews named the Shaka Zulu Kings and the Nigger Twins. They did break dancing and rapping instead of gang banging. Bambaataa also formed the Zulu Nation—which some thought of as a gang, albeit a kinder and more socially conscious group than the Black Spades. With his crews Bambaataa started putting on rap shows in the parks around the Bronx.

Bambaataa had a match in a young Jamaican kid who had moved to the Bronx in 1967. Afraid of this new country, he would keep at home and so learned

American culture from the records of James Brown, the Rascals, War, the Rolling Stones, and Sly and the Family Stone. A group out of Harlem called the Last Poets, who put down some deep spoken word—including the epochal "Niggers Are Scared of Revolution" and the seething city poems "On The Subway" and "New York, New York"—over funky percussion beats also influenced him in 1970. By the mid-'70s he wanted to perform, so he took the name Kool Herc and came out with his Jamaican style of roaring to the streets, and he and Bambaataa became the fathers of Bronx rap. A club called Sparkle on 174th Street and Jerome Avenue opened in 1975, and the kids of the Bronx had a place to go to hear music invented by men from their own neighborhoods. As the late-'70s roller-skating craze hit, the Bronx Skate Park had a Rolling Skating Jam night with rappers spinning the tunes. While all the swells at Studio 54 in Manhattan were "getting down" to Chic, a crew of ghetto kids were charting the course music would be take up to the present day.

Thus developed a new B-Boy culture. The origin of the name can be debated, but when I first heard it used by some Zulu Nations dudes back in the 1970s it meant Bronx Boys because the blacks of the Bronx always felt slighted by the blacks of Harlem. They felt Harlem got all the props for black culture in New York, and they wanted Harlem to know that the Bronx was here and it was happening.

In the summer of 1975 I was working for the Parks Department, and my job one hot summer afternoon was to take a truck to a park on the Grand Concourse and set up a stage for a block party. My fellow workers and I put the platform up, and these neighborhood guys came and started setting up speakers, boom boxes, and turntables. I asked one of the men where their instruments were.

"You looking at them."

"Oh, you're doing that rap thing."

"That's right."

"So what's your name?" I asked.

"Grandmaster Flash."

I laughed. "Yeah, well, I'm the Lone Ranger, so if you need me we'll be over there playing basketball."

"Yeah, I'll send Tonto for you," he said and went back to work.

In 1982 when I heard the song "The Message," I thought that had to be one of the best songs of all time. I realized that that kid in the park in 1975 was one of America's musical geniuses.

Along with the Bronx Boys taking the lead in rap, they also invented another controversial art form: graffiti. Kids with spray paint attacked every train yard in the Bronx. A 4 train would be rumbling down the elevated tracks on Jerome Avenue looking like a crazed version of an acid trip. Every car was painted in pink, red, white, blue, and yellow with crazy-looking drawings and names—tags—like Red, Stay High 149, Super Kool 223, Tracy 168, and Futura

2000. Every handball court was "bombed" by graffiti artists, and it seemed like the whole borough had paint splashed all over it. After a while, when the novelty wore off, even the most ardent supporters knew it was becoming an eyesore. These days, although cipher-like tags are still common, graffiti are mainly commissioned for sides of stores or for memorials of those who died violently and too young.

*

Drugs played a large role in bringing the Bronx down in the 1970s. The Dominicans and Puerto Ricans handled the main cocaine dealing on 170th Street just east of the Grand Concourse. Every night the cry of "*perico*" would fill the air as hundreds came to buy. It was so crowded and dangerous that cops just ignored it.

But it was heroin that was the real scourge. Brook Avenue, further north on 183rd Street, and Creston were the main dealing spots of that deadly drug.

Acid was a mainstay of the Italians up in Wakefield, and every ethnic group sold reefer. But in 1979 the Jamaicans became the kings of pot in the Bronx when they came out with trey—$3-bags of weed. The Jamaican trey bags had the best weed and as much pot as any nickel bag you could buy elsewhere.

Heroin started to die off because of overdoses and killings over turf. AIDS came later and finished off the rest. Coke got too expensive and by the early '80s the drug scene was dying down. In 1983 the Bronx Borough President's office

began a campaign called "The Bronx is Bouncing Back." And it looked like it just might happen.

Then in 1986 crack invaded and tore apart any improvements that were made. Projects were taken over by crack teams, and stealing and mugging became an epidemic. Crack affected the whole city, but by the 1990s the NYPD was making a real effort to bust up the crack crews. But they concentrated on Queens and Washington Heights in Manhattan. Once again, the Bronx came in last. The problem with the police shutting down the crack trade in Washington Heights was that the dealers just moved east into the 52nd Precinct in the Bronx. The drug still causes problems in a few neighborhoods.

*

For all the crime, drugs, and violence, the borough kept up a strong religious presence. The Irish and Italians had their Catholic churches with Latinos slowly creeping in. Jews had their synagogues. Blacks had many storefront churches. I would walk by them and be impressed by the joyful singing and yelling out to God.

Latinos in the Bronx are mainly Catholic, but lately some are breaking away to Pentecostal church storefronts and others deal with Santeria. Around the banks of the Bronx River and the shores of Orchard Beach you can see offerings left to various saints and gods. I have seen a cow's tongue wrapped with rope—supposedly to shut up a witness in a criminal case. Also coconuts, dolls with candy, and little toys as offerings for sick children. Latino stores called *botanicas* sell statues of saints and gods to help with offerings. Then there are candles with saints painted on them; they are lit to receive good wishes from the saint. There are herbs and potions for protection from evil. I never met anyone into Santeria, but every black, white, and Latin person I knew in the Bronx was scared to hell of it.

*

By the end of World War II there were over 600,000 Jews living in the Bronx. The borough's largest ethnic group, they accounted for almost half of its total population. Fifty years later their number has dwindled to a mere fifty thousand souls. In one of the greatest New York resettlements ever, over 550,000 people had moved on. In 2005 Bronx most of the Jewish population lived in Riverdale, Pelham Parkway, or Co-op City. In the South Bronx, where Jews once reigned supreme, there are only a handful of survivors left.

Recently I watched one old Jewish man beat it down the Concourse by 167th Street. He held his moth-eaten camel-hair coat closed tight with one hand like it was body armor. The old have a right to fear the Bronx. Scores of elderly victims have been beaten, raped, and murdered by cowardly thugs who target the weak. If there is a definition of hell on earth it has to be growing old stuck in a neighborhood like the South Bronx.

But the Jews who left couldn't take the bricks and mortar of their faith with them. At one time the Bronx was home to almost seven hundred synagogues. Today that number is down to thirty-four. The borough is littered with former synagogues. Some of these have morphed into churches, government buildings, and grocery stores. Others couldn't be sold and sit abandoned on dark blocks that house no Jews. Their doors are chained shut, and the walls have graffiti on them.

Recently I visited an abandoned synagogue on Morris Ave and 196th Street formerly known as the Beth Shraga Synagogue; it closed in 1999. On the corner a group of Hispanic teenagers hung out eyeing anyone that walked by. I stood in front of the closed temple and saw the Star of David carved into the stone above the chained gold doors. The brick front was filled with graffiti, and a small metal sign hung by a window announcing that the synagogue was for sale.

I later talked with Eliot Markson, a retired schoolteacher and now a Brooklyn resident, about abandoned synagogues in the Bronx. Markson is a bit of an expert on the subject as his father was the principal of the Hebrew school at the Adath Israel Synagogue on 169th Street and the Grand Concourse. Markson was bar mitzvahed there in 1955—as was the Bronx serial killer David "Son of Sam" Berkowitz in 1966. The temple was closed in the '70s and is now a Seventh Day Adventist church.

"They haven't changed the temple much," Markson told me. "It looks pretty much the same, only now it's not Jewish."

*

As synagogues faded, the Catholic Church managed to hang on. The Bronx can be a strange place. Time collapses there, and the past runs into the present. Recently the baseball legend Babe Ruth and a small man from Tanzania led me back to my great grandfather.

On a late Sunday morning I walked down Morris Avenue and 163rd Street—the heart of the South Bronx just a few blocks east of Yankee Stadium. I stopped at the corner and looked into an oasis in this urban desert. A black wrought-iron fence hemmed in a small park in front of St Angela Merici Church and grammar school. The trees were maple and oak, and the buildings were old and solid and had to have been built by experienced masons, as the brickwork was perfect. I walked into the church parking lot as the last cars were pulling out from the last morning Mass.

A while back the church and school were burglarized four times. The loss totaled $40,000, $40,000 more than the church could afford to lose. After word got out, good-hearted New Yorkers rallied to aid the congregation; even the Yankees—the wealthiest and most penurious team in the city—chipped in. Most of the equipment and church vestments were replaced, and it survived.

I took an interest in this because my father had grown up in the parish, and the place always held a dear memory for him. Since the Sullivans had come over from Ireland—my great grandfather Eugene led the charge to Amerikay in the 1880s—this had been their home. My father loved to tell his children the story about how he would watch Babe Ruth at Mass, and legend had it that the Babe had donated the altar at St Angela Merici.

I walked into the dark church, and a small, lithe man met me. Smiling beatifically, Fr. Peter Mushi shook my hand and told me how he wound up in the Bronx.

"I am from Tanzania and have been at this parish for the last three years. I love this parish. It reminds me of Africa. Here the people have so many problems . . . so many, here you begin from point zero." Mushi led me to a magnificent marble altar and showed me a dark brass plague on the side. There were about fifty names, but he ran his finger over one: Mr & Mrs George "Babe" Ruth. The other names of donors—which I couldn't read—were forgotten.

"See that is how this parish came to be. One donation at a time. There is a great history here, and people still come back. It has been here since 1899. and this was always the home of the poor."

I asked Mushi if any Yankees ever walk down the hill for a visit. He laughed and shook his head.

"No, but I'm looking to hook up with the Yankees in a big way. They could work more with the neighborhood. A lot of Yankees are Dominicans, and that is what this parish is mostly. If they would come here for one day and show the people that there is hope and raise some money for the school. One day, one visit is all we would need." Mushi paused and took a breath. "This is a very poor parish. This may be the poorest district in the nation. The poor begin here. They learn how to move on. From here they learn to be Americans.

"Come, let me show you Angela." Mushi led me to a statue of the saint in the lobby of the school. Down the hallway I saw a photo of the class of 1942. The faces were all Irish. The boys were dressed in military-type uniforms and the girls wore prim dresses. Mushi stopped in front of the icon of a woman pointing down to a scroll that a young girl was holding.

"St Angela's mission in life was that poor children should get a good education and that is our promise. We have 560 children in the grammar school and the tuition is $2,200 a year. This school is the only choice for the people that live around here. The public schools in the area are not good, so this is it for them. They need this school."

I thanked Mushi for the tour, but before I could leave he led me back into the church and up the stairs to the altar.

"Look again at the names. Take your time. Maybe there you will see something. Something you want to see."

I strained to read the names, but it was too dark. I pulled out a Bic lighter and scrolled down. A few names under Babe Ruth I saw it: Mr & Mrs Eugene Sullivan. "Holy shit! That's my great-grandfather and grandmother!" I said, then quickly muttered an apology for cursing on the altar.

Mushi just smiled at me. I looked back at the name and said a silent prayer to the man whom I'd never met yet who'd given me the gift of America. I wondered what old Eugene's immigrant eyes would have made of this small African priest and St Angela Merici *circa* 2005. I am not sure, but I know he would have to be pleased that his name and the altar are still there in the Bronx.

*

The future of the Bronx will not be found in its politicians.

The new-school Latino and black power base has now replaced the old-school white ethnics who did a terrible job for the borough. The only problem is that the new boss—(Borough President Adolfo Carrion, for example, who sold out South Bronx locals for a new Yankee Stadium and a shopping mall) is just like the old boss.

The Bronx will be saved the same way it was built: by the people who live there and call it home. Like the Gambians and Senegalese braving their way from Africa to start businesses in Morrisania. Or the Cambodians who survived Pol Pot and who are now reviving the Grand Concourse. The Mexicans who traveled ten days in the desert heat so they could start a new life in the Fordham Road section and work in almost every restaurant in Manhattan. If the Mexicans in the Bronx went back home, the people in Manhattan would starve. They keep this city eating.

These are the unsung heroes of the Bronx. These tough people who work make today better than yesterday. To them the Bronx is hope. To them the Bronx is the American dream. Just like what Al Jolson sang about in 1927.

My Life in Graffiti

Joseph Anastasio

Ditmars

On the subway again. Morning. Rush hour. I get on every day at Ditmars in Queens. The clean silver train is always there waiting to go. The car cleaners have already swept off the litter, and the conductor is at the ready by the intercom. "Partner got the line up?" he blurts out, and the voice crackles back over the speakers and says, "Yes." "Next stop Astoria Blvd, stand clear of the closing doors." The dialog is always the same; the trains all look more or less the same. The passengers, well, they all look the same, too. Everything is always routine on a weekday-morning commute. Robotic, boring. Devoid of life, really.

There was a time when it wasn't quite this way . . .

I remember the 1980s, the good old days of New York, when each and every subway car bore an exterior top-to-bottom coating of layers upon layers of graffiti. Each car was a unique blend of colors. Some were painted from one end to the other with artistic "pieces," cloaked in bright letters and mystery. Even the windows were covered with paint, sometimes giving a cathedral-like quality to the interior lighting. There were ugly "toy" (beginner) tags with no stylistic merit, making the trains look a mess, and then there were tags that'd make even the best calligrapher wet herself. There were some ugly pieces, and then there were some that resembled oversized versions of something you'd see on a museum wall. Each car was unique. Each one colored with paint, sweat, and life itself.

I remember growing up and riding the subways a lot with my parents, and being inspired by all of this artwork. Graffiti looked and smelled a lot like being a rock star. If you did it good enough and got your name up enough, everyone in the city would know your name. When the book *Subway Art* came out back then, it put a public face on the movement. It showed the artwork and the people behind it, helping lay a path to art careers that some still enjoy today. If having your name up all over town wasn't Rock Star enough, getting your work in such a book sure did the trick. Part of me wanted to be a rock star. I'd never learn to play an instrument well enough, but I could draw damn good.

I was pretty young when graffiti on the subways were in their golden age. The subways were full of crime back then. You'd always hear about people getting mugged or beat up on the subways at night. As I got older I became much less fearful of the crime. I came to enjoy just riding around town and, eventually, hanging out in some of the tunnels for hours at a time. I remember hiding out down there and watching these two guys paint a train that was parked on some unused track, being inspired by their boldness. I wasn't old enough to even walk into a hardware store to get some paint without raising an eyebrow, but time would soon take care of that.

30th Avenue

I remember tagging up on 30th Ave station. I was still young and brash, and more importantly I was free. I could stay out late no questions asked. My teen responsibility was to be irresponsible. I could get my hands on paint any time. I could get away with being a graffiti-writer now, and I went for mine.

Back when I was hitting this station, the graffiti in, on, and around the NYC subway system was dead, or so the MTA thought. Us writers weren't having it though. Rooftops became hot. To get up on a rooftop facing the elevated subway line was prime real estate, a surefire route to fame. The stations themselves became targets, too. The MTA just couldn't paint them as fast as kids were bombing them. Back then there were at least fifty to a hundred active writers in the neighborhood, some just wannabe toys, others more serious—and everyone was trying to get their tags up on these stations weekly. Those were the days; today you'd be lucky to see maybe a dozen people hit these stops during the course of a year.

Broadway

I remember 1991, when all the neighborhood writers hung out on the corner just outside Broadway station, and the cops would come around and harass us for no other reason than because you could tell everyone there was a bad apple. The first US invasion of Iraq had started, and one night the cops rolled up and started frisking the notorious writer Crime SWC. They felt a spray can in his jacket pocket and asked, "What's this?"

"It's a SCUD missile, motherfucker!" he replied. It may as well have been. Spray cans were the weapon, and we were at war with society. We were at war with other gangs and other writers. Fighting to make a name every single day.

Years later I learned that another infamous writer, Sane, was a station agent at this stop. I probably bought tokens from him and didn't even know it. That's how it was back then. Everyone was a writer, and a lot of the really hardcore dudes you'd never know about or recognize unless you ran in the right circles.

36th Avenue

I remember coming up here one night while I was still young but not entirely naive. I was with three other writers. They started tagging up the station and I was just thinking, "What are they, stupid?" We knew the Vandal Squad cops were hiding out in the "lay up" trains—subway cars parked in the middle track during off-peak hours. We knew the cops were watching, or at least I thought we all did. The cops were waiting to catch themselves some collars. Make some arrests, meet the "Performance Standard" (because there's no such a thing as a quota). One cop came up from the only exit on the station, the other from the tracks behind us. It was a trap, and in an instant it wasn't a game anymore. It was over. I was going to jail. My parents would disown me and I'd have to pay some big-ass fine I couldn't possibly afford . . .

They were big men with badges and guns, and they had us on the ground getting their frisk on. But they were human, and luck was on my side. Let's just say I was the only one to protest some of their search tactics, and that resulted in the cop not being very thorough. They never found the brand-new never-used can of pink Krylon up my coat sleeve. I suppose it helped too that I was a dirty-looking metal-head kid. Every writer I knew shared more or less the same fashion style: fade haircuts, phat sneakers I couldn't afford if I tried, triple-fat goose jackets, and of course beepers. Let's just say I didn't look that way. With my long hair, fucked-up jeans, construction-worker boots, spiky bracelets and .50-caliber bullet shell that I used for a necklace, I looked a lot more like someone out of a death-metal video than a hip-hoppin' graffiti-writer. When a train came, the cops told me to scram. Everyone on the train going home from work

was looking out at these little kids in handcuffs on the station with these two big burly cops standing over them. Then the doors closed and suddenly everyone on the train was looking at me, white as a ghost.

I started walking through the train, got off at the next stop, and walked for miles that night. I couldn't go home, I had to wear off the adrenaline. I didn't want a criminal record or grief from my parents and all the other associated stigmas of getting caught. But then again I had a can in my hand, and I knew I had to empty that shit. I bombed and cleaned that can out, and then I retired from the game, or at least that's what I tried to tell myself.

Queens Plaza

I used to always catch tags on Queens Plaza, too. One night I was with my boy and these two guys came up to us—using the universal tagger greeting, "Yo, you guys write?" It was Seus and Spook. I remember them guys . . . Seus was coming out all over the neighborhood and in the subway tunnels in a big way. I remember a few weeks later when Spook was electrocuted on a power line while out graffiti-bombing some tunnel. He lasted a while in a coma before dying. He was just sixteen. A few years later I heard that Seus was randomly stabbed to death one night. The streets, the tunnels, this graffiti game ... it takes a heavy toll sometimes. But when you're young, and when the economy sucks and the crack epidemic is in full swing, you just accept that death is waiting for you. Death might come on any given mission, any given night. You could get stabbed, mugged, beaten, or shot just coming home from hanging out on the subway.

There were a dozen ways to Sunday to get fucked up real bad back then, so bombing and living every night like it was your last was just what you did—and you'd do it without regret.

At Queens Plaza, the train finally ducks underground. It leaves the station packed to the gills with passengers. Standing room only, and some of them people are standing uncomfortably close to each other. You'd think maybe people would find another way to get to work besides the subway-sardine option, but they don't. They're persistent, doing this shit day after day after day, just like some taggers.

I remember persistence. The word was defined by a name, and that name was Sane Smith. Throughout the '80s, no matter what part of the city you went to, you'd see a Sane or Smith tag, and if you didn't, you'd see some of their boys, Ghost, JA, Bruz, etc. I was impressed by this persistence and the daring tactics some of these writers employed. 60th Street tunnel was a perfect example of this.

The "60th Street tube" is a long, straight, narrow unforgiving place. Unlike most subway tunnels, there's no place to hide down there should a train come. Smith and Bruz rocked it though, with tags under each light along the tunnel walls. With lights perhaps every 20 feet along this mile-long tunnel, you can do the math.

"It was a mission to hit every light," Smith says. "But we weren't going to leave any space for anyone else to get up. We wanted to claim it." Laying such a claim rarely comes without complications, though. "A worker train came, so we had to run to the next emergency exit—it was a like a slow speed chase. We hid there behind a door and they just went by, and we went back to work." Persistence is the quality that makes mere mortals into legends of the graffiti game.

59th Street/Lexington Ave

Getting off the train at 59th Street/Lexington Ave, I look across—across the platform, past the newly assigned cop stuck in his little "Omega" guard booth in the middle of it, across the northbound track—and stare for a split second at the wall. It is dull, gray, and utterly lifeless.

I remember when Gridz hit that wall. It was a simple piece—-white, blue, and green, but it shined like a pearl. That shit ran for months and always brought a smile to my face. It takes balls to get up right there on the platform—to do a quickie piece at such a busy station.

So much has changed since then. Post-9/11 paranoia mandated the police booth, guarding the cross-river tunnel as best they can. With this twenty-four-hour watch, you won't be seeing any new tags under them lights in the tube anytime soon, and you'll probably never see another piece on that dull gray wall again.

I go down the stairs and transfer to the downtown 5 train. It too consists of nothing but nice new shiny subway cars, complete with digital displays and automatic voice announcements of each stop. A more rote and predictable ride you cannot find. I board the train.

Grand Central Station

I remember the passage of time—the two years between my close call with "the man" and realizing I wasn't done yet. I came out of retirement, if one can ever truly quit this game. By this point I had been practicing on paper religiously and had developed my "handstyle" real good. I wasn't a toy-ass bastard anymore, and I had a new fast-acting super-sticky tag to slap all around town like your drunken mom's face at 4:00 AM.

I wouldn't do it alone, though. I was talking with this girl and she was all bent on adventure. I suggested taggin' up. I showed her some styles. Having an artistic flare, she took to writing like Koch to a crowd. It wasn't too long before we were bombing, taking the streets of Manhattan by storm. I think she even wrote "how 'm I doin'?" in one throwy.

The tag names we used, that's not important. What was important was the fun and adventure we had, the smell of the paint, the adrenaline rush, the aerosol-junky life. Scamming cans wherever we could by day, going out and bombing the town by night. We hit it and hit it big for a hot minute, and when word was going around that the man had their eye on trying to find out about us, we quit it. We emptied out our last cans on a wall in an abandoned lot in

Hell's Kitchen. Doing it on the down-low and never bragging about it at the time. That's the only way to really do graf and not get bagged by the man. Keep your mouth shut and do the work.

14th Street

I remember finally feeling satisfied after that. Like I had done what I wanted to do with graffiti and was done with it. I also remember bringing along a camera more and more. I had always been a photographer, but I never really had the cash for a lot of film. By now I was getting older, working, and realizing I could achieve the same effect of graffiti, saying, "Hey, I was there" by taking photos of some of these crazy places we went. For me, the camera replaced the spray can. My handstyle became my shutter style.

*

By this point the crowd on the train has thinned out a bit. The Lexington Avenue line that the 5 train runs on is considered to be one of the most overcrowded in the city. This crowding is due in no small part to the fact that the city has never completed building the Second Avenue line, which is eventually to run parallel to the Lex Ave line and hopefully absorb some of the riders from it.

I remember Second Avenue and meeting up with fellow photographer Mike Epstein and us being the first photographers to explore the abandoned northern half of the 63rd Street station. The station itself is part of the 63rd Street tunnel, though one can easily argue that the northern side of the platform was built as a provision for (and therefore a part of) the Second Avenue tunnel. Most people don't even know that there is a whole other half of a station laying abandoned behind the wall at 63rd and Lex, but sure enough it's there.

Just like everywhere else, a lot of graffiti artists had come and gone before us. According to Swatch, a graffiti artist who was the first to hit a lot of these Second Avenue spots, they went so far as to throw a New Year's party down here. The days of such parties are pretty much gone, but the tags remain. The taggers, though, they still go down there. A graffiti artist who recently went was Jedi 5. "Painting spots of this nature makes graffiti feel worthwhile," he told me. "I don't really care about street bombing, even though it's lots of fun. Coming to exclusive spots like this makes me feel I'm really putting effort into it."

Putting in the effort, finding the spots, and then rocking them in your own special way. Swatch and Tyke did it. Scope and Nuke did it a lot, and now Jedi & co are at it. Graffiti is a cycle, and it does not stop.

I also remember exploring the Chinatown segment of this Second Avenue subway line. I remember me and Clayton gearing up and going in. It was a nice feeling, being in a subway spot that so few have gotten to see. I remember the marvel of all the extra space they had built in there for utilities and ventilation.

Even the trackshelf, that little catwalk running alongside where the tracks go, was wider than you'd find in any older subway tunnel.

What will happen to this spot when the Second Avenue tunnel is finally built is unknown. Several of the current plans for routing the tunnel downtown do not use this stretch of tunnel at all. It may very well become an orphan, disconnected from the system, a monument to the fiscal crisis of the '70s that brought an end to the construction of the original Second Avenue line.

*

The train keeps moving, now going past the abandoned Worth Street station.

I remember not that long ago going to Worth Street. I remember running down the tracks to photograph this station late one weekday night. We were originally going to go to 18th Street, but the track-workers were out and about. I remember how we had to hide from passing subways on the platform, and how I found an old set of block letters from Rebel.

Rebel remembers that spot well, too. "We came out of that tunnel filthy," he said. "I had soot in my *ears* from that place. We ran out at like 3:00 AM and thought the station we were coming out onto was empty, but there was a guy right there at the end, and when I stepped onto the platform I was right there in his face. He stepped back and almost had a fucking heart attack—his eyes were like dinner plates!" Every real graffiti artist who's ever rocked a can has dozens of memories like these. They are the best urban stories you'll ever hear.

*

Brooklyn Bridge

I remember exploring all the tunnels near Brooklyn Bridge just a few years ago. One night I was down there with Maria, a fellow photographer and a woman who just plain ain't afraid to get down and dirty. We were wandering around down there for a few hours and getting ready to leave. We were waiting for a train to leave the J-train platform so that there wouldn't be any MTA personnel staring at us once we climbed up and out of this hole, but the train just wouldn't leave—and when it finally was about to, we heard work bums walking down the tunnel right toward us. The gig was up and it was time to go—we started running alongside the J train as it headed northbound towards Canal Street. We kept pace with it some-how, arriving at Canal just as the train pulled out continuing northbound. We jumped on the platform and ran out of the station just as some extremely loud buzzer went off on the tracks. Some guy was by the token booth saying, "What's that alarm sound?" We got out onto the street and we ran, finally stopping a few blocks away in a parking lot, where I proceeded to cough up some of the steel dust we kicked up for a good five minutes. You just can't pay for an adventure like that.

*

Fulton Street

I remember the war on graffiti. I remember when they singled out people like the brothers SaneSmith and tried to vilify them as best they could. The battle continues today, only more so. Even toy kids these days are getting their names in the paper when they get caught for catching just a few tags around town. To the powers that be, graffiti is a sign not of art but of trouble, of crime and a loss of control over the mindless herd of citizens. It is a precursor to more crime. The broken-windows school of Gestapo-style law enforcement. Graffiti is ugly and destructive, and for some writers, that's just the point.

"I came out of retirement because I lived in a nice neighborhood and soon found I couldn't pay the rent," proclaims FE One, a man that used to tag the trains back when they were hot in the '80s. "I'm just trying to bring the property values down. At this rate of gentrification, they just keep pushing us back further and further to the outsides of the city—they're pushin' us out into the ocean, and I don't want to be livin' that *Waterworld* life!'

You could say that the graffiti artist's story is every New Yorker's story. It is a struggle to survive in a city of ever-increasing rents, ever-increasing luxury for the rich, while the poor just keep getting pushed aside.

Wall Street

I remember just last weekend, being on a rooftop in Brooklyn. It's a hot spot, lots of tags in a prime location, and I was just sitting back, watching a new writer get his paint on. I was like a movie critic, thinking his tag's too long, takes too slow, his style isn't fully developed, and if he gets nabbed, how severe are the penalties? Before, you could get caught writing and get community service. Now, they're trying to stick even toy newbies with years in jail just for catching a tag.

On the one hand, graffiti get to be a frustrating game to watch as you get older. You see these kids coming up who don't practice enough, don't have skills, and don't know how to stay off the radar. For a cat like me, I *know* I could do it better. I could come out and rock shit pretty hard and get away with it. But I won't, and I don't, because the other part of getting is older is how much less doing stupid shit is worth the risks. You got bills to pay, a girl to keep happy, jobs you don't want to lose, a clean record, and let's be real, no matter how good you think you are, luck might turn out to be a bitch instead of a lady on any given night. It's easy to hate on the toys coming up, but hey, at least they're getting up, and getting up under increasingly risky circumstances.

Bowling Green

I remember being on vacation looking at time-share property with my fiancée. Out of curiosity we looked through the catalog to see where their NYC property was located. I nearly had a heart attack when I recognized the address. Their nice new multi-million-dollar building was built right on the abandoned lot where perhaps ten years ago I dropped my last tags on a wall.

Investments, bills, falling in love, getting married, having kids, cars, babies—all of these are reasons why people like me stop being so bad . . . but the temptation . . . it's always there. And while maybe I won't be picking up a spray can anytime soon, I sure as fuck won't stop running around the tunnels and abandoned parts of town taking my photos any time soon either.

The subway car I'm in only has a few riders at this point. Bowling Green is the last stop in Manhattan, and it is where I get off. In another four or five minutes I'll be in the office, at my desk, putting in another eight or nine hours of routine, rote, boring work, passing the time really, waiting for the sun to set, the weekend to begin, and the next adventure to begin, because this, this commuting, this sitting in an office all day . . . this isn't life. Graffiti, exploring, going on crazy missions . . . that's what life is, and I'm gonna live my life every damn chance I get.

Commerce

Luc Sante

Every sign of human progress entails a rent increase.
—Georges Darien

What this country needs
is a good two-dollar room
and a good two-dollar broom.
—Captain Beefheart

One morning as I was walking up First Avenue, a dog ran past me with a dollar bill in its mouth. A few seconds later a fat man came puffing by in hot pursuit.

*

Preparing to go do laundry, I accidentally knocked a box of detergent off the windowsill. I dashed downstairs to retrieve it, but by the time I got to the sidewalk it had already vanished.

*

For years I bought my produce at a place on First Avenue called The Poor People's Friend.

*

My friends J. and P. worked at an agency located in the basement of the Empire Hotel, across from Lincoln Center, that assisted foreign students traveling in the United States. They often had to come to the aid of travelers who had spent all their money and lacked carfare to the airport. Frequently students would barter small items for bus tickets; one day somebody traded them a car. It was a tiny car, perhaps Japanese (I don't recall the make), and clearly on its last legs. It was ugly in an unobtrusive way, its body freckled with rust spots. The argument against

possessing a car in New York City had mostly to do with parking problems, but this car was immune. We merrily parked it on corners, at crosswalks, in front of churches and fire hydrants, secure in the knowledge that it wouldn't be towed, let alone stolen. Tow-truck operators would take one look and realize that nobody would be paying ransom. We kept the car for almost a month, until, probably, some dutiful cop couldn't stand it any longer.

*

Second Avenue, south of 14th Street, was at that time deserted after sundown. One of the few sources of illumination, apart from streetlights, was the row of spotlights shining down on the sidewalk from the East River Savings Bank branch between 6th and 7th streets. One night J. and I were walking along when we saw, carefully lined up in the glow of the spots, the complete works of Wilhelm Reich, in chronological order of publication. We each took two books, feeling a bit guilty about it, since they seemed intended for some purpose. We joked that they were meant to greet visiting flying saucers.

*

One day, walking my dog on 13th Street between First and A, I noticed that among the sidewalk habitués every man, woman, and child was wearing identical Kenny Rogers t-shirts. Few of them would have figured among the singer's target audience. The shirts had perhaps, as they say, fallen off a truck.

*

Among the many curious enterprises on Elizabeth Street was a grocery store that only opened at night, approximately between midnight and dawn, and only stocked a handful of items, chiefly canned garbanzo beans. The store was run by an old woman dressed in black. We never managed to catch her eye, and never heard her speak.

*

There was a shoe store on First Avenue that you couldn't enter. It was down a short flight of steps in what is known as a French basement, and you couldn't enter because it was crammed to the ceiling with shoe boxes in a sea of dust. Only the owner could negotiate the narrow alleys between the towers. He would bring out the shoes and you tried them on and transacted business on the stoop. It was in effect a vintage shoe store, but it had not originally been one; the stock had been acquired new and then, for some reason, been left to sit there for a few decades. I still have the store's business card, which is not only illustrated with an engraved depiction of a man's lace-up boot, *circa* 1914, but also lists the telephone number (GRamercy 7-5885) and address (New York 3, NY) in ways that suggest it was printed no later than 1962.

*

I also sometimes bought shoes from a man named Jerry, from whom I sometimes bought drugs, too, mostly pills. Those were his twin enterprises. When I arrived at his apartment, he would invariably be wearing a sleeveless undershirt and pegged trousers, and just as he invariably would be ironing something on a board identical to my mother's.

*

If you sat in the right bar long enough, sooner or later someone would offer to sell you something—a tape recorder, say, or a supply of disposable diapers. The vendor would move from table to table with exaggerated stealth, opening the brown paper bag under his arm just enough to permit a glimpse of the item's packaging. Once I scored a portable hairdryer at the Gold Rail on 111th Street and presented it to my mother on Christmas. A few years later, my friend D. gave me, for my birthday, an 8-mm movie camera and tripod, as well as a film-cutter that was, however, meant for Super-8 stock. I knew instantly that he had purchased those items in the men's room at Tin Pan Alley, a bar we favored on 49th Street.

*

Everybody envied м. his job. Once a month he traveled to Kennedy airport, where, at a set time, he would receive a call on a particular pay phone. A voice would read him a list of numbers, which he would note down. Moving to an adjacent telephone, he would call another number and read the list to the respondent. A few days later a courier would bring him an envelope full of cash.

*

For many years there were numerous commercial establishments that sold marijuana. Some were candy stores, some social clubs, some *bodega*s. What they had in common was a slot in a rear wall into which you would push your money, generally $10, and from which you would collect your little manila envelope. The most famous were probably the Black Door and the Blue Door, which glared at one another from opposite sides of 10th Street. One was an empty room, the other featured a pool table; one marked its bags with a Maltese-cross stamp, the other didn't.

*

By the late 1970s, the fabled Fourth Avenue district of used bookstores had dwindled to fewer than half a dozen, most of them no longer even located on Fourth Avenue. One of the most venerable, Dauber & Pine, had moved to University Place, where it was selling its remaining stock and no longer acquiring anything new. One day the store suffered a fire, which was quickly contained but which left residual smoke damage. The damage was heaviest in the foreign-language department. The store owners tackled the problem by filling shopping bags with afflicted French books, each bag priced at $2. The books, however, not only were varyingly charred and smelling of smoke, but they had been in poor condition to begin with. Furthermore, they were almost uniformly nineteenth-century yellow-backed boudoir trash, the works of Paul de Kock and Xavier de Montépin—Madame Bovary's reading material. Nobody ever bought the bags, as far as I could tell, though they constituted merchandise so ineffably conceptual that they could have commanded thousands in a gallery setting a few blocks to the south.

*

One day I was sitting in the pastry shop, in a booth. I could hear every word being spoken by the large party at the table in the center. They were reminiscing about racetrack scams of the past. A small man with a raspy voice deplored modern telecommunications. At one time, he recalled, he and his brothers had rented a house overlooking the finish line at Pimlico, or maybe it was Hialeah. One of them hung out the window with binoculars. The instant the winner came across, he flashed a hand signal to another brother on the phone. Their man in New York would then signal to a confederate standing in line at the pari-mutuel office, who would bet large, since the official results would take another two minutes to be posted.

*

Until the 1990s I never paid more than $180 in rent. Still, given the condition of my crumbling building—of all the buildings I inhabited over the years—I felt that anything over $100 was high. I knew that R. kept an apartment (he seldom visited it, spending his time in other beds) on 3rd Street, in the Men's Shelter block, which because of the street's dangers was only $50 a month. My colleague H., for that matter, had inherited her lease from a dead aunt; her 7th Street apartment was a mere $38. And once I met an old-timer who paid $30, but he was bitter about the annual increases imposed by the landlord lobby—when he had originally moved into his 2nd Street tenement in 1960, the rent had been $10. We agreed that ten bucks approximated the value we derived from the neighborhood and its housing stock.

*

Once, while visiting my parents in New Jersey, I ran into a high-school classmate I hadn't seen in years. When he found out where I lived, he told me he visited the neighborhood sometimes in his capacity as freight agent for a large-scale marijuana importer. The outfit rented an apartment a few blocks away from me that was employed as a depot for goods being moved from one distant city to another. Years later, N., a friend who was a musician and a carpenter, told me he had spent the previous three months refitting a nearby apartment for a pot dealer. The circumstances were different, though. Prices had increased significantly and so, correspondingly, had apprehension. This dealer, a wholesaler for local traffic, had engaged my friend to put in numerous false walls and invisible compartments and sliding panels, as well as a booth by the door for the guard, with a hole through which he could poke the muzzle of his piece.

*

For years there was a general store, of the most traditional sort, on 9th and Second. I did my photocopying there, bought aspirin, string, drywall screws, mayonnaise, and greeting cards on various occasions. You could not imagine that they could possibly carry the exact spice or piece of hardware or style of envelope you needed, since the place was not enormous, but invariably an employee would disappear into some warren and re-emerge with your item in hand. In my memory I am always going there during blizzards. Another sort of general store stood on the corner of 14th and Third. It may have had another name, but its sign read "Optimo." It was cool and dark inside, with racks of pipes and porn novels and shelves of cigar boxes and candy. Of its two display windows on 14th Street, one featured scales, glassine envelopes, and bricks of Mannitol—the Italian baby laxative favored by dealers in powder for stretching their merchandise—and the other held shields, badges, and handcuffs. I often wished that Bertolt Brecht had been alive to admire those windows.

✳

Once after leaving the World, a club on 2nd Street, I was riding in a taxi with J. and R. Rounding a corner, we saw a mutual acquaintance, using a coat hanger, breaking into a parked car. We knew he did things like break into parked cars, but none of us had ever seen him in action. It was like watching a nature documentary—or better: it was exactly like looking out the window and seeing an egret building its nest.

✳

Usable objects not worth selling could be disposed of easily. You just put them out on the street and they would disappear, within minutes, as if they had been thrown into a river. Depending on the building, a similar result might be obtained by putting the stuff in the lobby or a stairwell. When I finally threw out my old green couch, though, nobody would touch it. I felt personally insulted. It was admittedly a little ragged, but its springs were all present and intact, and it was long enough to serve as a comfortable spare bed. The cushions, of course, were nabbed immediately, but the rest of it lingered on the sidewalk until someone stuffed it awkwardly through the back door of an abandoned car and set it on fire.

✳

Bodegas sold mysterious little bags of dime-sized cookies decorated with pastel florets of frosting. The bags cost a quarter, and every time I went to a birthday party I would buy one and tape it to my present. As far as I know, nobody ever ate even one, and no wonder: while they looked soft, they had all the resilience of marble.

✳

For years the local bookie occupied an actual hole in the wall: a storefront only as wide as its door and maybe 10 feet deep. He didn't hang out a shingle reading

"Bookie," but then he didn't need to. For some reason he abandoned this space in the early 1980s and relocated to a back table in the pizza parlor.

*

In Washington Square Park, a pot dealer walked around holding up notebook pages covered with scribble. "These are testimonials from my satisfied customers!" he crowed.

*

When I felt that prices in Manhattan were getting too high, I would cross the river to Hoboken, where you could still find $1 shirts and $5 suits long after those items had risen in price tenfold at home. One day I passed the window of a residence on the main drag in which two or three old paperbacks were displayed along with a scrawled sign saying "For Sale Inside." I knocked and was admitted. In addition to a couple of revolving racks of fantastically gaudy crime novels from the 1940s and '50s, the room also contained three generations of a family, apparently Southern, from a babe in arms to a grandmother sprawled hacking and gagging on a couch, with a sheet twisted around her middle. Something was cooking on a hot plate. No one spoke. At least five pairs of eyes regarded me hollowly. I browsed in record time, paid, and fled, feeling like a census taker.

*

Down the street from me was a store called Coffee and Dolls, run by two blond brothers in their forties to whom we referred as "Jimmy Carter" and "Billy Carter." The store's name was accurate, apparently—the window displayed dolls and sacks of coffee beans. No one was ever seen buying either item, however. The fact that the storefront provided a thin cover for the permanent ongoing poker game held in the basement could not have escaped the attention of many people, perhaps not even the police.

*

When I walked my dog around the block we would sometimes meet a German shepherd and his walker on 13th Street. The dogs liked each other and would play, not a small matter since my chow did not like many other dogs. The owner of the shepherd was a thin guy with a mustache, about my age. I don't remember much conversation, although he was pleasant enough. One day I found myself on Fifth Avenue, near St Patrick's Cathedral. Up ahead I spotted a mendicant in a wheelchair, with a blanket covering his lower extremities, his neck and torso contorted by cerebral palsy or something similar. When I got close enough to see his face I was thunderstruck—it was the owner of the German shepherd! I thought I must be mistaken, that there was really no more than a

general resemblance, but when I walked past him—carefully keeping a line of pedestrians between us so he wouldn't see me—I was sure. It was definitely the same guy. Had he been in a terrible accident and lost his livelihood? As it happened, I had just been reading about the "cripple factories" of the early twentieth century, where able-bodied men and women were taught to fake blindness and other handicaps to increase their take as beggars. The very fact that I had been reading about such things convinced me that I couldn't possibly be witnessing a present-day equivalent. I felt guilty for not reaching out to him or giving him money, although I couldn't persuade myself to go back. A few days later, however, when I walked my dog around the corner to 13th Street, there was the shepherd— and there was his master, as hale and cheerful as ever.

*

z. had come from Germany to make his way as a musician, and after a few years his career was progressing admirably. He played in three or four bands, all of them admired, some measurably in advance of what the other outfits on the scene were doing. He had also, over the years, become a heroin addict. As addicts will, he was driven to ever greater exigencies to raise money to support his habit. His musical employment gave him little financial advantage; as far as I know, none of his bands was ever recorded. He therefore became a burglar. One night he set out to rob the apartment of a former girlfriend. She lived on the top floor of a tenement, her bedroom window—which z. knew to be unlocked—located on the rear, about 4 feet from the fire escape. Grasping the railing of the fire escape, z. swung his legs over to the window ledge. He inserted the tip of his right sneaker beneath the top of the frame of the lower sash and pushed upward. The window, as he hoped, slid gently open. When he had raised it as far as he could, he dangled his feet inside and gave a mighty push with his hands, hoping that momentum and gravity would propel him in. He had fatally miscalculated, however, and dropped five stories to the concrete surface of the back court. Everyone immediately knew what had happened, even people like me who had not been close to z. A day or two later, the *Daily News* covered the story in an inch-long column filler. "ROMEO FALLS TO DEATH," it was headed. It told the poignant story of a young émigré musician who was such a romantic that he contrived to slip into the bedroom of his beloved as she slept. Sadly, he met with misadventure.

*

Sooner or later everybody I knew tried to buy something from the deli on Spring Street, and everyone had the same experience. Usually it was a hot day, and the store hove into view just when the need for a can of soda presented itself. So you'd enter, go to the cooler, pick out a cold one, and take it to the counter.

"Five dollars."

"Excuse me?"

"You heard me."

Some people left meekly; some tried arguing, to no avail. If the owner didn't know your family, he didn't want your business, and that was that.

*

The Late Show was one of several $3 clothing stores that flourished in the neighborhood in the mid-1970s. Everything in the store cost $3, whether it was a t-shirt or a three-piece suit in cut velvet. The place was run by Frenchy and Angel, surviving holdouts from the methamphetamine culture that had ravaged the area half a decade earlier and driven out the hippies. Frenchy had once been wardrobe manager for the New York Dolls; he walked with a cane and moved as if he was fifty years older than he was. Angel was so thin she could have hidden behind a telephone pole. She wore ordinary dark glasses that looked outlandishly oversized on her. One day I took my ditsy friend F., visiting from out of town, for a shopping trip there. Since she had arrived unprepared for the weather, I had lent her my brown leather bomber jacket. She carelessly threw it in a corner and went to work, stepping up to the counter hours later with an enormous haul. After she paid we went to look for my jacket and couldn't find it. It turned out that, while our attention was elsewhere, someone had come in, tried it on, and bought it.

*

Among the peddlers on Astor Place, the same set of the works of Khrushchev (Foreign Languages Press, Moscow) circulated from hand to hand for at least a year. Nobody ever bought it, but every day it would appear in someone else's stock.

*

Inflation. On August 6, 1979, I hit the street clutching a $10 bill. With that sum ($9.98, to be precise) I bought three slices of pizza, a can of Welch's Strawberry Soda, a pack of Viceroys, six joints, two quarts of orange juice, two containers of yogurt, and a pint of milk. For some reason I was moved to enter those details in my notebook. I often revisited the entry. On May 29, 1981, I noted that the shopping list would cost around $12 at current prices. On March 24, 1983, the sum had risen to $13.50, and a year later to $15. On August 2, 1986, I calculated the cost as $39.35—loose joints were rare on the street, and by then a dime bag of marijuana yielded about two joints. On December 1, 1990, the cost had reached $72—$12 minus the marijuana. On March 28, 1993, I figured it had attained $92.75, or $22.75 for everything but the pot.

*

One day when L. went to buy heroin on 3rd Street, as he often did, he was hijacked. That was not unusual either, but this time the thieves maneuvered him into an abandoned building and took not just his money but also every shred of his clothing. He was forced to make his way home naked. Fortunately he only lived about ten blocks away.

*

The last time I saw w., he was selling records on the sidewalk on St Mark's Place. He told me he was disposing of his property to raise funds for a trip to Asia. I don't remember buying anything from him—his tastes tended toward the impressive-looking but unlistenable—but unless I was broke I must have thrown some dollars his way. His travel plans sounded so grand—months apiece in Kashmir, Thailand, Bali, etc.—that I wondered whether he would ever realize them. A few weeks later I got word that he had committed suicide, in his apartment.

*

"My dream," v. told me more than once, "is to come upon a parked truck transporting Kodak film. Think about it: film is small, light, untraceable, easy to dispose of, and proportionately expensive. It's the ideal score. A find like that could set you up for years to come." I lost track of v., so I don't know whether he ever fulfilled his dream.

*

When s. inherited his father's estate, although it was not a major sum, he promptly retired. That is, he quit his job, moved into a room in the George Washington Hotel on 23rd Street, and took his meals at the donut shop on the corner. He read, wrote, strolled, napped. It was the life of Riley. He might have continued in this fashion indefinitely had he not made the acquaintance of cocaine.

Who Walk in Brooklyn

Brian Berger

Who knoweth Brooklyn? Stranger, oh, stranger, I answer you. I will answer you that only the hungry-hearted manswarm, the dreamers of dry dreams in the wind-spanned womblocked avenues called Pitkin and Church and Neptune and Ocean and Blake and Rogers and Tilden—
—Wallace Markfield, *To An Early Grave* (1964)

You can get Spanish fly on Union Street.
—Gilbert Sorrentino, *Steelwork* (1970)

I came here to rectify
Brooklyn Zoo, terrify
—Ol' Dirty Bastard, from "The Stomp" (1995)

There's the world, and there's the underworld. Then there's Brooklyn, which offers each in such abundance that distinctions between the two are almost meaningless. Scale is just part of the story: 2.6 million people, 70-odd square miles, and dozens upon dozens of distinct yet shape-shifting neighborhoods, almost all of them engaging in their polyglot, furious, and voluble ways. Geography, politics, real estate, crime, and a jumble sale of forgotten history tell the rest. If there's a single thing that defines Brooklyn today, it's the constant leaps of disjunction required to catch even glimpses of the whole.

Brooklyn's waterfront stretches from the poison sludge of Newtown Creek in the north down along the East River to New York Harbor and then out to the littoral islands of Jamaica Bay on its southern shore, with ugliness and beauty juxtaposed nearly every step of the way. Brooklyn rises most impressively from the water in Sunset Park and again up to Queens from Cypress Hills and Highland Park; on a clear day, you can look across the sprawling flats of East New York and New Lots to the Rockaway peninsula and the churning Atlantic Ocean beyond.

Packed within this diverse territory are tenements, rowhouses, brownstones, bungalows, shotgun shacks, stables, homeless encampments, and mansions in almost every imaginable style, including some, in Mill Basin, that defy simple description. There are one hundred public-housing projects in Brooklyn and, in recent years, fancy glass towers have risen where before there were none. The hulks of Brooklyn's once galvanic industrial base loom over sidewalks from Bush Terminal to Bushwick as abandoned trolley tracks tease through patches of worn macadam and salt marshes ripple in the afternoon breeze. I can walk through East Flatbush and Brownsville without seeing a white person for hours; had I the language skills, I could live here with only Russian, Arabic, Bengali, Urdu. There are day-labor guys sitting on milk crates at the corner of Fort Hamilton and 36th Street, and there are trust-fund kids sitting in cafés who'll never have to work a day again.

Brooklyn is infuriatingly bourgeois and achingly impoverished. Brooklyn will beat your ass and still offer you some kind of crazy wisdom. In Brooklyn, the haves and the ain't-got-shit can be equally ignorant. Here in Brooklyn, the erstwhile City of Churches, Santeria, Vodou, Yoruba, and Jah can roll with Jesus, Allah, Yahweh, and that most powerful god of all: money. Moschiach is coming to Brooklyn, but the bistros, boutiques, and patisseries beat him to it. (Brooklyn was a Dutch colony, then British; never French.)

The Warriors (1979) began and ended in Brooklyn, as did the life of its greatest writer, Gilbert Sorrentino (1929–2006). Here is where legends like

Randy Weston, Max Roach, and Joe Maneri came from and Meyer Schapiro, Tuli Kupferberg, and Ramblin' Jack Elliott too. Jazz heroes Cecil Taylor, Betty Carter, and Lester Bowie all settled here, as did Okie Woody Guthrie, and Jamaica's Clement "Sir Coxsone" Dodd. Puerto Ricans such as writer and activist Jesús Colón moved to Brooklyn and actor Henry Silva was born here, although he's often played Italian. Brooklyn is streets and the dark hip-hop sounds of AZ, Black Moon, M.O.P., Smif-n-Wessun and Papoose. Earlier, the streets gave us Al Capone, Lepke Buchalter, Bugsy Siegel, Barbara Stanwyck, Willie Sutton, Emmett Grogan, and Mike Tyson. Watch closely and you'll see Gene Hackman dressed as Santa Claus run past the corner of Ellery and Tompkins as he and Roy Scheider chase a perp into an empty lot in *The French Connection* (1971), with the Broadway el just in the distance.

*

Taken together . . . there is no Brooklyn, singular. To a large extent, it was always thus—cities are a complex space and, as anyone who's seen *Welcome Back, Kotter* (1975–9) can attest, Brooklyn is the "4th Largest City in America." Of course, Brooklyn wasn't *really* a city then, but the conceit was important. Ever since 1898, when our forebears made the highly contentious decision to join a so-called Greater New York, Brooklyn has struggled not just with its own conflicting identities, but those of America's *largest* city also, of which it was now a mere *borough*.

A populous borough (Brooklyn was pushing three million people by 1950), but not a glamorous one. That suited us just fine, and when John Richmond's *Brooklyn U.S.A.* (1945), began "In Defense of Brooklyn," it celebrated what the borough *was*, not what others wished it to be. For all the affection Bushwick-native Jackie Gleason garnered for *The Honeymooners* (1955–6), and however many people took disco lessons after *Saturday Night Fever* (1977), neither inspired anyone to move to Bensonhurst or Bay Ridge. Despite a small body of great Brooklyn literature from Walt Whitman onwards (Henry Miller, Hart Crane, Charles Reznikoff, Djuna Barnes, Louis Zukofsky, Robert Kelly) and the largest black population in New York, trumpeter Don Cherry could wryly title a 1969 album, *Where Is Brooklyn?*

If the particular provincialism of Brooklyn made some of its natives restless for more—and it must be said, many left; by the year 2000, the borough was 38 per cent foreign born, barely 41 per cent white—it also had the salutary effect of keeping rent down. The paradox is, the moment you split, Brooklyn had changed, but if you returned, Brooklyn was still . . . *Brooklyn, motherfucker.* Some might choose a more decorous way to say it—the battle between the street and gentility goes way back—but it *still* wasn't Manhattan nor, until recently, did it much resemble chain-store age America.

It's like reminiscing about chop suey joints and egg creams but, until the late 1980s or so, nobody from elsewhere in America—not a solitary soul—moved to New York City with the intention of moving to *Brooklyn*. Or, let me qualify that—nobody except *a lot* of black folk and Puerto Ricans (who have been American citizens since 1917).

*

Brooklyn's mythical peak begins in the 1930s as the US emerges from the the Depression, and continues until the early 1960s, when the Brooklyn Navy Yard was being phased out. That the alleged decline of Brooklyn coincides with a radical population shift is something the mythmakers rarely address, yet there's no denying the influx of Southern blacks and the Great Migration of Puerto Ricans after World War II transformed the borough. Indeed, whole neighborhoods changed complexion. Fort Greene, Bed-Stuy, Ocean Hill, Brownsville, and East New York became almost entirely black. Sunset Park and South Williamsburg went Spanish, which was then more or less synonymous with Puerto Rican (this too would change). Bushwick—an exceptionally tenacious Italian community aside—became black *and* Spanish, while a large area called South Brooklyn became even more Spanish than it already was. Everywhere, Robert Moses' highways and slum clearance projects bashed their way across the streetscape to disorienting effect.

It took the early films of Spike Lee to bring black Brooklyn into popular consciousness, and *Do The Right Thing* (1989) effectively schematized racial tensions of the time. Less remarked on but perhaps the greater achievement was the range of blackness DTRT portrayed—profane and pious, conscious and less so, Caribbean and African-American. This should *not* have been necessary forty years after Brooklyn became the Black population center of black New York, and while flawed, as a mass-media artifact DTRT could have been much worse. Conversely, as a postcard for keeping Brooklyn for *Brooklyn* (motherfucker), it could hardly have been better: black folk are scary! Even three years later, Gang Starr, inviting us to "The Place Where We Dwell," had to nudge some:

> Don't be afraid to venture over the bridge
> Although you may run in to some wild ass kids
> Take the J train, the D or the A if you dare
> And the 2, 3, 4, 5 also come here.

Little did they know. At a juncture when the borough is being reinvented by and for the wealthy as never before and many want little more than for the city (Brooklynites all call Manhattan 'the city') to leave us alone, a little fear could go a long way. If the primary myth of old Brooklyn—that people were

more closely bound by class and locale than separated by ethnicity—can be disputed, it's remarkable the *idea* (and not-too-crazy rent) of even a roughly egalitarian Brooklyn lasted so long. The worry is how the marketing of Brooklyn as a destination for the affluent threatens the social conditions that made *some* Brooklyn, *all* of these Brooklyns possible.

*

My Brooklyn is South Brooklyn, though few call it that anymore. For ten years now I've lived nearly equidistant between the Gowanus Canal and the former Anthony Anastasio Memorial Longshoremen's Medical Center at the corner of Court and Union. I'm writing this in a rent-stabilized apartment in a building over a century old. The date on the cornice of the pizzeria at Smith Street and 2nd Place reads '1877'. Nearby, on 4th Street between Hoyt and Bond, a single story wood-frame home sits alone amid a block of warehouses and small factories. It lies outside the local historic district, although it might be the sole residence remaining from when this part of South Brooklyn comprised an eccentric Irish shanty-town called Slab City. On warm summer nights you can still smell the Gowanus just around the corner.

Not many people who've moved here recently know of Anastasio, or his brother Albert—boss of the Brooklyn docks—or Joey Gallo, who Bob Dylan wrote his *longest* song of the 1970s about. All of them lived around here, as did

Eli Wallach too, over at 166 Union. The neighborhood was called Red Hook then, or South Brooklyn. In the late 1960s some real-estate types had the idea to rename it, something fancy that might obscure the neighborhood's tough Irish, Italian, and Puerto Rican roots and cut themselves off from its Red Hook identity as surely as the Battery Tunnel and Gowanus Expressway cleaved it in practice. Other South Brooklyn districts were doing the same thing, thus "Cobble Hill" and "Boerum Hill," each featuring vistas of near dead-level blocks all around.

I'm in so-called "Carroll Gardens," ostensibly because some of the buildings in the area are set back on their lots; thus front gardens (or driveways, for those who later made curb cuts) and small backyards. They're fine, if hardly exclusive to this neighborhood. The Carroll part is more interesting. The simple version has it that Charles Carroll (1737–1832), a politician from Maryland and the only Catholic to sign the Declaration of Independence, sent some troops here during the Battle of Brooklyn (1776) and we—especially the Irish who settled this part of South Brooklyn—have been grateful ever since. A street was named after him in the 1840s, and one of Brooklyn's oldest parks soon after. The truth—which no official New York City source nor book about Brooklyn mentions—is Charles Carroll was one of the wealthiest men in Maryland. His estate was called Mount Clare, and among Carroll's other possessions were over one hundred slaves. Some worked the fields, some were domestics, while others toiled in the iron works Carroll owned in Baltimore, just five miles away. *Brooklyn By Name* (2006) by Leonard Benardo and Jennifer Weiss is the latest reference work to omit this aspect of Carroll's biography. *The Neighborhoods of Brooklyn* (1998), by the Citizens Committee for New York City, declares Carroll "a fitting emblem of the neighborhood's proud heritage." *Caveat lector.*

I mention this not to start a debate on judging people out of their time. Rather, in the wake of the racial turmoil of the '60s and '70s it's odd a figure with such a tenuous connection to Brooklyn would again be honored. Surely it wasn't to remind people that, until 1830 or so, Kings County—which Brooklyn today is contiguous with— itself was heavily reliant on slave labor.

*

It was dumb luck I ended up in South Brooklyn. The first place I saw was a ground-floor apartment next to Monte's, the oldest Italian restaurant in Brooklyn (1906), on Carroll Street between Nevins and Third Avenue. The burglar bars were painted white, but probably weren't needed, for, while hard-scrabble Gowanus was where crackheads and wild dogs were common, this block was solidly Italian and, by all appearances, quite close-knit. The Glory Social Club around the corner was (and remains) Members Only, and since I didn't know anyone to get me in, I took this place instead. It's on what's termed "a leafy block" and in the fall, when Chinese women with poles come by to shake the branches of gingko trees and gather the fallen fruits, it smells just as awful as the Canal ever did.

Soon after moving in, I started reading the two community newspapers that served South Brooklyn. One had classifieds filled with Russian and Chinese brothels, but the stories I most recall were about the reconstruction of the 9th Street lift bridge across the Canal, which was *years* behind schedule, and the long-delayed repair of the Gowanus flushing tunnel. The history of Gowanus is twisted, but briefly, a saltwater creek amid marshes was, in the 1860s, turned into a canal to serve the growing industrial needs of Brooklyn. As quickly as it became the busiest waterway in the country, the Gowanus also became the scourge of South Brooklyn for the effluvia pouring into its water and air. Some called for the Canal to be filled in, but that never happened, nor did the conditions prevent people from living nearby. Although numerous nineteenth-century buildings remain, the thousands of squatters who once called the area home are long forgotten.

Also forgotten, or ignored, since it broke in the 1950s, was that pesky flushing tunnel. Built in 1911 and running underground from the East River to the Canal's terminus at Butler Street, the idea was that pumping (relatively) clean water in from the river would ameliorate the smell and maybe bring the waterway back ecologically. That it took almost fifty years for this to occur says everything about Brooklyn, the environment and class war; the rest is detail.

When the tunnel was repaired in 1999, there were excited dispatches from the Canal zone. *Look, algae! (It's a start.) Fish! Birds! Let's try oysters—there used to be oysters everywhere . . . oysters!* I remember one sad, sick seal who wandered up and died shortly afterwards. Then the flushing tunnel broke, again, and while I've seen claims it's fixed, reports of the Canal's health are suspect, as raw sewage still pours in when it rains and a skein of fuck-knows-what *and* fuel oil coats the surface of the water. When it rains *a lot*, the Gowanus floods, quickly, especially at high tide, and if a hurricane hits South Brooklyn, most people near the Canal are going to be under it.

*

At first, it was almost pure wonder: there was Mas Que Pan, Latticini Barese, the Yemen Cafe and three Chinese live poultry markets over by Columbia Street. There were botanicas, discount clothing stores and Puerto Rican social clubs.

My neighbors—Pete, the Old Crow, and an interracial gay couple, Dale and Sam—were all crazy and often drunk, as was the super, a PR dude who grew up here and lived in the basement of the adjoining building. I bought a spaghetti pot from Dave's all-in-one department store on Court Street and loved the baked clams at Helen's Place, where they always had the Mets, Knicks or oldies on the radio. A car service was busted as a fencing operation and a body found in the trunk of a car at the Red Hook impound yard. When my beater Volkswagen died, I went to Holy Land Auto Repair—Palestinians. The only nightspot on Smith Street was a Spanish sports bar called The Grid that featured Latin jazz and salsa on the weekends and until it was taken down a few weeks ago, the fading, handpainted sign of the ghetto record store on Hoyt across from the Gowanus Houses advertised funk, gospel, hip-hop, and reggae.

Things change—both the present *and* the past. Dale drowned in his bath-tub; Sam was evicted six months later. Pete was dead for almost two weeks before the smell got so bad anyone thought to check on him. In July 2006, I could read, in the *New York Sun,* that Smith Street was "derelict" until 1999, which is simply untrue. The erstwhile Smith Street "revival" began two years earlier and if you accept that Puerto Ricans and Dominicans, Italians, and Arabs can do anything *not* derelict, then Smith was just one more vernacular Brooklyn strip among numerous others, neither fancy nor terrifying. Of course, not every-one saw it that way. When the boutique Stacia NYC opened up a block from the metal fabricator that's since become an American Apparel, not only did she eschew borough pride, it was also the first Brooklyn store I saw with a buzzer—presumably to keep out any local riff-raff curious how the other half dressed.

In July 2005, the College Bakery—which made a great black & white cook-ie—closed after 74 years. Thankfully, there's still Esposito's Pork Store (since 1922), roast coffee gods D'Amico (since 1948), the amazingly ramshackle Community Bookstore, and Vinny over at the Smith Union Market, whose father owned the store before him. Vinny's in his 50s now, attended St Francis College downtown and is sort of the Mayor of the locals, who include Dante, a *Daily Racing Form* savant, and Billy, who used to work down on the docks. There's also the girlfriend of the Spanish kid who got his head blown off in a Carroll Park drugs assassina-tion back in '98 and the brother of one of the guys sent to prison for beating a black UPS worker on his way home to Red Hook the year before, but I don't know them personally. While not everything new is bad—the trattoria Frankie's 457 is inspired (and neat geo-specific complement to the Yemeni 145 Luncheonette, also on Court Street)—it's been difficult seeing the neighborhood's eccentric Brooklyn identity decline. Things are different in places like Gerritsen Beach, City Line, and Kensington—there's even the unpaved Old Mill Road in New Lots—but there's nothing pure out there, really. It's just . . . different.

*

All kinds of different. While walking down Lee Avenue one steamy summer evening, a Hasid asked if I'd help with his air conditioner; it took a few moments to realize he wanted me to turn it off, since his inscrutable faith forbade him to. The quiet Sabbath streets of Borough Park and Midwood also delight, although I recommend skipping the zany array of simulacra Kosher cuisines they offer after sundown Saturday and hitting DiFara's on Avenue J instead for Brooklyn's best (and slowest) pizza, with all due respect

Totonno's in Coney Island and Ciccio's in Gravesend. I could live on Lebanese food alone in Bay Ridge (Beirut to knowing wags), Pakistani in Bath Beach. While there's only one Miss Polonia of Greenpoint each year, Polska Agencja signs can be found in many parts of the borough. I've seen Día de los Muertos parades down Myrtle Avenue, shrines to S. Cono on Graham and portraits of Padre Pio nearly everywhere. Last week a hustler was working the shell game on Pitkin in Brownsville and he had his rap down: "I'm from Mississippi, man . . ."

On the streets—ones named Himrod, Junius and Old New Utrecht—you see everything: memorial murals, graffiti tags and torched cars, Let Live Meat, Nouveau Prosthetics and the eye-catching BJ 99¢. Cyclists race around Floyd Bennett Field, a former Naval Air Station, and the Imperial Bikers motorcycle gang chill in their clubhouse on Franklin Avenue. Up the block is Kelso Dining, a Panamanian joint, and nearby, on the side of a Dean Street warehouse, is a Studebaker palimpsest. Closer to home there's one for Citroen. On 18th Avenue in Bensonhurst you can get marzipan clams at Villabate and Joe's of Avenue U is Brooklyn's best focacceria, although I hear it's now Russian-owned. Brighton Beach itself has been going upscale for a while now, with bungalows razed to make way for condos, but it hasn't lost the weird energies that made Wallace Markfield's Brighton-set *Teitlebaum's Window* (1970) Brooklyn's greatest, most riotous Jewish novel. The Russian mob is no laughing matter but it's unwise to ask too many questions, and who can talk anyway with a mouth full of plov and garlicky Uzbek french fries?

In *Last Exit to Brooklyn* (1964), Red Hook native Hubert Selby claimed "there's a Spick joint on Columbia Street," and it's true, the popular Latin singer Tony Molina grew up there, no matter he's all but unknown to borough historians. Indeed, it was the quiet displacement of South Brooklyn's Spanish-speaking peoples—none of the Ecuadorian kitchen workers or Salvadoran nannies live *here*—which made me concerned for all of Brooklyn's multi-ethnic future. Rent

stabilization (in buildings with eight or more apartments) slows but doesn't stop the efflux, so I appreciate each Puerto Rican tire shop and the hundreds of hair salons exclaiming "Dominican Style"; likewise all the Spanish record stores and panderias that have opened almost everywhere *but* South Brooklyn. I eat weekly at La Asunción, a restaurante Mexicano on Fort Hamilton where, no matter what else is happening in the world, there's always soccer on or the juke-box blasting. The *club de futbol* they sponsor is named Piaxtla, after their hometown in Pueblo.

*

Mi Español es un poco loco so Brooklyn's vast black population is a bit easier to access. The bad news is the number of African-Americans in Brooklyn is said to be declining. A sign in a real-estate office on Church Avenue in Flatbush summed the trend up simply—"Live Cheap in Georgia!"—and for those who still have family to ya'll down there, it's very tempting. On Atlantic Avenue, across from the Carolina Country Store is a little Georgia farm stand, the proprietor of which has a BK to GA moving business also. Other signs of Southern Brooklyn can be seen, mostly in Bed-Stuy (the Down South Café, Tar Heel Auto Repair, Tar Heel Adult Center) but there's J-Soul in East New York, the House of Southern Flavors ("For a taste that's truly Southern!") in New Lots and the genius Chesapeake-style Rencher's Crab Inn at Flatbush and Avenue O. I first discovered them when they had a small takeout window on Myrtle Avenue in Fort Greene—now it's probably a wine bar or something. Far better are old-school taverns like Vern's Happiness Lounge on St John's and Randy's Hide-A-Way on Bergen, around the corner from which is aspiring rapper Boo Blades' All Star Barber Shop.

Thankfully, West Indian Brooklyn is thriving and to spend time there is to fall deep into the world of post-colonial identity and immigrant nationalism. Local and imported newspapers keep people abreast of news from the islands, little of which is good, especially in Jamaica, Trinidad and Guyana, the countries most represented in Brooklyn, followed by Haiti. As each nation's history differs, so too their cultures and cuisines in Brooklyn. Vegetarian Ital shacks cater to Rastafarians and smoke from cut oil-drum grills is one of the great joys of Brooklyn streetlife, along with a deliciously inventive use of English: hops bread, bake and shark, doubles, lead pipe, soursop, bus'-up-shot, front end lifter, Ting and the Bajan national dish of cou-cou (especially at Cock's on Nostrand) can all get pulses racing. Reggae and its progeny remain popular, calypso and soca too, with Mighty Sparrow especially on the scene; his 1990 single, "Crown Heights

Justice," might be the only worthwhile thing to come out of Brooklyn's most vexing ethnic flare-ups. Brooklyn's West Indian nightlife exists entirely outside mainstream attentions: clubs, concerts, and parties are advertised by posters and lavish full-color postcards placed in local businesses.

Relations between Brooklyn blacks is a complex, touchy subject. While West Africans largely keep to themselves, rivalries and prejudices between West Indian and American blacks are more evident. That said, *Rude Awakening* (1998) by Cocoa Brovaz is a remarkably embracing outline of black Brooklyn—aka Bucktown, aka Medina— loaded with funk, patois, and sharp observations of 'hood life relevant to everyone with an ear for the streets.

*

On Duffield Street, just off of Fulton, something called the Downtown Brooklyn Development Plan threatens two mid-nineteenth-century homes. One is owned by a black woman, the other by a white man. For decades, both have invested their lives and businesses in the community. Local historians believe the basements of these buildings might have been stops on the Underground Railroad. If the evidence is inconclusive, it's not like Underground Railroad stops were *advertised*, so it's certainly possible. By contrast, since the battle began in 2004, it was clear the city wanted only to condemn the land. Why? To create parking lots for the many office and luxury apartment buildings that might someday rise nearby.

Most among the many is something called Atlantic Yards. Included in the project's 22 acres are office towers, condos, and a basketball arena designed by Frank Gehry. A classic example of media obeisance to real estate was given by *New York* magazine, which in May 2004 described the arena as developer Bruce Ratner's "glittering gift to Brooklyn." Gift? A curious choice of words for a project loaded with public financing and which would, as on Duffield Street, seize private property for the benefit of the wealthy. This is especially galling given that Ratner has left his mark with disreputable projects already, including Metrotech—which looms as imposingly over old downtown Brooklyn as a Midwest prison surrounded by cornfields—Atlantic Center Mall and Atlantic Terminal Mall.

In the summer of 2006, fury over Atlantic Yards was reaching a peak. The arguments boiled down to three issues: economics, design, and scale. It's almost impossible to find a neutral—which is to say unpaid—observer who speaks in favor of Ratner's previous work. Unfortunately, he's a supremely connected billionaire whose errors don't face market consequences, as the sham agency known as the Empire State Development Corporation covers him all the way. The last question concerns the project's effect on Brooklyn's predominantly low-rise character. While I bemoan the Galleria Mall-ready Smith Street, it did evolve organically; when Uncle Pho (shamefully ersatz Vietnamese) and Club Sushi (directly across from Wasabi) closed, at least they were *allowed to fail.* Ratner isn't, and he's become obscenely rich in the process. That's not capitalism, it's oligarchy.

Whatever happens—and the game is so rigged in favor of Ratner, it seems only the courts can stop or restrain him—the wounds are already deep, laying bare the mendacity that defines illiberal city (and state) politics. (See also a corrupt public-land-for-condos scheme called Brooklyn Bridge "Park.") Bertha Lewis, the blustery Brooklyn leader of ACORN, a previously well-regarded advocacy group, supports Ratner, as does the imperious Rev. Herbert Daughtry, both of whom claim that a token number of "affordable housing units" (most of which are for those with incomes of $56,000 and above) represents a victory for the "working people." City council members Letitia James of the Working Families Party and Democrat Charles Barron, a self-described "black revolutionary Christian socialist" are against it.

*

Almost ten miles down Flatbush Avenue, Brooklyn's first mall, Kings Plaza, opened in 1971 on the wetlands outskirt of Marine Park and Mill Basin. The names are important, as the beauty of Brooklyn's meandering southern shoreline is frequently forgotten, and even more often abused. While I love Coney Island in all seasons—especially the back (non-boardwalk) side's windswept dunes—the salt marshes, cordgrass and cattails here are a welcome retreat from urbanity. A little inland, Zappa's Rock Palace on Quentin Road was *the* Brooklyn punk venue of the '70s and early '80s; with the metal-oriented L'Amour in Borough Park and PIPS Comedy Club in Sheepshead Bay, Zappa's represented a unique strain of white ethnic culture since lost to Williamsburg and Park Slope hipster-yuppie hegemony.

Back at Avenue U and Flatbush, it's hard to imagine when this was a sleepy corner of the borough, with open lots, small farms and, through the 1930s, even squatters. All my Brooklyn-raised pals have odd memories of King's Plaza—it was a *novelty*. Today, despite being on the edge of Jamaica Bay and Gateway National Park, a big-box style expansion of King's Plaza is underway. Although this part of Brooklyn is thought of as rather conservative, angry remarks from NY State Senator Carl Kruger tell another story: "We warned City Planning not to arbitrarily approve a use for this site that will erode an already perilous traffic situation, destroy neighborhood mom-and-pop businesses and allow a historically bad neighbor to further thumb its nose at the community. Once again, the administration has demonstrated where its priorities lie—in keeping big business happy."

When the first public hearing on Atlantic Yards was held on August 23, 2006, I accidentally stumbled upon a pro-Ratner rally on Jay Street. There were burly black construction workers in screaming bald-eagle hardhats, plus some middle-aged women and kids obviously there as props. I read in the paper that two multi-millionaire New Jersey Nets—neither of whom live in Brooklyn or the city—appeared later to rally the crowds. Surprisingly, a couple weeks before, *New York* magazine woke *way* up: "In looking at Atlantic Yards up close, it's outrageous to see the absolute absence of democratic process," wrote political reporter Chris Smith in their August 14 issue. "There's been no point in the past four years at which the public has been given a meaningful chance to decide whether something this big and transformative should be built on public property. Instead, race, basketball, and Frank Gehry have been tossed out as distractions to steer attention away from the real issue, money."

Meanwhile, a thriving Fulton Street repudiates the contention that a "new" downtown Brooklyn is necessary, except that this Brooklyn is mostly *black* Brooklyn. There's already rumbling—quiet so far but just wait—about how downtown businesses aren't well integrated with the increasingly affluent residents around them. Not that Brooklyn needs more jewelry, cell-phone or sneaker stores, but better them than another upscale baby emporium, bank branch, or realtor. For the time being, visitors can lace up their Timberlands and relish every psychic, black nationalist bookseller and African DVD vendor hawking the steady flow of films from Nigeria. Fulton Street is also the place to see the three secular icons of ghetto Brooklyn: murdered rappers Notorious B.I.G. and Tupac Shakur and, oddly, Tony Montana, the character Al Pacino played in *Scarface* (1983). In the pre-Atlantic Yards era, the highest point in the borough (512 feet), the dome of the nearby Williamsburg Bank Building (1929) looms over all. Formerly home to hundreds of dentists' offices, now it too is luxury condos.

*

Few things demonstrate the changing fortunes of Brooklyn more than its relationship with local industry, which was exceptionally close and often affectionate. Even now, the South Brooklyn Casket Company is the most beloved of Gowanus' many small manufacturers—Crusader Candle ("They Burn Better") is another favorite—and as of this writing, you can still stand on Van Brunt Street and watch the giant cranes of American Stevedore moving like spiders to unload cargo ships. The Sunset Park waterfront in particular is an awesome industrial-gothic streetscape of towering lofts, cobblestones, and railroad tracks. In 1946, Lucky Luciano bade farewell to America from Pier 7 here, and scores of post-9/11 detainees were held at the Metropolitan Detention Center, Brooklyn's only Federal prison. Many local factory workers come from up the avenues. One of Brooklyn's two Chinatowns is on Eighth (the other is on Avenue U), Fifth is mostly Latino, and Third, cruelly bisected by the Gowanus Expressway, is notable for junkyards, live poultry markets, and xxx-video stores.

Elsewhere, Brooklyn's past remains impressive, from the Port Authority Grain Terminal in Red Hook to Domino Sugar (closed after 150 years following a bitter strike) in Williamsburg and, painfully, the Civil War-era Greenpoint Terminal Market, set ablaze by an arsonist in May 2006. In Gowanus, the old American Can Factory at Third Avenue and 3rd Street houses studio space, while

a group of artists bought the National Packing Box Factory on Union Street to save it from future developers. Although the future of Pfizer's plant on Flushing Avenue is unclear (it's scheduled to close by the end of 2008), a film studio recently opened at the Brooklyn Navy Yard, and parts of East New York and Canarsie in particular abound with warehouses and factories.

Such was an era not-so-long-gone that a utility company, Brooklyn Union Gas

(BUG), could be a source of pride and bemusement. One example can be heard in song, for in 1978 BUG released a promotional 7-inch disco record called "New Life in Brooklyn" with the refrain "Brooklyn is cookin!" In 1997, Brooklyn Union Gas changed their name to Keyspan Energy—appropriate for all future dystopias (it's no coincidence Keyspan is a tenant at Metrotech) but a far cry from BUG. On a warm July morning four years later, two of the iconic structures of northwest Brooklyn, the 400-foot tall Greenpoint gas tanks (one built in 1927, the other 1948), were brought to the ground via implosion. Now, everyone loves an implosion, but people loved the gas tanks too, which were silver with a red and white checker-board pattern around the top to make them more visible to passing airplanes.

More glaring contrasts between old and new can be found on the other side of Williamsburg. The Gretsch Building, former home to the esteemed manufacturer of guitars and drums, went luxury condo in 2004. At least the Gretsch—like the Williamsburg Bank Building—remains. The F&M Schaefer Brewing Company was an iconic presence on Kent Street between South 9th and 10th Streets in 1915, when Brooklyn teemed with breweries. Schaefer spon-sored the Dodgers—many of whom were said to be fond of its product—and even hired Queens resident Louis Armstrong to cut their jingle:

> Schaefer is the one beer to have
> when you're having more than one.
> Schaefer's pleasure doesn't fade
> even when your thirst is done.

> The most rewarding flavor in this man's world
> for people who are having fun
> Schaefer is the one beer to have
> when your having more than one.

In 1976, the Schaefer plant in Williamsburg closed, and production was shifted to a more modern facility in Allentown, Pa. Approximately 2,500 Brooklyn jobs were lost.

Thirty years later, the promotional material reads thus, and precisely:

> Extraordinary attention to detail and quality are everywhere to be found. The 24/7 concierge-attended lobby—with its sophisticated interplay of slate, stone and wood—is a dramatic study in modern elegance. The inviting, lushly landscaped private courtyard offers a soothing, restorative retreat. Inside and out, Schaefer Landing inspires a life of comfort and luxury.

✴

In the midst of a historic explosion in Brooklyn housing values (and costs), 25 percent of the borough lives below the poverty level. Even here in almost hyper-gentrified South Brooklyn, signs reading "We Accept EBT and WIC" are common, even if few who don't participate in those programs know what they mean, social workers excepted. I was at the Red Hook post office the other day, across the from the Red Hook Houses—Hubert Selby lived at 626 Clinton, and rapper Shabazz the Disciple is from here too—standing in a long line of people waiting to get money orders. (Few of the impoverished have checking accounts and the post office charges less than the check-cashing store.) A black woman broke the quiet impatience of everyone when she exclaimed "Shit, man, they should have three windows open on Saturday—don't they know this is the ghetto?!"

Ghetto is one of those words that means different things to different people. A block away, at the corner of Court and Lorraine, *ghetto* means a garbage transfer station, where 18-wheelers with "Municipal Solid Waste" stenciled on their sides trundle in and out. Clinton and Lorraine each offer the ghetto standards: discount liquor store, laundromat, storefront church, bodega, barber shop, Chinese take-out. In May 2006, there was a big drug bust here, with 153 people arrested, some of whom were later released without charge. "They'd turned the housing development into a drug zone, attracting drug addicts from across Brooklyn and beyond," said Police Commissioner Raymond Kelly, a claim which strained credulity, given that parts of Red Hook Houses are at least a twenty-minute walk from the subway and there's around a billion other places poor people can buy drugs in Brooklyn and beyond. (Those better off have *prescriptions*, or get their dope delivered.)

Meanwhile, the other side of Red Hook is the latest Brooklyn neighborhood to be hyped by the press. Before that it was Bushwick—pimped twice by the *Times* in six months, like a few hundred white kids in lofts merit more attention than 100,000 Latinos and blacks. There's a giant Fairway grocery store in an old warehouse at the end of Van Brunt Street and quite a few restaurants and bars have opened in the last five years, but so far Red Hook's isolation—which is part of its great attraction—has kept things relatively low key. Construction of the largest Ikea in the US will likely change that, bringing tens of thousands of cars each weekend, and if the Port Authority succeeds in throwing American Stevedore off the docks to make way for some kind of mall catering to cruise-ship passengers, it's over.

Or it may be already. In June 2006, a happy couple posed for a *Daily News* article about their recent one-million-dollar home purchase on Pioneer Street. "Like many other 30-something professionals who've fled Manhattan for increasingly talked-about Red Hook, the Dituris wanted more space for their buck," the paper reported. "We love the East Village, but we wanted extra space, and Red Hook reminded us of how the East Village was 15 years ago: young people coming in doing interesting things and putting their own stamp on it."

Food stamps maybe (which is what the EBT stuff is about). As we puzzle why anyone would publicize such fortune when *more than 45 percent* of their neighbors in Red Hook Houses live below the poverty line, Brooklyn's poor aren't going anywhere—not here, not in Brownsville and not in Farragut Houses, whose residents can see the new luxury towers of DUMBO rising. If they knew about it, these folks *could* dig on Three Guys From Brooklyn, the 24-hour produce market on Fort Hamilton and 65th that advertises itself as "The Original Poor People's Friend." It might be a trip but they'd know they're welcome.

Everyone-and-Everything in Queens

Kevin Walsh

Although Queens is the largest borough in terms of area, if you walk into a bookstore or library and check out the New York City section, you won't have an easy time learning about it. Most New York City guidebooks treat Manhattan as the only borough in New York worth mentioning—while Brooklyn, the Bronx, Staten Island and Queens are all lumped together as the "outer boroughs" or places that are "further afield." Both city airports are in Queens . . . further afield from what?

*

Queens' history and its neighborhoods are represented by only a couple of prosaically titled books: *Old Queens, NY in Early Photographs*, by Vincent Seyfried and William Asedorian, and *Discovering Queens! A Useful Guide to Queens, NY*, by Steve Reichstein. Ellen Freudenheim has just chimed in with *Queens: What to Do . . . in New York's Undiscovered Borough*, a compendium of restaurants, parks, museums and historical tidbits. The small Arcadia Press also has a few Queens

titles featuring old photos, much like the Seyfried/Asedorian tome. Seyfried himself should be a national treasure; now in his eighties, this longtime Queens resident has been compiling borough history and annotating old photographs for years. Reichstein's book is a disappointment, as it seems mainly to be an advertisement for Queens real estate. While it discusses most neighborhoods, and there are large sections on ritzy Bayside and Douglaston as well as historic Astoria and Jackson Heights, Reichstein ignores Maspeth, Middle Village, Woodhaven, Ozone Park, and most of southern Queens, too. Glendale, Ridgewood, and Maspeth, for example, comprise a huge section that has generated absolutely no media coverage anywhere . . . except when crime occurs there or, in the case of Ridgewood, when real-estate flacks hype it as the next stop on the M train for Williamsburg and Bushwick refugees who've been priced out of Brooklyn.

*

Celebrities from the biggest borough have seemingly played down their Queens heritage, though that may be more because Brooklyn casts a large shadow and because its geographically larger neighbor has trouble competing. Despite "Rockaway Beach," one of their two 45-RPM waxings to make the *Billboard* charts, Forest Hills' finest, the Ramones, aren't closely identified with where they came from but rather with the Bowery, where they made their name. The roots of perhaps the city's greatest rockers ever go back to Queens, too, to Newtown High School in Elmhurst, where John Genzale (aka Johnny Thunders) played in bands with Arthur "Killer" Kane, Billy Murcia, and Sylvain Sylvain. Together with Staten Island native David Johansen, they were the New York Dolls.

Hank Azaria, Burt Bacharach, Tony Bennett, Jimmy Breslin, David Caruso, Rodney Dangerfield, John Frusciante of the Red Hot Chili Peppers, "plumbing-supplies dealer" John Gotti, revered Knicks coach Red Holzman, corporate raider Carl Icahn, fashionista Donna Karan, Cyndi Lauper, Lucy Liu, John McEnroe, insult-meister Don Rickles, Edward G. Robinson, Susan Sarandon, Martin Scorsese, Jerry Seinfeld, Paul Simon *and* Art Garfunkel, Paul Stanley and Gene Simmons of KISS, Donald Trump, and Christopher Walken are all from Queens.

Although often stereotyped as the white blue-collar borough because of sitcoms like *All in the Family* (Carroll O'Connor grew up a Woodsider) and *King of Queens*, in real life it's Queens' African-Americans who have perhaps left the biggest marks in worldwide culture. Louis Armstrong and his wife Lucille moved to a small brick house on 107th Street in Corona in 1942. They never left, and their home is now a museum. Pops, along with Dizzy Gillespie, who lived a few doors down, are buried in Flushing Cemetery. Beginning in the 1920s, Addisleigh Park, a tree-lined region in St Albans, became home to dozens of musicians, including Count Basie, Ella Fitzgerald, Milt Hinton, Lena Horne, Illinois and Russell Jacquet, Fats Waller, and even the hardest-working man in show biz, James Brown. Different eras of hip-hop stars have also called Queens home: Run-DMC (Hollis), L.L. Cool J (St Albans), Mobb Deep (Long Island City), and, most recently, 50 Cent (South Jamaica).

*

Until 1898, Queens was much larger than it is today, since it also encompassed what is now Nassau County. The towns of Hempstead, North Hempstead, and

Oyster Bay seceded to form Nassau when Queens became part of New York City. And, though it was Brooklyn that offered the stiffest opposition to consolidation, passing the measure by only a couple of hundred votes, it's Queens that today maintains the *most* independence. You never mail a letter to "Queens," you mail it to Ridgewood, to Flushing, to Sunnyside, to Rosedale. It's partly a question of Queens' vastness, but it also may be that residents feel more genuinely "suburban" than people who live in Manhattan, the Bronx, and Brooklyn, and prefer to associate themselves with a small-town community ideal. In his recent PBS-TV special, *A Walk through Queens*, historian Barry Lewis claimed residents in one part of Queens knew or cared little about other parts. Bayside, one of New York City's premier residential neighborhoods, falls in line with Queens' tendency to retain its small towns as self-contained entities, with most businesses clustered around the main drag, Bell Boulevard. Bayside was home to movie stars such as W. C. Fields in the early part of the century before the industry decamped to Hollywood, and famed boxer "Gentleman" Jim Corbett's house still stands there. Crocheron and John Golden Parks provide necessary surcease from . . . well, there's no big-city stress here, but even the quietest neighborhoods need parks.

*

The thing about Queens is that more and more of it disappears every year, and I'm not talking about global warming-engendered rising water levels swamping the shoreline. I'm referring to nearly any building built before 1950. When I moved to Queens in 1993, the borough still had quite a number of relics from a golden age.

In Astoria, for example—an incorporated municipality as part of Long Island City from the 1880s through the 1910s—there were block after block of Victorian-era "painted lady" houses, each with different architectural elements and painted a different color. In Queens, one-family homes are no longer consid-

ered worth building anymore; Astoria's widely varied stock is disappearing fast, most often replaced by what I call Fedders Specials: cheaply built bland, brick boxes without lawns, style, or the slightest trace of humanity.

Other parts of Queens have suffered, too. The beautifully mosaicked front of Forest Hills' Trylon Theatre was recently jackhammered into oblivion. In 2005, Maspeth lost the famous German restaurant Niederstein's (built in 1855, and an after-funeral favorite until its closing) on Metropolitan Avenue; an Arby's was built on the property . . . an Arby's! Alas, time and again the NYC Landmarks Preservation Commission has failed to protect the borough's worthy landmarks. Community efforts are hampered by the fact that real-estate developers give wheelbarrows full of cash to local politicians, who are therefore disinclined to support most preservation efforts.

*

Flushing was once a community of tidy Victorian-era houses all painted different colors, with spacious lawns festooned with bric-a-brac and peopled by families, blue- and white-collar workers commuting to Manhattan, and cat-stroking grandmas in rocking chairs. Walking the streets of Flushing today would make you cry. In its western sections it is now a collection of towering, anonymous brick apartment buildings. Lately, plans have called for gleaming malls, condos, and office buildings, along with a new Mets stadium and the cleanup of the beyond-filthy Flushing River. The new stadium, Citifield, is already under construction, as are some of the towers.

Oddly, while much of Flushing's twentieth-century history is endangered, it does preserve more seventeenth- and eighteenth-century buildings than any other neighborhood in New York City. (Manhattan's Dutch architectural relics burned down in an 1835 fire; Brooklyn fared somewhat better, but Dutch structures are still very few in number.) At Northern Blvd and Linden Place—the boulevard dates to antiquity as an Indian trail stretching across northern Long Island—the Friends Meetinghouse has been used nearly continuously for Quaker meetings since it was constructed in about 1695.

Flushing Town Hall, built in 1862 by a local carpenter, is an example of Romanesque Revival and a reminder of the days before Flushing became a part of Queens. Frederick Douglass, P. T. Barnum, and at least two presidents appeared here during the building's heyday. After consolidation, Flushing Town Hall became a municipal courthouse, but it suffered from neglect and deterioration; attempts to turn it into a museum of anthropology in the 1970s came to naught. When I first moved to Flushing, it was a rundown heap protected by chicken wire from ever-present vandals. Happily, Town Hall was magnificently restored in 1995 by the architects Platt Byard Dovell and is currently the seat of the Flushing Council on Culture and the Arts, the magnificent building a vibrant locale for local arts programs and jazz concerts.

Asians rescued Flushing. By the 1970s the deterioration of its downtown area and the hard "stagflationary" economic conditions prompted many neighborhood residents, primarily Italian and Greek, to move out, and immigrants from eastern Asia began to trickle in to fill the void. At first, it was just a collection of Indian restaurants and clothing stores along southern Main Street, but by the mid-to-late 1980s Flushing had become the city's second Chinatown. Today, signs and awnings in Chinese and Korean (especially in eastern Flushing) dominate the area, which just elected its first Chinese city councilman (John Liu) and assemblyman (Jimmy Meng).

*

Long Island City and Astoria have always been identified with New York City manufacturing and industry, as well as with a gritty, determined spirit. Perhaps the best known example of LIC grit today is the popular hip-hop artist Nas, who grew up in Queensbridge, a sprawling public-housing project just north of the 59th Street Bridge. His debut 1994 album, *Illmatic*, is considered one of the best hip-hop albums of all-time, and it's amusing to hear fans who don't know the city try to explain exactly where he is from.

South of Queensbridge in Long Island City, there's something called Queens West, a massive development that will ultimately occupy 74 acres along the East River. Plans call for fifteen residential buildings, three office towers, and the ubiquitous hotel and conference center. My populist tendencies bristle at redeveloping our waterfronts as housing for the wealthy, but so far, so good: Gantry State Plaza Park has preserved the titular structures from which goods were loaded onto a Long Island Rail Road freight spur, and even some of the rails themselves. The forty-five-story sea-green Citibank office tower, completed in 1989, is Queens' tallest building. Although out of scale with the surrounding neighborhood, it's arguably one of New York's most beautiful skyscrapers.

When I was a child, "Silvercup" referred to a common brand of bread; these days, Silvercup Studio is where Tony Soprano is filmed planning his latest whacking and then whining to his psychiatrist about how frustrated he is. Astoria became an unlikely hotbed for the motion-picture industry in 1920, when Astoria Studios was built by Paramount at 35th Avenue and 36th Street. After the film industry moved west, Astoria Studios was used by the US Army to make training films. Beginning in 1982, the studios were redeveloped by George

Kaufman as a modern production facility featuring seven sound stages (including the largest one outside Los Angeles). The American Museum of the Moving Image opened in 1988 and, odd as it may seem, is the only museum in the US devoted to the history of film. Elsewhere, despite almost twenty years of being hyped as the next "hot" neighborhood, Astoria maintains a remarkably heterogeneous character: a well-known Greek population thrives alongside Brazilians, Colombians, Egyptians, Albanians, and Croats, as well as a tolerable—because they are far outnumbered—population of Manhattan refugees.

*

There are places about equidistant from Manhattan in both New Jersey and Long Island where the city's towers appear to thrust above the horizon like battlements of an alien fortress. Only from these places can the King of All Buildings truly be appreciated. The Empire State Building's size and majesty simply cannot be fully perceived from midtown or Brooklyn, only from hamlets like Blissville and Laurel Hill. Stand on Laurel Hill Boulevard, the eastern flank of Calvary Cemetery, in the morning hours, for full effect. The sun glistens on the shiny Machine-Age battlements of the giant tower. It's one of the reasons I can be found in Laurel Hill (also known as West Maspeth) rather frequently.

Blissville is the small wedge of Queens positioned between Newtown Creek, Calvary Cemetery, and the Queens-Midtown Expressway; it takes its name from Neziah Bliss, inventor, shipbuilder, and industrialist, who owned most of the land here in the 1830s and '40s and whose Novelty Iron Works supplied steamboat engines for area vessels. Blissville's spine is Greenpoint Avenue, whose highlights include the Queen Anne-style Calvary Cemetery gatehouse at Bradley Avenue, the City View Best Western Motel (an establishment which, if

you're in the area, functions well as a hot-sheets joint, although it's not as notorious as other Queens love nests like the Kew Motor Inn and the old Mets Motel), and Foxie's Exotic Cabaret, serving nearby industrial and cemetery workers.

Laurel Hill, east of Calvary Cemetery and south of the BQE, first developed by Augustus Rapelye in 1853, was named for the laurel trees then growing in abundance there. Even today, it's an isolated little village, featuring heavy industry interspersed with ancient one-family houses that, despite the gritty location, retain their original charm from the late 1890s and early 1900s.

*

Jamaica, Queens, is far from its namesake Jamaica Bay. Both the neighborhood and the body of water are named for the indigenous Jamaica Indians (neither has anything to do with the Caribbean island). A vast component of southern Queens, Jamaica has recently achieved world-wide fame as the place where rapper 50 Cent grew up. There's coincidentally a West Indian population in Jamaica that gives the place an almost Brooklyn-like feel at times. Indeed, the single largest West Indian music store in the city is here, VP Records, founded by Jamaicans of Chinese descent. Jamaica's downtown is bustling with shops and architectural treasures abound, such as the Art Moderne La Casina nightclub on 160th Street. Just to Jamaica's northwest you will find Richmond Hill, a traditionally Irish and Italian neighborhood (Jack Kerouac lived here with his mother for a spell in the '50s) that now boasts both a significant population from the Indian subcontinent and a huge Guyanese one. Most but not all of the Guyanese are of Indian descent, and Hindu temples abound. Richmond Hill is nothing if not diverse: there's a mosque on Liberty Avenue, and just off the Lefferts Boulevard stop on the A train is an Ecuadoran lunch counter, Pique y Pase, which was acclaimed one of the city's best Latino restaurants in the *Village Voice* a few years ago.

*

People living in Broad Channel and denizens of the communities along the Rockaway peninsula can't be blamed if there's a slight feeling of neglect by the big town. If New York City were the solar system, they're Pluto. Until the past couple of decades, Broad Channelites did not own the land on which their houses were built. It was owned by the city, and they had to make do without sewers; even now, a volunteer fire department douses blazes. Broad Channel is smack in the middle of Jamaica Bay. Amazingly, the NYC sub-

way serves it, on a line purchased from the Long Island Rail Road after a 1950 fire. (The fact that communities like Co-Op City, Marine Park, Throgs Neck, Glendale, and Hunt's Point are without subway service and Broad Channel *is* is a delicious paradox in the New York City transit story.) Jamaica Bay Wildlife Preserve is here, too, a mecca for local birders.

Rockaway is also served by the A train, as well as being connected to Broad Channel by the Cross Bay Bridge and Brooklyn via the Marine Parkway Bridge, but a strong sense of isolation remains. Rockaway has communities with names like Neponsit, Belle Harbor, Rockaway Park (the "Irish Riviera"), Seaside,

Hammels, Arverne, Somerville, and Edgemere, but they are known almost exclusively by residents. There's also Breezy Point, along with Sea Gate one of the city's only two privately owned communities, at the tip of Coney Island in Brooklyn. (I haven't yet tried getting past the guards but have instead "headed south" and walked along its approximately 2 miles of beachfront. The next land south of here is Mexico.)

Along the peninsula, Fort Tilden preserves the concrete-shielded gun placements that were built to protect NYC from fire from enemy warships. Riis Park features the city's largest parking lot, along with an unofficial nude beach. There's still a "Playland" el station, but no Rockaway Playland: it closed in 1982, and the bungalows that surrounded it soon died off as well. Far Rockaway contains a jumbled street system more typical of the Nassau County small towns to its immediate east, but that's the only way in which it resembles the neighboring—and much more affluent—Five Towns.

*

Ridgewood's row upon row of brick brownstones, many built by developer Paul Stier (who has a one-block Ridgewood alley named for him), housed a couple of generations of German immigrants in the early twentieth century, many of whom worked in the neighborhood's breweries such as Eurich's, Welz, and Zerweck. When Prohibition arrived, the breweries quickly left. Today Ridgewood is a stable middle-class neighborhood centering on its main drags, Myrtle Avenue and Fresh Pond Road, the latter named for a body of water that was filled in as the city began to press upon the area's fields and forests in the early 1900s. Ridgewood still has a distinct German cast, not only the whiff of the extinct breweries but Platz Hardware, in business on Forest Avenue for over a hundred years, and Karl Ehmer Meats, for decades on Fresh Pond Road. Romanians, Bosnians, and Albanians have moved in, joining older Italians, as well as an increasing number of Mexicans and other Latinos. Bosna Express, right by the elevated J-train station, is the city's premier *cevabdzinica* (basically a Balkan grill), while Joe's Restaurant ("Eat at Joe's!")—a pizza-and-hero joint on nearby Forest—is one of the treasures of old-time Ridgewood gastronomy.

*

The 7 Flushing subway line was designated by the White House as a National Millennium Trail in 2000, in honor of the dozens of nationalities that flourish in the neighborhoods just to the north and south of Roosevelt Avenue, where the line runs. Romanian, Irish, Filipino, Indian, Colombian, Cuban, Mexican, Pakistani, Italian, Chinese, Korean, and many other enclaves can all be found along its route. Delicacies and religious appurtenances of nearly every belief represented here can be gleaned from a stroll along Roosevelt from 48th to 111th Streets—a long walk, admittedly, but rewarding for the reflection of the diversity

that separates New York from more homogenized burgs. This in a borough that gave rise to caricatures like Archie Bunker, who never met a non-white Anglo-Saxon Protestant he liked. (The house used to represent the Bunkers' in the opening credits of *All in the Family* can still be seen in Glendale, on Cooper Avenue near Metropolitan.)

The Flushing Line's teeming everyone-and-everything atmosphere inspired one of the more infamous moments in New York sports history. It was 1999 when Statesboro, Georgia native and Atlanta Braves star relief pitcher John Rocker described to *Sports Illustrated* the trip from his midtown Manhattan hotel to Shea Stadium in his inimitable style: "Imagine having to take the [Number] 7 train to the ballpark, looking like you're [riding through] Beirut next to some kid with purple hair next to some queer with AIDS right next to some dude who just got out of jail for the fourth time right next to some 20-year-old mom with four kids. It's depressing." A great number of Met players, however, notably Ron Darling and John Olerud, routinely took the 7 to work, embracing the concentrated atmosphere. As most Met fans, or Queens residents, would say, imagine having to live in Statesboro. It would drive any New Yorker insane.

The Homeless

Margaret Morton

In 1989, when my documentation of New York City's homeless communities began, there were more homeless New Yorkers than at any time since the Great Depression. Twenty-five thousand homeless poor sought beds in city shelters each night. Thousands more slept outside. Highly visible homeless encampments filled vacant lots and public parks, lined the seawalls along the East River, and perched at the ends of the Hudson River's crumbling piers. More than two thousand men and women lived beneath the city's streets, hidden in subway and railroad tunnels.

The economic, political, and social shifts that led to this massive dislocation are complex, but several key events of the 1970s accelerated the crisis. Tens of thousands of chronically ill patients had been discharged from state mental institutions, many without provision for housing or community-based treatment. People wandering the streets and sleeping in public places soon became visible beyond the Bowery. The decade marked a dramatic reduction in manufacturing jobs, particularly in New York City. Many low-skill jobs disappeared, casualties of automation and the use of cheap labor abroad. Soaring unemployment coincided with a sudden decline in the real-estate market. In the wake of the city's 1975 fiscal crisis, stringent revisions to property-tax laws were instituted. But the city's plan to increase revenue had an unexpected effect: a significant number of landlords, particularly in the South Bronx and on the Lower East Side, responded with arson or abandonment, leaving some five hundred vacant properties in neighborhoods where low-rent housing was desperately needed.

By the end of the '70s, the real-estate market had begun to recover. Rapid gentrification in the city's low-income neighborhoods further reduced the number of affordable apartments and single-room-occupancy (sro) hotels, thus inflating the housing market. While the economic expansion that continued through the 1980s brought a surge of wealth to the élite of New York, the outlook for the poor became dismal. Rules governing eligibility for welfare were tightened, especially for single adult men. Those who succeeded in navigating

the tangled bureaucracy received public-assistance checks that were inadequate in the face of escalating apartment rents.

A landmark lawsuit filed against the city in 1981, settled as the Callahan consent decree, guaranteed single homeless men the right to shelter. Subsequent litigation extended this right to women and families with children. More than twenty-eight thousand children and adults were residing in shelters by March 1987. Converted armories, such as Fort Washington in Upper Manhattan and the Atlantic Avenue Armory in Brooklyn, slept as many as twelve hundred men, billeted on floors once used for military drills. The crowded and dangerous conditions led thousands more to sleep outside, huddled in plastic bags or discarded refrigerator boxes, seeking protection in empty doorways, and finding warmth on top of sidewalk steam grates. As the situation worsened, a startling phenomenon occurred: homeless people began to improvise housing for themselves. Shantytowns soon became visible in vacant lots on the Lower East Side. These encampments also appeared in public parks, under highway exit ramps,

along the rivers, and beneath the streets. Residents clustered their dwellings into small villages that provided a sense of community and security.

The largest of these encampments was in Tompkins Square Park in the East Village, where 150 homeless people had set up tents by the late 1980s. The 10-acre park was also a nighttime gathering place for punk-music fans and activists resisting the neighborhood's gentrification. On the night of August 6, 1988, a large crowd lingered at the park's band shell after a concert. At a nearby entrance protesters rallied against news that the police would enforce a curfew. Police arrived. A bottle-throwing skirmish erupted into a bloody melee. Over a hundred complaints of police brutality were filed by protesters and bystanders, and over forty people, including more than a dozen police officers, were injured. Afterwards the homeless individuals quietly returned. They were again swept from the park by police in July and December 1989. Each time, they made their way back. But on June 3, 1991, a phalanx of police in riot gear routed them from the park and closed it for renovation. When it reopened in

August 1992, a curfew was imposed. The homeless community was never rebuilt.

Over the next six years, homeless New Yorkers continued to be pushed out of their fragile, self-made dwellings by politics, police, and bulldozers. Some homes were demolished after only a few weeks. Others survived for several years and gradually expanded into more permanent settlements.

The most longstanding of these communities existed for more than twenty-three years in an abandoned railroad tunnel stretching for 2½ miles under Manhattan's Riverside Park. Joe, an army veteran, found shelter there in 1973: "I know how it is to be a tunnel rat. I did that tour in Vietnam." Cathy, a young woman he had met in Riverside Park, joined him. They made a home together, the equivalent of eight blocks into the tunnel, in a pre-existing cinder-block room. Joe added a door and furnished the room with a bed, a nightstand, and a cupboard that he scavenged from the streets "upstairs." In addition to furniture, the refuse discarded by residents of Upper West Side high-rise apartments supplied Joe with used books and magazines, which he sold along Broadway, and with beverage cans that he redeemed at nearby recycling centers. Cathy, who suffered from asthma and epilepsy, cared for their pets: eighteen stray cats and a pit bull named Buddy. Throughout the 1980s, other homeless men and women found their way into the tunnel. They clustered plywood shanties beneath air vents, where shafts of daylight punctuated the darkness. Visiting graffiti artists painted elaborate murals on light-washed walls. Loners perched themselves on narrow ledges high above the tracks. Meals were cooked over fires that also served to combat winter's damp chill. The community relied on an underground water source. When it was suddenly shut off, tunnel residents were forced to walk miles below and above ground to obtain water and food.

While Cathy and Joe's community burgeoned, Bernard Isaac found his way into the tunnel through a broken gate twelve blocks north. He hand-picked other homeless people to share his refuge, and by the late 1980s his "camp" of seventeen men and women formed the nucleus of a separate tunnel community. Larry joined Bernard's group in 1986. "I was walking down by the river and I saw the gate was open," he said. "This has been my home for five years out of the nine or ten that I've been roaming the streets."

Esteban, who had fled Cuba during the 1980 Mariel Boatlift, worked as a security guard for a building on 90th Street where Bernard collected cans. "I'd been down here sometimes and had visited Bernard. But the job ended. Then everything ended." Esteban moved into the tunnel. Bernard befriended Bob at an Upper West Side soup kitchen where they both volunteered as cooks. Underground, Bernard cooked all the meals over an open campfire.

In 1990, Amtrak crews discovered more than fifty people living in the tunnel. Many of the residents refused to leave, continuing to live in their underground homes until June 1995, when Amtrak police informed them that they were trespassing and threatened them with arrest. Cops padlocked most of the entrances. Tunnel residents, undaunted, regained entry by digging "rabbit holes" and cutting the locks with hacksaws. In the late spring of 1996, through the combined efforts of Coalition for the Homeless and Project Renewal, twenty-six of the tunnel residents were offered Federal housing vouchers. Cathy and Joe moved to a subsidized apartment in Spanish Harlem. Bernard lives in north Harlem but returns to the Upper West Side to earn money assisting the superintendents of luxury buildings and walking dogs. Bob lives in an SRO near Times Square. Esteban still lives on the Upper West Side, but now he sleeps on the streets.

*

In the late 1980s, fourteen homeless men from Puerto Rico made a community in a vacant lot on East 4th Street. They cleared debris, searched for scrap building materials, and constructed plywood houses along a central path. The men continually embellished their homes with additions that stirred memories of the place they had left behind: a front porch, brightly painted rock gardens, an interior courtyard, an inflated plastic palm tree, a Puerto Rican flag. Pepe built the front porch out of red plastic bakery trays and framed his entrance gate with bedposts he had found in the trash. He connected his roof to his vegetable garden with a *marquesina*, or covered walkway, paved with marble left over from a local apartment renovation. Metal window grates cut from shopping carts protected his home from break-ins and vandalism. Pepe added a tool room where he made money repairing lamps, radios, TVs, and turntables for residents of tenements on 3rd Street and Avenue D. Over a period of four years, he transformed his plywood shack into a five-room home. Juan, one of the earliest residents of "Bushville," as the community came to be known, built a 16-by-8-foot plywood house using the exterior of a deserted building as the fourth wall. Above the front door he nailed a prized wooden sign: SPICE ISLANDS. Juan was found dead inside his home in 1991, following an illness. Evelyn, his widow, sold his hut for $100 to Gumiscindo, a neighbor, who rented it to newcomers Duke and his companion Tanya for $40 a month. Duke, a Vietnam veteran, complained about paying rent to live in a homeless community, but he had already endured four evictions and needed to find more stable shelter than his cardboard-and-plastic lean-to along the FDR Drive.

Despite its look of permanence, the community could not last. After the abandoned apartment buildings that overlooked Bushville were renovated as housing for low-income families, the new tenants complained about the homeless. Early on December 15, 1993, Bushville was demolished. The residents had been warned of the impending destruction but had nowhere else to go. As the bulldozers arrived, people quickly gathered their belongings. The noise of the heavy equipment was

deafening. Massive shovels wrenched the small houses from their foundations, held them high, then hurled them to the ground. Tanya and Duke lived for seven months in a stripped van up on blocks in a vacant lot on East Ninth Street before moving into an abandoned building in the neighborhood. Tanya's mother tends their baby. Pepe, the only Bushville resident offered subsidized housing, died four years later at age seventy. Another evicted resident, Mario, slept on the sidewalk around the corner from his former home until he died in 1998. He was sixty years old. The vacant lot is now a community garden.

*

Fourteen blocks southwest of Bushville, a group of sixteen homeless men and women pieced together homes on a triangular knoll that bordered the Canal Street off-ramp of the Manhattan Bridge. Bypassed by the steady stream of traffic from Brooklyn that pours into the heart of Chinatown, "the Hill" gained renown for its unusual dwellings.

At its crest, just before it narrows to a ravine and plummets toward Forsyth Street, stood the curious home of Mr Lee, an immigrant from Guangdong Province in China. Lee, who arrived at the encampment without a word in 1989 carrying his possessions in a sack, soon astonished his neighbors by constructing a house without pounding a nail or sawing a board. Instead, it was bound together with knots. Bright yellow plastic straps wrapped his soft, rounded hut, binding old mattresses and bedsprings into walls. The exterior was festooned with red bakery ribbons, paper lanterns, and castoff calendars that celebrated the Chinese New Year. Oranges, symbols of prosperity, had hardened in the bitter cold and hung from straps like ornaments. Mr Lee died in his home on May 29, 1992, in a fire set by an arsonist seeking revenge on another resident. Detectives searching through the ashes found bundles of charred photographs of Chinese families, hand-crafted passports for invented relatives all named Lee, and a large slate inscribed with cryptic ideograms. In the months that followed, every attempt to build on the site of Mr Lee's house of mysterious knots and messages was also consumed by flames.

The community continued to evolve: some people left the Hill; others arrived. Louie, the earliest resident, built houses for the newly homeless, charging $5 for each one, "Though no one ever paid me." But after another rash of fires, the city razed the settlement on August 17, 1993.

Louie piled a few possessions into a shopping cart and wheeled it down Forsyth Street to join a group of men and women who had pieced together a row of plywood shanties along the seawall bordering the East River between the Manhattan and Brooklyn Bridges. Most were refugees from homeless encampments that had been destroyed. Several of the men had been evicted from Tompkins Square Park. Others had been expelled from vacant lots, public parks, or abandoned buildings. Two had fled the arched ramparts of the Brooklyn Bridge; another had been routed from an underground tunnel. Some sought respite from the city's shelters, others

asylum from oppressive foreign regimes. Soon girlfriends arrived, the population grew to thirty-five, and stray cats and dogs were adopted as pets.

Louie, who had been nicknamed "the architect" when he lived at the Hill, never built a hut for himself along the river. Instead, he shared the tents of friends or slept beneath mounds of blankets on the edge of the seawall. He lost his balance and drowned in the East River on May 18, 1995.

For others, the sense of community at the river offered stability. Wooden pallets, left behind by local delivery trucks, provided fuel and building supplies. Residents of neighboring projects disposed of an endless supply of cans that the men redeemed for a nickel apiece. As the years passed, the makeshift huts were transformed into more permanent structures that evoked memories of childhood homes: a roof of equal pitch, a rope porch railing, a nameplate over an entrance, a weather vane. On May 10, 1993 the city demolished "Little Puerto Rico," the north end of the encampment. Ten residents lost their homes. The sense of community was fractured, and tensions erupted among the remaining men. The following spring Mark made plans to leave. "Of the original guys that came here, I'm the only one left. That's telling me it's time to go. With this new crew down here, I don't know. I just don't feel right with them." Mark was murdered, his body found at the bottom of a recycling cart on June 4, 1994. He was interred in the potters' field on Hart Island. He was forty years old. Bulldozers leveled the river encampment on July 1, 1996.

*

Other homeless men and women found refuge along the Hudson River. Angelo Aldi built his hut on a massive concrete pier that stretches out into the river at West 44th Street. To the north, tourists swarm over the *Intrepid*, a World War II aircraft carrier. To the south, visitors board the Circle Line sightseeing boat. Angelo and the six other men who lived on the wharf ignored these activities as they went about the work of building their homes.

Twenty-five blocks north, JR found refuge in a rusting metal structure that rises 45 feet above the Hudson at the end of a rotting pier. The reward for his perilous climb to the chamber atop the floating bridge, built 120 years ago to transfer boxcars arriving by barge to inland tracks, was solitude and a safe lookout against any intruders. But the bitter cold of January 1994 forced JR from his outpost and into the narrow confines of one of twenty-seven concrete vaults that lined a desolate stretch of railroad track nearby. Over the next three years, thirty-five more people found shelter in this ruin, all that remained of an elevated track once used by the New York Central Railroad. Police forced the residents to leave on February 26, 1997. Within hours, bulldozers had buried the last homeless community in Manhattan with dirt and debris excavated for construction of Donald Trump's luxury apartment complex, which now overlooks the rail yard.

*

Since then, the number of homeless poor has not diminished. In January 2006, Coalition for the Homeless announced that throughout the first half of the decade an average of 32,609 New Yorkers slept in homeless shelters each night, including 7,640 families and 13,616 children. Ironically, the city's building boom now provides temporary shelter for the dispossessed beneath construction scaffolding; cardboard boxes and bedding are concealed moments before morning work crews arrive. Only early-morning joggers, dog-walkers, and park employees see the homeless poor bending over water fountains to brush their teeth, shaking dirt from their sleeping bags, and bundling their possessions into backpacks. An all-night journey through the city finds urban nomads forever on the move: riding subways across the night, sleeping on the streets, tucking themselves into decaying structures along the waterfront, and disappearing again before dawn.

CITY LIFE

Among the most common misconceptions about New York is that it's a very 'liberal' city. It's not. New York is divided in almost every way, and the city's characteristic vigor—its fluid mix of worldliness and provincialism at all levels of society—shouldn't be mistaken for much besides the constant play of uncountable opposing forces. Among them is religious pluralism. The thousands of botanicas, storefront churches and, other, more imposing houses of Christian worship, have their place, but their effect on civic life is slight. This isn't true of Judaism, as befits the world's second most Jewish city, but with a population ranging from radical secular to ultra-Orthodox, from the indigent to a billionaire Mayor—generalization is impossible. Mosques are easy to find (look for the word *masjid*) in numerous areas, Hindu and Buddhist temples less so.

With religion playing only a small role in city governance, it's ironic few New Yorkers pay attention to local politics. The effects of this disinterest are many—that Yankee Stadium deal being a recent example—none salutary, except for those with the money to game a corrupt system to their benefit. This explains how luxury developments receive tax subsidies and why New York will have had *sixteen* years of Republican Mayoralty when 48 of 51 City Council seats are held by Democrats. The Yankees faced overwhelming community opposition, yet political reaction citywide was largely quiet. Bronx Borough President Adolfo Carrión Jr lives on City Island, which is as far from Macomb's Dam Park as he can get, but his future is secure: the machine knows he plays ball. While malfeasance is especially dramatic in the Boogie Down Bronx, dissatisfaction with the city is widespread. Indeed, the truest measure of New York might be its cynicism, perhaps the only thing shared equally by both the rich and the disenfranchised. It's apt, therefore, that the classic novel of American mendacity, *The Confidence Man* (1857), was written by a native son, Herman Melville. Such is the city where mob boss John Gotti became a folk hero and, ten years after Paul Castellano was gunned down, another Staten Islander, Wu Tang Clan member Raekwon, could identify with "Gambino niggas who swipe theirs."

Even those excitedly moving in on the real-estate boom are learning the truth: their condo is shoddy; illegal construction nearby has cracked their walls; an understaffed Department of Buildings a joke. It shouldn't have been a surprise. While journalism about how New York *really* works is rare, important exceptions include *City For Sale* (1988) by Jack Newfield and Wayne Barrett, *Subway Lives* by Jim Dwyer (1991) and *The Short Sweet Dream of Eduardo Gutierréz* (2001) by Jimmy Breslin. *City For Sale* details the corruption scandals of the Koch years, culminating in the suicide of Queens Borough President Donald Manes, who plunged a knife into his heart barely two months after cops stopped his car and found him bleeding from a slashed wrist. Manes' initial claim he was hijacked shocked a city familiar with violence. An unlikely hero of *City For Sale* was the then US Attorney Rudolph Giuliani, a role he wouldn't reprise as Mayor in Breslin's book about the death (drowned in concrete during a building collapse) of an all-but-anonymous Mexican laborer at a Hasidic-owned construction site in Williamsburg. For their part, both Barrett and Newfield later authored books debunking Giuliani.

It's no longer provocative to say 9/11 was the best thing that ever happened to Rudy Giuliani. Before that morning, the Mayor's apparent descent into madness was nearly complete. Having presided over a reduction in crime (claiming credit many thought due to the police), Giuliani took on more elusive enemies: smut, blasphemy, mosquitoes . . . He flirted with a run for Senate (against Hillary Clinton), only to withdraw claiming prostate cancer. An ugly divorce followed, and an NYPD security detail was assigned to his mistress. Kevin McAuliffe compiled *The Sayings of Generalissimo Giuliani* (2000); its design was an homage to Mao's *Little Red Book*. A pet project of Giuliani's was a new Emergency Operations Center. The press quickly dubbed the exorbitant facility—to be built in the same World Trade Center complex that was bombed in 1993—"The Bunker." The Mayor was not amused. The empty bunker and the rest of WTC 7 collapsed at 5:21 PM on September 11, 2001. In the days following, a term-limited Giuliani offered to remain as Mayor, although there was no legal authority for him to do so. Assured by both Federal and local officials that a smoldering Ground Zero posed no health risks, many who toiled there or lived close by continue to fall ill.

Today, Mayor Bloomberg and Police Commissioner Raymond Kelly are almost co-executives of the city. While Bloomberg is far less antagonistic than his predecessor, he's equally self-assured. The city promotes truck-intensive development while the Mayor pursues a radical anti-smoking agenda—for the benefit of New Yorkers' health. Access to Chinatown remains limited by NYPD road closures around One Police Plaza, despite repeated calls for the streets to be reopened. In 2003, demonstrations against the impending Iraq war were met with official resistance every step of the way. The following year, amid a failed campaign to attract the 2012 Olympics, Bloomberg welcomed the Republican National Convention to New York. Thousands of protestors were arrested, and the city has since paid millions to those illegally detained. Despite Kelly's public image as an anti-terror obsessive, the facts speak of a Police Commissioner—and presumptive Mayor—who will assert his desire for social control through any means necessary. These include the widespread use of police surveillance cameras, the harassment of photographers, and undercover operations of questionable necessity and improper supervision. So Amadou Diallo, Patrick Dorismond, Ousmane Zongo and Sean Bell died for what?

The Other New York Awaits its Leader

Tom Robbins

By the time Mayor Michael Bloomberg stepped onto a stage crowded with supporters on election night in November 2005, the only question remaining about that day's vote was the size of his victory. The communications tycoon had spent a staggering $80 million at that point, a casual splurge for a multibillionaire but one that crushed any lingering hopes harbored by backers of the hapless Democratic candidate, former Bronx Borough President Fernando Ferrer.

For his part, Ferrer had managed to scrape together less than $10 million, almost half of it from the matching funds supplied him under the city's public campaign-finance system, a program denounced by his wealthy competitor as a giveaway to professional politicians. In the crucial last weeks of the election, Ferrer had spent just $600,000 for television advertisements; Bloomberg had shelled out more than that just to keep his troops in coffee and pastries.

Even without his Leviathan-like spending, Bloomberg was viewed as a sure thing long before election night. In the months leading up to the vote, in the best tradition of the clubhouse pols he claimed to abhor, he had employed all the powers of his incumbency. He had doled out awards and projects, announcing a new police precinct here, new housing there. He had protected his left flank by reaching long-stalled contract agreements with a half-dozen major city employees' unions, including cops, teachers, firefighters, and sanitation workers. He had stoked the dreams of the city's real-estate and construction industry by calling for a broad swath of development, including, before he was done, new sports stadiums in Manhattan, Queens, Brooklyn, and the Bronx. He had eased the anxiety of the city's home-owners by continuing his practice of mailing individual $400 property-tax rebate checks, a kind of continuing apology for the sharp tax hike he had imposed during his first year in office. Politically, he had managed to maintain an alliance of convenience with the conservative leaders of the Republican Party, who were only too happy to have him on their ballot line even if everyone knew he carried their label in name only. He had also somehow managed to convince most of the media that his ongoing association with the

cultist, quasi-Marxist, overtly anti-Semitic officials of the Independence Party, who had provided him with his crucial narrow margin of victory in his 2001 election, wasn't really worth noting or pursuing.

"Mayor Mike"—as the buttons worn by the hundreds of people wedged into a huge midtown hotel ballroom dubbed him—was shooting for a blowout, a landslide that would even eclipse the huge re-election tally achieved in 1997 by his most important ally, former Mayor Rudy Giuliani. If there were any doubters still wondering how broad his support was, they needed only to take a look at the crew assembled on the stage in the vast Metropolitan ballroom of the Sheraton New York Hotel on Seventh Avenue. Stacked on risers like football cheerleaders, the better to be seen by a score of TV cameras, a rainbow of diversity had been carefully assembled by Team Bloomberg. The black pastor of one of the largest Baptist congregations in Queens stood next to an Orthodox Jewish assemblyman from Brooklyn's Borough Park; leaders of the hotel workers and the plumbers' union stood next to a labor-wary Republican congressman from Staten Island; a Puerto Rican councilwoman from the Lower East Side, an avowed lesbian, was placed next to a bearded, conservative Jewish representative; Giuliani, whose election-night parties were notable for the overwhelming whiteness of his supporters, stood next to another former Mayor, Ed Koch, who once wrote a book entitled *Giuliani: Nasty Man.* Leading the cheers, as Bloomberg quick-stepped onto the stage, was basketball star-turned-entrepreneur Magic Johnson. As the newly re-elected Mayor raised his hands above his head in a victory salute, a black gospel chorus sang "Ain't No Stopping Us Now."

The soul anthem was an odd choice. The song's boisterous melody and lyrics depict a dogged drive toward black liberation: "I know that you refuse to be held down anymore . . . don't let nothing, nothing, stand in your way . . ." The tune came out in 1979 and was sung outside City Hall by blacks protesting budget cuts and police brutality. Back then, New York had only recently been

declared to have a majority of minority residents. When demographers noted that high-water mark, the working assumption among political analysts was that the crucial next step had arrived for what was to be an inexorable march toward minority empowerment. The juggernaut of racial change was considered the defining element in the city's politics. If blacks, Hispanics, and what was then just a smattering of Asians had achieved numerical superiority, it was only a matter of time before the hands at the reins of City Hall would change color as well. It wasn't just a question of ethnic succession. Fundamental political change required new leaders, drawn from the ranks of those who experienced inequality first-hand.

And yet, three decades later, here was the New York electorate, even darker in complexion than it had been in the late 1970s, bestowing an overwhelming plurality on a white Jewish man who hailed from a Boston suburb. In doing so, it had rejected a native son, an affable, Bronx-born Puerto Rican, a man of progressive views and values in both social and fiscal affairs, someone who had carefully worked his way up the ladder of the city's Democratic political organization, the party that still outnumbered Republicans by a 5–1 ratio within the five boroughs.

In the wake of Bloomberg's victory, critics focused on the fact that Democrats had now been shut out of City Hall in an astonishing four straight elections. But while the GOP's continuing electoral success in a city where its national leaders are loathed was surprising, the failure of black and Latino empowerment was even more so. If once upon a time there had been "no stopping us now," the path to political power had been at least diverted if not blocked altogether.

*

What had happened?

Standard political orthodoxy held that voters had simply gotten wise to racial hype. Pointing to Bloomberg's improved showing in both black and Latino districts, critics of minority empowerment insisted that the Mayor's overwhelming re-election—he topped Ferrer by almost 20 percent—was explained by color-blind voters who had opted for competence and security over a risky and unproven alternative. But that was nothing new. Minority voters had always been willing to cross racial lines and support white candidates; it was white voters who were hard to woo in the other direction. On Staten Island, the smallest and whitest of the five boroughs, Bloomberg won his largest percentage of the vote in 2005, just as he had done in 2001, and just as Giuliani had done in the 1989 and 1993 elections versus David Dinkins. Moreover, the overall turnout for the 2005 election, the first time an Hispanic had become the nominee of a major party, was the lowest on record.

Another explanation held that Ferrer's undoing had come at the hands of a black political establishment that had remained cool to his campaign. Why hand City Hall to an Hispanic pol, this reasoning went, when a black official stood a decent chance to win the next time? Under term limits, Bloomberg would be out of office in four years. At that point, at least one African-American politician, the bland and non-confrontational city comptroller William Thompson, was almost certain to run.

*

If blacks remained aloof from Ferrer's campaign, it wouldn't be the first time they declined to make common cause with a popular Puerto Rican. In 1985, Harlem leaders, including Dinkins, Representative Charles Rangel, and former Manhattan Borough President Percy Sutton, had refused to support Herman Badillo, the ex-congressman who had offered himself as a progressive minority alternative to Mayor Koch, then seeking his third term. Badillo's saga was the stuff of dreams for a political pitchman. Orphaned as a young boy in Puerto Rico, he had been shipped to family members in New York. There, he had pulled himself out of poverty with the help of free tuition at City College and gone on to earn a law degree. Like Ferrer, he had worked his way through the ranks of the Bronx's Democratic organization. His reward was a job from then Mayor Robert Wagner with the city's department of relocation, helping families dislocated by urban-renewal projects. Badillo doggedly pursued a career in politics. It wasn't easy. Bronx Democratic boss Charlie Buckley derisively suggested that he couldn't be Puerto Rican because he was "too tall."

Badillo first sought the Democratic mayoral nomination in 1969, emphasizing the need to rebuild the city's neighborhoods. But instead of holding down the left-liberal wing of the party in a city aflame with anti-Vietnam war passion, he found himself upstaged by novelist Norman Mailer's futile bid. Four years later, Badillo ran again. He forced city comptroller Abe Beame into a runoff but lost. When Beame's City Hall foundered amid an increasingly desperate fiscal crisis, Badillo tried again in 1977. Aside from Beame, a pure product of the Brooklyn clubhouse who retained the backing of the city's still-powerful Democratic political machinery, the race for the nomination included many of the party's brightest stars. There was Bella Abzug, the feisty congresswoman known for her fierce anti-war and pro-feminist stands. There was Mario Cuomo, an eloquent state official from middle-class Queens who had the blessings of his patron, Governor Hugh Carey. There was also Percy Sutton, the elegant African-American official who had fashioned alliances with many of the city's white power brokers.

But even with the wealth of talent in the contest, Badillo stood out. He was the only candidate willing to openly suggest that the city should go toe-to-toe with the giant financial institutions that were demanding massive cuts in the municipal workforce, the closing of municipal hospitals, and the end to free tuition at city colleges. Ending the 130-year-old policy of helping the poor reach the middle class via a free college education, the lifeline he himself had grabbed as a young man, was, in Badillo's view, "not only stupid but also cruel . . . It sells out the future of so many young people; as usual the poor are being used to bear the brunt of the city's mismanagement." Badillo also angrily denounced the "planned shrinkage" theory broached by investment banker Felix Rohaytn, whose advice guided the Beame administration and who openly suggested that the South Bronx be leveled and turned into an industrial park. Such talk was echoed in editorials in the New York *Times* which suggested that essential services in poor and "marginal" neighborhoods be eliminated in an effort to reduce city costs. Badillo denounced such talk as racist. "The poor do not count in this city," he told Nat Hentoff in a lengthy *Village Voice* profile. "They have no clout." The solution, he said, was political power.

Badillo's tough talk got traction in the early weeks of the campaign as the candidates debated the causes of the fiscal crisis and the policies that might end it. Then it stopped. The 1977 campaign quickly descended into a racial brawl in the wake of the Blackout riots that erupted over two days in mid-July. Although no one was killed (violent crimes even briefly fell), the lawlessness brought renewed public calls for reinstatement of the state's death penalty. Leading this appeal was Koch, a liberal bachelor congressman from Greenwich Village desperately looking for a way to distinguish himself in a formidable field. Amid the late-summer heat, Koch began walking into senior citizens' centers and street festivals in white neighborhoods, yelling, "Hi, I'm for capital punishment. Are you?" Often he would call for a quick plebiscite on the matter, asking all those who supported bringing back the electric chair to raise their hands. Campaigning at the Battery as rush-hour commuters streamed from the Staten Island Ferry, Koch shouted through a bullhorn, "How many of you think the National Guard should have been called out in the blackout?" as he thrust his own arm high in the air.

Koch's media guru, David Garth, who had piloted John Lindsay, a charismatic liberal (and anti-death penalty) Republican, into office in 1965, was now using his former client as a campaign punching bag. Garth had provided Koch with a memorable slogan: "After eight years of charisma, and four years of the clubhouse, why not try competence?" To this, Garth added a series of TV ads in which Koch emphasized his law-and-order demands. Koch's poll numbers soared. When reporter Denis Hamill asked him in late August why he dwelt so much on capital punishment, Koch responded simply, "Because that's what people want to hear."

Badillo responded to Koch's babble by saying that while he personally didn't oppose the death penalty in all instances, it was irrelevant to the mayoral race since the decision was up to state officials. While Badillo's approach was rational and reasonable, it left him as an also-ran in the campaign as the eloquent Cuomo took the lead against Koch's pro-death chant. In the ensuing

Koch–Cuomo runoff, the death penalty became the key issue in a series of televised debates.

After Koch's election, Badillo briefly worked in his administration but quit in a bitter dispute, insisting that the city's minority neighborhoods were getting short-changed by City Hall. Badillo sat out the 1981 race as Koch easily sailed to re-election. But in 1985, invoking his credentials as an effective minority leader who had fought for neighborhoods and the poor, he put himself forward as a popular and qualified alternative. His rationale for running couldn't have been clearer: only an effective alliance of black and Latino political power could hope to counter the New York that Koch was shaping, a city in which the concerns of a wealthy élite and outer-borough middle-class whites, fearful of racial change, were primary.

No one has ever fully explained why the black establishment, which viscerally detested Koch, rejected Badillo. The decision may have been motivated by the same strategic thinking that helped strand Ferrer in 2005: that while Koch was still a potent foe seeking a third term, his star would be likely to fade by 1989, when an attractive black candidate could run.

Whatever the thinking, the Gang of Five, as Charles Rangel and his black colleagues were dubbed in the press, rebuffed Badillo. In a mockery of the political agenda they had claimed to champion, the group handed its support to Herman "Denny" Farrell, a passive and undistinguished black assemblyman from Manhattan. Farrell, a dapper man fond of double-breasted suits, never broke a sweat as he went down to a thunderous defeat in the primary. As for Badillo, he never recovered from the slight. He began a steady drift to the right, eventually finding a home in the Giuliani administration before making a final sad bid for the mayoralty in 2001, this time as a Republican.

＊

By 1989, the stars were nonetheless in alignment for a minority candidate, even if the man positioned to take advantage of them was an unlikely choice. David Dinkins, known for his reserved style and courtly manners, presented the mirror image of Koch's increasingly frequent and seemingly out-of-control rants. Elected in 1985 as Manhattan Borough President, Dinkins had become the city's most prominent minority politician following Badillo's eclipse. His high profile couldn't have come at a better time. Elected three times—twice by landslides— Mayor Mouth, as Koch was dubbed, had run smack into a massive municipal-corruption scandal that had boiled up from long-buried deals he had cut with the city's political chieftains to win the first time in 1977. Although the scandal lapped dangerously close to his own door, as witness the indictment of Bess Meyerson, the former Miss America who had held his hand in public throughout that first election, effectively silencing suggestions that he was gay, Koch was never personally tainted.

Dinkins, himself a product of a political machine, was the last person to voice outrage over the scandals. "Those people were friends of mine," he said of political hacks who'd been caught ripping off the city when I interviewed him for a 1988 *Village Voice* profile. If not for the brutal late-summer racial slaying of a black youth by a white gang in Bensonhurst, Koch still might have squeezed past Dinkins. The murder of Yusuf Hawkins, and Koch's ham-fisted response (he was heavily booed when he appeared at the wake), underscored his own racial insensitivities, which had been on display, in varying degrees, for much of his three terms. As a result, he lost a thin but crucial strand of white liberal voters who decided to make a leap of faith by choosing the decent, if unexciting and unproven, Dinkins.

Even that victory would never have been possible had Jesse Jackson not conducted the second of his presidential bids the year before. Squadrons of volunteers, many of them new to electoral politics, had registered new voters throughout the city's black neighborhoods for Jackson's race. Helping to orchestrate the get-out-the-vote push for the Democratic long shot was a rotund ex-labor organizer named Bill Lynch, a Dinkins aide who already had his eye on a City Hall office for his boss. In a nod to Jackson's Rainbow Coalition, and to emphasize his theme of racial harmony, Dinkins dubbed his own campaign a "gorgeous mosaic," as non-threatening a slogan as could be offered. Jackson won a huge turnout in black and Latino districts (as well as a surprising 16 percent of the white vote), and Dinkins and Lynch set out to build on that success. Dinkins' supporters were able to galvanize many of the same minority voters who had turned out so enthusiastically for Jackson's historic bid.

But if he was the first candidate carried into office by the political yearnings of the city's emerging black and Latino majority, once there Dinkins proved himself a reluctant warrior. Although he chose a talented staff comprised of aides selected mainly on merit, he was a decidedly hands-off manager, ducking rigorous discussions and leaving most of the toughest decisions to them. The press noted, however, that the neatly turned out Mayor relished the ceremonial aspects of his office. His ability to change in and out of tennis whites in the morning, and tuxedos in the evening, unfairly (or not)

became a hallmark of his administration. In good times, New Yorkers have been highly tolerant of such mayors, most notably when Jimmy Walker lived the Roaring '20s high life every night and rarely arose before noon. Dinkins had no such luck. A fatal racial blowup involving blacks and Jews in Crown Heights, Brooklyn following a fatal auto accident in which a young black child was killed showed his hands-off style at its worst. The August 1991 outbreak accompanied a spike in the murder rate, a climb that had begun under the Koch administration with the advent of crack cocaine in the ghettoes.

"Do Something Dave!" headlined the New York *Post*. Stung by the criticisms, he did. In what was to be a major accomplishment of his administration, Dinkins, working together with City Council leader Peter Vallone, was able to win a special tax hike to put more cops on the street. That move began the steady decline in the city's crime rate over the next decade. Dinkins, however, got no credit for it. Instead, Giuliani, a former prosecutor who had lost to Dinkins in 1989, focused his second campaign squarely on crime, an issue that inevitably emphasized racial fears.

Again, outside events intervened. Residents of Staten Island had succeeded in placing a referendum on the ballot that year calling for the borough to secede from the city, a move bolstered by the presence of a black man from Harlem in Gracie Mansion. The referendum was of dubious legality, but that was something to be settled later in court. What was more important was that it drew huge numbers of voters to the polls who also threw the lever for Giuliani.

This time Dinkins lost by nearly the same margin that he had won by in 1989, less than fifty thousand votes. Much of Giuliani's victory was achieved on the strength of those Staten Island votes where he swamped Dinkins by a 7–1 margin and where voter turnout was one-third higher than the prior mayoral election. Notably, Giuliani also won votes in liberal electoral districts in Manhattan's Upper West Side and in Brooklyn's brownstone belt. The tallies suggested that many of the same white liberals who had turned away from Koch in the Democratic primary four years earlier now did the unthinkable, casting their votes for Giuliani, a Republican.

*

That pretty much took care of minority empowerment at City Hall for the next sixteen years. As the new Mayor, Giuliani never wasted an opportunity to blame everything from the city's budget problems to the crime rate on prior administrations. The subtext of his caustic remarks was that the Democratic Party had been captured by radicals and minorities who cared little for the concerns of middle-income (i.e. white) taxpayers. In 1997, Ferrer made a brief effort to win the Democratic nomination against him, but he lost heart half-way through, yielding to Manhattan Borough President and West Side liberal Ruth Messinger. It was just as well. Giuliani trounced his opponent and would have had a good chance at winning a third term if not for the implementation of term limits.

Ferrer's 2001 campaign became his own hard-luck story. He had watched and waited in the intervening four years, lining up support among top black leaders, including the popular if irascible Reverend Al Sharpton. By primary day, September 11, most of his supporters believed they were on an unstoppable roll. Instead, the primary election, scrapped early in the day of the attack on the

World Trade Center, suddenly became totally irrelevant in the eyes of most New Yorkers. When the contest was held three weeks later, Ferrer's troops had lost much of their forward momentum. He still edged out Mark Green, his veteran white liberal opponent, but not sufficiently to avoid a runoff.

Mobilizing the city against further terror attacks suddenly became the preeminent campaign issue, a question none of the three surviving candidates— Ferrer, Green, and novice Michael Bloomberg—were equipped to handle. Still, it provided Ferrer a stand-out moment in which he offered a quiet profile in courage that surprised even many of his supporters.

The moment came when Giuliani, at the height of his post-9/11 popularity and openly seeking a way to remain in office despite the term-limits law, demanded that each of the candidates agree to leave him in charge for an additional ninety days beyond the end of his term to handle the emergency. The move was Giuliani chutzpah at its zenith. Anyone who agreed would appear weak to the electorate. On the other hand, a candidate who refused risked the wrath of a sitting Mayor whose poll numbers, which had sunk prior to the attack, were at record highs. Bloomberg agreed immediately. Green took a little longer but then said he would grant the unprecedented request, a decision that stunned many of his backers.

Ferrer met with Giuliani, thought about it, then said no. "You are either ready [to govern] or you're not," he explained to a meeting that day of the transit-workers' union, which had endorsed him. "Why is a candidate wasting the time of the electorate if he is not ready for a crisis?" Although few knew it at the

time, Ferrer had made his decision against the advice of his most important
supporter, the health-workers' union leader Dennis Rivera, who had put thousands of troops in the street for Ferrer and had helped bankroll his campaign.
"I told him I didn't like it, but that he should probably go along because Giuliani
was very popular and he would try to hurt him politically if he didn't agree,"
Rivera told me shortly after the event.

But if Ferrer held the moral high ground, it didn't do him a lot of good.
When Green was accused of using anti-black flyers to mobilize support in
Jewish neighborhoods in Brooklyn, the runoff degenerated into another racial
brawl, this time one within party lines. Green won, only to go on to suffer a
narrow defeat by Bloomberg, who spent an unprecedented $74 million in that
first campaign.

The blowup over the leaflet, which consisted of a reprint of a New York
Post cartoon depicting Ferrer kissing Sharpton's posterior, overshadowed another,
far more weighty discussion in which the questions of race and political power
had surfaced. Ferrer's theme in his 2001 campaign was that he sought to represent "the other New York." Although it later backfired on him, the slogan had
been adopted as a way to emphasize that a Ferrer administration would be far
more inclusive than Giuliani's had been. For Ferrer and his team, the "other
New York" was intended as a kind of umbrella under which he could gather
potential supporters—many of them black and Latino but working-class and
middle-class whites as well—who felt either alienated by the eight years of
Giuliani's iron-fisted rule or left behind in the rush to prosperity. The slogan
also allowed Ferrer to invoke the New York from which he himself had emerged,

a cold-water tenement walk-up on Fox Street in the South Bronx, where he had been raised by his mother and aunts. Ferrer's other New York was a place where the old urban remedies—free health care, affordable housing, public education—still had a crucial role to play.

The slogan itself had reached Ferrer via his late friend Jack Newfield, the muckraking journalist who had served as an informal adviser to a score of politicians he admired. Working the phones as hard as any county political leader, Newfield had championed Badillo's failed attempt to challenge Koch in 1985. The newsman had also promoted Dinkins' 1989 candidacy although he later soured on the Mayor. Although he never said it publicly, Newfield supported Giuliani in 1993 and remained close to him through much of his two terms in office, only offering public criticism towards the tail end of his administration.

Newfield's slogan also carried an historical homage. The late social critic Michael Harrington, who had been writing for the *Village Voice* in the early 1960s when Newfield was starting out there, had famously entitled his book on the nation's enduring poverty *The Other America*. Harrington, in turn, had adapted his title from an even more famous account of the needy, Jacob Riis' 1890 *How the Other Half Lives,* the exposé that rallied a generation of urban reformers.

But the catch-phrase that had served for more than a century, in one form or another, as a kind of readily understandable ideological short-hand, quickly became a major political liability for Ferrer when he made it his chief campaign theme. Was he tailoring his race just for minorities? Would whites have a role in his City Hall? Would Manhattan be on the outs in his administration? When the New York *Times* sat him down for an interview with reporters and editors in July 2001 (later reprinted in a full-page story), the first question put to him was whether he intended some kind of ethnic exclusion by the phrase.

Ferrer gamely tried to describe it as an expression where issues of color, class, and outer-borough geography coincided. "I really appreciate the question," he said, going on to describe the typical other New Yorker as someone with a job but without health insurance. He went on to say that "they are largely white New Yorkers," a claim the *Times* staff, correctly, didn't buy for a minute.

But even had he been more eloquent in his explanation (an adjective rarely used to describe Ferrer), he probably never had a chance, and he had made a crushing mistake by assuming good will on the media's part. For the duration of the campaign, the daily papers, with the liberal *Times* in the lead, proceeded to hammer away at him. By the time they were done, even sympathetic white New Yorkers were saying they took umbrage at a phrase that seemed to suggest they wouldn't be invited inside if Ferrer was elected.

In fact there were legitimate reasons to be dubious of Ferrer's capabilities. He had long surrounded himself with advisers, chief among them former Bronx Democratic Party chairman Roberto Ramirez, who had focused more on patron-

age than policy, seizing advantage of their opportunities in much the same way their white political predecessors had done. And if Ferrer achieved a reputation as a supporter of key progressive urban values, he had also managed to flip-flop disturbingly on such issues as abortion, capital punishment, and—most fatally in his third and presumably final run in 2005— the question of criminal indictments for the police officers who had mistakenly fired forty-one bullets at an innocent unarmed Bronx resident named Amadou Diallo, killing him. But even if all those doubts could have magically been waved away, the nub of Ferrer's difficulty in conveying his slogan lay elsewhere, in the form of a problem he couldn't directly address without raising a hubbub likely to foreclose the hope of winning any white support. This was the simple fact that minority empowerment, just as it had been for Badillo in 1977 and Dinkins in 1989, was crucial to his bid for election.

By 2005, however, Ferrer had learned his lesson. In an effort to avoid the hits he'd taken in 2001 and the political booby traps he'd encountered, the "other New York" phrase was noticeably eliminated from his 2005 run. Even as he became the first Hispanic to win the nomination of a major party, an historic first that Badillo had tried heartbreakingly hard to win, Ferrer avoided direct invocation of the aspirations of his race. The result was a lackluster campaign that ignited few sparks. It was only in the final days that, lagging in the polls and given virtually no chance to win, he once more trotted out the phrase. "There are two New Yorks and I've lived in both of them," he told his audience in the last week of October. "Born in one, I crossed the bridge of hope and opportunity into the other, right here to this place. But I have never forgotten where I came from." He went on observe what everyone else was already saying, that his chances of success were dim. But, like Badillo and Dinkins before him, he suggested that his campaign represented something far larger than his own narrow electoral opportunities. "I may win or lose this election," he said, "but I will speak for those who can't speak for themselves and I will be heard."

NYPD

Leonard Levitt

Perhaps my most important discovery in twenty years of reporting on the New York City Police Department is how little the public—top city officials and supposedly knowledgeable police reporters included—knows about what goes on inside it.

Police folk are by training and disposition not a talkative lot. Often, they don't communicate with each other. Their silence rarely serves the citizenry.

Over the past decade, the former Mayor Rudolph Giuliani, who is credited with drastically cutting the city's crime rate, virtually closed the department to the public. Despite the current Mayor Michael Bloomberg's campaign promise of more "transparency," the department under its current commissioner, Ray Kelly, is more secretive than even under Giuliani.

Hovering over it is the 2001 World Trade Center attack. Fear of attack now serves as a blanket hiding what the department is doing, or not doing. And the city's media, which began serving as cheerleaders as crime fell during the Giuliani years, has gone into a post-9/11 swoon, all but relinquishing their critical faculties.

Each police administration I have covered—including the current one—has had a back story, a largely unreported, behind-the-scenes dynamic with invariably far-reaching consequences. I discovered this early in my police-reporting career when, in 1983, I opened *New York Newsday*'s bureau inside the fourteen-story red-brick building known as One Police Plaza. Ed Koch was mayor then and Robert McGuire was the police commissioner. As McGuire prepared to retire, Koch, who had antagonized virtually all black New Yorkers, bypassed his logical successor—the NYPD's highest-ranking uniformed officer, Chief of Department Patrick J. Murphy—and announced the appointment of Benjamin Ward as its first black commissioner.

It is difficult to overstate the racial antagonism Ward faced just two decades ago. Phil Caruso, the Patrolmen's Benevolent Association's President, publicly referred to Ward as "Bubba." The insult had a prototypically racial overtone: as Deputy Commissioner of Community Affairs a decade before, Ward had released

a dozen black suspects in the murder of a white cop at a Harlem mosque.

As it turned out, it wasn't Ward but Chief of Detectives Al Seedman who had released them. This information was discovered by Gerald McKelvey, a fellow *Newsday* reporter, in a secret police document known as the "Blue Book," which, according to the case's grand-jury report, had been circulated only among the upper ranks of the department.

When I caught up with Seedman, then head of security for Alexander's department stores, he acknowledged having released the suspects. When I asked why he hadn't owned up to it, instead allowing Ward to twist for a decade in the wind, Seedman asked me, "What good would it have done?"

Newsday's story dissipated much of Ward's opposition, and he served as commissioner for the next five years. Nonetheless, questions remain. Was it happenstance that the Blue Book had never surfaced before? Or had the department protected one of its own? I have my suspicions. Had the situation been reversed—had the Blue Book exonerated Seedman, a white chief, and blamed Ward—I suspect *that* information would have appeared long before.

This led me to my second discovery, reinforced a year later: that there exists but a thin line between silence and cover-up.

On the rainy Sunday night of April 15, 1984, a few months after Ward's appointment, I was one of a half-dozen reporters outside a house in the poverty-stricken Brownsville section of Brooklyn, where ten women and children had been murdered—some shot at close range, one a baby in his mother's arms. The

largest mass murder in the city's history, the killings became known as the Palm Sunday Massacre.

Because I was the only reporter there who covered the Police Department full-time, I noticed something the others didn't. Standing in the rain, I watched as every top police and mayoral official, Koch included, arrived—everyone but Ward.

Back at One Police Plaza, I asked where Ward had been. I was told he was on vacation and unreachable.

Not until six months later did I discover where he'd been: traveling with a girlfriend to motels between Baltimore and Washington, DC on an alcohol-fueled binge. City Hall had been unable to locate him for three days.

When my story appeared, Koch claimed he did not know that Ward had been missing. Then he implied that Ward's absence was inconsequential. That the police commissioner of New York City failed to respond to the largest mass murder in its history, and that the Mayor couldn't locate him for three days, were hardly inconsequential.

Ward's disappearance reflected the back story of his administration: a volatile police commissioner and a mayor afraid to discipline him because of his delicate political position vis-à-vis black New Yorkers. This failing would lead to predictably troublesome consequences for the department. However, these would not become apparent until years after Koch and Ward left office.

In 1993, under Koch's successor, David Dinkins, a full-blown corruption scandal was brewing. It had begun the year before with the arrest of a police officer, Michael Dowd, who for years had headed a ring of drug-dealing cronies in his Brownsville precinct, coincidentally the same precinct in which the Palm Sunday Massacre had occurred.

In New York, such scandals are said to occur in twenty-year cycles. The previous one, in the early 1970s, had resulted in revelations of payoffs or "pads" at every level of the department, including inside the commissioner's office. All this had occurred under the supposedly watchful eye of Manhattan's revered District Attorney, Frank Hogan—"Mister District Attorney," as he was known—whose office was but a stone's throw from headquarters.

One of the reforms that had followed that scandal had been the reconfiguration of the department's Internal Affairs Division into a much-vaunted corruption-fighting entity. Dowd's arrest, however, had been made by Suffolk County police on Long Island, where he lived. The IAD played no role in either his investigation or his apprehension. In fact under Ward, the IAD had ignored all warning signs.

The explanation for this was revealed at a public hearing that provided me with a chill of insight. Chief Daniel Sullivan, whom Ward had appointed the IAD's commanding officer, testified that he had hidden all major corruption problems from Ward because, said Sullivan, he feared angering him.

*

Damaging as the Dowd corruption scandal was, it was the least of Mayor Dinkins's police problems. As commissioner he had appointed Lee Brown, a Houston native who knew little about New York, less about the NYPD. A frequent traveler to law-enforcement conferences, Brown became known in the department as "Out of Town Brown." The unreported back story was about how chaotically he ran the department. Despite Dinkins adding five thousand more cops—increasing the department to nearly forty thousand—crime seemed out of control. In 1990, Dinkins' first year in office, the number of murders—the bellwether crime that police cannot cover up or dumb down—reached a staggering 2,245. It hovered around two thousand for the next two years as drug-dealing gangs terrorized city housing projects with random shootings. The city's fear and frustration were spelled out in a front-page New York Post headline: "Dave, Do Something."

To appease his chief of department Robert Johnston—nicknamed "Patton" after the World War II general—Brown established a bifurcated chain of command. This allowed Johnston to report to him directly, bypassing the first deputy, Ray Kelly, whose authority Johnston refused to accept. The result was a disconnect at the highest levels of the department that presaged catastrophe.

In the summer of 1991, the Crown Heights riots erupted. The proximate cause was the accidental killing of an eight-year-old black child by a Hasidic Jew in a city-sanctioned motorcade. In retaliation, a black mob fatally stabbed a Jewish rabbinical student. Other mobs terrorized Jews in their homes, their cries for help captured in anguished 911 calls that the police failed to answer.

A report for Governor Mario Cuomo spelled out some of the reasons for the department's failings. When the riots began, Johnston had just retired. His successor was on vacation and made no attempt to return. With a broken chain of command, the riots continued for three days. The report blamed both Brown and Kelly for not taking immediate charge. But it left unanswered the question why both men failed in their responsibilities. Nor have answers been forthcoming to this day. Within a year of the riots, Brown returned to Houston, where he ran successfully for mayor, leaving Kelly as his successor. At a public breakfast shortly after his appointment, I questioned Kelly sharply, asking whether Brown had contacted him during the riot's first days or whether he had attempted to contact Brown. All Kelly would say was that Brown had kept him "out of the loop."

*

With Crown Heights as a backdrop, Rudy Giuliani, a Republican in a Democratic town, defeated Dinkins for mayor. In part because of his background as a prosecutor, in part because of his personality, in part because of Koch's experience with Ward and Giuliani's experience with *his* first police commissioner, he would exercise more control over the NYPD than any previous mayor.

His first move was to dismiss Kelly and appoint William Bratton, whose single-minded mandate was to reduce the city's crime rate. And Bratton delivered. By the end of 1994, murders had dropped to 1,561; by the end of 1995, to 1,177, the lowest in two decades. While skeptics pointed out that crime was falling across the country, Bratton countered that the steepest declines were in New York. His supporters maintained that he had effected nothing less than a cultural revolution within the Police Department.

What no one disputed was that Bratton had revolutionized the role of police commissioner. He dined at the uptown literary haunt Elaine's. He appeared in the gossip pages, hobnobbed with journalists, and was praised by academics for his crime-fighting tactics. He signed a contract with Random House to write his autobiography. In short, he became a celebrity, eclipsing the Mayor.

The back story was that the better known Bratton became, the angrier Giuliani became. A year after Bratton's appointment, Giuliani fired a shot across Bratton's bow by cutting the size of the department's public-information office by two-thirds and forcing the resignation of Bratton's department spokesman, John Miller.

Bratton ignored the warning. On January 15, 1996, after some covert lobbying, he appeared on the cover of *Time* magazine, personifying its story of nationwide crime reductions. Giuliani was barely mentioned. Giuliani then announced an investigation into unspecified conflict-of-interest charges involving Bratton's autobiography. In April, Bratton resigned. He had served as commissioner for only two years.

Giuliani would appoint two more police commissioners in his eight years as mayor. Both would be cronies. Never again would he select someone he could not control. Just as Koch had bypassed the department's logical successor to his first commissioner and appointed Ward, Giuliani bypassed Bratton's first deputy, John Timoney, a twenty-eight-year department veteran, and appointed Howard Safir, whom Giuliani had known from his prosecuting days in Washington. Their sole concern was outdoing

Bratton in reducing the city's crime. Safir referred to Bratton as "some airport cop from Boston." When murders fell below a thousand, Giuliani lauded Safir as "the greatest police commissioner in the city's history."

But Safir's sole focus on crime reduction led to perhaps the most flagrant racial abuses in department history. One case involved Patrick Dorismond, a black New Yorker who argued with undercover officers attempting to sell him drugs. After Dorismond refused to purchase them, a fight ensued and an undercover shot him dead. To justify the shooting, Safir produced Dorismond's sealed juvenile record to show, as Giuliani put it, that Dorismond was "no altar boy."

Then there was the fatal shooting of Amadou Diallo by four white cops from the department's vaunted Street Crime Unit. Before the shooting, Safir had tripled the size of the unit, praising it for its effectiveness in taking guns off the streets by stopping and frisking citizens—primarily young black men. Diallo, an unarmed African immigrant with no criminal record, was shot nineteen times in the vestibule of his apartment after Street Crime cops mistook his wallet for a gun.

Finally, there was the case of Abner Louima, which not even veteran police officers could believe actually happened. Louima, a Haitian immigrant, was sodomized with a broomstick by a white officer in the bathroom of Brooklyn's 70th precinct. The officer, Justin Volpe, was sentenced to thirty years in prison.

Safir also played to the worst of the Mayor's flaws, not the least of which were his secretiveness and his distrust of the media. Routine questions, such as the number of officers on patrol in a precinct, went unanswered. Virtually no information could be obtained from the department without a formalized written "freedom of information" request, which took months to resolve. The quarterly list of overtime earners was deleted to avoid revealing the highest ones—the detectives in Giuliani's police detail, one of whom guarded the Mayor's girlfriend and future wife.

Safir even did the Mayor one better when it came to the media. Whereas Giuliani disdained reporters, Safir baited them. At a dinner at Police Plaza for wealthy department benefactors, he introduced the *Times*'s two police reporters as "slime." He and his spokeswoman Marilyn Mode—who brought her little white dog to work, sometimes taking the animal with her to crime scenes—misled reporters or made up facts. After Safir's wife was involved in a minor fender-bender on the Queensboro Bridge, he sent detectives from his police detail to question the offending driver, Monica Nascimento, a hotel concierge. He explained that he had done so because he feared Nascimento was a "security" threat. He then feigned ignorance of a $1.5 million suit his wife filed against her, claiming "loss of consortium."

I brought a Bible to Safir's next news conference. Before he began to speak, I asked him to swear he would tell the truth.

Safir's unpleasantness was not merely personal. It would cost the city millions of dollars in lawsuits, including a million-dollar discrimination settlement to Sandra Marsh, a black deputy commissioner whom Safir had fired because she refused his order to rewrite a report critical of a white chief. Even more costly was the $17 million agreed by Michael Bloomberg to settle some twelve hundred claims of discrimination against black and Hispanic officers.

*

Giuliani may have called Safir the greatest police commissioner in the city's history, but he ignored Safir's recommendation that *his* chief of department, Joe Dunne, a thirty-year veteran, succeed him. Instead, Giuliani appointed Bernard Kerik, a third-grade detective with only seven years on the force and no college degree. Apparently, Kerik's more important qualification was that he had served as Giuliani's driver and advance man in his mayoral campaigns.

On the surface, Kerik appeared amiable and easy-going, a welcome change from the surly Safir. Black and Hispanic cops felt he treated them with a respect Safir never showed. Reporters described how while touring the city, Kerik stopped to personally make arrests. Negative stories seemed not to bother him. I wrote about his having ordered miniature plaster-of-paris busts of himself to be given as gifts to friends. After an initial groan, he burst out laughing. Like Bratton, Kerik obtained a contract to write his autobiography. The book, *The Lost Son*, described his hardscrabble New Jersey childhood and his search for his mother, whom Kerik maintained had been a prostitute and possibly murdered.

When the World Trade Towers fell, Kerik stood with Giuliani at Ground Zero. Over the next months, he appeared in the Mayor's shadow, his presence reassuring a shocked and frightened citizenry. So popular was he that when Bloomberg ran to succeed Giuliani, he asked Kerik to remain as commissioner.

Instead, Kerik allied himself with President George W. Bush and the so-called "War on Terror." The White House sent him to Iraq, where he supposedly trained Iraqi police; he quit the job four months into a six-month appointment. Returning to New York, he lectured on terrorism and American foreign policy. One of his talks was sponsored by a group of conservative intellectuals known as the Manhattan Institute. It was held at the Harvard Club. Kerik—who had recently obtained a correspondence degree in public administration from Empire State College—spoke for thirty minutes on the necessity of the Iraq war. His listeners responded with prolonged applause.

It was all an illusion. In 2004, the underside of Kerik's life was laid bare. Nominated by Bush as the Director of Homeland Security, his past was revealed to have included personal bankruptcies, associations with alleged mobsters, a series of mistresses, and an undisclosed marriage—described as "The Lost Wife" by *Newsday* reporter Sean Gardiner, who discovered her.

There was a final indignity. In the days after 9/11, Kerik had been given the free use of a Ground Zero apartment, supposedly to recuperate from eighteen-hour workdays. Instead, the married Kerik rendezvoused there with his girlfriends, one of whom was Judith Regan, *The Lost Son*'s publisher.

✳

Instead of Kerik, Bloomberg selected Ray Kelly, who had served as commissioner during Dinkins' last year as mayor. A businessman of scant acquaintance with the police, Bloomberg would defer to Kelly in all police matters, making him the most powerful commissioner in the city's recent history.

During Giuliani's eight years as mayor, Kelly served in Washington under President Bill Clinton, first as an undersecretary of the Treasury, then as Commissioner of Customs. But the Ray Kelly who returned in 2002 was not the man who had departed New York in 1994. Bitter and vengeful, he never forgave Giuliani for dismissing him or Bratton for replacing him. When Bratton, now chief of the Los Angeles Police Department, c ame through New York, Kelly refused to take his phone calls. When Bloomberg discontinued Giuliani's detective detail, Kelly transferred the detectives to assignments as far from their homes as possible. Only Giuliani's intercession with Bloomberg led Kelly to reverse himself and assign them closer to home.

Kelly had been police commissioner during the first World Trade Center attack in 1993 and had appeared on national television, standing shoulder to shoulder with Jim Fox, the head of the FBI's New York office. Their presence then had been as reassuring to New Yorkers as Giuliani's and Kerik's eight years later.

Returning to the NYPD four months after 9/11, Kelly would set the department on a new course, positioning it, at least in his mind, at the center of the country's fight against terrorism. Instead of welcoming the FBI and other Federal law-enforcement agencies as allies, he would make them his antagonists, stating both in private and in public that the Federal government had failed to protect New York City from terrorism.

Other than myself, no one asked why Kelly seemed intent on alienating the very agencies he might otherwise have welcomed as partners.

Similarly distrustful of the department's top brass, Kelly would rely on two civilians he had brought from Washington. The first was David Cohen, a former top CIA analyst; the second, Michael Sheehan, a former State Department terrorism expert who before 9/11 had unsuccessfully urged bombing the camp of Osama Bin Laden in Afghanistan. Cohen would become the head of the NYPD's revamped Intelligence Division. Sheehan would become the department's head of a new counter-terrorism bureau.

Some of their initiatives seemed nothing less than brilliant. Cohen's Intelligence Division recruited New Yorkers fluent in Arabic and other Middle Eastern languages. Their sole job was to troll the internet, seeking to infiltrate jihadi websites to monitor future terrorists. Other initiatives seemed comical. On at least three occasions, "Intel" detectives conducted undercover operations outside New York City's jurisdiction without informing local authorities or the FBI On the Jersey shore, Intel detectives staged a telephone sting of scuba-diving shops to test their vulnerability to bribes by possible terrorists. When the local authorities learned of this from the diving-shop owners, they were furious. They ordered the NYPD detectives out of New Jersey.

Intel detectives also appeared in Carlisle, Pennsylvania after explosives were reported stolen there. Checking for a terrorist connection, they began interviewing residents, who alerted the local authorities. The town's police chief suggested that the detectives return to New York and leave the investigation to the FBI.

Without informing the FBI, Intel detectives also turned up in Boston, infiltrating a church meeting of protesters intending to target the upcoming the Republican national convention in New York. The FBI, which had been monitoring the meeting, followed the detectives, unaware of who they were. On the Massachusetts Turnpike, they stopped the NYPD detectives for speeding and nearly arrested them. This out-of-state foray to observe a political protest group that had not acted illegally was but the tip of the iceberg. More recently, the New York *Times* reported that the NYPD had conducted surveillance around the country and the world of scores of protest groups that the police feared might demonstrate at the Republican National Convention in New York City.

Kelly also stationed Intel detectives overseas, competing for intelligence with the FBI and the CIA. The problem was that overseas postings for the NYPD are not included in the city charter. Kelly circumvented this by engaging the

Police Foundation's wealthy benefactors to finance them. Invariably, the detectives again bumped up against Federal agents. In a glaring example of high-level law-enforcement discord, Pat D'Amuro, the head of the FBI's New York office, publicly admonished Kelly for crediting an NYPD detective for the arrest of a terror suspect in London. It was the FBI, D'Amuro corrected Kelly, in conjunction with NYPD detectives, that had apprehended him.

Kelly also has used his counter-terrorist measures to make himself and the Police Department laws unto themselves.

During the first anti-Iraq protest demonstration in March 2003, the police made mass arrests. Detectives then interviewed protestors in their jail cells, telling them their release was contingent on answering questions about their political and social affiliations. Their answers, known as a "demonstration debriefing form," were then inputted into a data bank. When the New York Civil Liberties Union went public with this information, Kelly ordered the data bank discontinued. But he defended the questioning, saying that the protestors were "debriefed" as part of "the arrest process." For that, he was publicly admonished by Federal judge Charles Haight.

During the Republican National Convention in the summer of 2004, the Police Department arrested two thousand people and placed them in a West Side bus depot-turned-holding pen. Virtually every charge against them was subsequently dismissed. When protestors filed complaints with the Civilian Complaint Review Board (CCRB) against the police supervisors who had ordered their arrests, Kelly prevented the officers from testifying, a violation of the city charter, which mandates police cooperation.

Last year Michael Pomerantz, the head of the Mayor's Commission on Police Corruption—the city's only formal check on the department besides the ineffectual CCRB—resigned after the department refused to provide records it sought. Pomerantz was after the records to determine if crimes were being downscaled to show more positive crime numbers, as two police unions had charged. Kelly has also denied the records to Pomerantz's successor. Although this is a mayoral commissioner, Bloomberg has said nothing.

I came to know Kelly during his years in Washington, or at least I thought I did. I was one of a number of reporters invited to his swearing-in ceremony at the Treasury Department. When he visited New York, we met periodically for lunch. "You're the only reporter in New York with balls," he would say, referring to my columns critical of the department during the Giuliani years. A year after his return, however, Kelly found my columns critical enough of him that he drove out to *Newsday*'s headquarters on Long Island to complain to the paper's top editors. Assistant Managing Editor Les Payne, who attended the meeting, never told me the specifics of Kelly's complaints. All he said was, "Kelly wants your head on a platter."

It only grew worse. After I left *Newsday* and began writing an on-line column about the department, Kelly barred me from the building on security grounds. In fact, my mug shot was posted at the security desk alongside those of true miscreants, such as people who had threatened Kelly's life. Only my writing about this caused the department to back down; I am currently permitted to enter the building.

*

Perhaps the harshest criticism directed at the city during and since the 9/11 attack has been the lack of coordination between the police and the Fire Department. The 9/11 Commission cited this lack of communication, suggesting that a more coordinated response might have saved many firefighters' lives. It recommended that the Fire Department become the lead emergency-response agency, as it is in every other major American city. Instead, Bloomberg made Kelly and the Police Department primary, infuriating the firefighters.

Seen in a certain light, Kelly's aggressive actions might be viewed as single-minded determination to protect the city from terrorism. Seen in another, one might ask whether his fight against terrorism involves a settling of scores and a maniacal insistence that he—and he alone—control all aspects of that fight. One might also ask whether the city is actually safer because of this.

Unfortunately, no one in New York City is asking these questions.

Then in November 2006, five undercover cops fired 50 shots at three unarmed black men, killing one and seriously wounding the others because they mistakenly believed one of the three had a gun. Despite his focus on terrorism, it appears that the NYPD of Kelly, in reacting to the threat of a gun that has not been found, may not be so different from that of Safir.

The Practice of Everyday Life

Jean Thilmany

I'm from Iowa. In New York, that seemed the main fact about me that was worth knowing. It explained a lot: my blond hair, my preference for Brooklyn over Manhattan, my once-in-a-great-while penchant for overalls. New Yorkers inferred the rest. When I announced my home state, they assumed I'd grown up on a farm and that I was a hick. Not true. Though I have some tendencies toward hick-ness (I've been to a tractor pull, for instance, and I once helped judge pet rabbits at a county fair), I never saw a cow up close until my late teens.

I worked then—and by then I mean right after the 1999 internet crash, an adequate way of pinning my New York in time—in a Manhattan cubicle located in what I referred to as a prefab skyscraper, diminutive in the shadow of the Empire State Building. It was constructed of cheap building materials, same as the McMansions sprouting elsewhere in subdivisions all over the United States. I wrote for an engineering magazine. Despite having had no interest in this topic in college or after, I did well, writing up wing-test-study results and clearing up convoluted academic language. The job impressed no one, though I liked it fine.

"Why are you even here?" a man once asked me in a bar. He leaned in close so I could smell his beery breath and opened his eyes wide with the strangeness of it. A recent graduate of the New York University film school, he couldn't comprehend living a small daily life in New York City, a life spent without trying to break into documentary film or make visual art from found objects. "Everyone's here to be famous," he said, contemptuous of my stark lack of ambition. He grabbed his beer and moved off.

*

So it was probably my feeling of outsider-ness that lead me to seek out what my native-Manhattanite friend termed "deepest Brooklyn." I felt at home there in the three-story, six-unit, pea-colored apartment building occupied by born-and-bred Brooklynites who had no need to fake it. These included elderly play-boy Frank, his wife Josie of the bright, dyed-red hair, the screaming Mary, and a large, lonely, mentally slow man who lived above me and paced continually. The pacer kept his radio tuned day and night to a station that played hits of the 1970s. Brewer and Shipley, The Captain and Tennille, and Tony Orlando and Dawn all drifted down through the ceiling, an unrequested soundtrack.

After my Manhattan workday, I'd crowd into the L train and push for standing space among the vintage-dressed twenty-year-olds bound for Williamsburg and the less bedazzled blue-collar folks who'd take the train to the end of the line in Canarsie. I'd get out at Graham Avenue and came above ground at Metropolitan and Graham to a broken-down expanse of shoved-together squat brick stores that sold fifty different shapes of pasta and tins of olive oil the size of boot boxes. Rows and rows of three-story apartment buildings sporting green or yellow siding—a testimony to the time salesmen came through in the 1970s pushing tin, I'm told—lined the side streets. An endless line of garage trucks trundled deafeningly down Metropolitan on their way to a waste-transfer station just down the road. On hot evenings, the older women on my block arranged webbed lawn chairs up and down the curb to trade memories back and forth: "Remember how we used to take the train on Saturday nights to those dances? We'd dance in Keds. And those white shirts, like a uniform shirt? They'd stick to our backs and become almost see-through?" I smiled at the women as I threaded through them on my way home. I studied them secretly, like an anthropologist. In Iowa we had something very similar, only the women there played cards around oak tables, remembering barn dances out on the rural route. "Out where those condos are now."

That's the New York City I like to think I inhabited, always on the outskirts like a stranger peering into a shop window: shrieking Brooklyn women (and they always seemed to be shrieking) in faded housedresses they'd purchased who knows where (actually, probably in an ancient bra-and-housedress shop I'd seen in Greenpoint); the perennial church sale—same in Brooklyn as at any financially teetering church in Iowa; Frank and Josie eating dinner at their dinette set in front of the television. The universality lulled me while the differences were enough to make me seem to myself like an explorer. I sought out these small Brooklyn details to soothe my homesickness the way other friends sussed out a newly hip restaurant. I noted each one.

*

Sometimes on warm end-of-winter days I'd head out for a jog around McCarren Park and spot the pacer huddled in his blue winter coat against the squat brick building next to ours. He'd still be there when I returned. That building next door housed Manhattan Special, manufacturers of the first (since 1895!) coffee soda drink, and on those early Saturdays you could hear the bottles clinking and clanking reassuringly along the conveyor belt. Although a local treat, I thought it tasted like Seven-Up cut with coffee, horrid and undrinkable. Instead, I rounded

the corner for coffee at Caffe Capri, decorated like a Brooklyn Italian living room, dark with paneling and claustrophobic with tightly packed photos and paintings of the old country set amid the cakes, candies, and tins of coffee. Frank Sinatra was always singing at Caffe Capri, and the proprietor, Joe, was always behind the counter ready to pour out the excellent iced coffee or fill a canolli shell, sprinkling a bit of cinnamon on at the end. I had a bit of a crush on him and his stylish array of brightly colored button shirts, though he was probably more than twice my age. His wife usually sat at one of the tables idly fingering a napkin, or she puttered back and forth through a door I supposed led to their apartment upstairs. They made an odd couple, she rather frumpy with permed hair and a kindly face, Joe all angles and trim height, Brylcreem suave with a smooth accent.

Joe opened early and closed early too, so if it was after 7:00 I'd head up to Fortunato Brothers, a supposed Mob hangout. This rumor didn't seem particularly farfetched as I waited for my cappuccino to be made by the kindly, dark-haired Ecuadorian barista. We were surrounded by mirrored walls and aftershave wafting from the cackling middle-aged Brooklyn men in their loafers and cream-colored slacks. A young Italian woman in tight jeans waited on them while local Latino girls worked the bakery counter, filling bags with cookies, cakes, and marzipan and handing over cups of brightly glowing gelato.

To get to McCarren Park on Saturdays I'd jog under the Brooklyn-Queens Expressway overpass, then along a river of blood that ran perpetually along

the curb outside a live-chicken shop. I'd avert my eyes but never could block out that sweet, thick, cloying smell. I'd thread my way through nondescript squat warehouses and a few auto-repair shops duly guarded by ragged junkyard dogs. I'd wind through a small trash-filled park, sometimes inexplicably populated by mothers cheerfully babbling to their babies, and past the graffiti-scrawled brick walls of what might have been mistaken for an armory but that actually hid a now-closed swimming pool.

In those days, Hispanic boys played soccer in the sad pool's shadow. Once I stopped in at a lunch counter across from the park. It'd been around since the swimming-pool heyday (and has since been turned into the kind of recessed-lighting, designer-burgers-and-fries-in-a-high-quality-wooden-booth-type place you'll often see around). But that day I felt I'd opened the door and walked into a time capsule—the privilege and wonder of it. A kindly older man stood behind the counter polishing an ice-cream-sundae glass with a dish towel. He stood ready to make me an egg cream or black cow from the penned menu above his head. On the chrome bar stool pinned into the bar in front of him, a woman, her hair lavishly arranged and sprayed, talked loudly about the Brooklyn of her childhood. "We used to come over here for ice cream after swimming over there." She patted the stool next to me and nodded across the street toward the heavily graffiti'd brick walls and spun a story of 1950s childhood innocence and ice-cream splendor.

Another time after jogging I headed across the street to a flea market in the basement of the looming, domed Russian Orthodox church made famous in that Seinfeld episode where a nun almost converts for love of Kramer. "Oh it's you, it's just so perfectly you," an old lady shrieked at me when I tried on a London Fog raincoat from the 1950s. It wasn't, but I did find a box of eight-tracks—though I had no way to play them—that I bought from a graying man in a plaid suit-coat.

*

I felt the same about those eight-tracks as I did about all of Brooklyn around me: it was soon to be extinct, no longer needed now that developers were at work updating Williamsburg for the young and the newly rich. The old-timers held on much as they always had. What else could they do? Their neighborhood was changing around them—it had been for years, but now there were kids with money and little apparent interest in much beyond the next trend. In the face of this my neighbors took the shopping cart around the corner to the grocery store or gathered lawn chairs in front of their buildings to laugh and bitch about the invaders. The younger Brooklyn kids hung out on street corners, the teenaged girls razzing the guys in loud, hectoring voices. Same as it ever was.

Still, it seemed to me that a big part of this Brooklyn was not-so-slowly dying—the part where you're born middle or lower-middle class and grow up in a family in the city—and that I'd shown up in time to catch its last gasp. After World War II, property on Long Island had really opened up, making it possible for many Brooklynites to buy homes of their own. And who could blame them? At the same time, by trading a vital and thriving neighborhood— everything within walking distance—for the stereotype of a suburb, hadn't they cut themselves off from their past, their people, what Henry Miller called "a wild outer music of the streets," and done so deliberately?

And now there was the Williamsburg hipster invasion. It'd been going on for twenty years or so, but it seemed transformative around the Millennium. The sheer number of young artists and musicians was becoming untenable. Many people who just wanted a small, affordable neighborhood life were pushed to the edges of Bushwick and then out of Brooklyn altogether.

*

My grandmother Jean Van Drimmelen spent her whole life in Bellevue, Iowa, a town of about two thousand nestled on a flat strip of land between a particularly wide spot on the Mississippi and the encroaching river bluffs. As a child it seemed to me a blessed place full of stories. There's the one about Dora, who felt she'd been shortchanged in the little grocery store my great-grandmother had in her house. The day after that fateful transaction, Dora flung open the door, spat, and loudly put a hex on the entire business. Nothing happened. She returned to her squalid house. My great-grandmother continued to operate the only store in town. Later that month she brought over some produce to Dora that probably wouldn't be sold; they played gin rummy for several hours. Years later, Dora's daughter Maybelle would throw herself into the Mississippi after learning her husband Bim had been having an affair with Maybelle's much older aunt. Stately and imperial, the aunt had shown up fresh from her Chicago penthouse on the death of her second husband and taken up residence on Maybelle and Bim's plain sofa. After Maybelle's suicide, the pair married, but the aunt lived to be a hundred, nearly cheating Bim out of his rightful inheritance. He'd had to suffer her all those years, after all.

My apartment house in Brooklyn offered similar fodder. Take Mary, my eighty-year-old neighbor. I knew her age because she always loudly stated it. Her parents had immigrated to Brooklyn from somewhere in Italy. That's all I figured out about that. She'd grown up with her brothers right around the corner from our apartment building, but now she lived across the hall from me in a long, narrow apartment the mirror of mine—only with all-linoleum floors, the Williamsburg standard. (I ripped mine out to expose the hardwood.) Her neat and simple furnishings hadn't been changed since her mother's death twenty-five years earlier. In fact, she still kept her mother's bed made up in the middle room. On Mother's Day, she honored her mother by crying in front of a little poem on a wooden plaque tacked up in the kitchen: "You're My Mother, Bless Your Heart."

Mary shrieked at me through her locked door when she heard me clunking up the stairs after work, "Is that you, honey? Is that you? Open the door." I couldn't pretend I hadn't heard, so, roped in, I opened the door onto a homey scene: Mary in her housedress in the overheated room sitting at the oilcloth-covered kitchen table, a large glass of wine beside her. She spent her days listening to talk radio and, on Sundays, a station that said all-day Mass. She read the New York *Post* and commented foully on Giuliani. She'd send me on Byzantine after-work errands: "Run over to Model-t meats and get 25 cents worth of cut bologna. Only 25 cents." Then she'd give me two dimes. The quarter bought three pieces of thin bologna, but the gentle, doe-eyed butcher brothers at Model-t meats knew who'd sent me and threw in an extra few slices.

Another day I ran over to the Graham Avenue c-Town grocery store, deemed one of the filthiest grocery stores in town by a *Daily News* special investigation, to ask for the white ends of cheese from the deli case for her. I didn't know what that even meant but came back with two blocks of cheese at no cost and for little fuss. Which is exactly the opposite of what happened when I was sent to c-Town for a package of AA batteries. Two managers had to be called and one teenage shop girl enlisted before the entire crew remembered the batteries were kept on a high shelf behind the meat and would need to be removed with long-handled pinchers that couldn't be located. Undaunted, I walked across the street to the squalid little drugstore above the subway station. Its aisles were so narrow you had to turn sideways to fit yourself through, and always, always, no matter what the season, no matter what the weather, there was marked-down Halloween candy.

Mary received mysterious 1:00 AM phone calls from her cohorts in Italy. I know because they woke me up. Though the building was well over a hundred years old and of sound construction, I heard every cough, every stomach rumble, and other less delicate bodily utterances from my immediate neighbors. Mary's phone would ring each night shortly after I'd gone to bed, and she'd walk from the front room all the way to the 1970s rotary phone hanging on the kitchen wall. She'd ream whoever was on the other end, first in Italian, then in English. "Leave me alone. Leave me alone," she finally yelled one night. "I don't have any money."

Her Brooklyn relatives eventually set up a little second phone next to her bed, but by then I think the nighttime calls had ended. By then, too, she'd fallen a few times alone in her apartment and had undergone a two-month stay in a Brooklyn hospital. Mary was scared to death of winding up in a nursing home, but more and more that fate looked like an eventuality. The same relatives who installed the second phone sometimes sent their teenage daughter over to check

on her. They lived around the corner. The daughter would stand in front of our building, all adolescent saunter and ill-advised makeup, and yell up at the second-floor window, "Aunt Mary," a pause, "Aunt Mary, how ya doin?"

Interesting to me was how Mary would simply stick her head out the window and yell back, "Candy. Candy. Tell your dad to send over a pizza."

"Sure," Candy said and moved off toward a stoop down the block where a group of hooded-eyed teenage boys hung out. That was the entire extent of checking on Aunt Mary. But to be fair, Mary herself could simply scream out the back window, over the stunted 4-square-foot cement yards, the leaning cinder-block walls that separated them, over the crisscrossing washing lines, to Candy's parents across the way. Frequently they'd appear at their back window and shout the news of the day to her.

My elderly neighbor had only recently stopped riding on buses. Bad knees did her in; she could no longer climb the three steps. In fact, bad knees now kept her virtually housebound on the second floor of our building. Once, three male relatives came over to carry her down the stairs and to the apartment on the next block for Easter dinner. She came back crying and swearing. They'd had some sort of falling out. I got the impression the same sort of argument happened every year. She vowed never to return. Candy's visits and the yelled-over news exchanges continued, however.

*

One night I locked myself out of my place at 5:00 AM I couldn't sleep so I'd cleaned instead. When I took the recycling to the curb, the door shut behind me. I thought all was lost. It was winter and 15 degrees at 5:00 in the morning and me in my socks and bathrobe. If I could make it shivering in the doorway until 6:00, that was when I thought the pacer woke up and made his daily journey to the deli around the corner for the *Post* and the two gallons of milk he drank each day. But ten minutes into my vigil I knew I was lost. I was shivering and jumping in the doorway just to stay warm when there, like an apparition, was Frankie walking toward me down the street. "Hi, honey," he said as though we'd run into each other coming in at the same time after work. As if I was wearing everyday clothes. "I'll let you in, but you have to give me a kiss."

He was getting home from his mysterious Italian club. The one that had taken the sofa left in my apartment before I moved in. An empty storefront where Italian men gathered to play cards and drink rich red wine and listen to music and talk sports. At the age of eighty-eight, Frankie had gotten a job playing piano at the club he'd already been going to nightly.

"He's at work," Josie would say if you stopped by to report some dissatisfaction with your apartment: usually an ever-running toilet. I leaned in and smelled his boozy breath. I planted a kiss right on his lips.

*

That was three years ago. Frank has been dead two years now, Mary about the same amount of time. Even then, they lived in a city of ghosts, as we all do to some degree now and certainly will in our old age. Frankie at his club. Mary in her kitchen with her wine and memories of Mother, the voices on the radio soothing her through another sunny afternoon. They're all telling stories of long-ago times. Times when the cars had huge tailfins and no one thought to make them electric. When I visit my Williamsburg now, nearly every month, its Brooklyn-ness seems a little less each time. Fewer natives hanging on, more interlopers like me. I recognize myself in their faces. I hope they're as curious as I was.

At Least it's Not New York

Richard Meltzer

Hi. You know me. I'm the guy who hates this place. No, no change, I still hate it, but I've just got back from that 'other' place and would like to share with you how loathsome *it's* become. It's the North American Calcutta.*

Well, not "actually." There's still no leper colony, not an *official* one, and the principal religion isn't Hindu. Nor is the percentage of the total populace currently living in the streets quite as high as in that fabled Asian pus-pit—'scuse me, I don't mean to besmirch the Third World!—but it's getting there. It's gotten so you can't walk half a block without facing the face of misery. And by half-block I mean 'good' neighborhoods: Upper East Side, Gramercy Park. At 6th Avenue between West 3rd Street and West 4th it's more like every half-step.

And the face too: the face has evolved. It used to be, well, you could tell by the look on their face. There were distinctly different degrees and different flavours of despair. Junkies were always the hungriest, the hurtingest; they almost kind of *defined* New York Despair. Now it's down to one basic look for everybody, a single undifferentiated despair, an across-the-board urgency one full evolution beyond what you'd see in the despairingest junkie of yore, one *intensity*. Christ, it's intense.

There was one guy whose routine was "GIMME MONEY! I need money! Got to have money! If you don't gimme money there's no telling what I'll do!" (No one was giving.) A lot of them growl, "Hey, I'm asking *nicely*"—it seems like a standard operational riff. You keep walking and they keep talking: "Next time I won't ask so nice." One ragged hepster waved snapshots of his daughter ("Five years old! Her mother won't feed her! In Pennsylvania!"), another yanked at the leash of a scrawny eye-bandaged hound ("Blind!—I'm not making this up!!—'My dog needs an operation!!'"). Human blindos were everywhere by the *hundreds*. And of course cripples.

And just about everyone uses cups, like a paper soda or coffee cup. Cups full (or not so full) of coins. Coins-in-cup make a pretty good rattle. To accompany the pitch, y'know, the appeal. Paper money, you'd guess, goes straight in their pocket. Too gaudy, too risky to show, and too suggestive of windfall wealth: a bad ad for Need. I never saw any paper. I also noticed more pennies on the sidewalk, in the gutter, then I saw people with cups—a sure sign that pennies aren't worth *nada*. Or, per unit weight/volume, scavenging them's no longer cost-effective. I even saw occasional nickels.

But the cups though, often cups would be the first (or only) thing you'd see. Cups extended, then you'd see an arm and possibly a face. Some streets it's like the arm scene in *Repulsion* where Catherine Deneuve walks down the hall and they reach out from both walls grabbin' at her. Only these arms don't grab, if they grabbed they couldn't hold—or rattle—the cup. At night you're walking and suddenly cups pop out of nowhere, out of pitchblack ether—street lights shining on cups and nothing but. Or take a 2.00 AM, 3.00 AM cab ride and at every stoplight cups surround you, banging and tapping on the windows, like something out of *Night of the Living Dead* or the werewolf car scene in *The Howling*. Only it ain't exactly at that scale or tempo of physical "threat," nor after the second stoplight is it much of a "shocker"—just another chapter/scene in the ongoing round-the-clock tear-your-heart-out no-quit misery cup show. Most popular cup logo: I LOVE NEW YORK.

And the ethnic breakdown, the races involved here: all. Or most. I didn't see too many Micronesians. And nobody older than, say, 70. It's a young man's game, and by man I mean persons; there were women begging with babies in strollers, one (around 20) with newborn twins plus a two- and a three-year-old. (It might've been the neighbourhoods I hit but I didn't really see a lot of whores.)

Youngster's game: how could the old pull it off? Aside from the street exacting its toll, the brutal winters, the day-to-day ceaseless pain and ag, you've gotta be young just to keep up with all the fierce competition. Strictly on a bizness level, screaming need is not the easiest of sells even when you've got the frigging monopoly. (Imagine if Chrysler had to contend with 200 rival US automakers, and 411 Japanese. Once you've lost that good crisp youthful coin-rattle in the wrist, that loud booming youth-inflected GIMME MONEY! . . . you've lost it.

Even from the "buyer" side it's no snap, no easy light errand, y'know dispensing the monetary compassion. You look at a blockload of these fine folks, you count heads, and even if you're Mr or Ms generosity him/herself, how do you *in fact* divvy up the $100 in your pocket in quarters, half-dollars and small bills? (There's a scene like this in Louis Malle's *Phantom India*, the famous giver-splits-his-change-among-multiple-beggars scene, but why namedrop another dumb film? To put it in the proper numeric context, if you split your life income times twelve among all New Yorkers with a cup, among all those *south of 14th Street*, it wouldn't amount (per screaming unit need; per unit *second* of screaming unit need) to a flea on a whale's ass.

And then there's hundreds, *thousands* of these guys/gals who ain't even *on* the whale's ass; they're in the ocean. If you handed them ten bucks they wouldn't know whether to wipe their nose with it or eat it. I'm talking 'bout the ones you see conversing with phone poles, dressed for the Arctic when it's 102 °Fahrenheit, stooping to drink out of puddles of what . . . rainwater? . . . dogpiss? . . . gasoline? Hard to fathom how they get through a week, yet the dirt on their duds suggests months/years/etc. of ETCETERA. I saw literally THOUSANDS of these guys in a week of the Apple.

They're the most "conspicuous" of all the homeless, or maybe their "predicament" is, let's just say their plight is the most *topical*, so while I'm in town Ed Koch issues this proclamation to send swat teams of shrinks into the streets "to help these poor unfortunates" by carting them all off to hospitals. Wow, great idea. Bracket for a sec even the civil liberties issues and you're still stuck, for inst, with *where you gonna put 'em?* The joke while I was still there was, well, in a 200-story bughouse built by Koch's brother-in-law. Or Donald Trump. (It's *nice* to see a mayor as lame and realtor-owned-&-operated as our own, doncha think?)

OK, the rich-get-richer side. I was walking down Fifth Avenoo and I peek inside this normal-looking type clothing store, and I see this normal-looking leather jacket and I try it on—no big deal, normal. Just a jacket. There's not too much leather in your equivalent LA kind of store, it's too hot, so I figure as long as I'm here, why not, get a jacket. Black, try it on, fits, OK, how much? EIGHT HUNDRED AND NINETY-FIVE DOLLARS. Geez, if it had only been *seven* ninety-five (or even eight-fifty) . . .

Or: "In five years there won't be an apartment *as such* south of Harlem." A friend of mine said that. He'd just been conned into making some token down payment on the HUNDRED AND FIFTY-FOUR THOUSAND DOLLARS on his West Village apartment—no longer as such—will ultimately cost him to own as a goddam condo. And by apartment I of course mean medium-sized closet w/ an air shaft for a window. His girlfriend's closet on 10th Street and Avenue A with a caved-in ceiling, mouse-sized roaches and the floor on a 30-degree tilt is $750/month. Many units in this "gentrified" building contain fully-formed yuppies who when kids downstairs offer to sell 'em "crack . . . smoke . . . etc." decline *politely*.

The people I know who still live in New York live there 'cause if they ever abandoned their apartment they'd never, not even hypothetically, be able to replace it. To move is to move forever. It happened to me (fall '75), it'll happen to them. Meanwhile, re those who *can* move, there was this item in the Sunday

NY *Times* on the movement of rich bastards from Fifth Avenue to Central Park West. Condos on Fifth run, oh, five million while on CPW they're a measly three. Plus—the rich *always* have these pluses—"there are so many interesting shops and cafes on the West Side" (said one such flying piece of shit).

Shit . . . piss . . . I asked a cop in Union Square where I could take a piss, and he *courteously* directed me to a Wendy's where they don't lock the john. Ask an LA cop about urine and he'll bop you on the head. But I figure it's probably just the guy didn't want me pissing in the street. 'Cause the streets, well, when I still lived there the subways were already pretty much an extension of the sewer. Lots of fluids and stink and most likely the sewers even leak. Now, today, the sewer level's reached at least the street, first floor, and possibly even the second. When it reaches sky level, will the clouds rain piss?

Today's rats. I met this NY Parks Department guy who told me Central Park rats have evolved into something so tough and ornery they'll attack—and eat—full-grown *cats*. Says he's seen it. Seemed like a credible guy.

Great Moments in Irrational AIDS Fear. Buy a paper at *any newsstand* in Manhattan, try to give 'em the exact change, aim specifically for their hand, and they will not take it. Or maybe that's Fear of Cooties. I actually, by the way, saw five or six "AIDS beggars"—emaciated, scabby guys moaning, "I've got AIDS . . . feed me." (That must go over big.)

And what else? Well, the heartlessness. New York is basically no longer a city that "cares." Bernie Goetz (as hero) should have been the tip-off. LA *never* had a heart so in that regard they're even.

And? Well they got this sex station on cable, actually just a tit station although you do sometimes see pudenda. If I was 13 I'm sure I could dig it.

Newssheets? It's even worse than here. If you're not a stockbroker (i.e., if you don't read *The Times*) you've got a choice between Rupert Murdoch's *Post* ("Slut killed in Drug Deal Mix-up") and a *News* that *once* had naught but headlines— and now not even that.

Food? The food's still OK. If you don't mind spending $14 for a (damn good) pastrami sandwich.

Subways? Horrible but not quite a horror. No worse than the street. But I didn't use 'em much. Mostly I just walked and grumbled.

So, anyway, I was there and now I'm here, I get back and it's 100 °Fahrenheit. Two loathsome places—like a shuttle ride between Times Square and 42nd and Lex, horrible regardless of destination. I can't figure out how these bicoastal scumbags do it.

---

*In 1975, when I turned thirty, I left New York for no other reason than that I'd "used it up." Los Angeles, my new home, I used up in something like 30 minutes. It took me 20 years, however, to again move on—inertia is like that.

By the summer of '87, when I wrote "At Least it's Not New York" for the L.A.*Weekly*, I'd established myself as a snickering smartass, a pariah!, duty-bound to point out how loathsome and unlivable the palm-lines cesspool truly was. Amazingly enough, no-one else, at least not in print, seemed to notice.

Irony of ironies, in the dozen years I'd been gone, New York had become *even seedier than* L.A. And today, I hear, it's more *suburban* (ain't life funny?).

Fortunately, I now live in Portland.

New York State of Crime

Tim McLoughlin

On the eve of my nineteenth birthday, a group of friends took me out for a drinking tour of Lower Manhattan, the intent being to work our way south from Union Square until we arrived at the Brooklyn Bridge or passed out. There were about a dozen of us at the start of the evening, which, on a surprisingly civilized note, began with dinner at the Cedar Tavern. We stayed mostly on the East Side, veering as we moved downtown. Our second stop was a bar called Bridget's, on Second Avenue below 14th Street. It was a fairly rough place back then, with a colorful clientele. I was shooting pool against a local when a fight broke out at the bar. After some shoving and shouting, the toothless female bartender ejected one man with the assistance of a few of the patrons. About fifteen minutes later, our game still in progress, a shot was fired from the street into the bar, shattering one of the small panes of glass in the windowed front door and lodging in the back wall behind us. Everyone threw themselves to the floor, and for a moment there was only the fading sound of the gunshot and the thumping bass of the Silver Connection on the jukebox. Then I heard a voice from above my hiding place half under the pool table: "Shootin' pool or what?"

I slowly stood to discover that most of the other customers were returning to their seats at the bar or scattered tables. There was some discussion at the bar about the likelihood of the shot having been fired by the gentleman recently removed from the premises. The formidable barmaid resumed pouring drinks. A couple of people stepped outside and looked around, and one or two walked to the back wall and examined the bullet hole up close.

"Pool," my opponent urged again. Though it looked as if he hadn't moved, I was fairly sure he'd hit the deck with the rest of us and was merely taking advantage of having regained his composure more quickly. We finished the game and played another. I lost both and was thankful that the wager had only been one beer per game. We drank quickly and left shortly after I was thrashed the second time. Emerging from the bar tentatively, as if from a foxhole, we scanned the street. There were people and cars and neon signs, and absolutely no indication that anything untoward had recently occurred. There had been no conversation in the bar about calling the police, and none were to be seen outside.

Several of my friends took the incident as an omen and called it a night. The rest of us kept heading south. Sometime after midnight we arrived at the Brooklyn Bridge. Four of us, myself included, lived in Brooklyn and decided to walk over the bridge to clear our heads before going home. We'd just begun our ascent up the footpath when we noticed a flurry of activity in front of One Police Plaza. There were crowds milling and lights everywhere, and we surmised that a movie was being filmed. We turned back off the bridge and worked our way over to the crowd.

"What's going on?" I asked someone at the periphery.

"They caught Son of Sam," he said. "Bringing him in now."

Within a few moments a disheveled-looking young man with a passing resemblance to the songwriter Don McLean was rushed past to the accompaniment of popping flashbulbs, cheers and taunts, and shouted questions. We stood until he disappeared into the building, then resumed our hike over the bridge. On the Brooklyn side we split up and went home to our separate neighborhoods. It was early on the morning of August 11, 1977 and, other than being my birthday, just another summer night in the city.

*

I find it difficult these days to explain the crime vibe of New York City back then to anyone who wasn't there. The late '70s come to me now as snapshots:

Driving home from a girlfriend's house in surreal darkness the night of the blackout, stories of looting already coming in on the car radio. The short ride made longer by every driver's trepidation at each signal-less intersection. Arriving at my corner, Eleventh Avenue, to see cars parked on the sidewalk in front of several stores, the merchants sitting on the hoods and roofs with hunting rifles and shotguns, bracing for trouble that never arrived.

Going to concerts at Fordham University in the Bronx, then hanging out on the roof of a friend's dormitory building, eating rice and beans and getting stoned while watching fires move across the surrounding neighborhoods and listening to students speculate on what was being torched. *Dry cleaner's. Pretty sure it's the dry cleaner's. Fuck, no, it's the pizzeria. Shit, the pizzeria.* Much later, the subway ride home, sleeping in shifts so someone was always on guard duty.

As the '70s gave way to the '80s, as New York City teetered on the edge of bankruptcy but never fell in, most residents assumed they'd rounded some sort of historic bend and that there was light at the end of the tunnel. The '80s, of course, brought with them the advent of AIDS and the introduction of crack. We were still barreling down Dead Man's Hill, but now the brakes didn't work.

People had been freebasing cocaine for years, but the ability to buy crack in neat little $10 vials, precooked down to heart-stopping pure rock, changed

the landscape of drug dealing—and street violence—in dramatic ways. The War on Drugs has been and remains our generation's Prohibition; crack was the ultimate bathtub gin. Unlike heroin, regular coke, or weed, crack transformed every street-corner dealer with a couple of hundred dollars into an entrepreneur, and previously mellow junkies morphed into Wild West gunslingers. Add to the mix the Federal government's shortsighted decision to take the Italian Mob out of the drugs business, and it was exactly the recipe for disaster you would imagine. I suppose that if you're going to go to the trouble of having a war on drugs, it's probably a good policy to try to find out who the major players are and arrest them, but it is impossibly naive to assume that the drugs will then go away. After a series of high-profile sting operations and prosecutions like the Pizza Connection case (in which elements of the Mob used pizza parlors as fronts for heroin distribution), the Italians were knocked from the top spot in the narcotics food chain. Unfortunately the Asian gangs and Columbian cartels stepped in so quickly that in one notoriously embarrassing incident, the FBI confessed that it had dozens of hours of wiretap tapes that could not be deciphered because none of the Chinese interpreters in the Bureau were familiar with the obscure dialect of the gang under surveillance.

*

The way that crime affects the individual in a city like New York—if you are not being actively victimized—is in the small details of your life that change. (You felt it over time if you lived here, like the aging of a spouse or a relative you saw every day.) It is gradual for years, yet shocking overnight when illuminated a certain way. There are always neighborhoods you avoid, but gradually there are

more. People start putting "no radio" signs on their car windows. It begins as a hopeful deterrent to theft and vandalism, but quickly degenerates into a shameless advertisement for self-pity. The first signs that appeared were professionally printed stickers by manufacturers of security devices. *No Radio. I take it with me!* was the logo of Benzi Box, one of the first such designs. Soon, though, the signs became homemade, personalized, and increasingly desperate. *No radio* gave way to *No radio, you already got it* and, ultimately, *Window broken three times, radio and spare gone. You got it all.* And it enraged you because you were a New Yorker, Goddamn it. We didn't beg people not to steal from us. We told them they'd best not try. But there was your car, and there was your radio, and it was nighttime in Park Slope or on the Upper West Side, and you knew that green Volvo looked like an ice-cream cone to the crack-head who'd just jostled you on the sidewalk. So up went the sign and off you slunk home, spinning the cylinders on multiple high-tech locks behind you, the tumblers echoing in the empty space like the sound of cowardice.

*

The reaction to lawlessness in a civilized society takes many forms. There were vigilante movies like the Don Siegel-directed *Dirty Harry* (1971). Before that, Peter Boyle pulled the trigger out on hippie sex, drugs, and rock 'n' roll in the provocative counterculture exploitation flick *Joe* (1970). *Death Wish* appeared in 1974, the first film I can recall that dealt directly with New York City's escalating crime wave. It was a decade later when a guy named Bernie Goetz decided that life truly did imitate art and shot four young men who were trying to intimidate him on a subway train. I had begun my new career as a court officer in Brooklyn Criminal Court the year before, and though I considered myself a weathered New Yorker, I was overwhelmed by the steady stream of bad guys, assholes, rogues, and lost souls who filled the calendars. In my first year on the job we arraigned Joe Pepitone, the former New York Yankee, accused of weapons and drug charges, and hauled Al Sharpton in numerous times on one civil-disobedience beef or another. One day I obtained Tom Waits' autograph when he arrived at the courthouse—in a somewhat impaired state—to attend the wedding of two friends who were being married by a judge in chambers.

*

If you were middle-aged or older in the late '70s, you probably left town or wished you could, and that was a normal response to the escalating violence.

But for young people native to the city or transplanted from around the country or the planet, there is always an enticing world of possibility found in disorder. The term used in New York before gentrification for people moving into rough neighborhoods was *pioneering*. And there was a definite pioneering spirit afoot. The same lawlessness that sent so much of the middle class packing was fueling a no-rules freedom in the art world, establishing a vibrant above-ground gay community, and providing fertile soil for what would emerge as the biggest movements in pop music for the next two decades, hip-hop and punk. It was a crazy, out-of-control decaying-city energy. But it was energy.

If the '70s were about chaos, the '80s and early '90s were about meanness and drugs. Creative disorder had given way to nihilism, or maybe people were just getting worn out. It was a time when drug dealers and Wall Street inside traders got fat, and the rest of us stayed home.

The changes, as I've noted, come to you in small ways. By the late '80s I'd discovered how relatively easy it was to get a parking space on the street in Manhattan. Greenwich Village, the Upper East Side, and even the Theater District—areas that I would previously never have dreamed of driving to—began yielding spots pretty quickly. Racial tension, cyclically simmering and erupting here for four hundred years, flared dramatically several times. Paranoia over the fate of shrinking white enclaves led to the murders of two African-American men. One, Michael Griffith, was chased to his death on a highway by a white gang in the Howard Beach section of Queens in 1986; the other, Yusef Hawkins, was shot to death on a Bensonhurst street corner in 1989. Earlier that year a young white woman jogging in Central Park was gang-raped and beaten nearly to death. In 1990 a group of black activists organized the boycott of a Korean-owned fruit-and-vegetable store on Church Avenue in Brooklyn, alleging that the owners had insulted a black patron and falsely accused her of theft. The boycott became a blockade as protesters stood in front of the store entrance and intimidated any potential customers from shopping. A Federal court issued an injunction requiring that the protesters stand at least 50 feet away from the front door. The protesters ignored it. The police ignored the protesters.

The year 1990 was also when a young man in the Bronx, jealous that his girlfriend had gone out dancing, set a fire in the stairwell of the after-hours bar she'd gone to, then blocked the only exit. Eighty-seven people were killed in the Happyland Social Club fire, and since their deaths were the result of arson, they were all characterized as murder victims, bringing the city's homicide total that year to just over 2,200. In 1991 a young black boy was struck by a car driven by a Hasidic Jew in Crown Heights, igniting a race riot that lasted three days and resulted in the stabbing death of a rabbinical student.

I developed, suddenly, an oddly nostalgic longing for Son of Sam. Not for David Berkowitz, of course, but for a time when one man, killing seven people

over three years, could grip New York City with fear. He was a man of his time, and a lucky guy. If he'd struck in the early '90s he might not have been noticed, even with his letters to the *Daily News*. After Howard Beach and Happyland, the Central Park jogger and the Crown Heights riot, a plain old serial killer seemed kind of quaint to me. Middle American, like a town that still had a milkman and a doctor who continued to make house calls.

By 1993 the sinking-ship pathos was unavoidable, and New Yorkers had had their fill. Ed Koch, mayor for three terms, had vowed to become New York City's first four-term mayor, but in 1989 he was unable to secure the nomination of the Democratic Party, which went instead to David Dinkins, the Manhattan Borough President. Dinkins was challenged by a Republican upstart named Rudy Giuliani. Rudy had made his bones as a Federal prosecutor and had a reputation as a take-no-prisoners tough guy. New York was almost ready for him but not quite. In one of the tightest elections in city history, Dinkins defeated Giuliani and became New York's first African-American mayor.

The crime wave continued unabated, and if people had become frustrated by Koch's hands-in-the-air attitude toward anarchy, they despised Dinkins' fatherly social-worker stance. *There's no such thing as a bad boy*, his demeanor conveyed, often at a crime scene where grisly evidence was being carted away behind him. In the summer of 1992 there was a surge in sexual assaults committed against young girls at public swimming pools. Gangs of boys would surround them in the water, trap them in a circle, and grope them. The street term for this type of assault was *whirlpool*. As the number of incidents increased and media coverage became intense, Mayor Dinkins called a press conference. He unveiled a plan to appeal directly to the decency of the young men of New York City's streets. He displayed several advertising buttons with helpful slogans. The two most memorable were *Don't Dis Your Sis* and *Whirlpool Ain't Cool*. Dinkins beamed for the cameras. I have always believed that moment cost him the next election. In 1993 Rudy Giuliani won the race by the same slender margin by which he'd lost it in the previous campaign.

The first time I'd seen Giuliani on television was at a press conference years earlier, with then Senator Alphonse D'Amato. They had donned biker outfits, gone up to Washington Heights, and bought crack. Their intent, apparently, was to show that anyone at all could obtain drugs in the neighborhood, and to that end they were certainly successful. They looked like refugees from the Greenwich Village Halloween Parade. If someone sold them drugs, I thought, maybe we really did have a problem.

I confess to being among the early Giuliani supporters at the time of his election. We'd had enough, and it was time to fight back. Rudy's quality-of-life initiatives seemed silly, but cleaning graffiti, fixing broken windows, and getting rid of squeegee guys actually did create an impression that crime—or street crimes, at any rate—were no longer encouraged through municipal neglect.

The new administration was not without its critics. There were many complaints from the African-American community about the random stop-and-frisk of young men. The gay community was displeased with the crackdown on clubs and bathhouses, and in both Chinatown and largely Italian-American neighborhoods like Bensonhurst no one was happy with the zero-tolerance policy on fireworks.

As uneasy as many New Yorkers were with Giuliani's aggressive policies, the crime rate continued to plunge. Murder statistics dropped to their lowest point in twenty, then thirty years. In 1997 Rudy was re-elected with such an encouraging mandate that he expanded his platform. The war on crime had been transformed—at least for Giuliani—into a referendum on civilized society, and he was determined to mold one.

After crime, the next publicly identified threat to social welfare was commercial sex, at least at street level. Giuliani waged a successful war on pornography and topless bars—any establishment that sold pornographic material was required to devote two-thirds of its space to non-pornographic interests, and topless bars had to be located more than 500 feet from any residential housing. Many strip joints, especially in Manhattan, folded. The adult book and video stores that could hold on complied, resulting in stores with five thousand dusty copies of *The Sound of Music* and old crossword-puzzle magazines up front, the backs crowded with magazines, videos, sex toys, and lube.

The city thus safeguarded, attention turned to other important topics: jaywalking and motorists not properly seat-belted. Fences were erected at a number of mid-town intersections, those impudent enough to bound or walk around them threatened with arrest. Likewise, in a town where it is impossible to achieve speeds exceeding 12 miles per hour, priority was now placed on making sure that everyone was wearing their harness. Checkpoints were set up at random corners. I was stopped and pulled over by a foot patrol-man while waiting at a red light. (Fortunately, I was in compliance.)

There comes a moment in the movie *Bananas* when Woody Allen, having aided in that film's fictional South American country's revolution, stands proudly next to the rebel leader as he outlines the new government policy. Woody smiles and nods at each initiative until the leader states that every citizen must wear clean underwear, and that underwear will be worn on the outside from this day forward so that inspections can be facilitated.

Woody's expression in that scene was a lot like mine as I drove away from my random seat-belt stop in my new squeaky clean porn-free trigger-happy cop town. I was not alone. That expression was in evidence on the visages of many New Yorkers—a look that asked, *What next?*

⋆

Then came September 11, 2001. It is not my intent to dwell on the events of that day in political or even historical context. It was, however, the most devastating crime ever committed against the City of New York, and should be mentioned as such. Two close friends of mine lost their sons, and many other friends and acquaintances were similarly devastated. I was in my car, stopped at a red light, about fifteen blocks north of the World Trade Center, when the second plane hit. I saw it happen. I saw a huge chunk of the building tear away and fall. I ran the light and headed east for the bridge to Brooklyn, steering around slower-moving vehicles and not slowing for any traffic signals until I was safely over the bridge. I was wearing my seat belt.

Since 9/11 crime seems to be defined differently. Every reference to the pre-9/11 world—as bad as it may have been—seems hopelessly sugar-coated. There was a short period of time, weeks really, when rules just didn't matter. I returned home from work three days after the attack to find a fire engine parked awkwardly, half on the sidewalk, in front of my neighborhood bar. I entered to find a dozen or so firefighters, still in full gear, covered in ash, drinking silently. They had not been off-duty in thirty-six hours, and had lost an untold number of comrades. The entire city comported itself in a similarly shell-shocked manner for longer than any of us can realistically recall, until, bit by bit, there was a return. To parking tickets and burglaries. To littering and to muggings. To graffiti and drug dealing. To normal crime.

Never have a people so welcomed it.

Civil Rights: What Happens There Matters

Leonard Greene

Bigotry is a learned behavior. Proof of that can be found in the life of young Nicholas Minucci, a white teenage thug whose lack of tolerance, as demonstrated by a violent attack on a black man in his neighborhood, made him the unwitting bookend to a volume of ignoble incidents that defined race relations in the nation's largest city for more than a generation.

Minucci, nineteen at the time of the attack, was born in 1986, mere months before a gang of white youths brought shame and infamy to New York's Howard Beach community when they attacked three black men for being in their part of town. One of the victims, Michael Griffith, was killed by a passing motorist's car while trying to flee the onslaught. Although the incident stained the community for years, and made its name synonymous with racism, much of Howard Beach healed. Likewise, much of it did not, which is how, twenty years later, someone like Minucci could find himself on the other end of a metal baseball bat that had just opened a black man's skull.

Though the victim, Glenn Moore, twenty-six, and his friends admitted that they had come to Howard Beach in search of a car to steal, according to police Minucci and his accomplices knew nothing of their intent. The police also said Minucci and his friends shouted racial epithets at Moore and two of his friends who escaped unharmed.

Minucci was charged with assault in the first degree as a hate crime, which carries a sentence of eight to twenty-five years.

Unlike chief executives before him, New York's Republican Mayor Michael Bloomberg moved quickly to defuse the situation. "We will have no tolerance whatsoever for hate crimes against any groups in this city," he told reporters a day after the June 2005 attack, which he described as "racially motivated." "We have come a long ways in New York," the Mayor said, "and we are not going to let one incident divide this city."

Just how far New York has come is open to serious debate. Activists and some elected officials still cry out for a Civilian Complaint Review Board to independently investigate acts of police brutality in communities of color. Cops are still rarely punished when they abuse their enormous power in ways that hurt blacks and Latinos. And the prospect of again electing anybody but a white person as mayor—even though whites are slowly becoming New York's new minority—is as slim as a Metrocard. The economic divide, the true barometer of progress, remains as wide as a subway platform.

Still, the Howard Beach headlines did disappear from the newspapers, which, even to the most critical observer, is some measure of progress. Gone, though not completely, is the momentous tension that seemed to dominate everything going on in the city in the '80s. Pundits called it the "Me Decade." In New York, it was the "Anybody But Him" decade.

*

The era started with the election of Ed Koch, the Jewish liberal from Greenwich Village who became New York's 105th mayor in 1977. If Koch seems at all progressive now on matters involving race relations and civil rights, it is only because Rudy Giuliani would upstage Koch's lack of compassion. Koch did appoint the city's first black police commissioner, Benjamin Ward, but that historic selection hardly made up for the decade of racial unrest that went unchecked under the Mayor's watch.

In 1982 the decade's spate of race-related homicides began with the death of Willie Turks, a transit worker who was beaten to death by a gang of whites in Brooklyn's Gravesend section. Turks had stopped to get a bagel when a mob of whites from the predominantly Italian neighborhood pummeled him with baseball bats.

A nineteen-year-old unemployed weightlifter was convicted of "depraved indifference" homicide.

Halfway through Koch's second term, a young man died in police custody after being arrested for writing graffiti on a city subway car. Michael Stewart, a twenty-five-year-old black man from Brooklyn, was apprehended at Manhattan's 14th Street subway station in September 1983. Stewart lapsed into a coma while in police custody, dying thirteen days later. Though several witnesses testified that he was struck and kicked by the arresting officers, the six cops escaped criminal punishment, and only one was disciplined.

The following year, police were called to a Bronx home where an elderly grandmother was being evicted. There, they found a deranged Eleanor Bumpers, sixty-six, standing her ground with the aide of a 10-inch butcher knife. Cops said the 5-foot, 8-inch, 275-pound black woman lunged at one of the officers with the knife. Another officer leveled his shotgun and fired off two rounds. The first, according to prosecutors, shattered the hand with which she held the knife. The second hit her square in the chest. Bumpers died two hours later. She owed $417.10 in back rent on her city-owned apartment. The officer who shot her was indicted for manslaughter and suspended from the force. He was found not guilty, later reinstated, and promoted to detective. City officials were roundly criticized for not coming up with a better solution to resolve the rent dispute. Bumpers' family and community supporters wondered if there was a more sensible way for cops to subdue an elderly woman who, by several accounts, had difficulty walking.

Before the smoke had cleared from the shotgun blast that killed Bumpers, New York was embroiled in another racially tinged shooting. This time, it was no cop behind the gun. The shooter was a white electronics engineer adopted by many in the city as the righteous "Subway Vigilante." Bernhard Goetz, thirty-seven, pulled a .38-caliber Smith & Wesson from his jacket and opened fire on four confrontational black teens as they rode a downtown IRT train. By the time the train stopped again, Barry Allen, eighteen, Troy Canty, nineteen, James Ramseur, nineteen, and Darrell Cabey, nineteen, were all wounded.

After shooting Cabey, Goetz said, "You don't look too bad, here's another," and pulled the trigger again. Slipping away at the Chambers Street subway station, he rented a car and drove to New England, where he ditched the gun and his jacket in the woods. A week later, he turned himself in at a New Hampshire police station. By the time he returned to New York, the city was divided over whether he was a hero or a racist nut. Meanwhile, Cabey, who was paralyzed by the second bullet, slipped into a coma and sustained permanent brain damage.

Goetz argued that the four were out to beat and rob him, and that the shooting was self-defense. A jury believed him and acquitted him of attempted murder in 1987. Convicted on a weapons-possession charge, Goetz served eight months in jail.

Mayor Koch's open support of Goetz earned him boos before many black audiences. "I was denounced by black leaders for believing that he had engaged in self-defense," Koch said years later. "I believed it then, I believe it now."

But a lawyer for victim Darrell Cabey had a different view. "The verdict in the Goetz case the first time was a racial verdict," said attorney Ronald Kuby. "It was white America saying that white people could use whatever force they want against black people."

That message resonated loudly in Howard Beach on December 20, 1986. The ugly incident there began when three black men—Cedric Sandiford, thirty-six, Timothy Grimes, twenty, and Michael Griffith, twenty-three—were driving through the white community when their car broke down. Frustrated and hungry, they stopped at a pizza parlor to eat and plot their next move. When they left, a gang of about a dozen whites was waiting for them with baseball bats, some yelling "Kill the niggers." That was when Griffith was clipped by a passing motorist as he tried to run across the Belt Parkway in a desperate bid to escape. Within days, the attack made nationwide headlines, with demonstrators comparing attitudes in the provincial neighborhood with apartheid in South Africa.

The crisis also marked the political emergence of Rev. Al Sharpton and special prosecutor Charles Hynes, a former fire commissioner who, at the time, was an anti-corruption prosecutor in the Governor's office. Sharpton, along with the victims' lawyers C. Vernon Mason and Alton Maddox, advised the young men not to cooperate with authorities in Queens, whom they accused of "making a case" for the white defendants. Though their defiance outraged some more than the attacks did, the strategy forced a desperate Governor Mario Cuomo to appoint a special prosecutor. Within three weeks, indictments were handed up, and at the first trial, three suspects were convicted of manslaughter.

This outcome marked a major breakthrough on the justice front. Hynes rode the victory into the Brooklyn District Attorney's office, and it wasn't long before Sharpton, Maddox, and Mason had another opportunity to employ their successful strategy.

*

The same year the Howard Beach thugs were convicted, a fifteen-year-old black girl from Upstate New York told authorities she was abducted and gang-raped over three days in the woods by a pack of white men, one of whom flashed a badge. The case showed that the civil-rights movement, in the words of black scholar Manning Marable, "was coming unglued."

When Tawana Brawley was found in a trash bag in the courtyard of an apartment complex, she was covered with feces, her hair was cut and matted, and the words *nigger*, *bitch*, and KKK were scrawled across her body. Mason and Maddox replaced a local lawyer representing the Brawley family and, with the help of Sharpton, convinced them not to cooperate with authorities investigating the allegations.

Cuomo again appointed a special prosecutor, this time state Attorney General Robert Abrams, who launched an exhaustive investigation. Though the alleged abduction happened in Dutchess County, the saga quickly became a New York City story with demonstrators bused upstate from the five boroughs.

In the end, the investigation determined that the allegations were a hoax, but not before Brawley's advisers dragged the name of Steven Pagones, an assistant District Attorney in Dutchess County, through the mud, claiming he had been one of the attackers. Pagones, in a civil suit ten years later, won a defamation

judgment against Brawley and her advisers, but only Sharpton, with the help of high-profile supporters, has paid Pagones what he was owed. Brawley disappeared after the case, while both Maddox and Mason were eventually disbarred. Sharpton was widely discredited, though he managed to shake it off and come back swinging.

*

If racial tension was out of control, crime was even worse, and when the two crossed paths, the mixture was combustible. Such was the case in April 1989, when a young white female jogger was raped, beaten, and left for dead in Central Park. Not only did the attack demonstrate lawlessness at its worst, it also gave rise to a new term, *wilding*, which many African-Americans thought was inherently racist because of its obvious animalistic overtones.

But many whites in the city, beset by fear and frustration, did not care. So outraged was billionaire Donald Trump when five black and Hispanic teens were arrested that he purchased full-page ads in all the New York papers calling for a renewal of the death penalty. In these ads—which appeared in *Newsday*, the *Daily News,* the New York *Post*, and the New York *Times*—Trump called for the "roving bands of wild criminals" who "roam our neighborhoods" to be locked away and executed.

Trump got part of his wish. With questionable confessions that were quickly recanted, and not a shred of evidence that tied them to the victim, the teens—Yusef Salaam, Kevin Richardson, Antron McCray, Raymond Santana, and Kharey Wise—were convicted after two trials and locked away on a variety of charges including rape, sodomy, sexual abuse, riot, assault, and attempted murder. The convicts, none of whom had a record of violent arrests, professed their innocence for more than a decade until 2002, when another inmate, Matias Reyes, a convicted murderer and rapist, admitted that he alone was responsible for the attack. Reyes' DNA matched that preserved from the rape kit. The convictions of the "Central Park 5," as they were called, were overturned.

*

While testimony was being heard at the first Central Park jogger trial in 1989, a gang of white teens in Bensonhurst cornered sixteen-year-old Yusef Hawkins near a used-car lot and shot him dead. No one called these suspects animals. No one took an ad out in the newspaper.

Hawkins had gone to Bensonhurst with three friends to inquire about a car for sale. Sharpton, still reeling from the Tawana Brawley experience, was pelted with watermelons when he led a demonstration through the streets of Bensonhurst to protest the murder and the racism that created its climate. Even then, the only riot that broke out was on the silver screen in Spike Lee's powerful *Do the Right Thing*, which was released the same year. Lee would dedicate his next film, *Jungle Fever*, to Yusef Hawkins.

Before the year was over, New Yorkers had had enough. When Mayor Koch, already plagued by corruption scandals after twelve years in office, came up for re-election, voters rejected him in favor of the more conciliatory David Dinkins, who made history by becoming New York's first black mayor. Dinkins' lofty talk of a "gorgeous mosaic" as his vision of New York, a place that recognized diversity as a strength and not a weakness, was not enough. In 1990, a

black-led boycott of Korean grocers in Brooklyn over alleged racial epithets against customers created problems for the new Mayor, who refused to take sides, a decision that made him look aloof and out of touch.

But the fallout was nothing compared to the criticism that rained down on him after all hell broke loose in Crown Heights.

On August 19, 1991, two seven-year-old cousins, Gavin and Angela Cato, were playing near their home in Brooklyn when they were hit by a car that jumped a sidewalk on President Street. The car, driven by Yosef Lifsh, was part of a motorcade carrying Grand Rebbe Menachem Schneerson. Angela survived. Gavin did not.

A private Hasidic ambulance, reportedly on the orders of a police officer, removed the Hasidic driver, leaving behind the injured boy, who died a short time later. Outraged, an angry mob of blacks took to the streets, where, three hours later, Yankel Rosenbaum, twenty-nine, an Australian Hasidic scholar, was fatally stabbed by a black teenager, Lemrick Nelson, in apparent retaliation.

The unrest went on for four days, during which time Dinkins was accused of giving an order to hold back the police and let blacks attack Jews. He tried to set the record straight, but the angry city would not listen. When he ran for re-election in 1993, New York, a city dominated by Democrats, punished him by putting a Republican, Rudy Giuliani, in City Hall for the first time in twenty years.

But Giuliani was no healer. New Yorkers knew that before the election when the candidate failed to reprimand cops who called Dinkins a "washroom attendant" and held aloft signs reading "nigger" at a campaign rally. So it was hardly unbelievable that police officers could exclaim, "It's Giuliani time" before beating a man and shoving the handle of a toilet plunger up his rectum in the bathroom of a Brooklyn precinct.

That is what happened on August 9, 1997 to Abner Louima, a Haitian immigrant who was arrested after an early-morning fight outside a Flatbush nightclub. After being pummeled in the back of a squad car, Louima was tortured at the precinct, according to authorities who prosecuted the cops involved in the beating.

Louima won a record $8.75 million settlement from the city in 2001, and the officers involved were convicted on a variety of charges. Louima, it turned out, had embellished the "It's Giuliani time" part of his account. But he did not embellish his perforated colon, his ruptured bladder, or the broken teeth he suffered when the soiled plunger stick was shoved in his mouth. Neither did he exaggerate the tone set by a mayor who had allowed police to clamp down on civil liberties long before the Patriot Act would find favor in Washington.

*

At least Louima survived. In 1989, when the twenty-two-year-old African immigrant Amadou Diallo, returning to his home in the Bronx, crossed paths with cops from the city's venerated Street Crimes Unit, he wasn't so lucky. There was

no bedside press conference, no million-dollar settlement. In a case that took racial profiling to extraordinary new heights, the unarmed black street vendor was gunned down in a hail of bullets in front of his apartment on Wheeler Avenue by seasoned police officers who said they mistook his leather wallet for a metal gun. Cops said Diallo fit the description of a rape suspect who, it turned out, had already been captured. In the confusion over the weapon that never existed, they fired forty-one shots, hitting Diallo nineteen times. Twelve months and a change of trial venue later, a jury, which included several African-American members, acquitted the cops, and the Justice Department declined to charge them with any civil-rights violations. The incident and its aftermath sparked massive demonstrations against police brutality and racial profiling, protests that resulted in more than seventeen hundred arrests. The list of those arrested included the actress Susan Sarandon, the actress Ruby Dee, Jesse Jackson, and the former Mayor David Dinkins.

Nearly eight years later, in November 2006, the tally of 41 shots would be topped when a plainclothes police detail fired 50 bullets at a car of unarmed black men, killing one of the men, Sean Bell, just hours before his wedding. Bell and his two wounded friends were on their way home from Bell's bachelor party at a Jamaica, Queens strip club. The cops—one of whom reloaded and fired 31 shots—said they thought one of the men had a gun. A contrast in styles had emerged. Within days, Mayor Bloomberg said the shooting was probably "excessive," a bold declaration that had editors and reporters scrambling through their old Giuliani files. What they found spoke volumes.

Just weeks after the cops who killed Diallo were acquitted in 2000, the Giuliani legacy continued to build when another unarmed black man was shot to death by police. Security guard Patrick Dorismond was killed on a Manhattan street during a scuffle with undercover officers who—while on their way to an unrelated sting operation—asked him where to buy marijuana. Police said the gun went off accidentally.

Did Giuliani call the family to offer his condolences? No. The man who would later be called "America's Mayor" released the dead man's sealed, confidential juvenile criminal record as if to justify another senseless shooting.

Marital woes, a cancer scare, and a terrorist attack bought Giuliani somewhat of a pass on race relations in the final months of his administration. The attack on the Twin Towers on September 11, 2001 brought New Yorkers together across racial lines, and the heroic efforts and sacrifices of New York's Finest were hailed by white and black alike.

But the goings-on at Ground Zero were not enough to keep race from rearing its ugly head. Weeks after the attack, New York Democrats were divided by racial politics, and another Republican, Michael Bloomberg, became the city's 108th mayor. Bloomberg quickly opened his door to outcasts like Sharpton and consulted black leaders before his boxes were unpacked at City Hall. The outreach would help insulate the Mayor from the backlash that accompanied acts of police brutality and racial unrest.

It wasn't long before Bloomberg saw his share. In May 2003 Alberta Spruill, a fifty-seven-year-old black woman, died from cardiac arrest after police, acting on a false tip from a confidential informant, knocked down her door and threw a concussion grenade into her apartment.

A week later, a plainclothes cop shot and killed Ousmane Zongo, an unarmed African immigrant in a Manhattan warehouse, where police had raided a counterfeit CD operation. Zongo had no connection to the enterprise. Frightened, he fled, but not quickly enough to outrun the five bullets that killed him.

Less than a year later, Timothy Stansbury, an unarmed Brooklyn teenager, was shot on the roof of a housing project by a police officer on patrol. Police Commissioner Ray Kelly said almost immediately that the shooting was not justified, and Bloomberg visited the victim's family before speaking at his funeral.

Times were changing. How much they had changed became evident a year later, when camera crews found themselves back in Howard Beach doing stories about brutal beatings and Nicholas Minucci. But this one had a twist. Minucci was planning to use what lawyers were calling "a hip-hop defense."

Sure, he had called Glenn Moore a "nigger." But he didn't mean anything bad by it. "There's a very big difference in the hip-hop world that I come from," Minucci told a reporter months before his trial. "I was the only Italian in a school of 2,000 mostly African-American kids. All of my friends, ten or fifteen of them, were black. All of them. We hung out. We played ball. We goofed. A lot of us went to John Adams High together. And we always called each other 'nigga' all the time." The jury didn't buy it. The diverse panel needed only eight hours to convict Minucci on charges of second-degree assault as a hate crime, robbery and criminal possession of stolen property. A judge sentenced him to fifteen years in prison.

*

As I reflected on Minucci's twisted remarks and the cycle of bigotry that brought the focus back to Howard Beach, I thought about how events of the twenty years in between had affected my own life.

I came of age in the '80s, graduating from the same school in Brooklyn—Samuel J. Tilden High School—that gave New York Al Sharpton and Mets manager Willie Randolph. Much of what happened that decade shaped my life and honed my convictions. I took everything personally.

When the cops killed Michael Stewart, I grieved with his mother, who sang lead soprano in the choir of our church on Lafayette Avenue. Carrie Stewart was a wonderful woman who never wavered in her faith. She also never got justice for her son.

I took both Howard Beach incidents personally because of all the times my friends and I had been chased out of neighborhoods just like it. We couldn't ride our bikes through Canarsie without white boys hurling bottles and the n-word at us as we set speed records trying to reach a safe stretch of Remsen Avenue. My brother survived a baseball-bat attack in a white neighborhood. It might have made sense if they had robbed him. But the only thing they tried to steal was his dignity.

We grew up ten blocks from where the riots in Crown Heights started, in a house between two Jewish families. Every day I walked past the street where Gavin Cato died, on my way to Utica Avenue and Eastern Parkway to catch the train to NYU. Sure, there was tension in our community of attached houses, but the Poretskys and the Kahns who lived next door were our neighbors. They were our friends.

My favorite aunt used to own a house on the same street where Sean Bell's life ended. I can't even say his name without thinking of the Christmas celebrations my family had every year on Liverpool Street, especially when I know Bell died two days after Thanksgiving.

It was only natural that these experiences affected my outlook when I started writing for newspapers in New York and other cities. Not long after graduating from college, I earned the distinction of covering the Tawana Brawley story longer than any other reporter. Though it was my own story in the Middletown *Times Herald-Record* that cast the first doubt on her account of events, I still believed something happened to her.

I still do.

I also still believe in New York, which is why I continue to take what happens in the city so personally. Whether it's a terrorist strike or a City Hall takeover of the schools where my mother taught for thirty years, I am profoundly affected. What happens there matters to me. What happens there matters.

Speaking Truth to Power

Armond White

The *City Sun* wasn't New York's first black-owned weekly newspaper, but it was the first that anyone took seriously after the '60s, when black militancy made *The Amsterdam News* seem New York's closest thing to communiqués from the Front. When the *City Sun* proudly printed a cover story on the release of Spike Lee's *She's Gotta Have It* in 1986, it was an era-defining day. The Brooklyn-based paper had been in business for only two years, but the premiere of that particular movie—and its local fanfare—became a media watershed. It not only announced a fresh start for independent filmmakers depicting contemporary black culture but made clear that black journalism also had cultural importance, was more than just missives from a war zone.

Almost ten years later, Lee capitalized on his black independent-filmmaker image with *Clockers*, a Hollywood-studio-sponsored depiction of black American life that created a surprisingly different, deflating effect from the hipsterism of *She's Gotta Have It. Clockers,* the story of a white Brooklyn cop who investigates a crime cover-up by two young black men, was a tribute to the sanctity of the police and a rainbow-hued reflection of ghetto treachery. In short, everything the *City Sun* had celebrated *She's Gotta Have It* for not being. Ten years made a difference between Lee the black striver, using race pride as a calling card to get a foothold in Hollywood, and his eventual achievement of arrogant middle-class success.

*

Success for both the *City Sun* and Spike Lee belonged to a special period in New York's history. The mid-'80s gave rise to African-American pop communication more varied and prominent than had ever been possible before. In journalism and the arts, the mainstream witnessed the attitudes and ambitions of a social group that had seized upon advances foreseen in the objectives of mid-century education reform and arts consciousness and wrought by the civil-rights movements and black radicalism. The effects were widespread, from newspaper

ownership and filmmaker entrepreneurship to hip-hop music. The result was a popular culture that turned black experience and imagery into a new vanguard. Black culture came to fascinate media conglomerates, the fashion industry and academia; it also helped the profile of local politicians and small business folk. Iconic names cropped up across the city: Michael Jordan's restaurant in Manhattan; Spike Lee's Brooklyn emporium Spike's Joint; the Brooklyn offices of the *City Sun* itself. Black advancement was not monolithic. There were discrete visions of what this new, private black autonomy would mean for life in New York City: black rock bands like Living Colour, self-published guru-authors like Sharazad Ali, and machine-politics straw men like New York's first black Mayor, David Dinkins. This auspicious moment was not utopian; rather, it was unexpected proof of a now-fragmented dream—a quaking landscape of ideological monoliths.

This was confirmed by Lee's change of heart with *Clockers* and the *City Sun's* unavoidably disputatious reaction to the film. It was a small controversy, perhaps, but it illustrated that unpredictable dynamic between action and ethics. With *Clockers*, Lee sought to profit from a particular commercial depiction of urban and black American life characterized primarily by racial and class division. Only the *City Sun* stood between Lee and his Brooklyn striver's pose as the last word on black attitude. The two should not have been in opposition, but their clash demonstrated that another aspect of American plurality was cultural upheaval.

*

Following the wide range of black radical expression of the '60s and early '70s, white Americans' formerly abashed reactions to civil-rights progress dominated the media—especially New York tabloid journalism. With *Clockers*, Lee forfeited black screen time to portray a white authority figure's pent-up frustration—a sentimentality in which racist cops are not the products of bigoted indoctrination, just helplessly coarsened by the jungle/workplace. *Clockers'* police sympathy misrepresented America's—New York City's—basic white cop/black citizen tension.

In the film the police are the bearers of morality while black folks are the problem. Predictably, the white press loved this—*Clockers* was widely praised as Lee's best film to date because it appealed to the media brokers' own limited sense of social reality. Lee didn't instruct his viewers about conflicting urban racial philosophies; instead, by making the white cop Rocco Klein (Harvey Keitel) a man of heart, he played to his audience's prejudices by using the mainstream's familiar game of equal-time race sentiment, giving white bewilderment the same dramatic weight as black grievance. It was an erroneous quid pro quo that ignored the fact of unequal social power by which the Police Department's institutional racism was made to seem common-sensical.

Clockers was such a disappointing culmination of Lee's ten-year anniversary as America's foremost African-American movie maverick that it felt like a betrayal. The promise of a black cultural presence suggested by *She's Gotta Have It* was compromised by his willingness to co-opt the sorrow of black experience by subordinating it to the vanity of *Clockers'* white power figures. This peculiar prejudice could not have existed anywhere else but New York, the crucible of multi-ethnic mixing where black citizens toiled so long in the shadows of mainstream media controlled by others.

This marginal presence had seemed to change in the '80s. It can be safely said that Spike Lee had almost single-handedly wrestled Brooklyn mythology from the clutches of white public figures like Pete Hammill, Pat Cooper, and Rocky Graziano, who had made the place famous as an urban melting-pot, the fantasy utopia of America's multi-ethnic bonhomie. This vision was epitomized by comic Jews, Irish, Italians, Swedes, Germans—a sons-of-immigrants round-up. Mainstream media rarely presented Brooklyn as a home to blacks.

In a sense the movies are where American social identity thrives and matters most. If it didn't, there'd be no other reason to notice Lee. *She's Gotta Have It* didn't exactly put Brooklyn on the map, but it did put black Brooklyn on the map of the big screen. Before that, America had only gotten its information about New York's cultural census from the life habits and fond recall of upwardly mobile white performers. (The peak of working-class Brooklyn identification may have been Jackie Gleason's enduring TV series *The Honeymooners*.)

What was brash, impudent, and childlike about Lee's claiming New York turf came from his relation to the youth uprising of hip-hop music. In *She's Gotta Have It,* he cast himself in the role of a hyped-up b-boy, Mars Blackmon,

a caricature he also used in a series of television commercials for Nike. Although Lee's New York state of mind is still impudent, boastful, and defiant, in the '80s he forged this persona by portraying a jazzy Brooklyn and broadening its image to include the West Indian and Southern black migration pride that so define the borough. The black public profile that hip-hop created also embraced the career aspirations of the children of the civil-rights movement, the legacy represented by the *City Sun's* founders, local activist and journalist Andrew Cooper and his Trans Urban News Service partner, the Trinidad-born Utrice Leid.

*

For everyone in New York City during the '80s and '90s—especially those who kept their antennae up for what was going on in the black enclaves—it was an exciting time to be alive. From my position first as a freelancer, then as arts editor at the *City Sun,* the fascination and perplexity of rap, cinema, and journalism was a daily, weekly challenge. Following one form required keeping up with the other. The dynamic revealed what New York living really meant: artists and journalists continually vying for the harried public's attention; a constant struggle for power to address or correct the public's need for social identity.

This is how the civil-rights struggle turned into a struggle for privilege. Privilege is what was at stake in Spike Lee's career. This is why his big-screen imaginings of New York City were always more interesting viewing than Woody Allen's Big Apple movies in which privilege was no longer struggled for but taken for granted.

Allen's ascension was the latest expression of Jewish identity that had originated with the urban literary pioneers of the Depression era through the 1960s. His coronation by the New York *Times*—throughout the '80s, their critic Vincent Canby celebrated every Allen release in terms reserved for state occasions—was inordinate. Implicit in this coverage was the certification of Allen's rise from a marginal ethnic comic to a cultural potentate. Only the bracingly contrary voice of Pauline Kael in the *New Yorker* dared to question this development when her review of *Hannah and Her Sisters* mocked Allen as a new "cultural commissar."

While Allen aspired to mainstream sovereignty, Lee sought the pinnacle of New York's black subculture. This was a position of dominance that would parallel the mythos surrounding his New York University film-school idol Martin Scorsese, the son of Italian immigrants, who shared Allen's potentate status. Taken together, they were a diminutive, fast-talking, ambitious trio of strivers, their backgrounds announcing a strong challenge to the city's WASP-ruled cultural élite.

That these three kings didn't reign equally was apparent in the disparate measure of their public regard. Allen and Scorsese both won New York Film Critics Circle awards during this period but not Lee, whose career high point, *Do the Right Thing* (1989), lost to *My Left Foot* and Paul Mazursky's *Enemies: A Love Story*. The media were ready to restrict Lee as black more often than Allen or Scorsese was identified as Jewish or Italian. This was a practical fact of New York public life—that a black artist performed in circumscribed condition.

⋆

The *She's Gotta Have It* cover of the *City Sun* was an act of measured celebration but mainly an announcement that the city's cultural regime was changing. The story wasn't a promotional stunt but rather an example of advocacy journalism. The *City Sun's* motto, "Speaking Truth To Power," was proven by the paper's willingness to challenge the city's power brokers with the same intensity it devoted to marginal or unpopular people and positions. The paper's editorials were eye-opening to politicians and business leaders as well as to its own readership. This freedom of expression was taken seriously. The paper's principles were also sustained by the sense of responsibility that came from its staff's awareness of a committed, watchful audience.

Regardless of ethnic identification, the paper was enjoyed for its independence. Its commitment to black New York was never confused with its commitment to speaking truth to and for all of New York. The thrill of this was conveyed most spontaneously when culture writer Greg Tate urged *Village Voice* readers to "Read *The City Sun*!" This uncharacteristic gift from a rival publication signaled the fascination and novelty of what the *City Sun* brought to New York culture. It made a difference in how other journalists saw the city and the way they thought about their own jobs.

⁕

Likewise, anyone perusing the *City Sun's* decade-long chronicle of city history and black-community abuse by police would rightly wonder why, after the deaths of Michael Stewart, Eleanor Bumpurs, Kevin Laborde, Anthony Baez, Willie Turks, and Anthony Rosario, Spike Lee would have chosen to do a movie that valorized cops. These names haunt the memories of New Yorkers who witnessed the excessive police force and grievances of families of color during the '80s and '90s.

Rosario's case was especially shameful. He was shot in the back fourteen times by a police squad made up of two former Giuliani bodyguards. The quickly closed investigation became the subject of a 1995 documentary, *Justified Homicide*, by Jon Osman and Jonathan Stack that focused on attempts by Rosario's mother, Margarita, to reopen the case. The documentary features her desperate attempts to reach an incommunicado Giuliani until she makes a phone call to his local weekly radio show, in the course of which the Mayor berates her and then hangs up.

In this context, *Clockers* amounts to an anesthetizing work of propaganda. When a cultural figure as prominent as Spike Lee goes "right" this way—symptomatic of the class biases intrinsic in both bourgeois filmmaking and Afro-centric dogma—it becomes important to consider whether a black artist *must* conform to the style and messages of the mainstream when working under its aegis.

3 A.M. THURSDAY SEPTEMBER 15, 25 YEAR OLD MICHAEL STEWART IS ARRESTED BY THE TRANSIT POLICE AT THE 14th STREET/ 1st AVENUE LL SUBWAY STATION FOR ALLEGEDLY DOING GRAFFITI.

HOURS LATER HE IS BROUGHT INTO BELLEVUE BY 5 TRANSIT POLICE OFFICERS. BATTERED TO A PULP. D.O.A. RESUSCITATED BY LIFE-SUPPORT SYSTEMS HE REMAINS IN A COMA SUSPENDED BETWEEN LIFE AND DEATH.

PROTEST THE NEAR-MURDER OF MICHAEL STEWART BY THE TRANSIT POLICE / UNION SQUARE / 5:30 P.M. MONDAY SEPT. 26

What's missing from *Clockers* is a sense of black life lived—something Lee always pretends is his specialty. Its jacked-up hysteria about black pathology results in a ridiculous plot turn. The good brother Victor (Isaiah Washington) claims to have committed a murder that the police suspect was done by the bad brother Strike (Mekhi Phifer). The film offers white viewers the explanation that the good brother has held down a steady job, supported his single mother, his wife, and his two kids, and in general eaten shit for so long that he just explodes and kills a man. It offers black viewers the patronizing idea that the killing is a therapeutic form of "self-defense." In the end Lee's just telling the world that blacks are so sick and out of control that even the "good ones" are murderous.

*

Clockers embodied an unpardonable a shift in consciousness away from what the *City Sun* represented. Lee had achieved every New Yorker's dream of money and recognition. This upwardly mobile success story was epitomized when he appeared on Mayor Dinkins' wwwr radio show to protest the paper's disapproving cover story. Although Dinkins had already failed to win a second term as Mayor—even black voters had felt deceived by his overly accommodating public persona—he pretended to promote racial pride by backing Lee as the hero of his time. On the air, they tossed around such phrases as "race-traitor," besmirching the *City Sun's* integrity by arrogantly disregarding the paper's often lonely stance as the voice of black support during such conflagrations as the Crown Heights incident and Howard Beach killings.

Feeling personally attacked, I phoned wwwr and attempted to defend myself. Then, in an echo of the Giuliani–Margarita Rosaria incident, Dinkins pressed the off button on the call-in microphone.

That's what happens when free speech—challenged by Hollywood, challenged by money—gets manipulated by itchy fingers.

Clockers demonstrated the arrogance of power—a perversity that Spike Lee shares with many folks who, having struggled out of the underclass, achieve a level of status that they feel should set them above criticism. This defines the basic conflict between nouveau-riche black capitalists, who feel they are entitled to community celebration, and the valiant, truth-seeking credo of journalists and activists who struggle to maintain fidelity with the difficult, sometimes grim realities of African-American living.

By exchanging an independent perspective for Hollywood hegemony, Lee failed to attain the genuine New York vision promised by the black cultural-political-journalistic revolution of the '80s. Note how *Clockers* lacks an authentic black New York male's view of a cop, especially a white cop: the man in blue as potential aggressor, an unschooled wielder of inordinate force backed by an unfair legal system that threatens one's personal peace. The boisterous '80s hordes of hip-hop teens may have outnumbered the cops (as teasingly suggested in Walter Hill's 1979 New York City gang fairy tale, *The Warriors*), but no amount of hip-hop clamor could expunge the justifiably paranoid perception that is an indissoluble part of black New York life. That terror is not resolved

through drama or political revolution in *Clockers*. And it was pushed aside by the media-favored myth of Lee's personal bootstrap success.

Clockers reneged on speaking truth to power. When Lee's Hollywood victory proved unable to keep up with the responsibilities of ethnic diligence that would redeem mainstream success, it became clear that the auspicious opportunity of New York's '80s cultural wave had folded unceremoniously— just as the *City Sun* itself eventually folded. It was the end of an era.

In the years since then, the already empowered have been able to further broadcast their own version of "truth." Disenfranchisement can be felt by struggling artists, desperate neighborhoods, frustrated politicos, and average New Yorkers, who by now may have even forgotten that their frustration could be articulated and legitimized in print. The loss of the *City Sun* indicates that the spirit of the city is out of balance, a fact that can be attested by the foundering, since 1996, of Lee's film career. Such films as *Summer of Sam, Bamboozled, The 25th Hour, She Hate Me,* and *Inside Man* feel conceived without compass. Like so much in New York City since 9/11, newspaper readers and moviegoers are all left wondering what's next.

I Am a Renter

Philip Dray

I am a renter. I've spent the last twenty-nine years on the run. Gentrification, yuppification, luxury condos (are there any non-luxury condos?), latte shops, suburban kids asking which way to the Mudd Club. This time they have me for good.

A developer with all the right pull is building a twenty-two-story condo building in my backyard in Williamsburg, Brooklyn, blotting out the sky. No one in the neighborhood wants it. Not the residents. Not the shopkeepers. Not the Polish and Ukrainian people who have lived here their entire lives. Not the artists/writers/musicians. Not even the City of New York, which just rezoned the neighborhood with a six-story cap. But the developer—*he* wants it.

His name is Mendel. The Hassidic developers pretty much always get what they want. Why? The "electeds"—the Mayor, the Borough President, the city councilmen—wake up at 3:00 AM in a sweat, imagining forty-five thousand Jews marching into the polls and NOT voting for them.

So I'm the victim, I guess, but to be honest also part of the problem. For awhile I thought I could be part of the solution.

*

In the summer of 1976, I was living in Minneapolis, in a cheap apartment ten minutes' walk from one of the city's lakes. By coincidence, my building was owned by one of my high-school English teachers. It's weird when the same jerk comes into your life twice.

The city had about half a million people and one decent record store with about fifteen regular customers. With rock having been on life-support for several years, the first Ramones album, Jonathan Richman, the Berserkley bands, the Dolls, Television's single "Little Johnny Jewel," and the odd cut on the radio like "Radar Love" all meant a lot to us. We had a Bowie camp and a Roxy Music camp; a few people were into McCartney. We read *Creem*, *Crawdaddy*, and this new 'zine out of New York: *New York Rocker*. One night a friend from New York

called; did I want to take over the lease on his apartment in the West Village, $140 a month.

*

So I go. It's January 5, 1977, about 3 degrees below zero. For some reason my friend George and I decide to leave in this drive-away car at around 11:00 at night. We're keyed up to go and tired of saying good-bye to everyone. As a send-off, my neighbor presents us with an enormous joint.

In New York the $140 apartment is gone, but another one opens up at the corner of Hudson and Charles. One bedroom for $270 a month. I've left my girlfriend behind but brought my albums, a few clothes, and my electric piano. Each night I walk the length of Bleecker Street to CBGB's. Blondie and Patti Smith have already moved on, but Talking Heads, Ramones, Television are still holding forth; soon The Damned, The Jam, x-Ray Spex, and so on will arrive. I get a job working one of those Bob Cratchit jobs in a small book-publishing house. The first day my boss is dragging a heavy chair across a shag rug, and when I suggest we lift it so as not to leave any marks, she says, "What the hell do you care, it's not *your* rug!" Welcome to New York.

*

It's the spring of 1977. My girlfriend, based on my optimistic reports, decides to make the move as well, bringing our cat. Turns out we can't stay in the $270 place much longer, and she thinks it's too dark anyway, so with a gay friend we move to Chelsea. Rent is $600, but the place is huge, with nice floors. Chelsea, west of Sixth Avenue between 34th and 14th Streets, was kind of a bonanza then. From 23rd north there was a huge block of housing belonging to the International Ladies Garment Workers Union, just below 14th were some S&M bars, but the heart of the neighborhood was virtually untouched. Old nineteenth-century brownstones in decent condition, to the east still lots of active warehouses and small factories. There was a bar on Eighth Avenue for years called El Tropicana where somebody said they had seen Patti Smith, and I once stood behind Clem Burke of Blondie, who was buying smokes, but it was largely still quiet there and the rents fair. We had this landlord, Mr Brown, who fancied himself a mini-Donald Trump. His belt buckle was an enormous bronze dollar sign. That always worried me. He had fewer than four tenants so his place was not subject to the state's rent-stabilization laws, and he was very proud of himself for tracking the market and never failing to raise the rent substantially with each year's new lease.

*

In the spring of 1979, the girlfriend and I aren't getting along too good. We used to see it all the same way, but you know how it is, once you're in the big city everything changes. I think Jay McInerney made a fortune with that theme. Anyway, I want to spend evenings at Max's Kansas City with Mars, DNA, Teenage Jesus, and The Jerks; she's developed an interest in home furnishings from Conran's. Miraculously, I get a reprieve: she falls in love with the gay friend, who's decided to go straight. I sublet a place back down in the West Village, $200 a month.

*

By that fall, SoHo is getting very trendy. People are already talking about this new urban frontier: Tribeca. I should buy, but I'm oblivious. I'm no investor. First of all, I never have any money. It's the time before ATMs, and I spend my whole lunch hour every other Friday standing on line in the bank on Fifth Avenue and 55th Street to cash my paycheck, then grab an apple and a bag of Dipsy Doodles as I run back to my desk at Harper

& Row. Second, I have trouble anticipating the future. To invest takes vision. I have no vision.

This $200-a-month pad in the West Village suits me fine. I've never really lived alone, but it's not so hard, really. Bancroft makes these boxes of frozen fried chicken; you toss a leg and a wing in the oven for ten minutes, and you're good to go. I buy a bottle of Pernod, which is mentioned on that Bridget Polk live recording of the Velvet Underground at Max's. It's a dependable line: Want to come up for a glass of Pernod?

*

Having backslid into another relationship, all comes crashing down again in 1982. The sublet ends, and I'm forced due to rising real-estate prices to make the move I've dreaded—to the far East Village. I find a studio for $180 a month just east of Avenue A. My friends are afraid to visit me; we say good night at Second Avenue and I run the remaining distance home.

Truth is, the area is so "dangerous" that it proves to be one of the quietest neighborhoods I'll ever live in. I do my best to ease into the whole bodega culture—the storefronts selling nickel bags, the "loosie" cigarettes, even the characters hanging out on the corners begin to look familiar. I've never lived in a "bad" neighborhood before. It hits me that what's mostly bad about it is that it's been neglected. The people seem decent, just poor. There's a guy in my building everyone calls "Country" who sells heroin out of his apartment, but I come to understand his presence actually makes our address safe. A junky is watching over me. It's reassuring.

Strange things happen. I drift off to sleep one night to the sound of my neighbor demanding of someone, "Don't you like my breasts? What's wrong with my breasts?" I hear footsteps on the roof. Someone breaks in through my window and steals, of all things, my alarm clock. The couple right below me have a young daughter and two dogs—in a studio apartment. The ASPCA comes and insists they give up one of the dogs. Then one night they set a sofa on fire; there's smoke billowing out from under their door, but when the firemen rush up the stairs they refuse to let them inside. A week later the husband, who thinks I called the department, passes me in the hall and says, "I'm going to kill you." He means it. But I have to get to work.

*

Operation Pressure Point, 1983. The cops move in en masse and shut down the nickel-bag stores and the corner dealers, making the area safe for yuppification. "Country" gets taken away, fidgeting in the cuffs. Other neighborhood fixtures disappear—"Wolf Man," who howled at passersby and went barefoot 365 days a year; "Dirt Man," who was filthy from head to toe but so good-looking that people thought he was some kind of performance artist pretending to be a berserk

vagrant; and "Cop Seat Girl," this neatly dressed black gal who sat all day on a stoop outside a Con Ed plant under some graffiti that read "Cop Seat." First to arrive are the nightclubs, then the NYU students, then the suburban kids, a big-budget film shoot, and, finally, the beer-freaks, spare-changing from the tourists outside the Odessa (kielbasa and eggs, $1.39).

Someone announces a block-committee meeting to discuss the city's offer to put trees in the sidewalk. All the white people want the trees, but the Hispanics are against it, saying that prettifying the block will just drive the rents up. The whites are kind of numb—how can anyone not like trees?—but they're cowed. One Spanish guy who wears his shirt open and a ratchet on his belt is accused of bringing a weapon to the meeting. "This is no weapon!" he says, daring anyone to differ. "This is a tool!"

*

The new girlfriend and I are getting a bit claustrophobic in the studio apartment on the street with no trees. It's 1988. So I look at larger places in the neighborhood, only to find the $200 apartments of just five years ago are now $1,100. On a tip from a buddy we venture out to Williamsburg, Brooklyn, an area that since the early 1980s has gotten a reputation as a place for artists to score big loft spaces. The moment I walk into the available apartment, a large two-bedroom in the center of Northside Williamsburg, I'm sold. The rent is only $600 and the subway gets to First Avenue in Manhattan in under four minutes. For the eleven years I've been in New York, the idea of moving to the outer boroughs has been anathema—a kind of surrender, or suicide. But we move in.

Until the 1990s no one ever went to Brooklyn or Queens. Manhattan was the be-all, the end-all. Sure, it was fun to look down from the train on your way to Shea Stadium or Coney Island, but the actual side streets and little groceries and candy stores, places like Flatbush, Dyker Heights, Bay Ridge, Corona—no one would bother with them.

Anyway, we move in, and for two weeks I'm able to pretend I like it. I walk up and down Bedford Avenue—into the Hassidic area, back the other way to Polish Greenpoint—and I keep telling myself it's not so bad, this or that looks kind of promising. But one afternoon the creeping dullness of the place just overwhelms me. And then it sinks in: I've been forced out of Manhattan. The dream is over.

*

As in the East Village, I manage to adapt. Williamsburg enters a kind of golden age in the mid-'90s. Just enough new activity to make it interesting, and the mix is good. Artists, older Poles and Ukrainians, families, Arab shopkeepers. Someone told me when I first came to NYC that the city was really just a gathering of thousands of small towns. I see that now. There's an actual community here. The real New York is being priced out of Manhattan; now it's in the outer boroughs.

Unfortunately, this soon becomes apparent to everybody. Cobble Hill, Jackson Heights, Gowanus, all start filling up with Manhattan refugees. Williamsburg gets the worst of it. Its proximity to Manhattan, its old New York neighborhood corner taverns, and its large number of factories converted into clubs and theme restaurants spawn countless magazine articles about why it's the spot to make the scene. It's the "New East Village" but without the deviance. *New York Magazine* or *Time Out* even go to the trouble to print an article describing the "ultimate Williamsburg guy".

The neighborhood gets assaulted by hordes of sleaze balls. They take cheap booze, gussy it up as a "Cosmo" or whatever, and make a fortune selling it to young hepcats while generic trip-hop plays in the background. The loaded SUVs from New Jersey and Long Island start arriving each Friday and Saturday night about 7:00. The occupants eat affordable Asian food in one of the big theme restaurants, adjourn to one of the Olde New York neighborhood bars, and emerge around 4:00 AM, yelling into their cell phones.

The papers and magazines throughout New York all take the "spring-break" angle toward Williamsburg. In doing so they are, it seems, intentionally avoiding the real story, which is that the area is being overwhelmed by all manner of cockamamie get-rich schemes— high-rise buildings, an underground power plant, nightclubs and bars—and that the community is fighting back. The level of activism in the neighborhood is impressive. Half a century ago, some of the residents lay down in front of the bulldozers to try and stop the Brooklyn-Queens Expressway, which cut greater Williamsburg in two. Even now, the people involved tend to be very sophisticated. They have hand-held devices for measuring airborne toxins, that sort of thing.

*

The last hurrah comes in 2000. Some hip capitalist decides to open a huge rock club right on the area's most residential street. He's already infamous for refusing to pay the bands at a club he owned on the Lower East Side. When the community informs him the siting of the club is problematic, he tells us to shove it. Terrific public meetings are held . . . the old, the young, the artists, the local pols, even some priests, God bless 'em . . . all unified and ready to fight. People raise money, go to hearings, stand up and tell off bureaucrats. It's one of those Tom Joad experiences—"little people" taking on a greedy, heartless jackal. And we win! A judge says the guy's permit application was flawed, and a state agency denies him a liquor license. After the hearing, he and his investors go skulking off. Sweet!

*

It's 2002. Fact is, even with 9/11 and all that, everyone in the world still wants to live here. I'm no xenophobe. I love people. But they never stop coming—Japanese NYU students, refugees from the war in Kashmir, graduates of the Iowa Writers Workshop. I have this theory why the world loves New York City: unlike the rest of America, it was simply too big to be destroyed by the developers all at

once. Add to this the fact that, starting around 1989, the TV networks, who had long before stopped airing shows like *Naked City* and *Kojak* that depicted NYC as a hellhole, began showing *Seinfeld* and then *Friends* and *Will and Grace* and *Felicity*.

⋆

As of 2005, we're no longer just an exciting fringe neighborhood where the adventurous reader of the New York *Times* "Style" section can look for love, but a booming new residential belt. The factories are sold out or zoned out and converted into condos. A proliferation of liquor licenses turns North 6th Street into another Reeperbahn. Taking on one corrupt, unconnected nightclub owner required an all-out neighborhood campaign; for this you'd need the Red Army.

I still go to the community meetings. Mostly we are just a support group these days, trading horror stories. There's no place to park. A mom got run down by a red-haired *iPod*-ette on a skateboard. Someone else was brained by a Frisbee. A young Mexican roofer here illegally and sending $100 a month home to his family in Chiapas fell to his death at a construction site. Mrs Stanislau's flower shop is closing to become a Roy Rogers.

I walk home trying to remember a line from an Ian Frazier book. Something like: "Whatever neighbourhood I live in I manage to destroy."

Growing Up Unrented on the Lower East Side

Edmund Berrigan

I used to have this dream where I would descend a few of the concrete stairs out of my old apartment building at 101 St Marks Place, between First and Avenue A, not quite reaching the bottom where my brother and some of the neighborhood kids were playing whiffle ball in the middle of the street. I was about seven, a short, skinny white kid with messy brown hair and a white t-shirt on. I'd suddenly realize that I had no pants on, and I'd immediately head back upstairs towards the third floor where our apartment was, hoping no one would see me. I'd wind around the corners of the second floor, get up to the next landing, and look up at the gold number on the black square. Each time it read "four," and as I tried to descend to three the stairs would get longer, and my movements slower, until I wasn't moving at all.

*

My father, mother, brother, and I moved into a rent-stabilized railroad apartment in 1976, having lived previously in Chicago, where Anselm was born, and briefly in England, where I was born two years later, in '74. The rent was $180 per month, which seemed exorbitant at the time, so much so that initially my parents didn't take the place. But it remained un-rented for a couple of weeks, so finally they did. When we left in '92 the rent was a little under $400. Both of my parents were poets, Ted having established himself in the '60s with a book called *The Sonnets* that incorporated Dadaist, Cubist, and New York School tendencies and merged them with an intense Irish-American personality. He was a presence on the scene at that time around poets such as Allen Ginsberg and Frank O'Hara and artists such as Andy Warhol and Jasper Johns. Alice was eleven years younger and just at the beginning of her writing career.

Both my parents essentially only accepted work related to poetry, which tended to be teaching jobs or occasional residencies that never lasted very long. So we were mostly late with rent, and the generosity and friendship of others was crucial. If a younger unfamiliar poet wanted to come to the apartment, the

price of admission was generally a quart of milk or a loaf of bread. Ted was also slowly dying the whole time, but my brother and I were too young to know this, and there was enough ambiguity about the illness for our parents to not totally admit it. He finally did die at home on July 4, 1983, when I was eight.

Our apartment was at the front of the building. There was an air shaft next to the middle rooms, and steam heat warmed the place. The bathtub was in the kitchen, and there was no shower. Taking a bath involved moving all of the dishes from the bathtub cover and putting them on the kitchen table, then reversing the operation post-bath. The boiler was often broken in the winter, and we never had air conditioning for the hot, humid summer months. Our building was also completely roach-infested, and no matter how many times you might "bomb" the place, they would always come back. We would venture off on weekend excursions and on returning would find roaches all over the kitchen floor, scattering as we turned on the lights. Using the oven to heat the apartment—a common practice— produced many an overwhelmed roach stumbling out of the grill in a daze. I was always afraid to put my hand under the kitchen table, lest it return to light with a visitor.

Although the New York punk scene at the time was apparently quite prominent, I was mostly interested in *Star Wars* figures, at least until that day sometimes in the '80s when my brother, our great friend Byron, and I decided to burn them all in one last heroic battle. Our life was mostly concerned with poets anyway. After my father died, Allen Ginsberg gave my mom some office work to do in his home/office on 12th Street. This is a building that ought to be a landmark, the way the Bateau Lavoir is in Paris, the former residence of Picasso, Pierre Reverdy, Max Jacob, Juan Gris, and others. Then again, any number of buildings are worth the memories of the people who lived in them, though by now that quality of the East Village has been razed to the ground.

I walked into Allen's building once to pick up Philip Whalen and bring him to dinner that evening. I bumped into Allen's long-time friend Peter Orlovsky in the doorway, possibly smelling of alcohol. Peter recognized me, though he seemed a bit jumpy. He was wearing a denim jacket and jeans and was unshaven—it was nearly the time when the author photo was taken for his classic book of poems *Clean Asshole Poems & Smiling Vegetable Songs*, published by City Lights. "Oh, hi," he said. "Do you still play guitar?" "Yeah, I'm taking lessons." "Oh good. What about the banjo? Do you still play the banjo?" "Nope." "How about the mandolin, do you play the mandolin?" he said, making strumming gestures for each instrument. "Ukelele?" "No." "What about the fiddle? The fiddle?" "Nope, don't play the fiddle," I replied, a little dumbstruck by the lightning speed of the questions. "How about the autoharp, do you play that?" "Unh-unh." "Oh, you should pick those up," he said, and left.

Other people who lived (or still live) in the building included Richard Hell, Patti Smyth, Sylvia Morales (Lou Reed's first wife); the artists Rene Ricard and Richard Prince; the poets Alice Notley, John Godfrey, April Bernard, Simon Pettet, and Jim Brodey among others; and the novelists Luc Sante and Michael Brownstein. Sante wrote his book *Low Life* there. Legendary filmmaker, musicologist, collector and shaman Harry Smith also stayed at Allen's apartment for a period of time, until Allen got him settled at Naropa University in Boulder, Colorado for the last years of his life.

Our building on St Mark's Place, while not as heroically populated with poets, instead housed a number of old ladies who'd lived there for thirty or more years, and who often called on Anselm and me to help carry their groceries. Why did so many seventy-year-old women live on the sixth floor of an East Village walk-up? Most had rent-controlled apartments and paid less than $100 a month. One was Old Alice, who one time gave us two boxes of evaporated milk that sat on the top of our fridge for several months before finding the trash can. It's quite possible that contemplating those boxes of evaporated milk was my first metaphysical experience. I remember watching from the hallway one day as Old Alice was carried out on a stretcher. Did she have an oxygen mask on? That was the last time I saw her.

There were always a lot of people out on the streets, including a real mix of kids from different backgrounds whom we used to roam around with: Ukrainian, Portuguese, Italian, African-American, Puerto Rican, Polish. While the presence of that kind of diversity can still be felt, it has been somewhat driven

out by the skyrocketing rents, and there isn't the sense of a neighborhood where that kind of group could assemble in the same way. There were also a number of mostly harmless homeless men and women who were just as much a part of the neighborhood as everyone else. Fine in the summer but struggling to survive if they stayed for the winter.

In the late '80s Mayor Koch decided that homeless people didn't fit in with gentrification and established a curfew on park hours at Tompkins Square Park and had the homeless people removed. This was the park Anselm and I had played in as kids, and where my dad would sometimes score pills. On the night of August 7, 1988, there was a protest and then a riot. At one point, the protestors ran up St Marks Place toward First Avenue; I watched them from the front window. The cops chased after them on horseback and on foot, and a number of people were beaten, of course, including several who happened to be passing by.

By the time I was going to junior high and high school, a number of pot dealers had installed themselves on the corner of First Avenue and St Mark's Place. This began around '85 or '86, a couple of years after Ted died. I passed them every day on the way to the store or back from school, and we were (sort of) on a first-name basis. They would offer pot to anyone who went by, but one of them gradually got to know me and would apologize if he had solicited me before recognizing me: "Oh sorry, Shorty. What's your name?" "Edmund." "Eric? Stay in school Eric, don't be like me." They disappeared after a few years. I recently saw one of them in a gray suit, working as a doorman at a building off Avenue B.

My mother remarried in 1988, and things stabilized for a while. The neighborhood had changed but still had some of the same feel. An anarchist bookstore was opened by two partners in a spot where a tattoo parlor now exists. The attendees had a habit for a while of blasting music at 2:00 AM out on the street and banging on the lampposts. I would sometimes awaken to hear my stepfather, a British poet named Douglas Oliver, shouting out the window for them to turn it off. Eventually one of the owners ran off with most of the money. The other put a sign up on the bookstore that read "Shut down by the police." Doug was a good stepfather, an old friend of my parents. He lived with us in that apartment for five years and was very fond of his time in New York. For him, it culminated in a long satirical poem called "Penniless Politics" about a Caucasian man and a Haitian voodoo princess who found a third political party, have a sexual relationship, and spread via chain letter. They eventually come to power and rewrite the constitution. Doug had been a journalist in Paris for ten years, and had a habit of talking to cab drivers if he recognized their nationality from their name tags. It was in this way that we once discovered that we were being driven by a man who claimed to have beaten people in Haiti for the tyrant regime of Jean-Claude "Baby Doc" Duvalier. I don't remember if Doug tipped him.

Theatre 80 on St Marks Place was an old revival house for black-and-white movies. Anselm and I saw the Marx Brothers' *Duck Soup* there, and I spent a good hour afterwards trying to be as funny as possible. There's a pizza place now on the corner of St Mark's and Second. Before that it was a Gap. When the Gap opened in the '80s, it had a glass window but no gate. At least until some intrepid thieves from the street rolled a bowling ball into the window and stole what clothes they could, to be resold a little further down the block a day or so later. Before the Gap, the building housed the St Mark's Theatre, whose facade is shown for a few seconds in the Robin Williams move *Moscow on the Hudson*. In the film, an x-rated movie is playing, but I don't recall them ever showing pornographic films.

A classic example of the Disneyfication of the East Village would be the buildings at 19–23 St Mark's between Second and Third. At one time they comprised a club known as the Dom, where my parents (before they knew each other) both went to see the Velvet Underground play, including a performance by the Exploding Plastic Inevitable. Eventually the Dom closed, and for the longest time there was a social center which hosted regular Alcoholics Anonymous meetings. Now it's a shopping center with a Quizno's.

Simon Pettet and I used to play Scrabble for gummy bears. His wife Rosebud worked at a spice shop next to DeRoberti's pastry shop that sold them by the pound. Simon has a classic apartment in that same building on 12th Street, full of all kinds of recordings of poets and musicians, including a live record of the Cramps with a crowd shot on the back that happens to show one conspicuous red-headed British fellow dancing, that being Simon himself. One day we decided to play a round in Tompkins Square Park on a concrete chess table. A long-haired fellow walked by with a chicken on a leash—the kind of image that stays with you. This most likely was Daniel Rakowitz, who later cut up his girlfriend and allegedly ground her bones into soup that he fed to homeless people around the park.

In the early '80s the Rolling Stones came to our street to film the video for "Waiting On a Friend" from their album *Tattoo You*. I remember looking out the window and seeing Mick Jagger in front of a staircase, smoking a cigarette, encircled by a crowd several feet away. Ted sent Anselm down with an autographed copy of one of his books to see if he could trade it for Jagger's autograph. But the police wouldn't let Anselm through. In the end he came away with something

better. If you watch the video, at a certain point you'll see a shaggy-looking kid standing in front of a garbage can for about fifteen seconds, with Mick and Keith walking in the distance behind him. He probably had Ted's book in his hands.

The back cover of Ted's book *Red Wagon* has a photograph of him taken at Gem Spa by Gerard Malanga. Gem Spa was just a newsstand and a place to get a malted, but somehow it still stands on the same corner of St Mark's and Second. That was supposedly a prime spot to run into my dad and have him talk your head off for a couple of hours. I remember waking up quite a few early mornings to Ted returning from the outside world with chocolate donuts for Anselm and me. I don't think it was because he was an early riser.

*

Anselm and I managed to go to college after differing bouts with public high school. We went to the same elementary school, PS 19 on 10th Street and First Avenue. I went to junior high school down the street at JHS 60, across from Allen's apartment building. It was kind of a biblical experience, involving floods and fires, and I was among the minority for once as a white person in a mostly

Hispanic, African-American, and Asian school. We were city kids, full of all kinds of ridiculous curses and homophobic put-downs, and it was all a little scary and occasionally dangerous, though never that bad in the end. I was too meek to get close to trouble, anyway. Anselm went to JHS 56 down on Henry Street, and I imagine his experience was similar. We both went to engineering high schools that require entrance tests. He went to Stuyvesant and I went to Brooklyn Technical. I would take the N or R train from 8th and Broadway to Atlantic Avenue in Brooklyn and go work on a lathe, or shovel dirt for my foundry class, or any other number of strange tasks.

I never really was comfortable at Brooklyn Tech. At the same time, that's when I really began to comprehend what the death of my father had meant to me. I also began writing or thinking about poems every day after my mother gave me a blank notebook when I was sixteen. That was easy, having watched my parents for years just sitting around and writing. I understood what poetry could sound like. That a lot of this was happening in an engineering school was odd, but I also was attending (and occasionally taking part in) readings at the Poetry Project at St Mark's Church on the Bowery. I bought my first book of poems at St Mark's Bookshop, still the best poetry bookstore around. That was the collected poems of Dylan Thomas. I also bought a Claude McKay selected poems shortly thereafter. Being a poet or buying a book of poems seemed to me for a long time the only adult thing to do.

We had three Phillip Guston drawings from the '70s; I'm not sure how we got them, though one was used on the cover of one of Alice's early books. The other two were separately sold to cover Anselm's and my college tuition. Otherwise, our expenses had always been minimal, and we managed to survive for years in that cheap apartment, which was still cheap when my mother and stepfather moved to Paris in 1992. I suppose I could have gotten a job and kept it, but being eighteen and raised by constantly unemployed poets I had not the slightest inclination whatsoever to do so. I only wanted to be a poet. Really, too much had happened there, and it was just time to move on.

I went to Purchase College for four-and-a-half stony and beleaguered years, then caught a train to San Francisco, ending up in the Lower Haight for three years. It was as close to an East Village feel as I could get, and I wrote a lot of poems there. But as the dotcom craze skyrocketed, it became harder to get an apartment. This was somewhat troublesome, as I lived with eight people, two dogs, a cat, and a ferret in an apartment over the building on Haight and Fillmore where Jim Jones used to hold his cult meetings. I worked mostly in coffee shops with a short stint as a walking messenger. I remember pushing my cart around the busy streets of the financial district, making some pick-ups early and others late, so I could sit for a minute and cut up Dickens novels into sonnets. Walking one particularly crowded street I heard a thud next to me. I looked down and a sparrow had fallen out of the sky. No one else seemed to notice.

In 1999 I moved back to New York, where I've resided ever since. At the moment I live in South [Park] Slope in Brooklyn. I've also lived in Greenpoint, Williamsburg, North Park Slope, and Bushwick, and at several temporary places in Manhattan including three different offices. One was on Canal and Broadway. I paid $400 in cash for a couple of months to a seventy-year-old guy I met on a road trip to Texas. The room had no windows, there was no shower, and I had to pretend that I wasn't sleeping there. In another place, on 4th and Avenue C, I didn't have to pay rent but was caretaker for two pets: a rabbit named Farfar and a python named Buckwheat, to whom I fed freshly killed rats once a week. Farfar died of a heart attack after a couple months.

I've never thought that my upbringing was particularly unique. Whereas everyone else's upbringing I've encountered has seemed wild to me, an experience I couldn't possibly imagine. It's unfathomable to me to want to trade one set of mysterious and bizarre circumstances for another. All the same, the Lower East Side used to seem like a finely used piece of trash, the perfect rusted Tonka fire engine sitting on top of the wire trash can that you saw first, that you weren't sure you should grab until someone came up to you and asked if you were taking it. You later had no idea what it was doing in your apartment, but, as the Dude said in *The Big Lebowski*, "It made the room hang together."

THE THINGS WE DO

New Yorkers have almost nothing in common. We don't speak the same language, eat the same food, listen to the same music, or even share the same climate. (In summer, New York is divided between people with air conditioning and those without.) Some New Yorkers never walk up steep hills; others rarely taste salty breezes. The dominos games of Ocean Parkway are unknown on 7th Avenue in Park Slope; few accounts of the city even acknowledge Woodside, Woodhaven, Midwood, Midland Beach, let alone distinguish between them. It's a point that can't be made too finely, or too often. There may not be as many as "eight million stories in the Naked City" as the narrator of Jules Dassin's 1948 masterpiece *The Naked City* intoned, but there are *plenty*.

This isn't to imply New Yorkers don't share *anything*. Sex, drugs, gambling and money—or lack thereof—bind most of us, but as New York becomes ever more an international city, our collective totems are few. Children in the 1970s and '80s could share much with their peers—Cookie Puss and Crazy Eddie, Joe Franklin and 'Bowling for Dollars'. In the TV years before cable and the internet, such silliness could define us as New Yorkers. Today, even Marv Albert, the long-time voice of the Knicks, is no longer affiliated with a New York sports team. His former partner, the all-time swishin' and dishin' dude Walt "Clyde" Frazier, remains to bear witness to the team's ignominious crack-up. Despite the hard times, basketball is still the city's most popular sport—and by far the city's favorite *street* game.

Henry Miller described the streets as a "harmony of irrelevant facts that give your wandering a metaphysical certitude." This is the world of Ben Katchor's comic strip "Julius Knipl, Real Estate Photographer," and, like Miller, Katchor finds odd beauty amid the challenge of a changing city. CBGB's closing garnered much attention, but any true memorial for Downtown would include not just CB's best days but the Mudd Club, A7, Tier 3, Danceteria, Folk City, Tonic, and other, more fugitive venues. While attentions have shifted, naturally, to Brooklyn, we're a long way from Chain Gang's era-defining *Mondo Manhattan* (1987). New York remains a world capital for jazz and scuffling jazz musicians.

Since the 1990s, one of the most remarkable symbols of New York's creative foment is one of the most unlikely: the Queensborough Bridge , which looms over the city's largest projects: six blocks, ninety-six buildings. Perhaps *the* old-school rap battle was waged between Boogie Down Productions and producer Marley Marl's mostly Queens-based Juice Crew. "The Bridge Is Over," KRS-One taunted and, inspired by the challenge, Queens has been bringing heat ever since. Nas (son of trumpeter-turned-bluesman Olu Daru) is QB's favorite son, and with Staten Island's Ghostface Killah, maybe hip-hop's greatest lyricist. Other major

QB figures include Tragedy Khadafi, Cormega Capone, and Mobb Deep, who, at their pitch-black peak, are the grimiest thugs of all. Although filmed across the river in Jersey City, Jim Jarmusch's *Ghost Dog* (1999), with its inspired soundtrack by Wu-Tang leader RZA, *feels* like New York and usefully contextualizes a still widely misunderstood culture.

While hip-hop styles reign supreme and influence almost every ethnic group, a wide range of Spanish-speaking peoples are flipping elements of numerous cultures in their own fascinating ways. It's such a dynamic time that even those fluent in the language can only make provisional findings. Pedro Pietri (1944–2004), co-founder of the Nuyorican Poets Cafe, ranks with Edwin Denby, Frank O'Hara and Ted Berrigan among city poets, while salsa, bachata, reggaeton, ranchera and other musics blare from barrio to barrio. Just a few blocks from Maria's Tire Shop in the South Bronx, the Mott Haven-based arts organization 'Spanic Attack pursues what it wryly describes as "a pretentious failure, esp. re: various trends in Latino Art." Intellectuals and activists both, their humor ought not be mistaken for fatalism. Instead, it's an honest assessment of the futility of defining such a radically diverse population. In Brooklyn, on a restaurant wall previously decorated only with art and *futbol* memorabilia there now hangs a sign declaiming "Mexicanos—not Latinos! Latinos are the white people of Latin America. Not Hispanic—Hispanics are the people of Spain, Europeans. We are an Indigenous People!"

And that's New York. However disputatious—and goddamn, New Yorkers *love* to argue—the desire, and ability, of people to define, reinvent and sometimes disappear among the multitude is what makes living here uniquely exciting. It might be a hot gospel band wailing on a Bed-Stuy Sunday morning or stumbling across the Shostakovich School of Music in Bath Beach. The East Indian Music Academy in Richmond Hill offers instruction in "vocals, harmonium, sitar, sarod, Hindi, Sanskrit and Moral Education." A recent Andy Statman record is called *East Flatbush Blues*; Statman is a Lubavitcher Hassidim. Late-night hip-hop barber shops, 24-hour Korean BBQs and OTB, the skater kids, cricket fiends . . . the list is endless. The San Juan-raised, Highbridge-resident poet Urayoán Noel called his version "I'm Gonna Stay in New York (For the Fucking Record!)," and according to the author, *it's to be sung guaracha-style, backed by a cuatro and a Moog synthesizer*: "For the dead performance artists / For the sadness and the stardust / For your crazy Aunt Iraida / For where Flatbush meets Loisaida." *For all this and something more / I'm gonna stay in New York!*

Going Downtown (On an Uptown Train)
Paul Kopasz

On the wall of the squat at 8th and Avenue c was written, "Opium is the
religion of the people." It was a clever inversion of the Marxist maxim,
all the more charming for its being true. I was only just then, in 1989, becoming
a serious drug addict, but maybe that's not true—maybe I was already lost.
In either case, that slogan (and the dope) provided both wisdom and solace.

Not that I hadn't been gifted with plenty of this sort of cockeyed wisdom
before. I'd had plenty of experience with drugs before the squats. I'd been a pot-
head for years—since I'd been sixteen at least, when I was growing up in Detroit.
There was plenty of almost everything, especially acid and cocaine, during college
in Lexington, Kentucky. All that was missing was heroin. Sure, sometimes Dilaudid
(the monstrously powerful but short-acting morphine analog) would turn up, and
there were Placidyls in those days, too. You had to poke a hole in the Placidyl gel
cap to get the fluid inside to seep out and soak in to your gut more quickly.

For The Big h, however, it seemed you had to get to the East Coast, and to
me that meant New York City. Not many dope addicts will cop to it, but I have
to admit, I *wanted* to become a heroin addict. My jones wasn't just fed by Lou
Reed and Charlie Parker but by the endlessly glamorous images of gritty New
York films like *Panic in Needle Park* and *The French Connection.* Jim Carroll's
Basketball Diaries was my Rosetta Stone, mainly because it helped me decipher
William S. Burroughs' *Naked Lunch* which was, of course, the bible.

How could all of the greatest artists in the world be wrong? How could
they even be close to wrong? The art part is the key, though. I wanted to become
a junkie mainly to become a great artist. So it was that I made my way to New
York, trundling through the Holland Tunnel in a battered vw Beetle with vague
dreams, a pregnant girlfriend, some musical equipment, and just about zero
street smarts. I would try to carve out an existence and squeeze together a
decent band. Work? Art? What's the difference? Being a dope addict was the
hardest job I ever had.

*

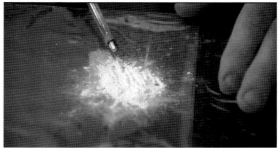

I started selling pot to friends from my $150/week bat cave in the Belleclaire Hotel at 77th and Broadway. Once a week a maid would pound on the door with clean sheets and towels; the bathrooms out in the hallway were communal. At the time, 1983 or so, the Belleclaire was an SRO— the type of place that attracted transients, marginal Broadway has-beens and never-wases, hookers, and a smattering of folks Ed Koch had let out of the local nuthouses for budgetary reasons. One of these was Chicken Man. He would occupy a corner in the neighborhood each day and make squawking noises at each passerby. When it rained, he would do the same on some randomly chosen floor of the Belleclaire.

Selling grass on a small scale doesn't bring in much dough, but it was a low-risk occupation and I'd have to say that times were good. Still, it was work, just as my many other New York jobs were work: telephone solicitor; foot messenger; bike messenger; microfilm retriever at Citibank; janitor at Macy's; handyman at SoHo art gallery; grunt-worker at a printing-supply house on East 18th Street; clerk at WNYC; building superintendent at 93rd and First, etc. The list might seem picaresque, but it just shows you what a then still young white man can achieve if he's willing to hand over 20 percent of his subsistence wage to Office Force, the loan shark of an employment agency that got me many of these fleeting positions.

Somewhere near the middle of that list—sometime in the mid-1980s—the jobs started to change subtly in that I began selecting them on the basis of the opportunities they offered for stealing. Thievery had yet to become my main job, but it would, and it was really just a part of the even larger job of becoming a full-time junkie.

By 1989, heroin had become my sole occupation as well as my one solace in the nonstop clang of a city that clearly had no use for me. Eighth Street and Avenue D was only a block away; that corner was *the* spot to buy in Lower Manhattan. It was cool to smoke grass in the squat, but shooting dope was strictly prohibited. Then again, it was supposedly prohibited by the Mafia, too. So what?

*

Before this came the relatively carefree days peddling Brooklyn dime bags to wimpy jazz musicians in the Village for $15. They were afraid to go into Bed-Stuy and Fort Greene or, God forbid, East New York. I wasn't. Hell, I'd been living in those places two years earlier; those neighborhoods never gave me much trouble. There were stores all over Brooklyn—former *bodegas* or shoe-repair places, their windows papered over with cereal or Pampers boxes—selling stuff right in the open. You'd go in, stick your money through a slot in the boarded-up wall where a counter had once been, and tell the nice man what you wanted.

Those days in Brooklyn take on a genuine rose-tinted glow now. After another wretched day of work I'd hop off the A train at Jay Street/Borough Hall rather than transfer to the GG, which would let me off at Clinton/Washington, which was closer to my pad at Steuben and Myrtle. I would plod up Myrtle—the locals had started calling it Murder Avenue, and me and my girlfriend were two of the very few honkies in the neighborhood—buying my drugs and sampling the local eateries and groceries and purveyors of goods of questionable origin.

Those treks up Myrtle sometimes took forever as I was loading up on all that good shit the neighborhood had to offer: grass, plantains, Cafe Bustelo, various hot peppers, chorizo, fake opium, those ubiquitous incense bundles, pizza, occasionally some coke. It was 1983, and between Jay Street and the end of the line at Myrtle and Steuben, I might have heard Grandmaster Flash's "White Lines" a dozen times: Freeze! Rock!

*

After a year and a half or so—just when my rent control had kicked in—I was forced to leave the Belleclaire when two band members mutinied and non-payment of rent became unavoidable. I bounced around for a while after that, sometimes sleeping on the trains and in Washington Square—you could do that then with little fear of being hassled, at least by the cops—until Steve Sacher, a bass player I knew, took me to a jazz musician-infested crash pad on Lispenard Street, a block south of Canal. The loft was close to Manhattan's first post office and above a joint called the Nancy Whiskey Pub, which is still there today, as far as I know. Every now and then, us "roommates" would play a gig down in that pub—rock and jazz standards and some R&B.

I was walking back on maybe the third day of my tenancy at Lispenard when I bumped into Steve at the front door. "I think your man Jaco is dead drunk in the gutter up on Grand," I told him.

"Well," Steve replied soberly, "we've got to go get him."

So we did. And that's how I ended up living in squalor with Jaco Pastorius for six months. It's funny that, with Charlie Parker in mind when I moved to the city, I ended up in a strange relationship with Jaco. At that time, to certain jazz and fusion cats, Jaco *was* Bird. He'd be—not the first one—but maybe the second to tell you.

"We built those towers," he said once to me, deliriously tramping around Washington Square charging Japanese tourists a buck or two to take his picture. "Me, and Bird, and Jimi Hendrix built those fucking towers," pointing up over SoHo at World Trade.

"Whatever you say Jaco, listen, man, I gotta grab an A train . . ."

Jaco would disappear for long periods of time and then return without warning and with every expectation that everyone nearby would continue to treat him like a musical god even though he was falling fast. It was booze, but mostly it was coke. He reappeared one Christmas Eve when all of the other guys (i.e., the ones who actually worked and paid the rent) were off on some senseless tour. I answered the door and Jaco came up the one long flight of stairs looking like Peter Tosh, his hair all greasy and nappy and clumped together in rubber bands.

I had found some window-pane-type LSD that afternoon while cleaning the apartment. It was what people called a "four-way hit" of "windowpane" acid. Whatever; I figured that meant that you should take all four of the small gelatinous squares, so I took three. I should have just taken one. (Actually, the stuff wasn't mine, and I shouldn't have taken any of it, but . . .) Jaco was mumbling, upset about God knows what, and while watching CNN we found out that the actor and *bon vivant* Peter Lawford had died. I'd had hundreds of acid trips but never tried this windowpane variety—this stuff was no bullshit. I got confident and started shooting my mouth off.

"Peter Lawford? For Christ's sake, that guy could never act . . . just 'cause he's a Kennedy in-law and he fucked Marilyn Monroe . . ."

"Shut the fuck up." Jaco got pissed. I was having a private evening—a holiday no less—with a master and I'd gotten him angry.

"Peter Lawford was one par-tay-in' motherfucker," Jaco informed me, with a reverence that seemed out of place but reassuring. Maybe he wasn't that mad at me. "That guy could go 'til dawn on the blow. And very generous." And then another snatch of anger: "What the fuck would you know about it?"

True.

I was scared now and tripping my brains out. I crawled out the window onto the fire escape, which faced south and offered a perfectly framed view of the World Trade Center, where I'd worked as a foot messenger just a few years earlier. It was freezing and I sat there cowering. I was afraid of Jaco and afraid of the city and afraid of music and scared of women and life and the two towers hovered over me changing color from blue to purple to pink and cycling back through again and again while I sat and shivered and tried to figure out why I was such an asshole that even Jaco got pissed off at me and whether there was any possibility at all that I could make something decent of my life. With the psychedelic towers glowering down at me and my family at home getting ready for Christmas back in Detroit, the answer was no.

A few years later I was sitting on a stoop in Alphabet City wondering if my heroin habit was getting out of hand. A street guy rolled by pushing a shopping cart filled with ragged clothes and empty bottles and cans. He looked at me and smiled, and his face morphed into Jaco's—the face of a dead man laughing at one comparatively ignorant. (Jaco had been severely beaten while on a bender down in Florida and had died, September 21, 1987; he'd been thirty-five years old.) It was as if he was saying to me, "Boy, you've made one dumb fucking decision—see what it did to me?" Then the ghost smiled in a cackling way and the face turned back. It wasn't Jaco anymore, and I just thought I was crazy or soon would be.

*

"Going downtown (rather than uptown)" as Rashied Ali (John Coltrane's last drummer and a regular on the Lispenard Street scene) and Jaco used to always say. We had a roommate later, a fairly well-known guitarist with a quite famous

group, who hung around all the time. He carried two different vials on him at all times and had 3-inch-long fingernails on each of his pinky fingers. He either went uptown or downtown. Each day, all day, until dinnertime he used his left pinky nail to scoop and sniff cocaine—heading uptown. After about 7:00 PM or so he would switch to snorting heroin from his right pinky nail. "The boy has been going downtown a little too much lately," was the consensus. I wasn't headed downtown just yet, but it wouldn't be long.

I was riding the subway nonstop to fill orders for small quantities of grass and hashish from these old places, orders that would, at the end of the day, yield enough profit for me to have my own grass, dinner—pizza or falafel—and some Häagen-Dazs. The temp jobs had become both unbearable and intrusive upon my lifestyle. With a free couch to live on, why bother emptying trash cans at Bloomingdale's?

When times got tight and customers cheated me, I would be forced to go out and try to find something to steal. I still had customers up at the Belleclaire, including a guy who worked at a fancy restaurant who gave me free lunches and brought the pot money to me at the end of each meal as if it were my change. It was on one of those visits to the Belleclaire that the desk clerk handed me a letter they had been holding for me for some time. It was from my patron saint of sorts—Bill Burroughs—and it included a recipe for a hash-based lozenge he had discovered in Morocco. I was re-energized in my commitment to the life of the chemical bohemian and righteous fuck-up.

The best-laid plans do oft go astray, though, and it should be obvious that mine were not particularly well laid. Instead of keeping a shitty part-time job and dealing on my low level, I was (I thought) rescued from this grind by the lucky opportunity afforded me to steal an ounce of cocaine from two hookers, old clients of mine in the Belleclaire. This endeared me deeply (and hopefully permanently) to those musicians down on Canal. I got away with the theft and made some new clients (I was going to say "friends," but I came to my senses) and a growing new habit. It wasn't the coke that was the immediate problem; it was the infrequent bag of heroin I occasionally employed to come down. Two years of confusion later, I was in the squats and sporting a pretty good habit.

*

Loisaida—the Spanish slang term for the Lower East Side when it was still a significant barrio—in 1989 was like the fucking Wild West. The drug trade seemed to be controlled by the Puerto Ricans, but there were plenty of black gangs pushing product and there were plenty of gunfights over on Avenue D, mostly involving interloping Jamaican posses.

I was commonly robbed in Alphabet City, and in spite of the low prices and near-round-the-clock availability, buying heroin there was daunting prospect indeed. Various gangs each had brand names for their junk, and their logos were rubber-stamped on the small glassine envelopes: Big Shot, Fatal Beauty, Untouchables (with a tiny picture of Robert De Niro), Century 21, Bad Boy, Grade A, Illusion, Mambo). The chop shop across the street had its own brand called Batman. There were knives everywhere and there were guys

walking around with facial scars everywhere. Below Delancey Street it was even scarier, harder to score without getting robbed or beaten up if you were white. I don't know how dangerous it was otherwise as I had no junkie friends.

I started buying dime bags and at first I could make one of them last nearly three days—I could precisely measure out my life by calibrating time in units of $10 heroin purchases. I could make projections of things like hours of labor, trips to the corner, and days between robberies. Later on, it took five or ten dime bags to get through a day, and that isn't even such a bad habit by ghetto junkie standards. I eventually became a full-blown addict with a couple of aborted attempts at withdrawal under my rapidly tightening belt. I was hitting the corners three times a day.

At first, the thrill of burglary supplied an adrenaline rush that perfectly complemented the heroin haze. Later, when I began injecting more cocaine along with my heroin, the adrenaline rush of burglary came to be superfluous and unnerving. It got scary. I was a good thief in the sense that I was conscientious and careful to steal only those items which were essentially valueless and replace-able. Not valueless to all, of course, or else I would not have been able to sell them. I was partial to jewelry because it's small, especially graduation rings, which most people never wear and don't even keep track of. Music was good, too, because I could selectively steal albums and tapes that contained music so bad no one should have purchased it in the first place.

My fences were a colorful and varied bunch: used record stores in the Village, the Strand bookstore, various shady uptown jewelers, and pawnbrokers in all five boroughs with poor eyesight, bad memories, and lousy bookkeeping habits. There were fencing sites that were more friendly than others, and I became fluent in the slang of all the asshole record collectors and rare vinyl traders in the Village, far from my victims' residences. Venus Records on 8th Street was my favorite back then, and it's inconceivable to me that they didn't know that I was selling them stolen goods.

The nadir came on a day when I couldn't score at any of the usual spots in Harlem and I headed back down to the East Village. The guy I found was a Spanish dude I'd never before dealt with. He took my twenty and started down Avenue D. He took some money from some others along his way, talking cordially with them and promising (as he did with me) to be back in fifteen minutes. When I, following, tried to talk to him, he pretended not to know me. Maybe he thought I was a cop, I don't know. What did become clear was that this man was not going to be returning with my dope. I kept following him, pleading (real stupid, I know) with him to just give me back my money, I'm getting sick, etc. The dealer would occasionally pause to turn back and glare at me trailing him by 10 feet, warning me to leave him alone or he was going to "fuck me up."

He only hit me once, but he broke my jaw instantly. I dusted myself off once the guy was a block away—now I really needed my medicine. I got up,

resigned to my loss, and did something I've regretted ever since. I went back to
the squat and burglarized the room of a person who had even less than me and
who had never done anything to hurt me. I had to crawl, lizard-like, along the
outside ledge of the old building (three stories up) in order to gain access. I
found a cigar box with the squat's communal funds in it and took the last $20.

That burglary, and the theft of my girlfriend's ring, were definite bottom
points, as were certain sexual tasks performed for what now seem startlingly
small amounts of money.

*

Harlem changed everything. If Alphabet City was a candy store, then Harlem
was a supermarket. With the plenty came plenty of opportunity, and stealing
class rings was nothing compared to the grand or so in loose cash I stole from
the two guys who came to find me one spring evening after I'd been to their
apartment to fix a broken refrigerator. The victim was himself an ex-junkie
(read: junkie) and had no illusions as to who had stolen from him; he shot me
with a stun gun about a dozen times as his friend held me down. I don't know
whether the gun needed recharging or if it was a crappy unit or if the electricity
was ineffectual because I was so heavily narcotized, but the pain was relatively
mild and fleeting.

I had to leave the neighborhood, and soon, one step ahead of the NYPD,
the state. It was time to get the hell out. I cleaned up at a friend's house in
Chelsea and then headed back to Kentucky. I felt great when it was over, but
I was flat broke, and when some old associates approached me about a small
smuggling job to Jamaica, I eagerly accepted. When I completed the mission,

I was paid, and even though I was clean, the first thing I did was return to Harlem for one last lost weekend. On my way back to Kentucky I was caught by the Federales. It was only at this point that I was finally able to leave the heroin alone. I had to do some time and then start all over again.

*

It is not painless getting shot with a Taser, though; let me restate that. It hurts like hell to be shot with a Taser. It hurts like hell to betray your loved ones and best friends as I did. Even those jazz cats who took me in off the street got robbed. It hurts to lower yourself so far you'd steal from the last few folks on earth who like you. The dope sure does feel good when it's going through you, though. Makes it a lot easier to forget all that other stuff.

It also makes it easy to forget large stretches of a whole life. Junk time is not normal time; it is a stoppage of time that lasts only until the dope runs out and the withdrawal begins. Once that happens, time skids forward, and work and robbery beckon. This schedule also makes chronology difficult. It becomes impossible to remember anything but the withdrawal symptoms as they occurred.

This cycle of pleasure and withdrawal *is* the demon itself, and the chief reason why recovery is nearly impossible. Programs for addicts who want to quit are a joke. When I tried to get on methadone, I was told to come back to Metropolitan Hospital up on First Avenue every morning at 7:00 and if I dropped five consecutive dirty urines I would be put on the waiting list.

"So, you're telling me I need to make sure I get high for the next five days if I want any chance of getting on the program?" I asked the doctor.

"We've got to make sure that you really are an addict."

"And then I get put on a list?"

"Yeah, and the line to actually get into the program stretches around the block."

Thanks, doc. And the cycle continued.

The cycle is very hard to beat. It's like the house odds at a casino.

*

There is very little from this time period of which I can be proud, although the whole experience was indeed terribly instructive. The dope didn't make me a better musician, either. It did instruct me in pain. It is an unfortunately unacknowledged secret (an open secret, in a way) that all the genius junkie musicians were geniuses in spite of their dope habits, not because of them. Contrary to legend, Charlie Parker's best stuff wasn't done when he was high; it was done while he was either in withdrawal or coming out of it. Same thing with Johnny Thunders. Same with Jaco. Same with me. Withdrawal makes you feel strong, like you've just slain a dragon. When you are living as if a character in your own novel—and the glamorous villain of the piece, at that—it is easy to mistakenly believe you are your own hero. These delusions inevitably result in tragedy.

I recall the worst of those times as cold street-corner mornings (usually Sundays, when it was much harder to steal and also harder to score) of relative hopelessness and abject fear of withdrawal. And yet they are kind and pleasant memories. The pain of withdrawal is, after all, a vivid reintroduction to the full world. Those cold, junk-sick mornings in Alphabet City and East Harlem, crying, crying in the gray rain, begging me to get my white ass back out on the street and hustle, scratch up some money or back a few bags or get to work, but for Christ's sake do something . . . those mornings when every tree was bare even if the air was warm . . . those sickly mornings of rain and grinding noise held a terrible, immutable, exacting beauty that I cannot accurately describe. It was something close to the pain of pure desire. William Blake said that the road to the Palace of Wisdom was paved with excess. I can safely say that that same road leads to many other places as well. It was all so miserable and degrading and guilt-inducing and I've yet to understand it, but somehow I miss it very much.

From Stonewall to Ground Zero

Robert Atkins

Gay culture and I came of age together during the '70s, hard on the heels of the Stonewall Rebellion. I was only a teenager on June 27, 1969, when Greenwich Village erupted in the first of several nights of anti-fag-bashing violence that not only threw butch mounted cops on the defensive but, in some cases, made them fear for their lives. It is said that this improbable event was triggered by the emotion-stirring funeral of Judy Garland, held earlier that day at Frank Campbell's Upper East Side mortuary, but it was also, of course, a response to years of smoldering resentment at police homophobia. Like the Stonewall riots, I was slow to ripen—it took me another five years and a move to San Francisco before I came out—but once out, I *slammed* the closet door shut. Nothing's been the same for me, or New York, since those riotous nights in 1969.

By the late '70s, the gaying of America was unmistakable, even well advanced in university towns and large cities on both coasts. Municipal ordinances prohibiting discrimination on the basis of sexual orientation vis-à-vis hiring or housing began to be passed almost immediately after Stonewall, while laws creating the statutory designation of *domestic partnership*, designed to grant basic rights to same-sex (and other unmarried) partners, began to be enacted into law two decades or so later. Of course these benefits, then as now, were not evenly distributed across the land. Nor was New York anywhere near the forefront of progressive political change in such matters due both to city council recalcitrance and to Albany's antiquated, patronage-ridden politics. But no matter. New York *was* the gay capital of the US. Things happened here.

One such emblematic happening was the 1979 investigation of President Jimmy Carter's chief of staff and campaign director Hamilton Jordan for allegedly snorting cocaine on the dance floor of Studio 54 the previous year. Although it isn't easy to imagine the staid-seeming First Family hanging out with Bianca and Andy, or Liza and Halston in the VIP room—much less dabbling in blow—it was gratifying to learn that Ham Jordan, the President's right-hand man, might be so in touch, so normal, so . . . well, gay.

253

But then, wasn't everybody who mattered? From discos to fitness clubs, from designer jeans to designer drugs, gay style and sensibility ruled. Homosexuality was transformed, in the words of many pundits, from the love that dare not speak its name to the love that wouldn't shut up. The more consequential products of contemporary gay culture, such as the Beat-era poetry of Allen Ginsberg and the Pop-art films of Andy Warhol, carried on a previously underground tradition of sexual liberation and libertinism. By the time of Stonewall, Puritanism, for once in America, seemed on the retreat.

A visit to Studio 54 or to the Continental Baths, where non-gay *chanteuse*/gay icon Bette Midler performed poolside, more or less placed gay life within the reach of hetero America. To dismiss these visits by the non-gay as mere voyeurism or cultural tourism is to grossly oversimplify. I'm reminded of several generations of white New Yorkers, between the world wars, motoring up to Harlem to eat and drink, listen to jazz or attend rent parties, and/or—not incidentally—meet a sweet and sexy somebody. Surely such personal encounters helped to chip away at the seemingly insurmountable barriers of race and class that separated everyone.

The cultural experimentation reflected in these experiences, in Stonewall, and by the general climate of sexual liberation helped soften once-rigid standards of behavior and thinking across America. Surprisingly transgressive non-gay movies of the era such as *Bob & Carole & Ted & Alice* (1969) and *Shampoo* (1975) suggest how far the center had shifted. They casually took as their points of departure the idea of marital fidelity as anachronistic and undesirable—a condition, like psoriasis, to be overcome. More mind-bending, in the parlance of the day, was the awarding of 1969's Best Picture Oscar to *Midnight Cowboy*, a genuinely iconoclastic film about an unsophisticated, sexually ambiguous hustler adrift in Sin City.

*

Unlike many gay Americans from the South, Midwest, or any small town or rural enclave, I came to New York not for homo-culture, gay companionship, or sexual opportunity but for their opposites: I came both to settle down with my sweetie and to focus on my career. I'd had a long-distance lover in Morningside Heights, near Columbia University, for two years, and in San Francisco I'd already, in my late twenties, brushed up against journalism's glass ceiling by writing for the *San Francisco Chronicle*, the city's main daily. The twin rationales were conjoined: as I joked at the time to my lover Steven W. and others, if I'd fallen in love in Detroit, that relationship would have been sacrificed to my career ambitions elsewhere.

I'd visited New York frequently during the late '70s. An art historian by training, I was entranced by the offerings of galleries and museums, their abundance and diversity; and the respect in which the arts were generally held. I wasn't used to a place where the announcement that one was a writer or artist garnered respectful interest rather than barely concealed disdain, even at Park Avenue dinner tables. This was a shock given that so much of my identity was bound up in a sense of myself as marginalized and alternative. I simultaneously came out and attended graduate school; both gaydom and the arts substituted for the more conventional politics in which I'd previously participated, beginning with the end of the anti-war movement during the early '70s.

Being from chilly San Francisco, I found New York's gay sex scene appealing primarily for the novelty of outdoor sex to be had in Central or Riverside Parks, on Fire Island, or on the piers or trucks of the Village and Meatpacking Districts. Otherwise, by the end of the '70s, gay bars everywhere seemed pretty much the same. Your choice was either the gritty, smoke-stained paneling and pool table of the levis-'n'-leather bars decorated with posters of the Marlboro Man and mustachioed guys who wanted to look like him ("clones" was the epithet of the day), or the more genteel and well-upholstered "fern" bars, where these droopy vegetal signs of post-war America hung over grand pianos surrounded by Broadway show-tune-belting homos who might, after Happy Hour, patronize the attached restaurant or available rent boys. (Ty's on Christopher Street and the Townhouse on East 58th Street, were—and remain—the prototypical levis-'n'-leather and fern bars, respectively.)

Hipper bars more suited to men in their twenties and thirties—the hippest of all had no name—sprang up in the East Village during the second half of the '80s, just as a burgeoning gallery and performance-art-in-bars scene arose just to the east in Alphabet City. By the turn of the twenty-first century there was

little energy remaining in gay bars outside of Queens' Hispanic dance bars; for pick-ups, the internet was a far more efficient way to play.

I was less interested in bars with their overpriced drinks and posing beer drinkers than in back rooms and sex clubs. I sampled many of them. The Anvil, a Meatpacking District landmark, was the kinkiest and hence my favorite. Public gay sex changed more during the first Giuliani administration, starting in 1992, than it had in the previous twenty years. Just as he had a problem with the First Amendment—Giuliani lost more than two dozen free-speech cases—Hizzoner seemed to have something against nightlife. His henchmen quickly shuttered numerous bars (gay and straight), dance venues, and gay sex clubs.

Under pressure, the homo body politic mutated. Suddenly, budding entrepreneurs began to host invitational pay-to-play parties at their lofts or apartments, or at rented spaces throughout Manhattan and Brooklyn. Today's gay visitor to the city might wonder why there aren't more available public-sex options. Few sex clubs reopened in an ever-gentrifying Manhattan, making gay life, in this regard, yet another casualty of the eradication of public space that characterized the end of the twentieth century in the US.

Having lived 3,000 miles apart for a couple of years, my lover Steven and I never pledged monogamy, nor did we quite believe in it. What was the point? We were savvy enough to know that what you think doesn't necessarily govern how you feel, but we knew that at heart we were liberationists and crafted a relatively unrestricted "contract." For twenty years, our only prohibited activities were—when the other was in town—sleeping elsewhere and entertaining at home.

*

I moved to New York on June 17, 1982, just a month before AIDS was officially dubbed AIDS at a meeting of scientists in Washington, DC. By that time, nearly 450 cases in 23 states had been reported to the Centers for Disease Control, and gay men in New York and California had founded three organizations to combat the threat—New York's Gay Men's Health Crisis opened during the first week of 1982. The unofficial but most widely used name for the disease at that time was GRID, or Gay-Related Immune Deficiency. (AIDS is technically not a disease but a virus-induced syndrome that weakens the immune system, allowing various diseases to overcome the body's defenses.) Among many gay men and others, the syndrome was known simply as the Gay Cancer.

No matter who called it what, the typical response was panic, especially after it was reported in July that hetero hemophiliacs and Haitians were among the afflicted. Until then, the media had tried to reassure jittery audiences that "we"—non-intravenous-drug users and heterosexuals—were safe from this plague. Denial and panic coexisted as the occurrence of AIDS among non-gays mushroomed, partly as a consequence of the homophobia that kept effective prevention information from reaching those in need of it.

The level of anxiety many Americans, and most American gay men, felt about the transmission of AIDS is difficult to imagine if you didn't experience it. Young men were dying—often within a few weeks of diagnosis—of pneumococcus pneumonia or Kaposi's Sarcoma, a rare and hideously scarring cancer previously found among elderly men. With their visible KS lesions and emaciated frames, AIDS patients were frequently treated as pariahs and outcasts, even by medical personnel who, over time, surely knew better. Many Lower East Side neighborhoods, with their large populations of intravenous drug users and gay men, felt like war zones during Carnival week; even a stroll to the supermarket could be stressful, depending on what—or who—you saw. The trick was to keep your eyes from lingering too long on the ravaged face of an HIV sufferer in order to avoid alarming you both.

This horror was compounded by fears of non-medical consequences conceived by Christian fundamentalists and other right-wingers determined to regain the political offensive and take back rights won by gays over the previous decade. No proposal, no matter how bizarre, was off-limits: be it editor/talk-show host William F. Buckley's plan to tattoo the buttocks of the HIV-positive; or the constant drumbeat for incarceration-like quarantine, an approach taken up by Cuba and China.

Although cooler, medically qualified heads tended to prevail in the formulation of AIDS policy in Albany and City Hall, such policy—and funding for it—mostly emanated from Washington. The gargantuan scale of Congress's and the Executive's task—the provision of housing, health care, and drugs—required superhuman responses from politicians who were anything but. The window of opportunity for gaining the upper hand over the HIV virus was lost as AIDS was transformed from a matter of public health into one of private morality. In the words of Dr Mathilde Krim, the Manhattan physician and founder of AMFAR (American Foundation for AIDS Research), uttered nearly twenty years ago, "Each step in the escalation of the AIDS crisis was predictable and could have been countered."

*

It is difficult to imagine another medical condition with such a far-reaching impact on non-medical matters as AIDS. For gay men (and lesbians) it has directly affected, or indirectly inflected, almost every aspect of daily life, starting with sex.

By 1985, AIDS-era sex had evolved into something appreciably different from sex of the '70s, different not only in the ways "hook-ups" were initiated and carried out, given that one or both players might be positive, but different even in the act of orgasm itself. Climaxing began to resemble nothing so much as pornography's iconic "money shot," the climactic moment when the male porn star—homo or hetero—pulls out of his co-star's mouth, anus, or vagina, and shoots, perhaps on his partner's face or torso. Instead of wet and explosive events taking place inside, gay men began to ejaculate on, rather than in, their partners. ("On me, not in me" became a mantra of safer sex.) Such visible and theatrical orgasms proved well-suited not only to film and video but to group sex play as well.

Dating, of course, was a source of high anxiety when so little was known about the causes and spread of the HIV virus—but then so was shaking hands, hugging, or greeting a friend with kisses on both cheeks. Gay men evolved elaborate strategies for determining if their dates might be HIV-infected. The most surreptitious one I was aware of involved the examination—through both touch and sight—of lymph nodes located on the upper neck, beneath the jaws and above the Adam's apple. Swelling signaled an immune system at work and the possibility of HIV infection.

When it came time to say good-night to a date, the seemingly clear guidelines for safer sex proved not so transparent after all. (This probably should have been inferred from the letter 'r' appended to *safe*.) Was kissing safe? It seemed so. Cock-sucking, on the other hand, was difficult to classify, its potential for danger rising or falling on the basis of numerous studies that failed to yield definitive answers. Unprotected oral sex, however, was known to be *safer* than unprotected anal sex, which consistently ranked at the top of this new hierarchy of dangers.

The biggest fear, however, was the knowledge that one's own body offered the greatest possibility for betrayal, making testing the scariest proposition of all. But why get tested when the single antiretroviral drug in use, AZT (which was finally approved by the FDA in 1987), was found to be toxic by so many? Or when a positive test result might mean the loss of a job and its accompanying health-care insurance? Why suffer the anxiety inevitable during the week-long period between being tested and learning the results? Or, in the case of those testing positive, during the probably limited duration of one's remaining, abbreviated life span?

Steven and I were tested for the first time in 1987, just prior to traveling to Spain. The negative results followed nearly five years of periodic funerals and nervous announcement of friends' positive tests. They were causes for both celebration and for a renewal of our safer-sex vows, which periodically, I'm afraid, had, in practice, lapsed.

Throughout the '80s and early '90s, AIDS also colored virtually every gay community event and activity. They included those, like the annual Gay Pride Parade, which had, since Stonewall, become time-honored affairs—in this case drawing hundreds of thousands of viewers to Greenwich Village each June—as well as one-time events. Of the latter, my favorite was the 1989 opening of the remarkable "Center Show," a commemoration of the twentieth anniversary of the Stonewall Rebellion at the Lesbian and Gay Community Services Center, which was housed in the sprawling nineteenth-century former Food and Maritime Trades High School complex at 208 West 13th Street.

In print, I concluded my paean of praise to the exhibition with a description of Tommie Lanigan-Schmidt's installation—he had been the only professional artist actually present at Stonewall—characterizing it as "a brilliant marriage of the personal and the political that gives meaning to the Latin entreaty 'Sursum Corda!' he's inscribed on the wall. It means 'lift up your hearts.' His deeply felt work helps get it up." His was a welcome message in light of the

emotional burn-out so many of us were suffering after too many years offering only the alternatives of utter despair and unbounded exhilaration.

*

I attended many public memorials and funerals during those years. In 1993, while researching a piece about AIDS and the media, I felt compelled to attend a service for Jeffrey Schmaltz, the New York *Times* reporter who'd died of AIDS and been eulogized by Bill Clinton for his coverage of the epidemic. It was an occasion for acutely mixed feelings. I disdained Schmaltz's closeted ways. Here was a reporter my own age who'd come out as a gay man with AIDS only after passing out in the newsroom of a paper notorious for its lack of investigative reporting about the epidemic. Might it have been Schmaltz's circumspection and lies of omission that made him the perfect *Times*man and accounted for the regard in which he was held by his colleagues? And which speaker at this memorial was more deceived: Columnist Anna "we-are-all-family" Quindlen, or activist-psychopath Larry "AIDS-is-intentional-genocide" Kramer?

After the death of the artist Keith Haring in the spring of 1990, an elaborate spectacle was staged in the Cathedral of St John the Divine, the world's largest Gothic-style church and a famously progressive institution. On the afternoon of May 4, an audience of several thousand mourners gathered for a program that began with the comments of Mayor David Dinkins and concluded with an aria sung by Jessye Norman. (Madonna, who'd performed at several of Keith's casually fabulous birthday parties, would have better reflected his musical taste.) In between, art dealers prattled and pontificated, and New York City Ballet dancers Heather Watts and Jock Soto performed.

Steven and I carried on, like people in wartime, despite the burden of accumulating grief. In fact, we thrived. We were HIV-negative; our careers were going well; we both wrote regularly for *New York Newsday*, a new daily paper published by Times-Mirror. Outlets for our political needs—at least that's the way I thought about them—were available and varied, too. Between 1987 and 1994, mammoth civil-rights marches and demos were staged nearly every year in Washington and New York. At the earliest of these, in October 1987, my life changed: I witnessed the breathtaking national debut of the NAMES Project Quilt (aka "The Quilt") and wrote about it for the *Village Voice*. After my article was published, I was asked by the *Voice*'s art editor, Jeff Weinstein, to write a regular column for that venerable downtown rag about precisely what interested me most: the conjunction of art and politics. I'd hit the jackpot! I imagined, well . . . *wholeness*—the possibility of integrating the previously separate parts of my life.

⋆

About six months earlier, ACT UP, the legendary direct-action group, had burst into being. On March 24, the group staged its first demonstration, a Wall Street action designed to protest pharmaceutical-company profiteering, which elevated the cost of a year's prescription of AZT to $10,000. The group's raisons d'être were cheap drugs and better access to them, and these demands would, along with pleas for more effective AIDS education and the eradication of AIDS-related discrimination, remain the group's core objectives.

ACT UP's art-for-the-streets performed several functions. It provided an informational context for the group's demands, often by giving visual form to the disturbing statistics emanating from the Centers for Disease Control. One wheat-pasted broadside, for instance, offered the alarming news that one in sixty-one babies born in New York was HIV-positive. The group's work also juxtaposed shockingly sexual images and irresistible humor in the service of safer-sex information. One agit-prop poster coupled a photo of an enormous, erect cock with the admonition to men to "Use Condoms or Beat It."

In the late spring of 1991, *The Red Ribbon*, a public artwork created by the artists' caucus of Visual AIDS (a group I helped found in 1989), made its television debut on the Tony Awards show. Intended to symbolize support for people with AIDS and to subvert the gooey jingoism of Gulf-War yellow ribbons, this was the first of numerous televised appearances for the *Red Ribbon* at concerts, awards shows, and sporting events throughout the world. The *Red Ribbon*, like

"The Quilt", empowered thousands to talk about AIDS, which remained, even fifteen years after the discovery of the HIV virus, a subject widely and inhumanely regarded as shameful.

*

If the Bush administration (1988–91) marked the high point of queer/AIDS activism, the beginning of the Clinton era in 1992 signaled its demise. There were several reasons for this. Bill Clinton's promises to expand health-care coverage and create a gay-inclusive military turned out to be (false) pledges the inexperienced President was unable to fulfill. Because queers had played such a central role in Clinton's election (especially deep-pocketed New York queers), we were understandably reluctant to part company with him, especially given the lack of alternatives.

In mid-decade, near-miraculous scientific advances—miraculous relative to those of the previous decade—began to provide longer lives and more robust health for people with AIDS. The so-called AIDS "cocktail," or combination therapy, also helped fuel the emerging controversy about the long-standing designation of the condition as an *emergency*. Surely an emergency couldn't last forever, especially in the face of mounting evidence that new treatment options meant dramatically lengthened lives, at least for people who could afford treatment. This "normalization" also implied a day when HIV disease would join medical conditions such as breast cancer and the perhaps even more virulent Hepatitis C under the "normal" rubric.

The '90s also brought back the good old days in the luxurious form of intra-gay-faction squabbling. The issue was nomenclature: Should *queer* replace *gay/lesbian* as our descriptor of choice? The younger generation favored the once-derogatory, now-recuperated *queer*, while the '60s liberationists tended to prefer *gay*. But the distinction ran deeper. Unlike the typical minority-group argument about linguistic signifiers, this one actually altered and enlarged the population pool in question rather than just renaming it. Embracing groups even more marginal than gays, such as transsexuals, redefined inclusion in the homo camp from a matter of sexual preference to the broader and ultimately far more complex matter of *sexual difference*.

This revolutionary shift resonated with many, but hardly all, elements of the community. It was engineered largely by Queer Nation, a group founded in 1990. Queer Nation's outrageous antics and tactics ranged from its distribution of an eye-popping broadsheet attacking straights at the 1990 Gay Pride Parade and its coinage of the now-familiar battle cry "We're here, We're queer, Get used to it!," to organizing angry demos to call attention to rising rates of anti-gay violence and bemused *Kiss Ins* at Long Island shopping malls in order to claim "queer space." The group's advocacy of outing—the practice of revealing the sexual identity of closeted gay and lesbian public figures who supported or

initiated homophobic policies for personal gain—was especially controversial. Queer Nation's successes, however, are undeniable, as is evident not only from university queer-studies curricula but from the location of the group's founding meeting: the now-renamed Lesbian Gay Bisexual Transgender Center on West 13th Street.

*

After nearly twenty years of live-in satisfaction with Steven, our relationship was in a holding pattern. Professional success, global travel, and sometimes extravagant dinner parties made us an ideal couple in the eyes of many friends. And so we may have been, although it didn't seem to matter much then. Near the end of it, our relationship had settled into a largely amiable, but increasingly distant, set of routines. We had come to know one another so well that middle age prompted us to wonder if this was all there was. And if there *were* more, wouldn't moving on be easier now than later? In addition, Manhattan's metamorphosis from museum capital into museum-of-itself made me restless for California with its more accessible light and air, and its longer vistas, which corresponded with the perspective I craved on my own life. I knew, however, that Steven would sooner lose a leg than leave New York.

A year after the new century dawned, the possibility of separating was raised and, in retrospect, seemed to indicate a fait accompli. But, as with so many other social arrangements in New York, it was 9/11 that precipitated the undoing of our relationship and my departure.

To term 9/11 *indescribable* is simply to acknowledge the pain it causes to describe it, which I do not intend to do. My private 9/11 began with a call the

following day, a Tuesday, from Dr G., our family physician. After confirming that we were alright, he asked me to visit his office that Friday to discuss some recent test results. I knew something was wrong since he always conveyed good news over the phone. Was it prostate cancer? Hepatitis C? HIV?

It turned out to be HIV, and, given my current relative good health, I tend to agree with Dr G. that HIV was the least troublesome, most treatable of the three diseases I'd feared.

My departure from New York on October 13, 2002 was a cause for intense introspection. When I'd arrived two decades earlier, the legendarily hedonistic post-Stonewall era was winding down, and AIDS was about to rear its ugly head. New York, like so many places, would be rendered yet another American tragedy. I made and buried friends; I now saluted others still living. I was humbled by both the psychic toll exacted by this veil of tears and fortified by the human capacity for survival and my own need to move on. I'd arrived twenty years earlier a young gay man in love, and I departed a middle-aged queer man, alone, although not really lonely. I left from JFK both relieved and heartsick, carrying few material possessions but bearing a treasure trove of memories. I'd miss the adrenalin-fueled pace and brainy ambition of the place, its exasperating hard edges and unexpected kindnesses, sometimes meted out by strangers, who like me, hailed from elsewhere. I sensed that I'd be back, realizing that in some ways New York *is* America, at its exultant best and annoying worst: Ever ungainly and unrefined, maddeningly fragmented and stubbornly ignorant of its own best interests, big-hearted and large-spirited, and—oh my, yes!—queer to the max.

Sex Before Dot.com

Kate Schmitz

New York has a reputation for being a land of sexual excess, and it was once. It still makes people think of things like Times Square, prostitution, and the Mafia underworld, but these have become somehow tame. Before Tompkins Square was rid of its homeless, and before the aesthetic changed from thrift store to pseudo thrift store, the big tourist attractions played second fiddle to used condoms and peep shows. People came to score dope as much as they came to see the Statue of Liberty. Hooker hotels like St Marks and a bunch of places way uptown housed those who lived day to day by thievery or peddling sex. People with no money could enjoy the all-window corner view at Disco Donut, elbow to elbow with the prostitutes who hung out there. On the 4th of July or Chinese New Year, the entire lower part of Manhattan was a firework-wrapper ticker-tape parade. Times Square was still alive, and neighborhood strip clubs like Billy's Topless were on corners all over the city. The city wasn't prettified, and mainstream corporate American consciousness hadn't spread to its outskirts. NYU hadn't knocked down The Palladium, Julian's pool hall and Carmela's to make more dorms. The city as a whole embodied naked, unrestrained, unapologetic, and not-ever-airbrushed sex in all of its textures— dark, unknowable, fecund, smelly, and viscous.

*

When I was about three, I had recurring nightmares in which King Friday would come up between the wall and my bed. We lived in Staten Island at the time but had to move when our neighbor was shot taking out the trash. The nightmare was the existence of King Friday. Who was he? Was he real? How did he have so much power? Like many New Yorkers, I was raised on mythology, fairy tales, and television. I anticipated and feared Saturday, when I'd get to go to the McDonalds on the corner of Broadway and 71st Street only after being subjected to mystery and aliens on *Star Trek* and *Space 1999*. Life in NYC was spooky and odd, especially to a hormonal pre-teen. The essence of my King

Friday fear lurked in Donna Summers' moaning, the strange sound of the song "Miss You" by the Rolling Stones, and ads for sex movies in the newspaper right next to Benji's smiling face. I watched as people, including my father, walked nonchalantly by marquees in Times Square advertising things that were private, sinful, and terrifying, and I didn't understand a thing. Men touched me as they walked by, a twelve-year-old painted into Sassoons, and it was as inexplicable as Brooke Shields' relationship with her Calvins.

I wore ripped fishnets and patent leather, lace-up, pointy-toed, stiletto-heeled boots from Trash and Vaudeville from the time I was fifteen—this is when I was living on the Upper West Side with my father. I routinely wore a platinum-blonde wig, on the gray side from when I tried to dye it black, because my father preferred it to my black dread locks. I'd never had sex. Insecurity made me pretend that I knew everything about everything (which never afforded me the opportunity to learn Anything). I was so afraid of anyone discovering I hadn't had sex that I wouldn't have sex, because it might give my secret away. I once told a guy named Arnoud that I couldn't have sex with him because I'd thrown my diaphragm away after my last, terrible boyfriend. I was seventeen at the time, and he, being French, believed me. By the age of seventeen, the French probably are old pros when it comes to sex. I lied and lied to cover all I didn't know, and I longed to be a stripper. I was ready for anything, in fact, the filthier the better, just to rid me of my naiveté and virginity.

In the early '80s, long, long (in my mind) before anyone else knew of it, MTV came out and cemented my belief, born of fairy tales and TV shows, that my life would inevitably be glamorous. And it was. I saw Woody Allen on the street on a regular basis. I walked on the same sidewalks and ate at the same restaurants and had my roots dyed and sat on the same park benches as the cool and famous did when they were slumming it. I realized that, in New York, there was so much possibility. It wasn't about finding oneself, it was about choosing, so I jumped around, looking. I never got comfortable with one job, one scene, one drug, or one relationship. My priority was to be at the right party with enough cigarettes and drugs. Beyond that, I sat back, waited to be discovered, earned money when I needed to. My friends were musicians and artists, and they were struggling toward recognition. I was a painter, and I worked in my studio (back then, fledgling painters could afford studios—mine was on Mercer between Prince and Spring), but being discovered was more important to me than my paintings, and I was more likely to be discovered out of my studio than in it.

I didn't realize how suspect my thinking was at the time . . . and how could anyone as drug- and alcohol-addled as I was be expected to?

*

I associated energy, dark violence, sex, and glamour with New York, and music embodied it all. There were many inexpensive places to live, and the poor and the people who wanted to be outside mainstream society lived there. Fourteen-year-old boys with terrifying faces lived next door to hapless musicians squatting for political reasons or because they were too strung out to hold down jobs. Occasionally someone visited by car, which in retrospect I see was a smart thing to do in order to avoid being beat up on the street for no reason (as happened to Laurie and Jennifer in Williamsburg at Metropolitan and Berry—smote for being a girl couple), or mugged and robbed on the G train (on the way to Bed-Stuy), or caught on a sidewalk moving with a million fist-sized water bugs (at East 11th Street, crack central). Of course, it's likely the car would be gone the next day, or torched, but at least the trip would have been more pleasant.

Someone would offer you drugs on every block—sometimes while minding their children ("sens, sens, sens—JIMMY GET OUT OF THE STREET!—sens, sens . . ."), or not minding their children, one of which was a five-year-old girl, always dressed in ruffled dresses, who skipped around singing, "Come and fuck me, I'm so pretty" next to my friend's doorway on 2nd Street and Avenue C. The primary colors of crack vial tops decorated the sidewalks, people talked about so-and-so getting caught in cross fire (which you heard routinely), and people looked mean. One way to live in a neighborhood like this was to dress in clothes that made it clear that you had no money and no prospects. I had remote control ready for surprise attacks no matter how crusty or saturated with chemicals my mind was, and by the time I was in my early twenties, I learned to hide girl features behind baggy clothes, never wear make-up, or groom.

I would go to gay bars like The Boiler Room on Second Avenue, where there were amphetamines and gay people, and no law or inhibition. No one seemed to care about the LES, and we had it to ourselves. Even when, in the mid-'80s, AIDS banged into the scene, it just added to the atmosphere of danger. People were either gay or sharing needles or both, and although a few pre-cautions became more or less ubiquitous, none of the behavior changed in any real way. If one of my gay friends was a little late to meet me, it would be understood that he'd passed a cute stranger on the street and ducked into a dark corner. Along with the crime and rodents there came a direct energy that was like a drug. I used to get an adrenalin rush just by making it home safely to my apartment from the subway. At its best, the dark outskirts of NYC back then had the camaraderie found among small enclaves of ex-patriots in foreign cities. There was even a bar called Beirut.

Anger, however, was the real zeitgeist in the New York I knew, and it was expressed in all the crime, music, and sex that was going on. People didn't only dress to make it clear that they didn't care what others thought; they behaved on a daily basis in a way that made it clear. Richard Kern's films were screened

behind bands and featured things like Kembra Pfahler of the band The Voluptuous Horror of Karen Black getting her pussy sewn up. According to Kern, it was "a badge of honor" for girls to come by his apartment unannounced and masturbate for him. If you found girls on stage it wasn't a love-and-hippies thing—they'd be painted blue or green, and they looked poisonous and mean.

The girl band Thrust performed their un-pretty horn-blowing cacophony naked, rolling around on filthy stages for once not dominated by men. It was clear expression—art in its pure state, unfettered by art-world demands. These weren't Vanessa Beecroft's high-heeled models, no more shocking in their nudity than Bloomingdale's mannequins. People shot up on the street. They ransacked cars (especially if their owners had had the audacity to install the super-sensitive new car alarms that arrived on the scene sometime in the early '80s), and on the Williamsburg Bridge they pushed you off your bike and sold it to someone just like you a mile away on St Marks Place. "*DIE YUPPY SCUM*" was everywhere, as was the upside-down, cocktail-glass graffiti of the anarchist band Missing Foundation.

The worse it got on the streets, the tougher the music became. It was the one thing that all the subcultures had in common. The music venues were a lawless free-for-all. On stage, people would be getting blow jobs or threatening to kill you or throwing brains and goat legs at you, in a non-ironic way, if you can imagine that. Everyone was angry, and music was a way for performers and audiences to express it. When you left, you'd be bruised and you would know you had bruised. Being kicked in the head by a mounted policeman or the sudden wham of a goat leg on your shin felt good; it was the only thing as strong as the music, hate, fear, and hormone-driven frenzy coursing uncontrollably through you.

*

My drug- and youth-fed lack of inhibition allowed me to drive stolen cars through red lights and across the Williamsburg Bridge thinking I was playing a video game, score crack outside the front door, throw a burning couch out our window, and, on a separate occasion, light the kitchen table on fire and watch it burn. We'd put back as much liquor as possible. A handle bottle of Duggan's Dew would just about hold me and my boyfriend. If anyone else came by, we'd have to scrounge up more alcohol. Wherever we were, we'd stay until all the alcohol was gone. Leaving an open bottle around was inconceivable. A liquor cabinet was an impossible dream—anything you bought to stock it with would be gone that night. Drinking, as you know, leads to the stupidest fights. My boyfriend and I fought on the street and in the subways like two animals or two stupid, fucked-up white kids, but it was all in good fun. I can't imagine anyone more obnoxious and stupid than we were. This culminated in a long story involving drugs, me nearly going blind, and my landlord from San Francisco throwing away all of my art work and my patent-leather stiletto-heeled boots, among other things.

After a year of unrepentant craziness, I moved from Williamsburg to Bed-Stuy. I shared the bottom of a brownstone next to a church with three boys from Queens, two of whom I dated. The other one I remember as a blur of rotating potheads (being a fan of amphetamines made it difficult for me to enjoy the company of potheads at that time). As far as I knew, the white interlopers didn't hang out with the black residents of the neighborhood. Pratt University wasn't far away, and there were little enclaves of white college-aged people and the bars they went to. It was a little like a war zone, and the different segments of the population did not mix. Necessities (i.e. cigarettes, booze, and Chinese food) were purchased from behind scratched, graffiti-covered, bulletproof glass. Run-ins on the streets and subway were often tense.

I got a job at The Palladium. It was in the late '80s, when hip-hop was huge and every one of its enthusiasts seemed to have a gun. I ended up taking tickets and fielding death threats at the front door in the hot summer of '89 when *Do the Right Thing* came out and people were in the mood to kill. After work we had to wait until the gunfire ceased to leave; it all ended with one injury and one fatality—John, the head of security, shot at the front door. Initially I'd worked in the ladies' room selling stuff. I think my actual role was to keep it from becoming a total sex-and-drugs kismet. I was too busy making six times the money I'd end

up making at the front door by selling various (legal) items like hairspray and condoms to care.

   After work I'd leave and take the subway home to Bed-Stuy between 4:00 and 5:00 in the morning, my green cookie tin with little red reindeer full of around $500 in singles and fives stuffed in my bag. Taking a cab never occurred to me, although those were violent times. A girl coming from her waitressing job at the South Street Seaport was killed for $27 on my doorstep that summer, and it didn't occur to me to change my habits. Instead I'd take the A to the G. It was a gruesome, long haul. They were the two worst lines in the system. I'd get home an hour or more later and do drugs and drink like crazy until it was time to go to work again. One night/morning I came home to find the entire backyard on fire. There was a deck off the kitchen window so I grabbed the dirty dishes that no one but me ever washed and whipped them through the fire so they shattered against the back wall. It was memorably cathartic. Then I moved back to Williamsburg, where I've lived ever since.

*

The new generation of white kids started living in Williamsburg in the mid-to-late '80s before the inlaid sidewalks and new trees. It was the best place in all of the five boroughs, according to me. Low buildings, sea gulls, wide streets, no traffic—just a sleepy town with beautiful sunsets and river breezes. And drug/turf wars, rampant prostitution, a strip club (on North 9th and Bedford), and packs of wild dogs. Williamsburg was covered with basic, old-man bars and memorable places like The Williamsburg Tavern and The Ship's Mast, which featured free hotdogs and movies. Nanette's on Grand Street was the best. Soon, enterprising early hipsters started opening places like The Bog and some place on Metropolitan which I hated going to because they only had wine and beer. That was in the Mafia-controlled Italian neighborhood, where you could only get beer at one deli that closed early. I don't think you could find alcohol outside social clubs in that neighborhood until the mid-'90s. On the south side there were underground clubs like Keep Refrigerated and other loft parties—the ones in the Gretsch Building were notable because of the spectacular view. All the new white people loved these underground clubs. There was a real feeling of living outside society, of being able to get by on a shoe string and not work for the man. Not working too much gave people time for indolence and heroin.

Heroin was an entire way of life (or death), like a career choice for some and a fun, dangerous game for others. Urban kids got their adolescent adrenalin rushes off danger on the street. Procuring the drugs was half the fun. Sneaking in doorways in Latino neighborhoods where I wished I could belong, braving genuinely strange things, sometimes inexplicable things, and not really taking note all the way because you were fixated on your mission and the butterflies that came with it. I'd walk through abandoned buildings where the Stations of the Cross had been set up or where people were having sex, creeping by headless animals, half-humans doing all kinds of drugs, used condoms, used tampons, discarded panties, *Naked Lunch*-sized cockroaches. Everything was spooky and out of proportion in the same mysterious way King Friday had once been. We were living in a counter-culture world where music, sex, and drugs were the law that differentiated us from materialism and conservatism, which seemed hypocritical and far more ugly than our dirty lives.

*

That was *circa* 1990, which seems as remote as 1890 now. The city has changed so much in the past sixteen years that it may as well have gone from coal heat, farmland, and horse-drawn carriages to the insane traffic nightmare it now is. The Bowery is home to luxury lofts. How long, for example, did the Bowery bum exist for the street's name to have become synonymous with bummery?— and now there are million-dollar black-granite-countertop closets there. Actually, The Bowery is a great example of how the disenfranchised held together before the dotcom, mall era of New York. The winos and smelly vagrants of the Sunshine Hotel mingled nicely with punk rockers at CBGB's Sunday matinees. Everyone was just hanging out, beer in hand. The city seemed open, free, and full of possibility.

In the spring of 2005 I saw the legendary band Chain Gang—the same

Chain Gang who spent the summer of 1977 trying to catch Son of Sam in order to get the reward money—at CB's. They were amazing and scratched an itch I thought I'd have to live with the rest of my life. As the band started its second song, however, a silver-haired suburban guy in his fifties packed up his teenage daughter and her friends from the stage-side table they'd been seated at and strolled out.

Perhaps that was the appropriate reaction in a city whose façades have been cleaned up beyond recognition. The seedy, intimidating Times Square that once perplexed me is a brilliant, colorful tourist attraction with popular musicals, chain stores, and theme restaurants. Sex is still alive, of course, but its public face has been tamed. Other parts of the city have followed suit and embraced conformity as though all of New York were a giant shopping mall. It's a far cry from places like Rose is Vintage, Alice Underground, and Domsey's—cheap stores where water bugs would fall out of the sleeve of a coat as you tried it on. Finding the right leather jacket was once difficult—now it's just expensive.

I remember walking down 9th Street near the corner of Fifth Avenue twenty years ago, listening to my friend's apocalyptic prediction that the city would one day be divided between the poverty-stricken and the rich with no middle class. The other day a one-eyed, local, limping Latino man on the street

in Williamsburg, who would have once put me on guard, complained to me about the new $750,000 condos he's a caretaker for. The two buildings he owns, in the South Bronx, were only around $350G each.

The rest of America's conception is that in New York everywhere you turn there's a compatible mate. Here you'll find the money-, culture-, and glamour-conscious of the world elbow to elbow with the bridge-and-tunnel-ers who comprise the singles scene, and it's true, if you like getting wasted enough to be one of the last at the bar you probably won't have to go home alone. In general, however, for longer-lasting love, you have to have to fit your beloved's criteria—job, wardrobe, apartment, car, family, piercings, musical taste, educational background. It's all advertised as available here, and people won't settle for less. They posture and lie to the point that they can get anyone they want, but no one is good enough for them.

A friend confided, without irony, that although she appears happily married to a great guy, her fatal mistake was to marry for love. This woman felt she was living like a peasant because she didn't live in Tribeca and her stairwell was shabby. Her husband is high every single time I see him.

An Incomplete History of New York Galleries

John Yau

Any history of the New York gallery scene will be incomplete. For a while, in the early 1980s, Jean-Noel Herlin, a book dealer and lover of art, had a small store on Thompson Street, just a block away from West Broadway, SoHo's main thoroughfare. One of his projects was to collect every announcement of every exhibition that had happened in New York since, I believe, 1960. He also collected posters and announcements for performances and events associated with the art world. He had filing cabinets full of ephemera, all of it in an order only he seemed to know how to decipher. Was it by gallery, artist, or both? I can't remember.

Herlin's collection was a library that, even if you didn't know how to navigate it, revealed riches at every turn. I often went there to ask him questions, to have him look something up, occasionally to buy an announcement card or small brochure, all of it drenched in history. His project comes the closest to being an actual history of the New York gallery scene; an institution eventually bought the collection, I believe. Before he moved from New York to Los Angeles, I think the poet-critic Peter Frank did something similar, except that his collection was limited to the announcements and cards he had received in the mail or picked up in galleries he had visited. The only other remotely similar experience I had was when I went to a place in midtown that sold movie ephemera, including cigarette and lobby cards, studio shots, and magazine reviews, all carefully stored in plastic sleeves. This is history told through its detritus, a printed record of exhibitions and events that, for the most part, are forgotten.

The *Village Voice* critic Jerry Saltz is this generation's Robert Parker, and, like the well-known oenophile, he has on one occasion at least published a diary of every single gallery he visited during the course of an art season. His stamina rivals that of Frank, who seemed to go to every gallery during the '70s, and William Zimmer, who popped up everywhere in the '80s. They are indefatigable gallery-goers, which is exactly what the art world needs. The father of these chroniclers is Irving Sandler, whose life was changed by a black-and-white

abstraction, *Chief* by Franz Kline, which he saw at the Museum of Modern Art in 1952. Sandler's *Sweeper-Up After Artists: A Memoir* is the most informative and detailed look at the New York art world that existed in the 1950s and '60s. In a recent conversation, Sandler told me that there were around two hundred artists in New York in 1960, and one could meet them all in a relatively short period of time.

Then came Andy Warhol, the ascension of Pop art, and the art boom. The blond-wigged Warhol, with his soup cans, silk screens, cool demeanor, and gnomic pronouncements, fascinated the public and introduced kitsch, glamour, and death into the art world's consciousness. In turn, oodles of money began flowing toward Andy and others. As Wallace Stevens coolly observed, "Money is a kind of poetry." And, whatever else can be said about art, it is a kind of money.

*

Of course, I had no idea that the boom was over when I moved to New York in the early 1970s, a decade before Arthur Danto, writing about Andy Warhol's *Brillo Box*, proposed that art history was over. In fact, I didn't know that I had gotten to town after the money and excitement had started to leave the art world, and that it was in a tailspin. In the late 1970s, just before that world took off again, a well-known poet-critic took a sadistic delight in informing me that I had missed everything important in both art and poetry, even the sex. His self-satisfaction was so evident that it was easy not to believe him. What he didn't lament, and what in fact he didn't need to lament, was the demise of bohemian life. By then, one was finding it increasingly difficult to be comfortably poor in New York.

Ruptures, shifts, and swift change—it never occurred to me that living on the edges was a way to tempt fate because it seemed that everyone I knew was in the same leaky boat. We wanted to become poets and artists, and we believed that we could find an inexpensive space in New York that would enable us to sustain ourselves literally, socially, and metaphorically. Everywhere I looked, there were juxtapositions without transitions, and the feeling that anything could be placed next to anything and, simply because of proximity, belong with it.

Directly above Fanelli's, a long established SoHo bar where artists and unlicensed and licensed plumbers looking for work liked to gather at all hours of the day, Betty Cuningham had a gallery that she affectionately referred to as the bowling alley, because it was long and narrow. She was being ironic, of course, because its uneven wooden floors wouldn't have passed muster in even the most downtrodden bowling establishment. The gallery was a short walk from the pristine spaces of Susan Caldwell, Paula Cooper, Leo Castelli, and Ileana Sonnabend. The link between Cuningham Ward and Fanelli's suggests that one could also write a history of the New York art scene seen through the lens of its bars and the long-gone but historically important places such as Barnabus Rex and Magoos, where artists used to gather. Magoos, which was the watering hole for those who lived in Tribeca, eventually went out of business, I suspect, because it lost its lease and the rent skyrocketed. The owners used to trade art for a tab at the bar and restaurant. The contents of Magoos—all the art and furnishings—ended up in Japan, perfectly preserved.

I used to spend my Saturdays going to the galleries, with possible stops at one or two museums. Speaking about his own early days in New York in the 1950s, Robert Ryman said that he "looked at everything" and that he "accepted it all." Like many before me, I knew that this would be my education about art, and that I had to go to as many galleries and museums as I could lest I miss an important lesson. If you planned your day right, you could go to galleries in the three areas in Manhattan where most of them were clustered: between 70th and 81st Streets, along Madison Avenue; along 57th Street between Sixth and Park; and in SoHo. This all changed with the rise of galleries in Brooklyn and Chelsea.

From the mid-1970s to the late '90s, SoHo was the heart of the art world, the place that generated the most excitement and interest. During the mid-'90s, ACE under the direction of Doug Chrismas had a gallery at 375 Hudson Street, just below Spring Street. This vast space was larger than many museums' exhibition spaces, and put on important shows by Norman Bluhm, Tim Hawkinson, and Robert Rauschenberg, and a performance/exhibition by David Hammons in which the viewers were the performers and, to some degree, the exhibition. Today, the center of the art world is Chelsea, which is much bigger geographically than SoHo, with spaces that are more various in size.

The biggest difference between Chelsea and SoHo, though, is not the size of the spaces but the placement of the reception desk, phones, and offices. If you walked into the back room at Castelli, which was open and accessible, you could see Leo in his office. The people working there were polite and friendly. Much of that friendliness and openness is gone, replaced by aloof workers and a more official, colder atmosphere. You are no longer a gallery-goer but an interloper, one of the rabble craning their necks to see how the other half (and it is surely much, much smaller than that) lives. Recently, I discovered that one gallery's back room, and its spaces for private viewing, was far bigger than the public exhibition space. The back room, where there were lots of works of art on the walls, was off limits to the public, and the person behind the counter politely asked me to leave. More telling is the fact that there really is no equivalent to Fanelli's in Chelsea.

In the 1970s, over the course of a day—this depended on the weather, of course—you could go to the Guggenheim Museum, as well as to Robert Elkon, Cordier and Ekstrom, Martha Jackson, Bykert, and Knoedler on the Upper East Side. Among these galleries, Bykert, which was run by Klaus Kertess, was an anomaly, as it showed artists one would have expected to find in SoHo: Brice Marden, Dorothea Rockburne, and Chuck Close. Bykert closed in 1976, by which time SoHo was firmly established. On 57th Street, you usually went to Andre Emmerich, Tibor de Nagy, Fischbach, Allen Frumkin, Betty Parsons, Pace, and Marlborough, with perhaps a stop at MOMA on 53rd. You would finish up your day in SoHo by going to Paula Cooper, Susan Caldwell, OK Harris, and Holly Solomon. Everyone went to 420 West Broadway, where Leo Castelli, Ileanna Sonnabend, and John Weber had galleries. Often this was the place you went to last. On other days, you might start off at the The Clocktower, a non-profit space in a city-owned building on lower Broadway, and work your way up to SoHo.

It was when you got to SoHo that you felt everything was cooking. By the time 112 Greene Street had moved and been renamed White Columns, two artist-run spaces, 55 Mercer and AIR, had opened their doors. And, although I wasn't yet aware of it, all kinds of change were afoot. Sometimes change is glacial, other times it is like channel-surfing in a hotel at midnight, with everything flashing by until you don't know if you are looking at a movie you haven't seen before or watching something you saw in some other hotel room on an equally frenetic sleepless night. This sense of vertigo was present then and, because of the sheer number of galleries and where they are located, is more so now. You simply had to accept that there would be shows that you missed and things you failed to notice. It was as if you were overloaded before you even stepped into a gallery, and these days that feeling increases moment by moment.

*

Although I didn't see it in any momentous sense, I moved to New York before the World Trade Center was finished, Battery Park was completed, and the high-rise apartments along the lower end of Greenwich Street rose into the air. New

York was beginning to reinvent itself in ways that none of us could foresee. But artists figured out how to use SoHo, that slightly out-of-the-way space, long before these revitalization projects were finished. For in the 1970s, when painting was supposed to be dead, the art world was not limited to what one saw in the galleries. The news was everywhere, and there were many competing events with accompanying narratives. Philip Glass gave a free performance in the rotunda of the Customs House. Terry Riley installed motion sensors in an abandoned structure that would soon be demolished. Suzanne Harris and others built temporary sculptures, and did performances, on the landfill along the Hudson. Gordon Matta-Clark snuck into an abandoned building on a pier in midtown and redid the entire interior. One day, I took the Circle Line around Manhattan so I could see the sheet-metal façade into which he had cut a large sign-like opening, all that remained of his startling interventions.

In many cases, the gallerists were decidedly eccentric. The galleries were their fiefdoms, the pulpits from which they delivered sermons on Surrealism, painterly realism, Pop art, Conceptual art, and early Modernists. For the most part, men presided over the uptown galleries, and intrepid young women began their own spaces in SoHo. What you dived into was an ocean of competing narratives, and it was bracing and delicious. In the Odyssia Gallery, which was on Fifth Avenue between 57th and 56th, I saw for the first time etchings and lithographs by Morandi, paintings and paste-ups by Jess, a shy, reclusive man who lived with the poet Robert Duncan in San Francisco, and paintings and pastels by Irving Petlin. Whenever I left one of the rooms to walk into the next, an assistant would turn off the light in the room I had just exited.

At the Pierre Matisse Gallery I saw my first paintings by Balthus, including the infamous *Guitar Lesson*, as well as his long, largely black paintings of a Japanese woman on her hands and knees, looking into a mirror. Later, I learned that his wife had posed for these late pictures. The magazines presented their narrative interpretations of the events portrayed, but it was the actual stuff that counted. If you looked, you could make up your own mind, or, if you preferred, you could defer to hierarchical judgments. As a viewer and later as a critic, I wasn't interested in ideologies that proclaimed the death-of-painting or in trying to become an ideologue.

Something should also be said about those galleries whose lives were as brief as a that of the fruit fly or, on a more exotic note, the night-blooming cereus. In the late '70s, on the corner of Grand and Lafayette, Robert Friedus had a gallery on the top floor of a building he owned. On the first floors was his tool-and-die business, and somewhere between them and the gallery was his apartment. Emily Sorkin, his gallery director, would have, for a short time in the 1980s, a gallery in her loft on Franklin Street. More recently, Tracy Williams, who had a high level position in a major auction house for many years, and who was the director of Zwirner and Wirth, opened a gallery in the garden apartment of a brownstone on West Fourth Street in the West Village. Like The Rivington Arms and other galleries in the lower East Side, this space is off the beaten track. The vitality and enduring strength of the New York art world is due to the enterprising nature of people like Williams, who believes in art and artists enough to stake all that she has on them.

*

If the poet-critic was right and the boom was over, and gloom and confusion were in the air, I thought everything was fresh and new. I saw lots of paintings by people whose names were never mentioned in the *Times*, and that was exhilarating. For me, one of the great things about New York was that you could see a painting by someone and it didn't matter if hardly anyone else seemed to know this person's work. This meant that you could actually learn on your own, and that you didn't have to accept conventional wisdom or received knowledge.

Everything began to change the day Ronald Reagan was elected President. Rents started climbing higher and higher. More and more galleries began opening on the Lower East Side as well as in SoHo. Mary Boone, who had once worked at Bykert, moved into the first floor of 420, and, with Leo Castelli, showed Julian Schnabel. While many in the art world celebrated the return of painting, others announced the death of the self and originality. The new orthodoxy that art historians established in the 1980s, and that continues to be influential today, was fervently anti-bohemian, not to mention anti-painting. There was a growing interest in photography and new media. The theories and writings of Jacques Derrida, Walter Benjamin, and Jorge Luis Borges replaced those of Clement Greenberg and Michael Fried. Younger critics such as Craig Owens had an enormous impact. The influx of Continental theory, and the rise of Post-modern jargon— "death of the author," "mechanical reproduction," "citation," "institutional critique"—inspired the replacing of such Modernist and formalist terms as "quality," "all-over," and "flatness."

At the same time, in counterpoint, an art scene began developing on the Lower East Side. In 1980, Group Material Gallery opened on East 13th Street. In 1982, Gracie Mansion and Sur Rodney (Sur) had opened Gracie Mansion on East Ninth Street, Dean Savard and Alan Barrows had started Civilian Warfare on East Eleventh, and Peter Nagy and Alan Belcher had opened Gallery Nature Morte on East Tenth. Other galleries that would open on the Lower East Side included Pat Hearn, International with

Monument, PPOW, and Vox Populi. Gracie Mansion had previously held exhibitions in a limousine parked on Saturdays outside 420 West Broadway, and had used the bathroom of her Lower East Side apartment to show art. The LES scene was devastated in the '80s by AIDS, drugs, and cancer, which eventually killed Jean-Michel Basquiat, Colin Deland, Jimmy Desana, Keith Haring, Pat Hearn, Robert Mapplethorpe, Nicholas Moufarrege, Cookie Mueller, David Wojnarowicz, Martin Wong, and many, many others. More than gentrification and fickle taste, the unrelenting wave of deaths helped bring the Lower East Side scene to an end.

Before AIDS became a plague, Haring was drawing in subway stations; Basquiat was leaving his graffiti tag "SAMO" on the walls; Richard Hembleton was spray-painting the shadow of a lurking figure in doorways, near construction sites, and on the sidewalks of lower Manhattan; and Jenny Holzer was pasting her "truisms" on walls around town. Standing on the corner of West Broadway and Spring Street, camouflaged in mud, face paint, and branches, Kim Jones became the "Mudman," moving silently and slowly, evoking his days in Vietnam. The art that took place outside of galleries in the '80s was different from what one experienced in the '70s, a sure indication that what was going in the galleries had also changed. Little street art takes place in Chelsea these days, but that doesn't mean it won't change as well.

*

Chelsea has established itself as the primary area to go to if you are interested in contemporary art. Everyone knows that it is unlikely that it will be able to

sustain all the galleries it now houses. Some have already come and gone. In counterpoint to the heavy concentration of commercial spaces, there are few artist-run spaces and just a handful of cooperatives, many of which seem to have lost steam. The rents in Brooklyn's Williamsburg have skyrocketed, but a number of galleries have weathered the change, and others have started up. Meanwhile, the larger, more successful galleries in Chelsea are both secure and convinced of their own authority. They mount large shows in their large spaces, and publish expensive catalogs documenting the historical importance of their exhibitions. Their haughtiness was inevitable. After all, post-war American artists started Pop art, Earthworks, Conceptual art, and Minimalism, profoundly influencing the direction of art history. Yet it is also true that many deserving artists have been neglected or marginalized, and that many narratives and discourses regarding the first decades of post-war art have not surfaced. The health of the art world depends on both retelling and subverting received history rather than reiterating known narratives. Intervention is necessary, by galleries as well as by artists and critics.

Certainly, for many New Yorkers whose lives are tied up with the art world, artist-run Williamsburg galleries such as Pierogi and Sideshow are exciting venues. Located in what was, until recently, a largely Polish neighborhood with many small houses, industrial spaces, and tenement buildings, these artist-run galleries have a far lower overhead than their counterparts in Chelsea and uptown. This allows them to take risks and to show young and upcoming artists.

And, whatever else galleries do, the constant showcasing of new talent is a necessary component. Like a river, the art world must constantly replenish itself.

The funkiness of Pierogi, Sideshow, and of other galleries such as Black and White, and A Clean, Well-Lighted Place, is reminiscent of those that flourished briefly during the early 1980s on the Lower East Side. Sarah Bowen has a gallery in a converted garage which has low ceilings and two rooms. There is both a beautiful symmetry and a delicious irony to the fact that this space thumbs its nose at those Chelsea galleries housed in former taxi garages.

Like the galleries that existed on the Lower East Side in the early '80s, many of the ones in Brooklyn are open on Sunday. There is a sense of community, and a commitment to something that goes beyond commercialism and sales. This sense of community is underscored by the existence of a free monthly newspaper, *The Brooklyn Rail*, which covers both culture and politics. Run by the artist and translator Phong Bui, *The Brooklyn Rail* covers the whole art scene, as well as local news.

★

If the New York art-gallery scene is to survive, then it must function as a site where the new can be seen, and be able to generate heated discussions about the future of art and culture. Galleries need both a sense of history and a commitment to the young and promising. They must always show the work of up-and-coming artists. In January 1958, Leo Castelli gave the then unknown Jasper Johns his first solo exhibition. The rest, as they say, is history. Instead of resting on their laurels, galleries have to keep embracing art and artists who have little or no public history. That spirit is still very much alive in Williamsburg, in pockets on the Lower East Side, and, with a few exceptions, in Chelsea, at galleries such as Zieher Smith, Derek Eller, Edward Thorp, and Baumgartner. Betty Cuningham, by the way, has a beautiful, spacious gallery there, and shows some of the same artists she first exhibited in her "bowling alley" nearly thirty years ago. She remains as friendly and direct as ever.

Scrapple from the Apple: New York Jazz

Allen Lowe

It all began the day I listened to a Charlie Parker record my mother bought in a local supermarket. It was 1968, and Bird was new and great and different to me, so I started buying more jazz records. One of those was *Worktime* by Sonny Rollins; it cost 99 cents at the Mays Department Store near my hometown of Massepequah Park. On it, Sonny played an Irving Berlin tune I'd heard Ethel Merman sing on *The Hollywood Palace*, "There's No Business Like Show Business." Ethel had pipes, but Sonny was something else again.

The effect on my life was cataclysmic. In pursuit of further revelations, I started to travel to New York on the Long Island Railroad so I could hit record stores like Daytons' in Greenwich Village, where jazz lps rarely cost more than two bucks. It might seem odd given I came of age in the late '60s, but I truly was a bebop boy.

Charlie Parker, who had lived on Avenue B right by Tompkins Square Park, was the center of it all. Bird was the Sun, God-like and unreal, so the musicians who had known or worked with him were deities by association. I knew their names from records and books, names like Al Haig, Tommy Potter, and Curley Russell. Bird died on March 12, 1955 at the age of thirty-four. Max Roach, Parker's greatest drummer and the genius behind the kit on *Worktime*, was still active, but what happened to the rest of Bird's men? I was crazed to find my bebop idols; New York City was like an ancient jazz dig site awaiting my archaeological efforts.

*

Among the first jazz giants I came to know was pianist Barry Harris, a wonderful player and among the very first progeny of the bebop generation I was so enthralled by.

Barry was originally from Detroit—part of the influx of Motor City musicians that included the Jones Brothers (Hank, Thad, and Elvin), Pepper Adams, and Yusef Lateef. Barry had little use for the avant-gardists who came to the city

after him, like Ornette Coleman and Eric Dolphy, but he was, nonetheless, truly charismatic and a direct link to the genius of Thelonious Monk and Bud Powell.

I first heard Barry in the early 1970s. He'd recently recorded with another bebop-inspired Michigander, the combative saxophonist Sonny Stitt, and was working at Jimmy's on the corner of 52nd Street and Sixth Avenue. Jimmy's was a bar owned by Mayor John Lindsay's flack Jimmy Aurelio, and Barry played in a duo with bassist Wilbur Little. "That was a good gig," Barry told me, though the patrons rarely listened. "I was able to get unemployment insurance when it ended."

This was good news because we were still in the middle of the lean years in jazz. With the rise of the Beatles and rock culture in general, jazz had lost a good deal of its cultural cachet and a lot of great musicians were scuffling. Others taught, took any gig they could find, or quit performing altogether.

*

It's the cliché that's true: Walking down Third Avenue one night in 1977, I felt as if I'd been struck by lightning. There, in the window of a corner bar called Gregory's, was a sign saying that Al Haig was playing that evening. Al Haig? Was he still alive? The standard jazz reference works wrote of him like he was an apparition, mysterious and wordless, an inarticulate survivor of the bebop holocaust. I knew Haig from his records with Bird and a handful of solo sides. Soon there *I* was standing at the bar, trying to drink one beer very slowly so as not to get kicked out or have to pay any more money than I had in my pocket. I listened, enthralled, and came back a few days later, this time deciding to splurge and sit at a table. I snuck in a cheese sandwich from a local deli to save money, thus leading to my first personal encounter with Haig, who looked up from the piano in the middle of a phrase and yelled, "Hey, give me a bite of that cheese sandwich!"

It took a few years to find out the story, but, as rumored, Haig had gone through intense struggles with alcohol. What I didn't know was that, at the end of one blacked-out binge, he'd found his wife dead at the bottom of a stairway. Haig was arrested, tried for murder, and finally acquitted. When I later met his attorney, the famous black civil-rights activist Flo Kennedy, she said to me that the only reason Al was even charged was because he was a jazz musician. This was, she said with characteristic and justified contempt for the legal system, "the niggerization of a white man."

My friendship with Haig was representative of my association with what was a small but growing cadre of New York bebop veterans. In varying ways, many of these men were like refugees from the furiously self-destructive life cycles of the bebop era. Haig was guarded but friendly, particularly as soon as he realized that I would not grill him about 1) Charlie Parker; 2) the good old days of bebop; 3) his trial. As a matter of fact, the only reference he ever made to that experience was to refer to "domestic troubles," and though he knew that I knew what had happened, there was no self-consciousness about our avoidance of the subject.

*

Maybe this discretion was the secret to my friendship with all of these musicians, like Davey Schildkraut, a brilliant white alto player best known for his 1954 recordings with Miles Davis. Davey had been praised by people like Dizzy Gillespie, Stan Getz, and John Coltrane, but he'd turned his back on it all to work a low-wage clerical job for the City of New York. Davey was a New Yorker born (1925) and bred who started playing alto (like Johnny Hodges) and then joined the Navy. When he came out, something different was in the air, and he started to wander up to Minton's Playhouse, a Harlem night spot where the early beboppers were starting to develop their new music. "I wanted to sit in," he told me. "[Trumpeter] Fats [Navarro] was playing and I said 'Fats, what tune is this?' As soon as he told me what chord changes it was based on, I was ready to go."

Davey was a true eccentric, who even back than talked about space aliens and seeing flying saucers. "Yes, that was Davey," Jackie McLean said to me years later, "and he was one of my favorite people on or off the bandstand." As the '50s went on, Davey's enthusiasm for playing waned. "I wanted to be with my family, and I started talking long walks around the city," he told me. "The calls stopped coming. But I loved New York and I loved those walks. Bird once said to me, 'Dave, I really admire you and the time you spend with your family.' I said 'Bird, you could have that too, but you're always on your way someplace to play.'"

Among those who played with Bird, I also found—in the phone book— Curley Russell, probably the most recorded bebop bassist of the 1940s. Russell (born in 1917) had been off the scene for decades, and was living with his daughter out in Queens. He had bursitis and the beginnings of the emphysema that would kill him in 1986. Bird's other bassist, Tommy Potter (1918–1988) had also disappeared, but it turns out he was living with his wife in a huge brownstone in Bedford Stuyvesant. A nice and mild man, Tommy never really

explained why he turned from steady gigging to menial jobs that probably earned him even less than he'd made as a jazz musician.

One bopper who did keep gigging was pianist Bill Triglia. Born in 1924, Bill was a friend of Davey Schildkraut who had recorded with Charles Mingus (check out *New Tijuana Moods*, 1962), played an actual Jewish wedding with Bird (much more interesting than the one depicted in the Clint Eastwood movie), and was a mainstay at Birdland in the 1950s. A jazz Zelig, Bill had played with what seemed like literally everyone, from Louis Armstrong to Lester Young to Sonny Rollins. Now he seemed perfectly happy to play lounges with the occasional bebop gesture followed by yet another version of the theme from *Mondo Cane*.

*

One thing I missed in those days was the avant-garde loft movement. Broadly speaking, this was the early to mid-'70s, when jazz musicians occupied industrial spaces downtown, sometimes producing concerts for themselves and others. Ornette Coleman had a place on Prince Street, and his 1970 lp *Friends & Neighbors* was recorded there. The brilliant saxophonist, pianist, and composer Sam Rivers (born in 1924) and his wife Beatrice had Studio Rivbea on Canal Street; a series of five lps called *Wildflowers* came out of that scene, and together they stand a remarkable document of an exceptionally fertile period. John Coltrane's drummer Rashied Ali was proprietor of Ali's Alley and put out music on the tellingly named Survival Records.

There were a few loft clubs in the 1970s that were more mainstream. The Jazz Forum on Cooper Square was run by a nice guy named Mike Morganelli who played the trumpet with more enthusiasm than aptitude. Reedman Mike Morgenstern (no relation to jazz historian Dan) was behind the Jazzmania Society on 14th Street. Mike was a good player in a Dolphy-esque manner, if somewhat below world-class, and my friend the great pianist Bob Neloms played there frequently. All of these clubs, which seemed to be doing well near

the end of the decade, became victims of rising real-estate values and the always-fluctuating jazz audience, and were gone by the 1980s.

Bob was a genius of sorts, and though I've heard some brilliant chord men, none could sit at the piano and rework a song like he could. Bob is also a superb raconteur who can tell stories of his years at Motown, where he was a staff musician from 1961 to 1963. "I was sitting on the steps with Stevie Wonder, and the guys came in with the shark skin suits—next thing we knew the Four Tops went from a jazz group to a soul group." Bob also recalled how, touring the South, the Motown bus got shot at: "they thought we were Freedom Riders." On playing with Charles Mingus, he said, "My mother never really approved of me being a jazz musician until she saw me playing in Europe for 10,000 people. At that point she figured I was a success."

Bob and I lost touch in the late 1980s, though I found him again just recently in Detroit. He and his wife had moved back to his hometown, tired of the New York grind and frustrated that the view from his old apartment, where he'd lived for twenty years, was now just another big building.

*

Another group of older musicians I got to know were those gigging at the West End Cafe up near Columbia University. The West End was booked by WKCR deejay and jazz historian Phil Schaap, and the forgotten talent he brought in was staggering—idiosyncratic trombonist Dickie Wells; the wondrous blues and swing pianist Sammy Price; tenor saxophonist Percy France; Basie-ite altoist Earl Warren; and another of the great white enigmas of bop, Joe Albany. "Hey, you know what they should call my autobiography?" Joe asked me one night as we drove along the FDR drive. "*I Licked Bird's Blood.* I used to shoot up with Bird, he'd take the needle out of his arm, and hand it to me—but first I had to wipe the blood off of the needle and lick it off my finger."

The West End was a quintessential New York City scene in those days, its bandstand populated by jazz vets who should have been legends but who had, somehow, been consigned to workaday status. Count Basie's drummer Jo Jones played sometimes, and Max Roach would be there when he did. Jones still had some swing left in him, although he was quite sick with alcoholism by then.

I got to know Eddie Durham in a casual way. Eddie, who'd been born in 1906, was a brilliant guy, one of the first to play electric guitar (he mentored Charlie Christian when they both lived in Oklahoma City) and a great arranger whose achievements were largely unrecognized. One night he confided that he'd just gotten a royalty check for $5,000 because some group had recorded a disco version of one of his swing-era arrangements. "I feel nigger-rich," he laughed. I was a little taken aback by the phrase, but it was wasn't long before I heard almost the same expression from another gentleman who often hung around the West End, Professor Snead. A former musician—he'd played bass with Billie Holiday—and a wonderful poet, Snead collaborated with Piano Red on the tune "Bald Headed Lena," which the rock-'n'-roll group The Lovin' Spoonful recorded in the 1960s. "That was nice," he told me. "I got a big check and I was suddenly what they call 'nigger-rich.'"

For a time Jabbo Smith was also a regular at the West End. Probably the only 1920s-trumpeter who could, in his prime, challenge Louis Armstrong, Jabbo was tired and faded, but he had the most beautiful singing voice I have ever heard, and on a good night would not only croon "Talk of the Town" and "Sweet Lorraine" like a more soulful Bing Crosby but would also blow a few choruses that showed he indeed still knew his chord changes.

*

In the 1980s, things were changing, both for me and for jazz in New York. Al Haig died suddenly in 1982—I can still feel the shock and sadness of his wife Joanne's call to me in Brooklyn on that morning. Al's bassist, Jamil Nasser, was with her, and she was so grief-stricken that Jamil had to get on the line to tell me what had happened. Haig's death separated me from New York in a way. Later that year, I got married and moved New Haven, Connecticut.

It was then that I picked up the tenor saxophone again, an instrument I'd hardly touched for more than a decade. I decided to get serious about playing again. I started to really open up to jazz outside bebop and to altoist/composer John Zorn especially. A native New Yorker, Zorn had been kicking around downtown since the mid-'70s, but it was his 1986 Ennio Morricone tribute, *The Big Gundown*, that convinced me this was something radical and compelling.

Today Zorn is an iconic figure, an industry unto himself and a scene-maker via his Tzadik label and the Zorn-affiliated music venue The Stone out on Avenue C. I sometimes feel that he is an inconsistent ideologue, but there's no denying he's also something of a throwback—a bourgeois-assaulting artist—and his often surprising reconsideration of common source materials is refreshing.

The next New York musician to transfix me was Julius Hemphill, who had come east from St Louis in the early '70s. Following in the line of the Chicago-based Association for the Advancement Creative Music, Julius was, along with Roscoe Mitchell, Anthony Braxton, and Henry Threadgill, among the first of his generation to understand that free jazz needed an injection of organization and compositional discipline if it wasn't to paint itself into a musical corner.

Julius was the one who conceptually organized the epochal World Saxophone Quartet. The WSQ at its late-'70s-to-mid-'80s peak ranks with the greatest African-American art, succeeding both as brilliant Modernist expression and as an open, freely associative comment on the tradition. The WSQ was Julius' baby, but over the years tensions within the group grew. I was in the city to rehearse with him the day he received a registered letter from the quartet's lawyer firing him; a depressed Julius asked me to give him a lift to the lawyer's office while he ran upstairs to sign the papers.

In 1986 I got a grant to hold a new-music seminar in New Haven; I'd recently heard clarinetist Don Byron, and, impressed, I invited Don to come on up. Still relatively unknown, he was happy to be there, especially since Hemphill and the legendary pianist Paul Bley were also on the bill. I'd just started to write in more open forms, and Don and I recorded several of my compositions. I had a good feeling about it; if he was accepting of my work, then I could get up the nerve to ask Hemphill if he would record with me. Julius listened to some things, seemed pleased, and came up to do a session. The recordings with Byron and Hemphill came out in 1989 on a self-released CD called *At the Moment of Impact*. One day I opened the *Village Voice* and was flabbergasted to find out that jazz writer Francis Davis had named it as a "Voice Pick Hit." I didn't become a star, but at least I was on the map.

*

New Music in New York in the 1980s was synonymous with the Knitting Factory, a club on Houston Street that was quickly becoming the focus of the downtown scene. For me, it was a place to focus on the jazz styles I'd missed in my bebop fervor. One of the first things I did was to see Cecil Taylor there. I also saw Don's new group, as well as Tim Berne and numerous others who showed me that it was time to wake up and smell the new music. Inspired, I put together a project called "The New Tango" based on some things I'd been listening to by Astor Piazolla. I got Julius for the date and a bunch of guys I'd been working with who were also in Anthony Braxton's music program at Wesleyan. We made a live recording at

the Knitting Factory. The legendary engineer David Baker did a great job and the session went well.

Julius and I had became pretty good friends by now. When he complimented my compositions, it was like being anointed by Duke Ellington—I truly felt Hemphill was of that stature. Ironically, many of his own records, both solo and with the wsq, were released on an Italian label, Black Saint. Other significant New York musicians whose work might have gone largely undocumented in the '80s had it not been for Black Saint and its sister label Soul Note included violinists Leroy Jenkins and Billy Bang; tenor-player Frank Lowe; and altoist Jemeel Moondoc.

Julius and I did two CDs together; a third recording was cancelled as he became sick. He lived in a loft downtown with his partner Ursula Oppens (the superb new-music pianist for whom Conlon Nancarrow had written pieces). Sometimes Julius didn't say much and I was intimidated by the long silences—until Ursula said, "Julius likes you and would love a visit." I realized then that the open spaces in our conversations were just Julius' way of being. The last time I saw him, he was weak and thin and on the list for a kidney transplant. That morning I'd been up to the Jazz Record Center on West 26th Street. Just as I was leaving, I ran into Frank Lowe. Frank said, "Hey, cousin, I been wanting to meet you to see if we're related." He laughed and we talked. When I told him I was going up to see Julius he hopped in the cab with me and we—really they—spent a nice afternoon talking about old times. Julius died on April 2, 1995.

*

Wynton Marsalis was in ascendance throughout the '80s, and while I had no use for him, his reactionary ravings about new music and the alleged tradition catalyzed my next project, "An Avant Garde Tribute to Louis Armstrong." We recorded at the Knitting Factory with a band that included octogenarian Doc Cheatham on trumpet and Loren Schoenberg on tenor. I'd known Loren since the West End days, when he was young and "chesty," as Percy France used to describe his somewhat confrontational personality. Equally brilliant on tenor and piano, Loren was a different man by this time and we'd become good friends. To me he represents everything that is good about the so-called "mainstream" of jazz, a *healthy* respect for tradition that doesn't hold him back from looking at everything new the world has to offer.

By this time, I'd also established a relationship with Roswell Rudd, who was getting back into the game after years off the scene. Rudd was the man who put the trombone on the avant-garde musical map in the 1960s, working with Cecil Taylor, the New York Art Quartet, and especially Archie Shepp. Rosie had been close to the revered pianist/composer Herbie Nichols (1919–1963), read A. B. Spellman's classic *Four Lives in the Bebop Business* for moving portraits of Herbie, Ornette, Cecil, and Jackie

JEMEEL MOONDOC QUINTET

Nostalgia In Times Square

McLean), and had in his possession quite a few of Nichols' compositions. After playing the Armstrong project with us at Sweet Basil in Lower Manhattan, Rudd made two CDs with me. I cannot adequately describe the feeling I got on certain nights from playing with Roswell: he seemed to levitate the bandstand. One time Loren looked at me after a particularly amazing Roswell solo and said, "Now, *that*'s the real thing."

I still kept some ties to the old school. Percy France, whom I regarded as one of the greatest mainstream tenors ever, advised me on horns and mouthpieces. Percy got sick with cancer, his recovery uncertain, when a car struck and killed him in Manhattan. A lot of people from my earlier New York days were gone—cancer took Dickey Wells in 1985, and in a truth-is-stranger-than-fiction moment, on March 6, 1987, Eddie Durham died on the way to Basie guitarist Freddie Green's funeral. Joe Albany began a paranoid descent into his own miseries, calling me a few times with angry accusations of exploitation. Pianist Walter Bishop, who lived across the hall from Joe in the famous subsidized artists' housing on 42nd Street, tried to help, but Joe was too far gone; he passed in 1998. My relationship with Davey Schildkraut ended similarly; he died, alone, the same year, forgotten by all but a few.

*

In 1994 I made one last attempt to grasp the straw of New York jazz fame. I got a contract with the German label Enja for a project I called *Woyzeck's*

Death. Roswell, clarinetist Ben Goldberg, and trumpeter Randy Sandke were among those in the band. The album was released without promotion and disappeared, although the *Penguin Guide to Jazz on CD* had kind words.

Since moving to Maine in 1996, my musical career hasn't been the same. I rarely gig, but I did take up guitar about five years ago and bought an alto saxophone, too. In April 2006 I returned to New York to record a new project with Randy, guitarist Marc Ribot, and pianists Anthony Coleman and Matthew Shipp. I'm particularly happy to have hooked up with Shipp. In our first conversation, I told him he sounded like a successful version of me, and he laughed, understanding immediately what I meant. Matt is everything that you hope for—and sometimes get—in a New York musician: hip in the deepest way possible, open to all things musical, approachable, and so damned smart it's a little scary.

That—and the potential magic of any bandstand—is the good side. Whenever I miss New York I look at Randy, who can play and write anything, is uncommonly intelligent, and a real nice guy, too. For all that, he rarely works in the city, few critics understand him, and he's a little burnt out producing and financing his own projects. As a matter of fact, you might say that he's a poster child for so much New York City jazz: neglected yet forward-looking and, when it comes to his own hometown, out of work.

Death and Transfiguration in New York Rock

Brandon Stosuy

> New York is a place of vast wealth, and between the whores and the business men there are the artists and the patrons of said art. Maybe waking up everyday and seeing all the seemingly unfathomable wealth, born of patronage, nepotism, skill, complicated criminality, luck and even talent and effort is too much; to embrace chaos is more attractive than to pursue a laid out pattern of how to dress for the job you want instead of the job you have. Who wants beauty when you and me can make the ugly?
>
> —Elisa Ambrogio, Magik Markers

In 1977 I was four years old and living in southern New Jersey. My parents had grown up in the city, but hanging in the rural Pine Barrens they never played the iconic '70s Big Apple sounds of the Ramones or Television, let alone their mysterious progeny DNA, Mars, and Teenage Jesus and the Jerks. Mom and Dad were into Bob Dylan, of course—a shared favorite was *Desire*—and oddly, my father had a black Velvet Underground t-shirt. I never asked him where he got it, but in retrospect, the pairing of Dylan and the Velvets makes perfect sense.

*

Nobody knew it at the time, but Dylan's 1960 move to New York from Minnesota could be viewed as one of rock history's big bangs. Another, generally less celebrated explosion occurred a few years later when a young composer, John Cale, arrived via Tanglewood and Wales. Cale hooked up with John Cage and threw himself into the early Minimalism scene. Violinist and filmmaker Tony Conrad was Cale's roommate for a while; both played with La Monte Young and Marian Zazeela in an intense, Indian-influenced drone ensemble called The Theatre of Eternal Music.

Cale and Conrad also joined forces with Lou Reed, a Jewish kid from Long Island. As the Primitives, they recorded an early Reed song, "The Ostrich." While Conrad left to focus on his art, film, and also solo compositions, Cale and Reed

stayed together; with drummer Angus MacLise and guitarist Sterling Morrison, Reed's friend from his student days, they became the Warlocks and, soon after that, the Velvet Underground. MacLise, something of a shaman, quit in 1965, to be supplanted by the androgynous floor-tom maven, Maureen "Moe" Tucker.

Setting lyrics about heroin and bondage to drones and blues-free rave-ups, the Velvets were participants in the scene around Andy Warhol's Factory. Warhol began managing them in 1965, bringing the art world into rock and vice versa. Besides publicity, the Pop art progenitor's main contributions to the band were Nico (for whom Dylan had written "I'll Keep It With Mine"), the ineffably cool Teutonic vocalist he foisted upon them, and the striking, innuendo-heavy banana on the cover of their 1967 debut, *The Velvet Underground & Nico*. Before the 1968 follow-up, *White Light/White Heat*, Reed fired Warhol and dumped Nico.

Not long after, Cale left as well, beginning an erratic, often brilliant solo career that continues to this day. His 1979 effort, *Sabotage/Live*, stands among the best documents of CBGB's peak era, as well as the post-Velvets record that most captures their original street-level energy and paranoid tension.

Since 1972, when he released both his self-titled solo debut and *Transformer*, Reed has produced a bewildering oeuvre, including a double album of feedback and noise, *Metal Machine Music* (1975). Derided at the time, it fits nicely alongside any number of more recent black metal or Japanese noise-core outings. Weirdly, as if thinking back to "The Ostrich," Reed followed it with the stripped-down good-time tunes of 1976's *Coney Island Baby*. Despite a few intriguing moments, including one called simply *New York* (1989, one of my father's favorites), Reed fell into self-parody, recording increasingly inessential collections.

Nico's post-VU output is highlighted by three art-song masterpieces, *The Marble Index* (1969), *Desertshore* (1970), and *The End* (1974), each arranged by John Cale, the last featuring the dark synthesizers of Brian Eno.

＊

Inspired by music, movies, and restlessness, adventurous kids from other parts of the country were drawn to New York in the early '70s. Among their number were Kentuckian Richard Meyers and Delaware native Tom Miller. They'd met at a Maryland boarding school and headed to the Lower East Side to be poets. Upon arrival they renamed themselves Hell and Verlaine, respectively, and formed a band called The Neon Boys. Around that time in Queens, rockers were trying a less overtly artful approach—first the New York Dolls, then the Ramones. A few years on, Hell co-wrote "Chinese Rocks" with Dee Dee Ramone; recorded by ex-Doll Johnny Thunder's Heartbreakers, it remains one of the great city-dope anthems.

The nexus of all these influences and activities was a Rimbaud-, Dylan-, Velvets- and Dolls-loving poet from Jersey named Patti Smith. Her debut album, *Horses*, produced by Cale, was released on Arista Records in 1975. The floodgates cracked. The Ramones, Talking Heads, and Richard Hell and the Voidoids all signed with Sire; Television recorded for Elektra; Blondie, who were poppier than the rest, landed at Chrysalis. In January 1976, New York cartoonist John Holmstrom and friends put out the first issue of an irreverent hand-drawn magazine mostly about music. Reed graced the debut cover, followed by Smith, Joey Ramone, and Iggy Pop. They called it *Punk*.

＊

Thirty years later, I have to admit, punk and its discontents aren't that important to me. Even as a teenager in the mid-'80s, I found the Ramones tired and rote, all gabba-gabba-hey'd out. I was drawn to noisier sounds, ones imagined as a reaction to punk, to new wave and to New York City itself. They called the clatter No Wave.

The idealistic plan was to shatter rock tendencies. It didn't always succeed, but even the failures are interestingly mangled. If No Wave bands had any

common aesthetic, it was a conscious movement, often by non-musicians, away from the past. Lydia Lunch described it a desire to "disregard influence." No Wave didn't last very long or produce much of a paper trail—in retrospect, that's a good thing. Because there were fewer records available, it hasn't been as fetishized as punk. Where the over-exposed CBGB's bands sound dried up and suburban these days, No Wave feels just as shadowy as tomorrow.

Stylistically, the bands scowled through a blitz of spastic free jazz, art noise, and anti-punk formalism. Vocals were often jarring, Dadaist shouts over a shredding guitar, and occasionally clattering broken dance rhythms—an amateurism that strikes me as technically dead-on today. Listen, for example, to the timeless antisocial raving of Chain Gang's "Son Of Sam," released before David Berkowitz was caught. Its immediacy is the stench of tunnel rot on a summer subway platform. Check the inarticulate, guttural howls of Arto Lindsay on DNA's "Horse" when he warbles, "Get out of here / go fuck yourself" at exorcism's end. It's this dark pre-language that feels especially New York—all concentration, texture, busted energy.

Equally as catchy is the name "No Wave" itself. Because its origins are a little murky, I decided to ask some people who were there. "I've always believed the term originated with NO, a fanzine that was published by Chris Nelson, Jimmy Sclavunos, Seth Cagin, Anene Kaye, and me, in 1977/78," said historian Phil Dray, co-founder of Information and The Scene Is Now, bands best known these days because Yo La Tengo covered songs by each. "On the cover of our second issue Chris put a photo of a surfer catching a wave with the caption 'New Wave, No Wave.' It was a joke on 'New Wave' and the name of our zine."

"My impression was that the connection between the name of the maga-zine and the musical movement/style was largely cemented due to the several connections between NO magazine and the New York Rocker, where I then worked as art director," added Dray's long-time bandmate Chris Nelson. "I'd frequently talk up the Teenage Jesus/Mars/DNA sound to my boss, Andy Schwartz, the editor and publisher of that much more established publication. Andy, whose sense of humor can tend to the acerbic, jokingly began referring to the group of bands as the No Wave, first in conversation, then in print—which I took partly as his estimate of the commercial prospects of the groups in question."

In 1978, Brian Eno, who'd recently started living in New York, compiled a scene sampler and called it *No New York*; it was released on the Antilles subsidiary of Island Records and contained four tracks each by the Contortions, Mars, Teenage Jesus & The Jerks, and DNA. In contrast to his own pristine ambient and pop work of the time, Eno's recording took a documentary approach that fit well with the bands' on-stage ravages. Keeping with the attitude, the lyrics were hidden on the inside of the record sleeve, so you had to tear it open if you wanted to shout along. Writing in the April 1979 issue of *Creem,* Richard C. Walls summed it up nicely: "This music has no future. But it does have a vindictive present."

Around 1981, most No Wave-ish bands disappeared, with fragments reappearing in a wide variety of cross-pollinating contexts. There was the downtown improv scene of John Zorn, influenced by jazz, punk, and the prodigal art-prog of British guitarist Fred Frith, who'd recently moved to New York. Massacre, Frith's band with Bill Laswell and future Lou Reed drummer Fred Maher, made one blazing statement, *Killing Time*, in 1983 and dispersed. Frith lived in New York for fourteen years; another of his bands, Skeleton Crew, paired him with cellist Tom Cora and harpist Zeena Parkins. Composer and guitarist Elliott Sharp was a polymath in the Frith tradition and also became a member of late No Wave survivors Mofungo, a sometimes folksy agitprop combo misnamed

after the plantain-and-pork gut-bomb found on the menus in the Puerto Rican restaurants once on the Lower East Side.

Composers-turned-punks Glenn Branca and Rhys Chatham led classically minded guitar armies, out of which came various rock bands influenced by these innovations: the Swans, Live Skull, Sonic Youth. There was also dance-punk disco via the Bush Tetras (with Pat Place of the Contortions), the Golden Palominos (Arto Lindsay took part), and avant-garde-cellist-turned-ecstatic-disco-composer Arthur Russell; the Del Byzanteens (a project that included Jim Jarmusch, composer Phil Kline, and lyricist Luc Sante); you name it . . . about the only common thread is that, via one course or another, most of this music emanated from lower Manhattan.

*

As a Misfits-loving South Jersey farm boy, I came to learn these things in retro-spect. In the early '90s, a friend of mine suggested that since I was so into Pussy Galore, I ought to give a closer listen to the Contortions. Here, I came to realize the significance of New York City. I had been frequenting record stores like Kim's and Bleecker Bob's from an early age, but until then—remember, this was the pre-internet era, where a nascent musical education came almost strictly from fanzines—I didn't really grasp the historical links.

Led by Jon Spencer, Pussy Galore began in 1985 in Washington, DC, and their early recordings were primal shit fests filled with so much sex and cursing that critics wondered if it was some sort of joke. In retrospect, it was an obvi-ous—yet inspired—mix of the Cramps (Ohio-to-New York rockabilly fiends) and Einstürzende Neubauten (serious German industrialists who played sheet metal in addition to regular instruments). Extremely at odds with the strait-laced Washington scene, the band moved to New York, where vulgarity and provocation were most welcome. I was especially into the records made after ex-Sonic Youth drummer Bob Bert joined the band: from *Right Now!* (1987) to *Historia de la Musica Rock* (1990).

Right Now! was produced by Mark Kramer, known to all simply as "Kramer." In the early '80s, he'd been one-third of Shockabilly, a disreputable folk-noise band with post-everything guitarist Eugene Chadbourne and drummer David Lichtenstein (ex-John Cale, future klezmer-revival hero). Later in the decade, Kramer ran a recording studio, Noise New York, and a record label, Shimmy Disc. (Perhaps the most highly regarded of his productions are the three albums by Boston band Galaxie 500.) Shimmy Disc put out a bewildering array of platters, including the early efforts of King Missile, led by John Hall, who emerged out of the roiling ABC No Rio open-mike scene. Records by other local bands like Fly Ashtray and Uncle Wiggly revealed a little-known pop streak in the New York underground, while Kramer's own projects, the almost glam rocking B.A.L.L, and Bongwater, a collaboration with downtown performance artist and Club 57 hostess Ann Magnuson, were great on their own unpredictable terms. An acrimonious breakup between Kramer and Magnuson in 1991 and subsequent business troubles marked the end of Shimmy Disc as a force in New York music.

∗

Hip-hop aside (and outside the bounds of this essay), I didn't care much about NYC music in the mid '90s. Nor, it seems, did many other folks—although Yo La Tengo (based in Hoboken but with a Brooklyn bassist and clearly of the New York tradition) made some terrific records, and the post-punk Chavez, fronted by Matt Sweeney, flew the flag for estimable if not earth-shattering guitar rock.

After graduating from college in 1995, I moved around some. Imagine my surprise in when I moved back to New York in 2001 and discovered the so-called NYC post-punk revival about to hit. Seems everyone was talking about No Wave again and specifically *No New York*.

During that period, bands like Yeah Yeah Yeahs and Liars dressed up as Max's Kansas City rejects and prospered, delivering secondhand Wave to folks from north Brooklyn. While the Yeah Yeah Yeahs at first seemed Pussy Galore-influenced trash rockers, their Siouxsie Sioux-meets-Deborah Harry front woman seduced photo editors everywhere with her mall-explosion fashion sense. Later recordings revealed the Yeah Yeah Yeahs to be no more than pop rockers in drag, media-savvy but empty (a common NYC affliction) LES-does-Brooklyn signifiers. Perhaps sensing their own aesthetic doom, the Liars moved to Berlin and graduated to gorgeously plain-clothes ambient Kraut-laced drone-rock.

My neighborhood even had its own imitation Club 57 in Luxx, an Alice-in-Wonderland-styled joint that tried to establish a genre called electroclash, a synthy, party-oriented new-wave dance sound that brought back bad memories of '80s cocaine hedonism and leg warmers more than the heyday of dark electronic rock music. Popular acts in this scene included Peaches, ARE Weapons, and Fischerspooner.

An easily gulled media also celebrated a simplistic, Velvets-derived group called the Strokes. Rich Manhattan kids dressed by stylists, the Strokes were a cause célèbre and bête noire almost upon arrival. Everyone I knew was indifferent. A scene-surveying compilation released by Vice Records around that time was the creatively titled *Yes New York*.

⁕

Five years later, there's yet another renewed fixation on the downtown NYC of the '70s and '80s, largely through group exhibitions at the New Museum and Grey Gallery and various book-length publications. Much of the interest is in the visual art of the period, though there have been a slew of reissues over the past few years, including recordings by Glenn Branca, Arthur Russell, Rhys Chatham, Mars, and James Chance. Even *No New York*'s available again under the suspicious aegis of the Lilith label, which claims to be from the "Russian Federation," where they master '70s records straight from vinyl. Meanwhile, most bands have jumped to Brooklyn; downtown Manhattan, a cultural incubator for hundreds of years, is near dead to the artist's life.

Despite a general disinterest in specific stylistic forebears (*very* No Wave, right?), there are plenty of historical threads connecting the new to the old. Indeed, it's these mutant hybrids that are most interesting: not facile attempts to recreate '77, or even '82, but groups pillaging what they feel like, then yoking the disparate elements into something all their own.

DNA's impulse toward intellectual destruction is especially present in Magik Markers. Only drummer Pete Nolan currently lives in NYC, but coming out of Connecticut, MM stalk the area enough to feel local. The trio doesn't translate well to recording, but singer/guitarist Elisa Ambrogio's manic charisma makes them one of the best live bands you'll ever see as she stalks the stage, bangs her head against the drum, speaks in tongues, destroys whatever comes into her sight. It's a feral diva thing, like the Germs versus Harry Pussy fronted by Patti Smith's worst Sufi nightmare.

Elsewhere, bands are taking a variety of cues from late-'60s communalism, often refracted through a German or hardcore filter. Groups like Mouthus (another crew showcasing a Harry Pussy vibe), Double Leopards, and GHQ (a trio that includes Magik Markers' Nolan and Double Leopards' Marcia Bassett) offer various degrees of slow-release drone. The scene's relative elders, long resident in Harlem, the No Neck Blues Band, recently collaborated with '70s Krautrock band Embryo. Wooden Wand & The Vanishing Voice, a menagerie of freak-folk dignitaries with psychedelic and noise leanings, deal in apocalyptic concepts and themes. Staten Island native Wooden Wand's solo debut, *Harem Of The Sundrum & The Witness Figg*, was more traditionally song-oriented and deserved more attention than it got. Art world insider Lizzy Bougatsos leads Gang Gang Dance, a group that composes outer-realm soundscapes that seem to incorporate the sirens of both the street and the sky. Then there's Prurient (aka Bushwick-based Dominick Fernow, who, in 2006, opened a metal-and-noise-specific record store in Manhattan), metal-edged drone-lords Sunn o))), bearded noise-rockers Parts & Labor, the female duo Metalux, Blood on the Wall (Mudhoney + *Daydream Nation*), Black Dice, Telepathe, Eystek, the DFA guys, USAIAAMONSTER, and dozens more.

*

Now New York: the gentrification that gutted the vital streetscape across the East River's wreaking havoc on waterfront Brooklyn. When I moved back East, I didn't consider living in Manhattan; Brooklyn's lower rents and active music and art scenes made it an obvious destination. Now, as the waterfront gets taller and "luxury" lofts are tucked amid old wood-framed row houses, affordable places are increasingly difficult to find. Hipsters are venturing outside Williamsburg into Bushwick, Gowanus, and the farthest reaches of Greenpoint and Red Hook—but there's only so far they can go, and no doubt the housing "boom" will follow, at which point the question becomes: Why stay?

It's difficult to predict how the dramatic rise in housing costs will affect the area's music scene. There's talk of people heading to Philadelphia, the so-called sixth borough. Last I heard, Philadelphia had the best heroin on the East Coast and rent is cheap, so . . . At the same time, I'm almost certain that bands like No Neck and Excepter (including ex-No Neck member John Fell Ryan) will stay, but what about kids who showed up following the scene's 2002 watershed and are faced with difficult financial choices?

Maybe it's time to get something going in Queens . . . Gabba Gabba Hey!

Sounds of the City

1. Television: *Marquee Moon* (1977)
Front man Tom Verlaine nabbed his surname from the nineteenth-century French poet Paul while worshipping at the altar of Rimbaud. The lyrics evoke urban epiphany; there's additional poetry in Verlaine and Richard Lloyd's dual carbolic garage-'n'-psyche guitar-scapes.

2. *Suicide* (1977)
Martin Rev and Alan Vega haunted the LES with guitar-free ominousness for six years before recording their debut. Rev's bassy synth and sputtering drum machines are the perfect undertow for Vega's living-dead vocal rockabilly. "Frankie Teardrop" is a desperate, evicted, and hungry twenty-year-old piss-factory worker who kills his wife and kids before blowing out his own brains.

3. Various: *No New York* (1978)
It's not a complete scene report, but No Wave's crews were best enjoyed in bursts, so Eno's decision to include four tracks each from just four bands makes sonic sense: treat it like a forty-three-minute collage of punk-funk static chaos and rampaging, implosive tribalism.

4. Glenn Branca: *The Ascension* (1981)
After the Static and Theoretical Girls, and playing elsewhere with fellow guitar general Rhys Chatham, Branca composed these pieces for four guitars, bass, and drums. The drone creates classical-tinged ice sheets; drums blast out Morse code, building unending, triumphant crescendo.

5. Swans: *Children of God* (1987)
Obsessed with human frailty, Michael Gira had already mastered the fire and brimstone intonation way back in 1982 (making Joy Division's Ian Curtis sound like a pistol-whipped soprano). Here, piano and acoustic guitar are added to the assault; the real weapon, however, is Goth diva Jarboe, her fragile, atmospheric folk tunes the perfect counters to Gira's manic heaviosity.

6. Royal Trux: *Royal Trux* (1988)
Ex-Pussy Galore, the underground's version of Keith Richards and Marianne Faithful, Neil Hagerty and girlfriend Jennifer Herrema blew through a decon-structed (or barely built) set of blues pierced with soul and spit and all kinds of skeletons. My favorite Royal Trux's the 1990 double album, *Twin Infinitives*—their *Exile on Main Street* and *Metal Machine Music*—but by then they'd gone to SF.

7. Sonic Youth: *Daydream Nation* (1988)
A Gerhard Richter muted candle marks the crossroads where weird tunings equals anthemic art rock and swelteringly chilly New York noise with the best writing of the band's career. "I see a falling snowgirl walking Broadway / Turns the corner at 14th and I know there's no way." Check.

8. John Zorn: *Naked City* (1989)
Zorn's free-jazz grindcore supergroup included Wayne Horvitz on keyboards, guitarist Bill Frisell, Fred Frith on bass, Joey Baron on drums, and vocals from the Boredoms lead howler, Yamatsuka Eye. Among Zorn's cartoon-like originals the band runs "The James Bond Theme" and Ornette Coleman's "Lonely Woman" through the blender. The black-and-white cover photo—head wound splayed on a city street—captures the zeitgeist.

9. Animal Collective: *Sung Tongs* (2004)
Adopting playful monikers—Avey Tare, Deakin, Geologist, Panda Bear—this Brooklyn (since dispersed) quartet started making insane zoological drone noise, then slowly worked Beach Boys harmonies and other pop influences into the celebration. The band's fourth album is their bubbling best, melodies askew and structures uncategorizable.

10. Excepter: *Alternation* (2006)
Shadowy urban-field recordings evoke the sound of rotting Sheffield as heard over old Faust records, '80s hip-hop beak-beats, and anything else that can be ladled out of the Big Apple melting pot labeled "Made in Bushwick." "(The Pipes)" was constructed by tapping the heating system in the band's loft pipe and laying down spare feedback hums as accompaniment.

BIG ART Inc.

Anthony Haden-Guest

When Robert Rauschenberg won the grand prize at the 1964 Venice Biennale it was seen as a sign that the Americans had finally whipped the sorry rump of what was left of the Ecole de Paris. Poignantly, Roger Bissière, the French contender for the prize, died later that same year and is now more or less unremembered. According to Serge Guilbaut, the French-Canadian author of *How New York Stole the Idea of Modern Art*, many European art-worlders believed that the Rauschenberg's dealer, Leo Castelli, had somehow got to the jury and put in the fix. Conspiracy theories ran wild. In one TV-movie-of-the-week-ready scenario, the Sixth Fleet, which was then in the Mediterranean, had been putting on a show for their boy.

Fast-forward. In 1999 Damien Hirst was offered a pavilion in that year's Venice Biennale. He turned it down, lickety-split.

I had called to ask why.

"Couldn't be bothered," he said, with his usual clenched, nonchalant mutter.

Hirst, who now works with an excellent business manager, Frank Dunphy, has an instinct both for the internal dynamics of the art world itself—knowing just what causes nostrils to twitch—and for the uses of media, both haute and base. And he was only ahead of his time.

Just.

Who needs fuddy-duddy Venice—in the words of that ethereal prima ballerina Alicia Markova "a smelly old city, falling into the water"— when you've got auction houses putting on museum shows (such as the Donald Judd show at Christies, New York, in the spring of 2006), art fairs going toe to toe with the auction houses, dealers funding multi-million-dollar art projects and combining to make promotions, hedge funds speculating on artist futures, and global museums acting like the giant retail chains, stocking up on the same brands, these brands being virtually critic-proof *Über*-artists? Why stick to the well-thumbed guidebooks when high-tech and market forces are reconfiguring the whole map?

*

Leslie Waddington, a doyen of London dealers, remembers a Picasso exhibition in the Maison de la Pensée Française in Paris in 1954. "I saw only four people there," he says. "And Picasso and his family." In 1959 he went to a Barnett Newman show at French & Co. on Madison Avenue. It was organized by the pugnacious protagonist of the Abstract Expressionists, Clement Greenberg. "I went four or five times," Waddington says. "There was never anybody there except for Greenberg and a secretary."

In the early '60s Dick Solomon, then a young dealer, now President of the Art Dealers Association and of Pace Prints, went to Rauschenberg's second solo show. "The after-party was in a loft," he says. "The complete American art world was there. Everybody! Artists, collectors, writers. Perhaps Andy wasn't there. He didn't like those things."

Jeffrey Deitch, the New York dealer, says, "When I began in the '70s there were five galleries that mattered. I knew everybody in the artworld. Not just the artists, the collectors. I knew the framers! I knew the people who sold the paint!"

As to the social order of the art world, well, there was a mini-scene in New York, captured with a cold, sharp eye by Tom Wolfe in his piece on the Pop collectors Bob and Ethel Scull, but it was a dealer-driven scene. You would be no more likely to see a collector lifting a paddle in an auction house than a Park Avenue grande dame at Hunt's Point vegetable market, prodding the eggplants. Auction houses only became the art-world Oscars during the late '70s in New York; that's when today's sensation-fuelled art world was born.

The '80s Boom. Heady times. Those were the effervescent days when well-heeled folk who had been burned in other markets took to snapping up art, the time when individuals came plunging in out of nowhere to open galleries, a time when the media began panting after Art Stars—some of whom took advantage of the super-heated market to speed work directly from the production

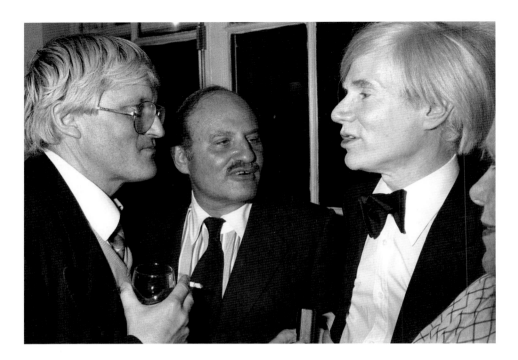

lines in their studios to the auction houses—and in particular a time when
sober financial institutions, with absolutely no prior interest or track record in
this notoriously dodgy and volatile field, began setting up every permutation of
art fund, twinkling with projections, cat's cradles of statistics and God knows what.

Hang on a moment. I just had the scariest flash-forward!

Could I just possibly also be describing ... now?

In 1989 at the Boom's height, the dealer Irving Blum was approached by
somebody with a terrific Warhol, a *Green Liz*. Blum already owned a Liz Taylor
with a red background. "I bought it from Andy for a thousand dollars," he says.
He believes the green is a marginally better painting. "They wanted one point
five million. No Warhol had ever gone for more than eight ($800,000). I said we
have to have it!"

Came the Gulf War, the Japanese real-estate collapse. Art went . . . pffft!

"Three months later it was worth 500,000," Blum says. "Citibank called in
the loan. I had to sell off some good work cheap. It almost did me in."

He hung on to his *Green Liz*, though.

The Art Stars were equally gutted.

"Artists used to have a joke back in the 80s," says Ashley Bickerton. "There
was an ad on television of a woman in a cocktail dress holding a champagne
glass, saying: I'm cleaning my bathroom bowl! Because they have this little thing
that sits in the toilet, cleaning it, while the woman was out and about, partying
with the glitterati. We'd all be out at these events, and joking to one another:
I'm cleaning my bathroom bowl! Meaning you have a horde of assistants in

there, churning away. Production was going on at your studio, while you were out, enjoying yourself."

Then the kissing had to stop.

"The town turned ugly. There was this incredible momentum to exorcise the 80s. Kill them off," Bickerton says. "So it's a cathartic thing. It's like stoning a culprit. Venting collective rage, public executions."

He left New York to make his work, first in Bahia, Brazil, currently in Bali. Last May he had a splendidly over-the-top two-gallery show at Sonnabend and Lehmann Maupin.

The smartest of the post-Boom artists were quick studies. "I was the first phoenix," says Sean Landers, who had his initial solo show at the Andrea Rosen Gallery in New York in 1992. "I rose out of the ashes. I started showing right after everything turned bad. I started showing very lean and mean stuff. Writing on yellow paper. No more expensive materials or slick ideas."

The '90s, then, began as a reprise of the early '70s but without the electric energy. Conceptual art had become the new Academy. Somewhere, you felt, a computer had been programmed with Duchamp, Beuys, and other blue-chip Conceptualists and was coming up with Situations Vacant. Artists set themselves to making barely saleable work, like installations and performance pieces—not a particularly daring strategy when nobody was buying anyway (I am talking about Contemporary art here. A few dealers, like the Nahmads, of London, New York, Switzerland, and wherever else, had deep pockets, and experience, and were buying Modern work cheap).

Video became ubiquitous. The first artist videos in the late '60s and '70s were stark exercises in time and space that seemed designed—as if to differentiate themselves from the seductions of the entertainment industry—to be as unentertaining as possible, preferably boring, and sometimes grating, like Bruce Nauman's screaming clown. In the '90s, though, video became self-indulgent, diaristic, a kind of kicky visual equivalent of Easy Listening music.

The art world's glutinous embrace of photography was even more obviously dealer-driven. It was fine when the photographer was a Nan Goldin, whose snapshot aesthetic made Robert Mapplethorpe's pictures, say, suddenly look as classical as Irving Penn. But it's a whole lot less fine when the bar of achievement is lowered to ankle level, so that nowadays no fashion or celebrity photographer is too facile, too tacky, or too commercial to get his or her gallery show. Photography, like video, has become an appropriate form for a culture with the attention span of a goldfish.

The strategic alliance between the worlds of art and fashion is another of our period's defining characteristics. It is by no means the first art-&-fashion love affair, of course. The Surrealists, in their late, social-climbing phase, designed costumery and table settings for affairs like a Rothschild ball, and Yves Saint-Laurent referenced Mondrian.

All that seems, so to speak, just the dress rehearsal. Now design houses have decided that art-world cred is a plus, and pretty cheap compared with, say, a major ad campaign. Hugo Boss backed the Ross Blechner retrospective at the Guggenheim, Tocca gave a fashion show at Julian Schnabel's studio, and Gucci's Tom Ford signed a check for the Ann Hamilton piece at the Venice Biennale. It's not just a matter of business and social opportunity—though it's that, too, of course. There's also a mutual benefit. Fashion, after all, is just garments, *schmatta*, however hopped up with sex, money, and celebrity. Art confers a touch of class.

Fashion-based art is about surfaces and sensation. Sometimes it is irony-coated, as when Sylvie Fleury made arrangements of fancy shopping bags, or as in Claude Wampler's 1995 performance piece *She Is High, True or False?*, in which the artist would circumnavigate a cocktail party affecting to be an eerily aloof High Fashionista.

Sometimes, it's post-feminist and complicated.

On April 23, 1998 I went to the Guggenheim to see a piece by Vanessa Beecroft, curated by Yvonne Force—who also, *piccolo mondo*, curated the art in the then Hop Spot, Lot 61. It was a weird evening. The air was humid, at once misty and glimmery with thunder-light. I walked along 89th Street from

Madison to Fifth Avenue. Of a sudden I saw the Beecroft piece, pieces, really, through the curving street-level picture window on the corner.

It was hard to miss.

Twenty fashion models, standing, with the sullenly impassive near-snarls of angry cats. Fifteen were wearing flimsy Gucci underthings, and five were wearing nothing but shoes, also by Gucci, who had underwritten the event.

I stood and watched. A few people passed me on the pavement, respectable East Siders, and nobody else stopped. As the *Post* gossipist Cindy Addams is forever writing, *Only In New York*.

I walked on and into the Guggenheim. Which, it seems relevant to add, began its life as "The Museum of Non-Objective Art." Mostly naked fashion models at that time would have been unwelcome.

*

There were several bad years. In New York the galleries were being shouldered out of newly high-rent SoHo by fashion, but the move to Chelsea, an area of big, squat, unprepossessing buildings occupied by garages and auto-parts suppliers, seemed iffy at first. Janelle Reiring, a partner in the gallery Metro Pictures, notes that they moved from SoHo to Chelsea at the end of the '90s. "There were about four galleries here," she said. "I promised myself to go to every opening. *That* promise lasted about ten minutes!" Another gallerist, Renato Danese, says, "There was a time when you could walk the streets here and there was a deathly stillness."

Then there were the fairs. Art fairs, like auction houses, used to be for the trade, and as unexciting as any other trade fairs. The first European art fair to show contemporary art was the Cologne fair. Ernest Beyeler, the mega-dealer, started Art Basel two years later. Andre Emmerich remembers that he was the only New York dealer at the first Art Basel. Among the work he took was a canvas by Morris Louis. "It didn't sell," he says. Emmerich noted that a few European collectors might show up, but it was an unusual occurrence. As for sightings of actual artists at an art fair, that was about as welcome as livestock wandering around a butcher's (that remains pretty much the case, by the way). Other European art fairs followed. NYC in Madrid in 1982. FIAC (the Foire Internationale d'Art Contemporain) opened in Paris two years later. The first major US art fair opened in Chicago.

Then four New York dealers, Pat Hearn, Colin de Land, Paul Morris, and Matthew Marks, came up with an inexpensive way of kick-starting some action: a hotel show. Thus in 1992 a slew of international dealers sold out of rooms in the Gramercy Park Hotel. I remember Jay Jopling of White Cube presiding while Tracey Emin sat on a bed, making (then cheap) spidery drawings and talking about the general awfulness of her life in an affectless monotone. Gramercy hardly seemed a threat to Chicago but grew year by year. In 1999 they checked out of the hotel and moved to larger venues, renamed The Armory Show after the 1912 exhibition that chucked out the Duchamp urinal.

*

So to the current boom or bubble, which makes its predecessor seem puny. Bubbles are much like love affairs. No two are quite the same. Some end in horrors, others in pleasant regret. And—importantly—each time one is convinced that this is the real thing, that it will endure forever. So it is with the contemporary art bubble. In the '80s there were about eighty contemporary galleries in SoHo. There are now almost three hundred in Chelsea. Thirty-six hedge funds are invested in art, and the auction houses have increasingly involved themselves in what used to be the prerogative of dealers: the mechanics of art careers. Some years back, Christie's, New York flew in Maurizio Cattelan, then the hottest of the hot, to install a piece, pre-sale. (It depicted Pope John Paul felled by a meteorite.)

Recently Christie's, London approached a young curator. "Why don't you talk to us about curating a collection that we could then auction off?" he was asked. "Call it the Unknown Collection."

The velocity has become an in-joke. I was with Jeffrey Deitch in the office above his SoHo gallery. Deitch, one of the best gallerists in the business, and certainly the one with the most antic program, was, as usual, costumed as a banker in dark suit, black tie, and lace-up black shoes, and he was cackling to himself as he played a CD 'I'm losing my edge . . . I'm losing my edge . . .' the singer mourned. "All these young French and German dealers," Deitch explained.

He gleefully punched replay.

There's a rationale. A world-wide boom in museum-building has meant that the world's pools of available art are drying out. Great Impressionist paintings? Forget it. Gone, mostly gone. Major Modernism is around but cripplingly expensive (a serious Jackson Pollock would fetch $100 million). So most speculative energies are focusing on post-war art, and sizeable sums are being put up. A few years ago, a German dealer was said to have ploughed $50 million into buying up the 1970s oeuvre of the painter Gerhard Richter and to have recouped their investment many times over. Now the targeted artists are getting younger and younger.

This increasingly means that the work of budding artists is up at auction a few years after it has left their studios. This is risky career business, but a generation of artists has been brought up in a culture of marketing and brief pop-star careers. As for today's half-dozen *Über*-artists, they can seem critically untouchable in a period when hedge-fund collectors would rather trust well-compensated consultants than drudge reviewers. Like few artists before them—the Christos come to mind—these artists control their own careers.

Two questions nag. One: When will the downturn come? The art market has never gone up forever. What will trigger the collapse? And how brutal will it be? Shit does happen, whether as mundane as a global property-market collapse or as ugly as a dirty bomb. "We're at the top. Or near the top," the canny private dealer Asher Edelman told me in New York before the Armory fair a couple of years ago. His reasoning was that he had seldom seen so many major pieces coming on the market.

Alexander Henrici, New York's best-known maker of artist prints, was also at the fair. "I've not been this busy since 1990," he told me. The Year of the Bust, that is.

"Asher's wrong," Leslie Waddington told me in his booth. "We're *at* the top. There's trouble ahead." He added, "But I could be wrong."

"Have you ever been wrong?" I asked.

"Yes. In 1990. And it cost me $200 million dollars."

"How wrong can you be?" put in Clodagh, his wife.

I conveyed these presentiments to a New York maestro dealer, Richard Feigen.

"I've always known what's going to happen," he said sagely. "But I've never known when."

Will there be a downturn, I asked James Mayor?

"Of course. The question is when that happens to the kindergarten art will it bring the rest down too?"

Anyway, will the new collectors—the hedge-fund whizzes with no memory of past bumpy rides, for instance—care? Perhaps art truly has become like fashion, pop, or celebrity, toss-able when out of style?

"It's so much fun now!" David McKee, a New York dealer, said to me at a recent Basel fair. "It's a whole scene. And they love it! They gamble! They don't care if they lose."

If true, that *will* be a first.

Nagging question number two concerns the future reps of our Big Artists. The needle of taste can take years to settle. "In the late 20s Derain was easier to sell than Picasso," says London dealer James Mayor. "In the 30s Utrillo was one of the most expensive artists in the world." Utrillo, a sentimental drunk, is now barely a footnote.

Irving Sandler, the art historian whose *The Triumph of American Painting* celebrated just that, was briefly the manager of "The Club," a group of mostly painters and a handful of dealers, Leo Castelli being one. Sandler calculates that there were 250 artists in the New York School when it bestrode the world. Most of their names will now, of course, be wholly unfamiliar.

"Do you know how many Pop artists there used to be?" asks Irving Blum. "Three hundred." Who now remembers such a once well-thought of name as Allan D'Arcangelo?

Some of the Art Stars of the '80s—Julian Schnabel, Donald Baechler—have crawled out of the rubble, but many are still MIA, their works seen only in low-level day sales, if at all.

*

Simone de Pury was at tea in the Carlyle Hotel on Madison Avenue. The former beau of Louise McBain, and co-owner of the auction house Phillips with Danielle Luxembourg, De Pury is typical of Big Art in that he morphs from one position to another. He had a gallery in Geneva, and he has set up one art investment fund, Sirius, and he was now launching another. The Gerhard Richter venture, he says, was just one example, albeit a striking one, of a number of maneuvers in the shallow sixty-year space of Post-War Art. Dealers find an undervalued commodity and buy it up cheap. "Now I hear they are buying up early Kenny Scharfs. And Julian Schnabel's plate paintings," he said.

Some weeks later De Pury was conducting his own sale in the Phillips space on West 15th Street. Phillips has a let's-put-on-a-show sensibility, and the back of the room buzzed like a hive. De Pury rapped his gavel to little immediate avail and the sale began.

A lot vaulted, with most bids coming in by way of the bid-takers. at their telephones. De Pury addressed them by name. "Michaela . . . Olivier . . . Robin . . . It is with Michaela," he said, with dramatic emphases. "008 . . . that's interesting," he said, taking the number of a successful bidder's paddle.

Auctioneers have different styles just as arena rockers do—Christopher Burge at Christie's, a Brit, excels at putting-the-rich-folks-at-their-ease money jokes—and De Pury is pure theatre.

A spirited duel sprang up between two bidders, both (unusually) in the room.

"Why did you stop? It was so nice," he sighed as one dropped out. "Try one more little bid," he coaxed as another lot faltered; then he dropped the hammer, intoning "Souuuuuuld!"

"Simone should get an acting award" said the Miami collector Don Rubell after the sale. "He squeezes without making people angry."

*

The boom continues improbably to crest and roar like a wave that won't come crashing down, so the players, whether artists, dealers, collectors, or curators, are increasingly graded like stocks. Larry Gagosian, who has galleries in New York, Los Angeles, and London, was number one on a Power 100 list in the *Art Review* in 2004—last year it was Damien Hirst—and he is the perennial focus

of most (not always friendly) interest. All gallerists entice artists away from the competition, but few do it with the panache of Gagosian. So his moves are watched carefully. A couple of months before, he had given Richard Prince (whose work had begun skyrocketing at auction after twenty years of coasting) a show at his Los Angeles gallery. Gagosian had let this be known by way of a billboard which stood for several weeks on Beverly Boulevard. This is a device mostly used to promote new movies and rock albums and was probably yet another art-world first. Barbara Gladstone, Prince's New York-based primary dealer, could be assumed to have taken note.

As I write, I hear that Gagosian has just detached two other artists from their galleries. For that matter, another *Über*-gallerist, New York's Matthew Marks, has just one of California's hottest artists, from the jaws of his gallery.

Note the ravening metaphors I keep drifting into. In boom times, the art world reminds me of nothing more than those old Natural History Museum dioramas of life in the depths.

"Everything has changed. It's a matter of scale. It's a money game," says Irving Blum. "Things are bigger. More legitimized." He meant that art is now considered a necessary item in any worthy portfolio. It takes "ten"—ten million per annum—to be a player as a collector, he said. I had been told it would cost $25 million to start a high-end gallery from scratch these days and mentioned this figure.

"You can't. Nobody can," Blum said.

He meant everything was locked up tight.

Oh, yes. There had been another chapter in his ongoing Warhol saga.

Blum had been approached by Lawrence Graff, the leading London jeweler, who is one of Britain's most fervid collectors. Graff had asked if the *Red Liz* was for sale.

"I said yes. For 9 million," Blum told me.

"That's too much" Graff said.

"Lawrence," said Blum. "You grade your jewels and I grade my pictures. Nine million is the right price."

No deal.

A couple of days later Tobias Meyer of Sotheby's was on the phone. He had heard—the art world is a listening gallery, filled with Chinese whispers—and offered Blum a ten-million guarantee.

Fine.

"Lawrence bought it for 12.6. He wanted a hard under-bidder," Blum says. Larry Gagosian takes an optimistic view of the still-surging boom, seeing art as a solid value in times of cultural melt. "It can't be pirated. It can't be digitized. There are no unlicensed reproductions," he says. "A painting is a painting."

Coffee, Cocktails and Cigarettes

Daniel Young

Back in New York for the first time in over a decade, the Italian businessman's first observations of twenty-first century Manhattan were mostly positive. "The coffee is 1000 percent better," he marveled over dinner. "Everything is so much cleaner. Districts I was afraid to walk in are now fashionable. It is a shame, though, about all the *putane* you now see in midtown."

"Prostitutes in midtown?" replied his startled American friend in a low whisper the Italian may have confused for curiosity. "You can't be serious."

"I've seen them with my own eyes, on Madison Ave., Third Ave., Fifth Ave., women without overcoats, barelegged and under-clothed, huddled by the entrances of office buildings, puffing idly on cigarettes. In the middle of the day no less."

To think of the Italian of this story as naive would be naive. He was no doubt fulfilling the obligation now felt by all good Europeans to ridicule a succession of no-smoking laws that have literally pushed junior stockbrokers, art-history students, and—could it possibly be?—the chain-smoking members of Alcoholics Anonymous out into the gutter. Indeed, his little joke might have had a sharper edge had he also taken notice of the single males cruising past the revolving doors of midtown and Wall Street towers, checking out the leggy cigarette breakers the prohibitionists had smoked out of their cubicles and, in more than a few instances, corner offices. Loitering outside the north entrance of the new Condé Nast building, Prada-clad editorial assistants as slim as their Marlboro Lights were altering pedestrian traffic patterns on West 43rd, all the while gaining a strategic edge over nonsmoking EAs not privy to these morning and afternoon powwows with similarly repressed colleagues further up the mastheads of *Vogue* and *Vanity Fair*. Rather than stigmatize smoking, the ban had arguably made it advantageous to the career and social aspirations of ambitious young New Yorkers to inhale.

Everyone agrees: the new and improved New York is a cleaner, safer metropolis than it was ten, fifteen, twenty, and thirty years ago. Coffee, that

most loyal friend of loners and insomniacs, daydreamers and night owls, that liquid power source as vital to the twenty-four-hour city as gasoline and, ounce for ounce, only twenty-five times more expensive, is in fact better. A lot better. Elegant, shapely cocktails worthy of Dashiell Hammett's martini-swilling Nick and Nora Charles have reclaimed their position on the skyline, restoring an ideal of Manhattan sophistication suppressed for years by tequila sunrises, frozen margaritas, wine spritzers, and yuppie microbrews. And, thanks to the anti-smoking hysteria, fat, smelly cigars, as well as the smelly fat cats who smoked them, have been swept from our favorite gathering spaces.

Disagreement nevertheless endures about whether better truly means, well, better. Yes, tobacco prohibition ostensibly protects the health and defends the airspace of, if not the smokers themselves, the supposedly clean-living innocents who either work beside them or serve coffee and cocktails to them. True, the comprehensive ban from public spaces means diners at the city's eighteen thousand restaurants can, for better or (oftentimes) worse, actually taste their food and see their companions. And, sure, the demonization of secondhand smoke might soon be easing the workload at such institutions as the Memorial Sloan-Kettering Cancer Center and Chris French Dry Cleaners.

But with the convenience of not having to repeatedly empty ashtrays and deodorize wool sweaters comes sacrifice. Many come to New York so they can act in ways they are forbidden to act at home. Historically, the city has been a haven for refugees fleeing intolerance. Through a creative brain drain, its artistic and intellectual communities are enriched by repression elsewhere. Any attack on personal freedoms, including the liberty to engage in unhealthy activities, is troubling.

Happily, the caffeinated city is not fraught with comparable dilemmas pitting libertarians against reformers. New Yorkers remain free to drink awful java, and many of them still do. Outcries against the opening of yet another Starbucks, as opposed to complaints about the less-than-outstanding coffee served there, are predictable and, to a large extent, boring. (At last count there were, in the East Village alone, 43,802 Starbucks stores.) There is nothing more

maddening than meeting a friend for coffee, only to have him or her go on and on about how the coffee-bar chain is ruining New York, or how it is playing with our minds by sizing coffees in the inflated manner of eggs so there is no such thing as a "small." No, I would reply, your complaining is ruining New York. Your talking about Starbucks is keeping that name in daily conversation. Please don't call me back until a new Starbucks actually opens inside your apartment. Now that would be interesting.

Coffee snobbery is a target with greater possibilities. At Via Quadronni off Madison Avenue, fashionably correct Upper East Siders shell out $4 for an admittedly great take-out cappuccino. A regular coffee at hundreds of other Greek-owned diners throughout the metropolitan area, poured into a blue-and-white paper cup adorned with a Greek key motif, gods and goddesses, and monuments or icons of ancient Greece, is only $1. These cups all carry a message of hospitality, such as "we are happy to serve you," "it's our pleasure to serve you," and "serving you is a pleasure." Shouldn't we be paying more for such neighborliness, not less? The surcharge at coffee bars for milk-added coffee drinks itself constitutes a cultural revolution. Can you imagine the old Automat cafeterias asking more for a light coffee than a black one? Why not charge extra for sugar, too?

To long for the New York coffee of our *film noir* fantasies, of Edward Hopper canvases and beatnik coffeehouses, is understandable: this was, typically, a burnt-tasting black ink of a blend kept scalding hot in the Bunn-O-Matic in which it was brewed, poured from a glass carafe into a thick-lipped, unbreakable cup, again and again. Two or three refills of this dirty water meant you were ingesting the caffeine equivalent of ten espressos, to say nothing of the diuretic attributes that also make uninterrupted sleep impossible. If the caffeine does not do the job, the multiple round-trips to the bathroom will. Is it any mystery, then, that gallons of decaf also keep you up all night?

Decent-quality, freshly ground, aromatic coffee, whether brewed by the drip method or under the intense pressure of an espresso machine, is now a New York must. A serious restaurant or café cannot get by with coffee that lacks body, flavor, some acidic brightness, and, in the case of espresso, the residual sweetness in the thick *crema*. This expectation of a pleasant-tasting experience already constitutes a major advance.

Espresso, however, remains problematic, largely because it requires an attentive barista keeping the machinery and workings clean and the coffee properly measured and compacted through tamping. Remembering that espresso is a method and a technique rather than a particular bean or a specific roast, a consistent result eludes New York practitioners, due either to their own negligence or that of misinformed or insufficiently demanding clients. The fashion for drinks prepared with espresso has outpaced the population's ability to access and appreciate them.

Forgive native New Yorkers our unusually high tolerance for bad-tasting espresso, bearing as we do the legacy of painfully bitter cups at Italian cafés, pastry shops, and social clubs in Little Italy, pre-1975 SoHo, Greenwich Village, the Belmont section of the Bronx, Corona in Queens, and the Brooklyn neighborhoods of Bensonhurst and, before it turned into a Seattle on the Gowanus Canal, Carroll Gardens. Those proud immigrants of Naples and Sicily punished us with pitch-black espresso so foul that a strip of lemon peel was served with it to rub on the rim of the demitasse and rub out the flavor. (This is known as Roman-style, never mind that no one in Rome drinks their coffee that way.) The ritual was seen as a rite of passage and a rather nasty test of masculinity, though some might easily have suspected the Italians of playing a cruel joke on

their Irish and Jewish neighbors. A teenager who could sip an unsweetened one without wincing had come of age. Women rarely touched their lips to such an espresso. Instead they sipped cappuccinos dusted with cinnamon or chocolate—ladies' coffee drinks the men secretly coveted but didn't dare order. The taste for strong, bitter coffee shared by more recent immigrants from Latin America is more conditional. They take it with two to four rounded teaspoons of sugar and a half-cup of hot milk.

Cafe con leche is a unisex drink, and it is unwise to suggest otherwise to any *hombre* who orders it.

In so far as cities and drinks can have genders, New York, the vertical city of skyscrapers, is clearly masculine and so is coffee. (Tea and all the rituals and paraphernalia that go with it are, if you had to choose, feminine.) It is hardly surprising, then, that New York is a coffee town. As a boy I recall Manhattan rides in my father's 1958 Impala, the uptown-bound sedan briefly crushing gushes of steam billowing from manholes, potholes, and cracks in the asphalt. I imagined Manhattan as one giant percolator feeding boiling coffee to the masses through an underground network of leaky pipes.

Unlike the world of coffee, the world of cocktails is divided less by gender than by race, with trends bouncing between brown (Scotch, bourbon, rye, dark rum) and white (vodka, gin, sake) alcohol. Still, if you had to choose, and understanding that there are no absolutes, the browns are for guys, the whites for gals. From the 1980s to the 1990s, allegiances within both sexes shifted from single malt scotches—stylish bars displayed collections as them in back-bar trophy cases—to vodkas, vodka cocktails, and vodka and gin martinis. The rise of vodka in the '90s was sudden and incredibly complete. Chic advertisements by Absolut and, later, their competitors sold an impossible idea: The drink that had no flavor had pizzazz.

Cocktails first came of age in New York in the 1920s and '30s, reflecting the giddy high times of the Jazz Age and later, following Prohibition and the great stock-market crash of 1929, as an antidote to and escape from depression. During this period, cocktails became symbolic of the New York intelligentsia and the literary life. The writers Dorothy Parker and Dawn Powells were big drinkers, knew big drinkers, and wrote about them. In the classic cocktail town, the New York writer is immersed in cocktails, and it is no giddy affair. Cocktails may be associated with Art Deco supper clubs, penthouse soirées, witty dialogue, and the whole glamorous business of going out on the town, but very often there is something dark and serious happening within.

The cliché of the 1950s encompassed the three-martini lunch and the man in a gray flannel suit who absolutely had to know how to make a perfect martini. During the '60s and '70s, the symbolic importance of the cocktail was greatly diminished. Writers explored hallucinogens, not gins. LSD, grass, heroin, and, moving into the '80s, cocaine were emblematic of that period.

The New York habit of going out for cocktails was revived by the young women either portrayed in or, more likely, influenced by *Sex and the City*. They loved the Cosmopolitan, the cocktail the show made famous, and they knew that colorless vodka did not stain their Prada tops and that everything dissolves in gin anyway. With glasses invariably filled so that they somehow hold a tablespoon of liquid over their intended capacity, spills and stains are commonplace. (A guy in a rugby shirt at the great burger bar J.G. Melon once told me there is more liquid in the top quarter-inch of a martini glass than in the bottom two inches.) "Tini" madness soon followed, the idea being that if you stuck that suffix onto the name of a white liquor (e.g., sake-tini) you'd have a hot drink.

Bartenders have supplanted DJs as the star mixologists at bar/lounges and clubs in Manhattan and the new Brooklyn. The more creative among them are experimenting not only with fruits and liqueurs, the traditional mixers, but also with exotic flavors like cucumber and rose water, saffron and *wasabe*. Their latest formulas are regularly featured in the hottest magazines. Some have been reporting that the rye Manhattan, that great New York cocktail, is a retro drink on the ascent. Whether they get such intelligence from bartenders or

liquor-company publicists is difficult to ascertain. Regardless, New Yorkers are drinking Manhattans again.

Cocktail fashion will come and go. Makers of both world-famous and boutique gins are doing everything they can to catch up with vodka and help maintain white-cocktail supremacy. Bartenders are inventing new drinks with different gin varieties, the spicing being what distinguishes gin from vodka. If the rye Manhattan becomes the next Cosmo, brown liquors are sure to stage a comeback.

Drinks and cocktails have not changed nearly as dramatically as the establishments in which they are dispensed. The New York bar itself, traditionally an Irish-owned, often Irish-named affair spanning the social strata from the working-class Brooklyn of Farrell's in Windsor Terrace (near Prospect Park) to P.J. Clarke's, the Third Avenue lair of Manhattan fat cats, is an endangered species. In leaner times, Clarke's was the bar to which Ray Milland returned for his frightening drinking sprees in the 1948 Billy Wilder classic, *Lost Weekend*.

In the 1980s, the gentrification of the Irish bar scene was most apparent on Amsterdam Avenue between 75th and 86th Streets. Seemingly overnight, this rundown stretch of *bodegas*, kosher markets, Irish bars, and tenement storefronts on the Upper West Side was converted into a pub crawl for rich college boys. Years ago, this crowd hadn't even known that Manhattan had a West Side. Now the Amsterdam bars were so popular it seemed you needed to flash a photo ID *and* a recent bank statement to gain admittance. Double-parked BMWs with out-of-state plates may have angered drivers of taxis and the number 7 and 11 buses, but they impressed the coeds on a year-long spring break.

In the 1990s, a similar if less complete transformation took hold of Ninth Avenue in the '40s, the heart of Hell's Kitchen. For sinners of the bottle, a bar was never more than 50 feet away. Neither was a church in a neighborhood once notorious for gin-runners and, later, gang warfare. Extending south to 34th Street, this crime-ridden area was once filled with railroad yards, breweries, factories, warehouses, docks, and the stinking 39th Street abattoirs, as well as squalid tenements. Now lounge bars with names like Vintage and Revolution were taking control, jacking up not only their own comparatively low rents but also those asked of the newer, younger, better-paid, and generally whiter tenants colonizing the area west of midtown.

Theme bars, a novelty in the 1980s, are still something of a factor now. Sports bars are so passé that it's hard to believe they were trendy, even fashion-

able, during the reigns of Reagan and Koch. The Sporting Club in Tribeca had approximately 1,321 television screens showing everything from NFL football games to mahjong matches from the Senior Center at the 14th Street YMHA. The best cleavages from the state of New Jersey could not get a second look from the overstimulated sports fanatics in these environs.

Cigar bars and cigar bar/restaurants caught on in the bullish 1980s as masculine places for celebrating—and spending chunks of—gravity-proof salaries, helium-powered profits, and soaring stock options. Humidors at these bars were renting for as much as $100 per month, which, on a cubic-volume basis, was eleven times more expensive than a Trump Tower penthouse. Some humidors were sold as condos. Already fading in the late 1990s, the cigar-bar fad was both crushed and salvaged by the new smoking laws. The legislation stipulated that cigar bars needed to have opened before December 31, 2001 to remain as smoking establishments. This loophole effectively prevented new competitors from opening while securing for the surviving fifteen or sixteen cigar bars and bar-restaurants newfound status as the last surviving refuges of the New York smoker.

The appeal of tapas bars, hotel bars, and wine bars shows no signs of slow-ing. Wine bars assume an educational role. You can't just go to one and order a glass of red. You must first be instructed on the merits of a particular wine pro-ducer and the characteristics of a grape variety. At Bar Veloce's three downtown locations, the instruction and coaching extend beyond the wine. Italian film

classics play silently on a plasma TV at the end of the bar. When your companion, existing or perspective, has his or her back to the screening of Fellini's *La Dolce Vita* (1960), the English subtitles are there for you like a cinematic Cyrano, feeding you good lines. Need an icebreaker? "It may seem strange but I already know you well" flashes across the screen. *Grazie,* Marcello.

The constant with cocktails, as with coffee and cigarettes, is that they double as eminently sociable and entirely solitary pursuits. This duality is at the heart of New York existence: to be with everyone, no one, or something of both. Regrettably, though perhaps for the greater good, the New York that smokes is losing that versatility. Another casualty of the cleaner, gentrified, and more antiseptic New York is the breakup of two classic pairings: coffee & cigarettes and cocktails & cigarettes. (A third configuration, coffee & cocktails, has a deservedly narrow constituency, Irish coffees and latte Kahlua martinis notwithstanding.) By forbidding smoking in the establishments where drinks and java are dispensed, the laws risk converting the most public of great cities into a community of private pursuits.

Worse still, tourists who smoke, our friend the Italian among them, may continue to tell bad jokes about women in doorways.

Writing New York

Meakin Armstrong

My East Village apartment is a shambles. A teetering stack of novels finally collapsed. Domino-style, they slammed onto a bookcase and caused still more books to fly. Hemingway and Richard Hughes shot out like bullets from the bookcase and toppled my mountain bike onto the floor, which upset my downstairs neighbor. An argument ensued. That neighbor and I are no longer speaking.

Such is New York. Everything here is jury-rigged and tenuous. In a typical Chinese-puzzle New York apartment, we live stripped-down lives. We haven't the space for spoon collections, much less the Library of America. Unread books must go, and it's depressing, because unread books are an indictment, a call to failure. They are a dust-gathering accusation, and a testament to the many distractions of this city.

I moved to New York to be a writer. At first, I was on the Upper East Side, in a one bedroom above a deli staffed with belligerent cashiers. My roommate lived behind a wall of crappy, custom-made bookcases. When I escaped that neighborhood in 1988, I ended up behind different set of (equally crappy) bookcases in Alphabet City. I've since carted books and detritus to all my apartments, up to my present holding pen on East 13th Street.

Many of my books, whether on the floor or still on the bookshelves, are set in New York. I read about this place, because this city is where "sister" Carrie Meeber met her downfall and where Miss Lonelyhearts listened to the lovelorn. A horror of New York's overcrowded streets was the driving force behind what made Sammy Glick "run." Beyond such writers as Theodore Dreiser, Budd Schulberg, and Nathanael West, its neighborhoods inspired writers as varied as Nik Cohn, Pietro di Donato, John Dos Passos, Ralph Ellison, Joseph McElroy, Isaac Bashevis Singer, and Gilbert Sorrentino.

When F. Scott Fitzgerald stood on the newly constructed observation deck of the Empire State Building and looked out over New York, he wrote that he had never suspected that his adopted city wasn't infinite, that it had an actual limit. Even today, his surprise is understandable—New York is labyrinthine, with a deep inner space that comes from so many people living atop one another. Here, jostling go-getters and slow-going daydreamers are mixed-in with slack-jawed tourists in a scattershot manner. One could live in a three-block radius in New York, and still experience the world.

This city's very nature requires a different sort of literature. We give up the wide-open spaces for competition, communion, and contact. Go back to 1855, when Walt Whitman's *Leaves of Grass* first appeared: it applied even then. The poet wrote of the city's energy, drive, and occasional sense of shared purpose among strangers and passersby. Whitman is still the city's greatest writer. He is its standard-bearer and what New York deserves. Of course, deserving and getting are different things.

*

Many of the books strewn across my floor were written after 1977, when this city went to hell. Writers whose works date from then have oscillated between enjoying the city's lack of supervision, to fighting against its decline. Others were wistful. New writers emerged as the city changed yet again. Start with the Bronx: it brought us Cynthia Ozick, Don DeLillo, and Richard Price.

Essayist, short-story writer, and novelist Cynthia Ozick believes those with firmly anchored personalities, the ones who are irretrievably principled, receive little but agony and bad luck. In her elegant 1997 novel, *The Puttermesser Papers*, Ruth Puttermesser is a lawyer "with a Jewish face and a modicum of American mistrust of it." Because of sexism and anti-Semitism, Puttermesser is consigned to the backroom of a white-shoe law firm until she leaves to work for the city as general counsel. She is promoted. She becomes vital to the city bureaucracy's spasmodic workflow until a political appointee shunts her off to irrelevance.

In Puttermesser's confused fury, she inadvertently creates a golem. Ozick's view of '80s and '90s New York City hangs heavily in the novel's background: it is a decaying, pre-dotcom bubble, vaguely hopeless place (and that's exactly what it was like), but—and perhaps this is something only a committed New Yorker can understand—it is still the only place in which to live.

Ozick isn't wistful for an imagined doily-draped past; she's gloomy for its future. Likewise, she doesn't object to the notion of an unfinished New York, the one Rem Koolhaas wrote of in 1978's *Delirious New York*: "New York is a city that will be replaced by another city." She wants a different matrix all together, a New York that allows for the civil and the smart.

Don DeLillo has become literary shorthand for the post-Pynchon novelist whose books brim with pop culture references and skewed contours of reality. His best novels, *White Noise* (1985) and *Libra* (1988) also have a sense of impending doom—be it an encroaching cloud of noxious chemicals, or the impending assassination of JFK. His *Underworld* (1997) begins in a dazzling manner, with perhaps the best first sixty pages of any novel. It's at the old Polo Grounds, and the Brooklyn Dodgers are playing the New York Giants in the third game of a tiebreaker; the winner will go to the 1951 World Series. With two men on base in the bottom of the ninth and the Dodgers losing 4-2, Bobby Thomson smashes a three-run homer off Dodger reliever Richard Branca. The crowds go wild. In the stands are Toots Shor, Frank Sinatra, Jackie Gleason, and J. Edgar Hoover. In the confusion, Gleason, drunk, vomits on Sinatra's shoes. Someone in the stands catches the winning baseball, but the next day no one is sure which person has the the actual ball that made baseball history. It simply can't be verified.

Here, DeLillo cuts away to follow Nick Shay, a Bronx teen listening to the game on the radio. Shay spends some eight-hundred pages trying to get the authentic game-winning ball. *Underworld* brims with rooftops and skyline. So much so, that when DeLillo leaves New York, it enervates. It's as though we are in that damned car with Shay while he drifts through the Western desert in search of that baseball. Those pages go on. And on. And still on, into the horizon, as seemingly endless as the desert itself.

In 2003, Delillo returned to New York for *Cosmopolis*, the story of a 28-year-old billionaire, his outrageously appointed limousine, an epic traffic jam, and an overpowering desire for a haircut. The novel journeys downtown, with a variety of characters entering and leaving the limo. The car may move by inches through the gridlock, but the story veers uncontrollably: *Cosmopolis* is New York

excess in satire; it's less of a Manhattan limo ride than one through a Coney Island funhouse: monsters appear, then quickly recede.

Richard Price grew up in Parkside Houses in the Wakefield section of the Bronx. Nowadays, New York makes only passing appearances in his novels. Arguably, however, Price writes about an imagined sixth borough because, even though his stories take place in the housing projects of a (fictional) New Jersey city, they nonetheless *feel* like '70s New York. His best novel thus far is *Clockers* (1992), which includes reportage on how crack is made and sold, how people get by in the projects, and how the police conduct homicide investigations.

*

To the rest of America, Manhattan *is* New York. It's home to New Year's Eve and Broadway tripe. Countless novels have also featured Manhattan, from *Slaves of New York* and *Bright Lights, Big City*, to *Bonfire of the Vanities*. Meanwhile, historical fiction writers such as E. L. Doctorow, Caleb Carr, and Michael Chabon have approached Manhattan through its past. It charms to read these books, especially Chabon's *Amazing Adventures of Kavalier & Clay* (2000). This novel brings the cityscape of the 1940s and '50s to light: men in suits and hats jostle at the street corners; the city feels un-air-conditioned. The novel is a pleasant diversion well imagined—but perhaps too much so: as the story moves on and becomes increasingly like the comic books its protagonists produce.

While New York nostalgia is undergoing a boom, another is 9/11. Done sincerely, as in Art Spiegelman's comic *In the Shadow of No Towers* (2004), such books convey agony and confusion, albeit in a scattershot manner. Sometimes 9/11 is used as an ironic set piece: a character's conflict has seemingly ended, the novel is about to conclude—when in the distance, the planes approach (see Paul Auster's anemic 2006 *Brooklyn Follies*).

Too often, however, these books are about self-possessed city dwellers who find spiritual release from disaster. Their characters learn the various home truths that others living elsewhere seemingly already know: stop and smell the roses, and so on. Thus far, 9/11 novels are tragedy porn. They are for those who fall victim to the Affective Fallacy, the belief, among other things, that good writing is what makes you cry.

*

Two novels published in the late '70s have managed to link Manhattan with Richard Nixon: *The Public Burning* by Robert Coover (1977) and *Jailbird* by Kurt Vonnegut (1979). Coover's *Burning* is one of the most imaginative novels of that decade. Here, Uncle Sam is real, the personification of the United States. When the President is at full-strength with a working mojo, he has more than the bully pulpit; he is *literally* Uncle Sam in his cracker-barrel glory. But Uncle Sam is in a death match with archenemy, the Phantom—the Soviet Union. Narrated by a young Vice President Nixon, *Burning* takes place in 1953. Ethel and Julius Rosenberg are to be executed in Times Square. The novel was controversial in its day, and rumors abound that it was pulled from the market at the urging of Nixon supporters—even though his callowness and lack of gravitas make him oddly sympathetic.

Coover's New York isn't meant to be realistic, except for its asides on the meaning of Times Square (he calls it the "ritual center of the Western World") and the harsh reality of the Rosenbergs' Lower East Side. This is done purposefully: the Rosenbergs are ordinary idealists, not the cartoonish Uncle Sam, nor the conflicted Nixon. They are people who died so that America could feel a momentary sense of moral vindication.

In Kurt Vonnegut's *Slapstick: Or Lonesome No More!* (1976) a near-future, almost-deserted Manhattan is called "Skyscraper National Park," and had the King of Michigan living at the top of the Empire State Building. For *Jailbird* (1979), Vonnegut ventures from underground catacombs to the top of the Chrysler Building. His protagonist, Walter F. Starbuck, is a former-everything: former Communist, former Nixon advisor on "youth affairs," and a former prisoner who wanders Gump-like through the last century's major events. Vonnegut weaves together the Nuremberg Trials, Nixon, Roy Cohn, Watergate, Sacco and Vanzetti, Whittaker Chambers, and relentless capitalism into a cohesive whole, held together by New York itself.

However, Vonnegut is a fabulist: the book isn't about the city we live in, except in the deepest sense. A single conglomerate, the RAMJAC Corporation seems to own everything in New York. In a city whose streetscape has become increasingly denuded by the faceless proprietors of Starbucks, Dunkin' Donuts, and the latest consulates for Banana Republic, the book is not too far from the truth.

*

In Californian Steve Erickson's fantastical novel *The Sea Came in at Midnight* (1999), the East Village is a ticky-tacky Hell. It's an area is for people too drug-addled and self-destructive to care. However, they're also privileged; they seek out this destructive environment as amusement, not because they need cheap rent. Any downtowner can attest to that area's pervasive truth.

Best known as a poet, writer and activist, Eileen Myles has often covered the downtown scene as a true bohemian. Her *Chelsea Girls* (1994) is a group of short stories, or "autobiographical fiction," about an alcoholic lesbian named Eileen Myles. It's laced with hypnotic sentences that flow like rivulets in the gutter, or down tenement windows. They are finely crafted, only seemingly top of the head. In her 1991 collection of verse, *Not Me* (1991), Myles writes in telegraphic reverie:

Brooklyn is just a
ride away. I'm hungry
again! While the ponytail
drips down my back &
I pull on the black shirt that's wet from
the pool, but so
what, it's August and
the six birds in
New York sing back.

Taken as a whole, Myles' work is part of an increasingly lost New York, where dissipation and production were still possible. "Downtown," was once an area without hall monitors, towering NYU dorms, and uninspired, so-called bistros.

In Harry Mathews' richly complex 1987 novel, *Cigarettes,* New York was where they once practiced total-control sadomasochism. Mathews is the cofounder of the journal *Locus Solus* (named after the Raymond Rousseau novel) with John Ashbery, Kenneth Koch, and James Schuyler, and in 1972 he was elected to the French writing group OuLiPo. The structure for *Cigarettes* is perhaps Mathews' most OuLiPian: each of the fourteen chapters examines the relationships between two of thirteen primary characters. Although a complex whole, the book engages on numerous levels: as an urban comedy of manners, art world satire, and threnody.

Downtown aspirations and energies feature prominently in Meredith Brosnan's *Mr Dynamite* (2004). Jarleth Prendergast, a thirty-seven-year old experimental filmmaker and copy-shop flunky, is awaiting an inheritance from a recently deceased Irish aunt. When Prendergast's inheritance turns out be a teapot instead of the much needed "cash fuel injection," he copes by drinking, a lot, reading the *I Ching*, and living in a whorl of cinematic and musical *noir* (*Point Blank*, John Coltrane and Johnny Hartman, Scott Walker). Prendergast's exploitation of trendy Celtic fetishism will also make you think thrice the next time you watch *Riverdance* or step in St Patrick's Day vomit. Interestingly, much of *Mr Dynamite* takes place in areas little served by literature: Inwood, Long Island City, pre-hipster-mecca Williamsburg—even the concrete plaza, brocade curtains, and men's room urinals of the Metropolitan Opera. Along with Turkish immigrant Erje Ayden's *The Crazy Green of Second Avenue* (1965, with introduction by Frank O'Hara), this might be the most honest novel about the discovery of New York.

*

Queens, the city's largest borough in terms of area, is also the most ethnically diverse county in the United States. It's a hip-hop capital and in the television

universe, the blue-collar worker calls it home. Strangely, except for Edwidge Danticat's *The Dew Breaker* (2004), which is concerned with the everyday life of Haitian immigrants (one of whom was a Duvalier goon), novels aren't generally set there.

A relatively new exception is *Paradise Travel* (2006) by Jorge Franco. It's the story of a young Medellín couple's journey to New York City as visa-less immigrants. When Marlon and Reina finally arrive in Queens, things go awry: they are quickly—and accidentally, or so it seems—separated. Marlon makes his way in the émigré community of Jackson Heights alone, never forgetting Reina, for whom he continues to search, deciding that he "would live through whatever hell New York had to offer" in order to find her. The book is somewhat slight (it doesn't have much by way of shading), but it performs an all-to-rare service— it lays bare the New York immigrant experience.

D. Keith Mano's *Take Five* (1982)—roughly comparable to the novels of William Gaddis and glowingly reviewed by cognoscenti—was a commercial flop. Few, including the publisher, seem to have been ready for a six-hundred-page, obscenity-filled and sacrilegious novel about a failed filmmaker who finds salvation while approaching death. Simon Lynxx is the misanthropic scion of an old Queens family whose grand old manse has been turned into a house museum. He drinks in its backyard, pelted by trash from the surrounding apartment buildings. He thinks about his filmic masterpiece, *Jesus 2001*, a Christian *Godfather*. One mishap after another ensues; Lynxx loses all of his senses. *Take Five* is reminiscent not only of early Christian writings, but also of Hermann Broch's *The Death of Virgil*. While an easier read than Broch, there is also its Rabelaisian spirit, freneticism, and its vacuum-packed prose. These things (of course) can either exhilarate or exhaust.

*

"Brooklyn is the new downtown," magazines breathlessly proclaim. But even though significant parts of the borough are nowadays manicured and populated with vw Touaregs and Bertini baby-strollers, there is nonetheless a distinct attitude that is Brooklyn. Perhaps it's best illustrated in Brooklynite Rafi Zabor's 2005 memoir *I, Wabenzi: A Souvenir (Aporia)*. When Zabor finds himself in a battle for a parking space with some privileged kids in a shiny new car, he leans out the car window and shouts at them in "a voice so full of a barbarian and pure Brooklyn savagery that it shocked even me: 'HOW'D YA LIKE A BIG DENT IN YOUR NICE NEW FUCKING MERCEDES!'"

Brooklyn is also (for better or worse) Paul Auster. He is prolific, popular, and Park Slope-identified. In *The New York Trilogy* (1985–6), Auster introduces us to his style: engaging, digressive narratives marked by strange, often untenable coincidences and disquieting word play. About his writer-detective Quinn, he writes: "New York is an inexhaustible place, a labyrinth of endless steps, and

no matter how far he walked, no matter how he came to know its neighborhoods and streets, it always left him with the feeling of being lost." Auster has his staunch supporters and impatient detractors. He is, however, the writer for the rising Brooklyn: the one of shimmering towers, yoga classes, and weekend retreats.

Jonathan Lethem's milieu is more working-class; often his characters, like the author himself, grew up in the realtor-christened area of Boerum Hill. His *Motherless Brooklyn* (1999) is a detective novel with a twist: the detective isn't a professional, but rather a townie among the gentrifiers. He also has Tourette's Disorder. While entertaining in parts, readers would have been better served by reading the likes of Ross Macdonald or Charles Willeford.

Fortress of Solitude (2003) was to be Lethem's masterpiece. In the *ur*-Boerum Hill we encounter the painfully named Dylan Ebdus, the child of hippie gentrifiers who force him to attend public school with African-American kids from the nearby projects. He's harassed ("yoked") on the street and robbed of his change. His mother leaves him. Eventually, he meets Mingus Rude (more straining at Significance), the motherless biracial child of a former R&B singer, who becomes both his friend and protector. Ebony and Ivory take up graffiti. Later, they become (in something of a plot lurch, due to the possession of a magic ring) superheroes. While there are strong, incantatory passages, *Fortress* as a whole is not unlike a slide show of someone's vacation, in which the host is a one-sided conversationalist and doesn't notice that you're glassy-eyed and looking about for an escape.

A straight-shot autobiography is better. Vincent Fedorchak's *Fuzz One: A Bronx Childhood* (2005) dispenses with magic rings to tell a similar story. Vincent, a white boy misfit, becomes a graffiti artist—and the book has hundreds of pictures to prove it. Of the homeless in the subway system, Fedorchak writes: "When they were bombed on that bum juice and the trains would fly by them, it was like watching TV, and the only channel they had was the New York City Subway . . . But I'm sorry to say that graffiti is gone. The die-hard bombers have passed on by . . . . New York city is different now. Somehow, we let it get away from us."

*

Perhaps we let New York get away from us, or perhaps we'd grown tired of what it had become. While living in New York has always been difficult, in years past there was a vital difference: the city had always seemed inevitable and *necessary*. It was the Big Time. Writers were drawn it not only for its opportunities, but also because it easily symbolized both the benefits of capitalism for those who won or the dire consequences for those who lost. As Robert Coover writes in *The Public Burning*: "New York was like some kind of Jerusalem, an El Dorado. There were picture books and photos in the papers, newsreels, stereoscopes, and later, Tru-Vue films, all those movies about the great Empire City. . . . [It was the] place where the melting pot melted . . . ."

From Blackout to Blintzes (and Beyond)
Robert Sietsema

When I first hit town in 1977 as a wide-eyed refugee from Madison, Wisconsin, I found my new East Village neighbors perched on a sand hill in a trash-strewn lot that had, only a year earlier, contained tenements. I was moving with my girlfriend, Gretchen Van Dyk, into a railroad tenement next door to the lot. Our building on East 14th Street lurked among a row of nine tenements built in 1897; Sylvester Stallone was said to have lived in one of them. There were four flats per floor, and the claw-foot bathtub was in the kitchen. The toilet, in a tiny room, was flushed by water descending from a copper-lined, oak box tenuously attached up near the ceiling and released via a pull-chain. Once in a while the box would tear away from the wall and deposit its liquid load on the heads of users below.

My new neighbors were having a barbecue, gleefully grilling garlic-laced Polish sausages over kindling found in the lot. As we sat down to eat our meal around the campfire like cowboys, the sound of fire engines ripped the night air, and, when we later went up on the roof of my building, we looked across the Lower East Side and saw fires burning in several locations. That was the Age of the Great Fires; one school of thought contended that they were set by welfare mothers trying to get out of their crumbling tenement apartments, having been promised a $3,000 relocation fee by the city, while another insisted the fires were started by landlords so they could kick out their black and Latin tenants, collect insurance, then yuppify the premises. The empty lots left by buildings that had been pulled down eventually became dozens of community gardens, half of which were later destroyed by Rudy Giuliani.

I arrived on June 10. A month later, on July 13, as I sat playing Monopoly with a couple of new friends, the lights flickered once, came back on, then flickered out more permanently ten seconds later, at 9:34 PM. It was the Great Blackout. There was no electricity for more than twenty-four hours, and it was with some delight that we stood on the roof and surveyed the darkened city, devoid even of streetlight. The Strauss store at the corner was looted by perps who lowered themselves through the skylight. We had water pressure, but, at

Stuyvesant Town across the street, where the middle class dwelled, people were replenishing their water supply by lowering buckets by rope to accomplices waiting below.

Near the Strauss store in one of our row of tenements, basked a sandwich shop of uncommon virtue. Jack's Nest specialized in long-roasted beef brisket, but the bread they served it on nearly overshadowed the fat-streaked and caramelized meat. It reeked of East Village *terroir*. Cut on the meat slicer, the bread was from a humongous loaf with a dark, rigid crust and an open texture, and the slices were so huge they had to be cut in half to make the sandwiches. Was there some sourdough in there? Not sure, but the bread sent the brisket sandwich, dripping meat juices, into orbit. In the early days of the hipster East Village, there were almost no restaurants that stayed open after 6:00 PM I know it's hard to believe, given the saturation of the current East Village with late-night cafes.

Luckily, there was Kiev. At the corner of East 7th Street and Second Avenue, Kiev was a Ukrainian restaurant that managed to stay open late into the evening, offering a combination of diner standards and Eastern European fare—principally blintzes, cutlets, soups, and *pierogis*. It wasn't long before Christina's, at 13th and First Avenue, appeared to catch the evening overflow, though it became most popular for late breakfasts. Hipsters—originally from places like Minnesota, Florida, and Upstate New York—would appear around 11:00 AM, rubbing their eyes, for Christina's famous *challah* French toast with extra syrup and a side of bacon.

Of course Katz's Delicatessen was open in 1977, but that was across the Houston Street frontier in a neighborhood that was still distinctly Lower East Side and remote from the East Village—a cognomen popularized by hippies but probably originally invented by real-estate developers. It took us a couple of years to discover Katz's, with its unctuous brisket-based sandwiches, but once we did, we'd splurge and share a sandwich once a week or so. Even then it seemed quaint and decrepit to us, a vision of old New York that we could grasp only faintly. I can't explain why we never patronized the Second Avenue Deli— now sadly defunct—except to say it seemed expensive and was thronged with very old people. B&H Deli also existed, but the food would have seemed too bland and cheesy to us. Anyway, St Marks was our counter-cultural strip.

From 1979 until 1993 I was in the Noise band Mofungo. The name was a misspelling of the Puerto Rican dish *mofongo*, which Phil Dray had misremembered from a menu. I wasn't really much of a musician, but at the time bands were the main social outlet for men in their twenties, as Italian and Puerto Rican social clubs must have once been in the same neighborhoods. Rehearsal studios were rented by the hour, and each hour required a surtax of a six-pack of beer, which would be guzzled at stray moments. I started doing my foodzine, *Down the Hatch*, in 1989 or 1990, with an eye toward reviewing ethnic restaurants that would be of interest principally to musicians, or so I thought. With a great deal of luck, I parlayed the foodzine (perhaps the first in the nation) into a restaurant-reviewing gig at the *Village Voice* some years later.

*

In 1977 Manhattan's Chinatown was confined to Mott, Mulberry, Bayard, Pell, and Doyers—five narrow streets that had defined the city's most visible Asian community for over a century. Though plentiful, eating establishments were almost exclusively in a Cantonese vein and fell into two basic categories. First were the humble tea parlors, typified by Mayfair Coffee House, a walk-down space at 20 Mott Street where the waiters wore somber black vests over their patched white shirts. They shuffled as they tossed huge bready dumplings called *char sui bao*—known to us as Chinese hamburgers—onto the tables on small white plates, and sluiced gallons of steaming tea from stainless-steel reservoirs into plain glasses that scalded the fingers of the uninitiated. The waiters often seemed to be in a bad mood. Other tea parlors of that era had waggish names like King Sun (11 Pell), Lucky Yue (172 Canal), and—a place at 25 Pell that persisted well into the 1990s, whose name I spent years pondering, though I never set foot in the premises—Pell's Dinty. *Dinty*, an ancient Irish word meaning "dainty," is still familiar in the Midwest, where a quick lunch might consist of a can of Dinty Moore beef stew. Had Pell's Dinty originally been an Irish place?

The patrons of the tea parlors were mainly Chinese men, often picking up a quick snack on the way to work as waiters at the second type of establishment: restaurants that specialized in Cantonese food aimed at non-Asians. The fare at these places ranged from cheap stir-fries and over-rice dishes to bigger-ticket entrees of pork, beef, shrimp, or—most expensive of all—whole fish. Diners often combined a trip to one of these restaurants with a visit to the curio shops that lined the streets, peddling mahjong sets, paper umbrellas, and Chinese pajamas embroidered with laughing babies. Vague memories of nineteenth-century opium dens and tong hatchet murders, as described by Luc Sante in *Low Life*, still lent a raffish air to the neighborhood and contributed to a sense of exoticism. According to Nick Tosches, the last opium den in Chinatown closed in 1957. But in 1977, the sickly smell of opium smoke still lingered in the air.

The Cantonese spots frequented by non-Asians omitted—on their English menus, at least—such beloved Chinese foods as shredded jellyfish, duck feet, and pig intestines, but they were also spawning grounds for a Chinese-American cuisine that had ping-ponged between Asia and North American ever since the California Gold Rush, generating such delectable standards as chow mein, chop suey, and egg foo young—the latter an omelet ramified with sprouts smothered with American-style canned gravy, fusion fare more cunning than any cooking-school-trained celebrity chef has yet produced. Just to demonstrate that Chinese-American food is still an evolving cuisine: the dish known as General Tso's

chicken, though named after a real nineteenth-century Chinese officer, was invented in the 1970s at a restaurant on East 44th Street called Peng's for an audience of non-Asians.

Apart from Chinatown restaurants and Midtown Chinese places like Peng's, there wasn't much in the way of Chinese food available in 1977 New York. The Sichuan revolution—which was to begin remaking our ideas of what Chinese food could be—originated on the Upper West Side around that time. One day in an East Village junk shop (these rag-and-bone shops, once a fixture, are now long gone) I picked up a copy of the *Insider's Guide to Chinese Restaurants in New York*, published in 1970 by William Clifford, a columnist for *Holiday* magazine. The fact that such a parochial volume had once been published by Grosset & Dunlap is a fact worth pondering on its own, but it shows the mythical status that Chinatown had attained among non-Chinese, and it offers statistical confirmation of my early impressions. Of the forty-nine Chinatown restaurants reviewed, only six fell outside the boundaries of the five streets: two on East Broadway, three on the Bowery, and one on Catherine Street—all suggesting the directions in which the neighborhood would eventually flow.

The modern visitor to Chinatown will find the '70s version—like an antique pearl in the middle of a three-bite oyster—quaint and almost laughable. Now the sprawling neighborhood extends from Church Street in Tribeca to Montgomery Street on the Lower East Side, and northward beyond Delancey Street, at the doorstep of the modern East Village. Altogether, Manhattan's Chinatown is twenty times larger than it was in 1977, and substantial new Chinatowns have materialized in Flushing, Sunset Park, and Homecrest. Clearly, there has been a massive increase in Chinese immigration.

The helium inflating this balloon was the Immigration and Nationality Act of 1965. Prior to its passage, Chinese migration had been limited by a xenophobic quota system dating to 1924 that vastly favored Europeans over Asians, and men over families, in an attempt to perpetuate the racial balance of early twentieth-century America. The punitive 1924 act followed sporadic anti-Chinese riots that had occurred on the West Coast since the 1880s. The effect of the quotas had been to limit Chinese immigration mainly to men, who sent money home to China and who were separated from their families for decades on end. But, even after passage of the 1965 act, it was to take more than a decade for the effects to be felt as the new flood of immigrants arrived, established communities, flourished, and eventually moved to the suburbs or to middle-class communities within the city.

Tourists with cameras around their necks still wander the original five streets, which in certain corners remain eerily the same as they were a century ago. Nam Wah Tea Parlor still exists in something like its 1920 state on crooked Doyers Street. But the balance of the expanded neighborhood, now centered on Grand Street from Mott to Essex, is not aimed at tourists anymore, and the non-Asian dining-and-curio dollar certainly constitutes a much smaller part of the overall economy. Along this route are markets that display their

wares in well-organized tiers. One type specializes in cheap fresh seafood, usually by the whole fish—and sometimes the whole fish is still flopping. There are turtles (a Fujianese passion) and live crabs (a Sino-Malaysian favorite) trying to hoist themselves out of their cardboards boxes or engaging in impromptu claw duels atop a heap of fellow crustaceans, a spectacle that draws a crowd. Another sort of stall sells green leafy vegetable, melons of every sort and size, and alien vegetables—like tomatoes—that Chinatown restaurants have only just begun to experiment with. Meat markets specialize in diverse small birds and pig offal, in addition to cuts of steak and pork that would look good even to an Upper Eastsider. Chinese shoppers take a break from work or commute from the 'burbs to buy fresh lichee nuts, barbecued duck, and pea shoots a startling shade of green. Young Asians throng tea parlors that sell bubble tea, the latest craze from Taiwan. Chinatown of today more closely resembles China itself than the Chinatowns of yore, though the range and quality of stuff for sale would put the old country to shame.

Nowadays, the range of cuisines available in area Chinatowns astonishes. Reflecting immigration from nearly every corner of China—much of it via Hong Kong, Shanghai, and Taiwan—the cooking styles include Sichuan, Hunan, Mandarin, Uighur, Guilin, Chiu Chou, Fujianese, Hakka, Shanghai, and a Hong Kong version of Cantonese that one-ups the old style. There are now nearly a dozen restaurants in Chinatown specializing in Shanghai fare alone, with its gravy-squirting soup dumplings and braised pork shoulders prettily ringed with baby bok choy. We also have food of the Chinese diaspora in Vietnam, Thailand, and Malaysia. Increasingly, Cantonese restaurants like Danny Ng, located at 36 Pell within the original five streets, are patronized not by Occidental diners but by assimilated Chinese from the suburbs who want to show their children and grandchildren what Chinese restaurant food was like when they were young. Our nostalgia has become their nostalgia as well.

The same period witnessed the constriction and, finally, the modern expansion of Little Italy, which was under real-estate pressure from Chinatown the entire time. In the late 1970s, only three restaurants remained along Mulberry Street, plus John Gotti's social club and a couple of tawdry shops that peddled curios. I remember one in particular, at the corner of Grand and Mulberry, that displayed a t-shirt in the window with a sausage, two meatballs, and a pile of spaghetti artfully arranged to resemble a cock and balls . . .

But Little Italy was able to pursue its own agenda even as Chinatown pushed from the east and south. Around 1990, the neighborhood came back with a vengeance, flogging the same overcooked, overpriced, red-sauced fare that had led to the area's downfall in the first place. Only now the public ate it up. The main reason, I'm convinced, was the downtown-ization of Manhattan in general, whereby tourists from around the globe, and visitors from Jersey, Long Island, and the outer boroughs were attracted to a series of theme campuses below 14th Street, of which Chinatown, SoHo, the East Village, the West Village, and even Tribeca soon became examples. It didn't matter if the restaurants of Little Italy were jive as long as they were listed in the tourist guides. Of course, Italian-American food has long been one of the consistently best dining genres in the city, available in several evolved forms, mostly originating in Apulia, southern Campania, and Sicily. Remember, pizza as we know it was invented in New York City at Lombardi's, an institution that has itself benefited from the tourist influx. (By the way, it's not in Little Italy.)

Still, even among turds one may find a diamond. Luna, at 112 Mulberry, was founded in 1939 and run by one Momma Luna for the better part of the last

century. It features the type of red-sauced fare you've come to expect in old Italian-American joints but with more clarity and a real sparkle to the marinara, and exceptional homemade ravioli. A signed photo of Walter Winchell still graces the walls. And here's the best part: it's never been in Zagat. (And sadly, it just closed.)

*

Though the legacy of the 1965 immigration act is most visible and quantifiable in area Chinatowns, it has had a profound impact throughout the city, extending to dozens of nationalities that had been embargoed prior to its passage. In 1994, when I published the first edition of my guide to ethnic food in New York, it included ninety-four restaurants in seventeen ethnic categories, the result of meals eaten in the preceding five years. I considered the list far-ranging and up-to-date at the time. The fourth and most recent edition of *The Food Lover's Guide to the Best Ethnic Eating in New York City* (2004) lists 110 cuisines and over 800 restaurants. Ethnic restaurants have come to constitute a major component of the local restaurant scene, and there are more kinds to explore than ever before, making this the greatest age for eating New York has ever seen, and the most democratic one, too.

While zooming rents have caused upscale restaurant prices to soar, many ethnic spots still charge retro prices since their patrons can't afford more. These places have become destinations not only for adventurous diners but for frugal ones, too.

This explosion of ethnic restaurants has given the hungry a vast smorgasbord to choose from, and finding and reporting on these places has furnished me with the best job imaginable. Several times a week I'll sally forth—by car, by subway, by bus, on foot, or by bike—to look for new and overlooked places. A visit to Bensonhurst, for example, might yield a Guerreran *taqueria*; a Hong-Kong-style dim-sum specialist, where Chinese and Russian immigrants sit amiably side by side and knock back plate after plate of dumplings and dainty tidbits of smoked fish; and a *focacceria* mounted by Sicilian immigrants serving spleen sandwiches that McDonald's is unlikely ever to knock off. (On second thought, maybe they will someday. They're making burritos now at their Chipotle subsidiary, right?)

A trip to Queens might yield a new South Indian place specializing in the fermented and potato-stuffed pancakes called *dosa*s; a tiny café with only three tables serving the tart and fishy cuisine of Isaan, the impoverished Thai region adjacent to Vietnam; and a northern Chinese restaurant aimed at Koreans that specializes in goat offal, including eyeballs in brown gravy and cumin-dusted kebabs cooked over charcoal, reflecting the Muslim influence on northern Chinese cooking. On Whitney Avenue in Elmhurst, a series of small cafés from Sumatra and Java are currently duking it out for culinary supremacy. Dueling *satay*s! Increasingly, you need an anthropologist or a travel writer to know exactly what you're eating, and one can easily imagine a gaggle of university professors untangling this welter of cultural identities and its ultimate meaning sometime in the future. For now, we can observe, eat, and enjoy without guilt.

The Bronx and Brooklyn are rich in African restaurants, and Brian Berger (one of this volume's editors) and I have spent countless hours combing both boroughs for new places. The first African immigrants who began appearing fifteen years ago were principally Senegalese and Nigerian. The former became street peddlers, while the latter, as a result of their facility with English, became cab drivers. As with the Chinese, the earliest arrivals were principally men; the Senegalese organized benevolent societies via their UN legation to bring women over to cook. The earliest Senegalese restaurants were fly-by-night kitchens in SRO hotels, where a single African woman cooked for a throng of robed Wolof men who would appear for their principal meal of the day—in all-you-can-eat quantities for $5—around 2:00 PM Eventually, these same women established tiny restaurants in Harlem, Hell's Kitchen, and Bedford-Stuyvesant.

Other Francophone Africans followed the Senegalese. At first, Wolof restaurants tried to accommodate new diners by making lackluster versions of other countries' favorite dishes, but eventually, the Guineans, Malians, Sierra Leonese, and Ivory Coastals established their own places. Meanwhile, Nigerian and Ghanaian cafés became prominent components of the dining scene in Brooklyn and Bronx neighborhoods. Even Staten Island got in on the action, harboring cafés from Liberia. And it wasn't long before we were trying to figure out how to eat giant Nigerian tree snails, so rubbery that they were nearly impossible to swallow. What American

kid wouldn't love mashes—the extensively pounded starches of West Africa made from rice, plantains, and tubers like yuca—smothered in peanut sauce. Eventually, some African cafés were using the mashed-potato flakes found in American supermarkets to make their own unique African-American mashes.

Fifteen years ago, Colombians held sway along Roosevelt Avenue in Jackson Heights, with dozens of bars, cafés, and chicken rotisseries. Then, according to legend, the floodgates opened when a Volkswagen factory closed in the city of Puebla, in southern Mexico. Massive Mexican immigration has not only changed our idea about Mexican food (before, we had only a smattering of indifferent Tex-Mex) but remade several traditional Latin neighborhoods. East Harlem has gone from being mainly Dominican and Puerto Rican to being largely Mexican, as you can see if you stroll along East 116th Street. Similarly, Brooklyn's Sunset Park now has a dominant Mexican presence, in addition to old Dominican elements and newer Ecuadoran and Salvadoran ones.

Moreover, small Mexican *taquerias* have appeared in many Manhattan and outer borough neighborhoods where Mexican laborers have found work. The most authentic wrap a pair of fresh corn tortillas—probably made at the twenty-four-hour factories on Brooklyn's Flushing Avenue—around fillings like pig ear,

face meat, tail, skin, or intestines, in addition to the usual *cecina* (dried beef), *al pastor* (pineapple-marinated pig on a rotisserie), and *carne enchilada* (stewed meat). While the earliest Mexican immigrants were from the state and city of Puebla, more recent ones have come from Guerrero, Oaxaca, and points beyond.

Meanwhile, Roosevelt Avenue remains the heart of Hispanic New York. Under a street darkened and deafened by overhead subway tracks thrives a cosmopolitan scene as thronged and vital as any in Bogota, Lima, or Mexico City. Meanwhile, a new Colombian strip has grown up several blocks to the north on East Elmhurst's Northern Avenue, where lunch counters with fronts open to the street flog *arepas*, *hamburgesas*, and pineapple-and-ham-topped pizzas. Even the Argentine and Mexican restaurants on this thoroughfare cater to Colombians.

*

Living and eating in New York City the last thirty years has been an embarrassment of riches, and it has often been that my friends and I didn't know which direction to turn next. While mediocre and expensive barbecues have been opening in Manhattan, Uzbeki and other Central Asian places, with the kind of dedication to charcoal that would make a Texan proud, have been opening in Queens and in the Russian sections of maritime Brooklyn. No better barbecued lamb is to be had than at Rego Park's Salut (later styled "Salute" as the proprietors became Americanized) and Cheburechnaya. In Brighton Beach, the ancient slinger of Jewish pastries called Mrs Stahl's Knishes was elbowed out of its space by a Uzbeki spot which also specialized in the Turkic dumplings called *manti* and in the *plov* that constitutes the national dish, a pilaf of lamb and carrots flavored with Asian cumin.

It was easy to play Marco Polo in these places, because the typical Uzbeki spot is a Silk Road-style teahouse serving green tea in Chinese cups, proffering a

limited menu of kebabs, dumplings, and noodle dishes. One place with the official-sounding name of Uzbekistan Community Center has an oven made of horsehair and mud imported from Central Asia. The waiters are Orthodox Jews, while their Muslim brethren run the oven, a class system transplanted intact from the old country. It's also a shining example of Jewish-Muslim cooperation, one that the Western world could well study. The long wheat noodles known as *lagman* are homemade, served in a thick soup with lamb and cilantro. These were the noodles Mr Polo discovered when he visited Samarkand in 1272, and it's likely they were the ones that eventually reached Italy.

When I first started reviewing ethnic restaurants, there was a small but vocal minority who considered my activities faintly racist, and the term *ethnic* to be code for "non-white." They viewed the act of critiquing these places as condescending. But in fact, the effect of reviewing has been quite the opposite. Through popularization, the longevity of such eateries has been extended through expansion of their customer base, while diners have learned much about the immigrants who've come to live among us, their diets, their folkways, and even a stray word to two of several foreign languages. In turn, the immigrants have been given the opportunity to study us in what is clearly a comfortable context. By seeking out ethnic restaurants, we voluntarily meet immigrants on their own terms. Restaurants, bakeries, and cafés have turned out to be a neutral ground where the many cultures of the city mingle, and both immigrants and long-time residents come away all the better for it, with an enhanced respect for each other.

Chronology

1964
Verrazano Narrows Bridge opens between Brooklyn and Staten Island – World Fair in Queens – riots in Harlem – Holy Modal Rounders self-titled debut released – 636 murders

1965
Malcolm X assassinated at Audubon Ballroom – New York November 9 blackout – Cross Bronx Expressway completed – the City Landmarks Preservation Commission is formed following destruction of Penn Station – *The Village Fugs* – Fred Neil *Bleecker & Macdougal* – Mayor Robert Wagner does not seek a fourth term – John Lindsay elected Mayor – Bob Dylan, "Positively 4th Street" b/w "From a Buick 6" – 631 murders

1966
Twelve-day transit strike – Brooklyn Heights is the City's first historic district – Metropolitan Opera moves from Broadway and 39th St to Lincoln Center, which was built on the formerly largely black and Hispanic neighborhood of San Juan Hill – Howard Leary named Police Commissioner – subway fare rises to 20 cents, the first increase since 1953 – Frank O'Hara dies from injuries sustained after being hit by a dune buggy at Fire Island – 653 murders

1967
Martin Luther King leads anti-Vietnam War protest from Central Park to the United Nations – 9-day garbage strike – *Hair* opens at the Public Theater – *Velvet Underground and Nico* – Tuli Kupferberg, *1001 Ways to Live Without Working* – 745 murders

1968
Student uprising at Columbia University – bitter two-month teachers' strike following controversy over "local control" in Ocean Hill-Brownsville – Shirley Chisholm of Brooklyn elected first black woman in US House of Representatives – Willie Colón Orchestra, *The Hustler* – Ray Barretto, *Acid* – Don Siegel dir. *Madigan* and *Coogan's Bluff* – 904 murders

1969
AFL New York Jets win the Super Bowl – Stonewall Inn riots inaugurate modern gay rights era – New York Mets win the World Series – Mayor Lindsay re-elected – Fugs, *Belle of Avenue A* – John Schlesinger dir. *Midnight Cowboy* – 1,043 murders

1970
First New York Marathon, then held only in Central Park – Herman Badillo of the Bronx elected first Puerto Rican in US House of Representatives – Robert Downey dir. *Pound* – Buck Owens, *I Wouldn't Live In New York City* – Gil Scott-Heron, *Small Talk at 125th & Lenox* – Last Poets self-titled debut – Patrick Murphy named Police Commissioner – Grateful Dead perform four nights at the 46th Street Rock Palace, Brooklyn – subway fare rises to 30 cents – 1,117 murders

population	Manhattan	1,539,233
	Brooklyn	2,602,012
	Queens	1,986,473
	Bronx	1,471,701
	Staten	295,443
		7,894,862

1971
All In The Family debuts – Frank Serpico testifies before the Knapp Commission about widespread corruption inside the NYPD – Off Track Betting (OTB) begins – King's Plaza Mall opens – Louis Armstrong dies at home in Corona, Queens – Allman Brothers, *Live at Fillmore East* – Fania All-Stars, *Live at the Cheetah* – *Eddie Palmieri & Harlem River Drive* – 1,466 murders

1972
Mob boss Joey Gallo is gunned down at Umberto's Clam House in Little Italy – Mafia war follows, as does, coincidentally, Francis Ford Coppola's *The Godfather* – John Wojtowicz and Salvatore Natuarale hold up a Gravesend, Brooklyn, bank for fourteen hours; incident serves as the basis for the 1975 film *Dog Day Afternoon* – Bronx Museum of the Arts open – *East Village Other* ceases publication – Gordon Parks dir. *Superfly* – subway fare rises to 35 cents – 1,691 murders

1973
Abraham Beame elected the City's first Jewish mayor – Staten Island Mall opens – *Kojak* debuts – Welfare Island, formerly Blackwell Island, home to prisons and mental asylums, is renamed Roosevelt Island; residential development will follow – *New York Dolls* – *Soho Weekly News* begins publication – first community gardens on the Lower East Side appear – Morton Feldman, *For "Frank O'Hara"* – elevated West Side Highway collapses at Gansevoort Street – Donald Cawley named Police Commissioner – James Brown, "Down and Out in New York City" from his soundtrack to *Black Caesar* – 1,680 murders

1974
French acrobat Philip Petit walks tightrope between the still-unfinished World Trade Center towers – Starrett City in Brooklyn opens – Duke Ellington dies; thousands attend funeral at Cathedral of St John the Divine – Michael Codd named Police Commissioner – 1,554 murders

1975
Fraunces Tavern in lower Manhattan is bombed by Puerto Rican nationalist group FALN, killing 4 people and injuring more than 50 – a bomb explodes in the baggage claim area of the TWA terminal at LaGuardia Airport, killing 11 and injuring 74; the perpetrators are never identified – Borough of Richmond is officially renamed Borough of Staten Island – *Saturday Night Live* and *Barney Miller* debuts – *Taxi Driver* opens – Jackie McLean & The Cosmic Brotherhood, *New York Calling* — subway fare rises to 50 cents – 1,645 murders

1976
David Berkowitz ("Son of Sam") kills first victim and wounds another – CUNY charges tuition for first time in its history – World Trade Center opens – New York City Marathon expands to all boroughs, in honor of the US bicentennial – *Ramones* – 1,622 murders

1977
Studio 54 opens – 25-hour blackout – David Berkowitz (Son of Sam) is charged with 6 murders – President Jimmy Carter visits Hunt's Point in the Bronx – Edward I. Koch elected Mayor – 1,553 murders

1978
Mob boss Carmine Galante is gunned down in a Bushwick, Brooklyn restaurant – Sid Vicious allegedly stabs his girlfriend Nancy Spungen to death in their room in the Chelsea Hotel – Lufthansa robbery at Kennedy Airport is largest in US history; the 1988 film *Good Fellas* follows its aftermath – *Taxi* debuts – Rubén Blades & Willie Colón, *Siembra* – Robert Maguire named Police Commissioner – Emmett Grogan dies of heroin overdose; Bob Dylan's *Street Legal* is dedicated to his memory – 1,503 murders

1979

Woody Allen's *Manhattan* opens, as does Walter Hill's *The Warriors* and Charlie Ahearn's low-budget *The Deadly Art of Survival* – self-aggrandizing, self-appointed vigilante group the Guardian Angels appear – residential construction begins in Battery Park City – Sugar Hill Gang, "Rapper's Delight" – 1,733 murders

1980

Eleven-day transit strike – John Lennon murdered – last trains run on High Line, the elevated freight tracks in Chelsea and the Meat Packing District – Kurtis Blow, "The Breaks," Funky 4 + 1, "That's the Joint," Spyder-D, "Big Apple Rappin" – subway fare rises to 60 cents – 1,812 murders

population		
	Manhattan	1,428,285
	Brooklyn	2,230,936
	Queens	1,891,325
	Bronx	1,168,972
	Staten	352,121
		7,071,639

1981

Simon & Garfunkel play a free concert in Central Park: half-a-million people sing along to "59th Street Bridge Song." – 1,000 passengers refuse to leave an out-of-service cc train at Hoy-Schemerhorn station in Brooklyn – "The Adventures of Grandmaster Flash on the Wheels of Steel" – in *Escape From New York* (mostly filmed in East St Louis, Illinois), the island of Manhattan has become a maximum security prison – *Fort Apache The Bronx* star Paul Newman denies that it is racist; terrible supporting actor Danny Aiello gets his pizzeria torched 8 years later in *Do The Right Thing*, so justice is served – subway fare rises to 75 cents – 1,826 murders

1982

Willie Turks, a black 34-year old MTA worker is killed by a white mob in Gravesend, Brooklyn – Westway, a planned underground West Side highway and related real estate developments – New York City adds a 718 telephone area code; Manhattan and the Bronx keep 212 – Long Island native Howard Stern returns to New York, broadcasting on WNBC AM – Charlie Ahearn, *Wild Style* – 1,668 murders

1983

Coney Island Mermaid Parade begins – Benjamin Ward is City's first black police commissioner; Diana Ross performs before 500,000 people in Central Park – hundreds of non-disco loving teens cause mayhem afterwards – Ted Berrigan dies – the bullet-riddled body of Mafia hitman Roy DeMeo is found in the trunk of his car in a Sheepshead Bay parking lot, one of 1,662 murders

1984

66-year old Eleanor Bumpurs is shot and killed by police as they tried to evict her from her Bronx apartment – Bernhard Goetz shoots 4 men on a subway; he said they tried to rob him – Run DMC self-titled debut – Benjamin Ward named Police Commissioner – UTFO, "Roxanne, Roxanne" – Roxanne Shanté, "Roxanne's Revenge" – Gary Winogrand dies – subway fare rises to 90 cents – 1,450 murders

1985

Mob boss Paul Castellano is shot dead in a gangland execution on E. 46th Street in Manhattan – Westway is finally cancelled – L.L. Cool J, *Radio* – Doug E. Fresh, "The Show" b/w "La Di Da" – MC Shan, "The Bridge" – Rockaway Playland closes – 1,384 murders

1986

Larry Davis wounds six police officers during a shootout in the Bronx; a fugitive for 17 days, he becomes a criminal folk hero – 23-year-old Michael Griffith and 36-year-old Cedric Sandiford chased by white mob in Howard Beach, Queens; Griffith is killed attempting to flee across the Belt Parkway – New York Senator Alfonse D'Amato and Federal attorney Rudolph Giuliani don outlandish "undercover" disguises and buy crack in Washington Heights; the City is not impressed – Ivan Boesky pleads guilty to insider trading – machete-wielding Juan Gonzalez kills 2 and wounds 9 on the Staten Island Ferry – subway fare rises to $1 – "Eric B. Is President" by Eric B. & Rakim – 1,582 murders

1987
City refuses to allow a Long Island garbage barge to dock – Oliver Stone-directed *Wall Street* symbolizes, or celebrates, '80s excess – MC Shan, *Down By Law* – Kool Moe Dee, *How Ya' Like Me Now?* – Chain Gang, *Mondo Manhattan* – 1,672 murders

1988
Bronx Congressman Mario Biaggi resigns in Wedtech bribery scandal – 22-year-old rookie cop Eddie Byrne of the 103rd Precinct assassinated in South Jamaica, Queens – *New York Press* begins publication as a free weekly paper – New York City is in violation of EPA Clean Air standards – Jungle Brothers, *Straight Out Of The Jungle* – Stetsasonic, *In Full Gear* – Big Daddy Kane, *Long Live The Kane* – Public Enemy, *It Takes A Nation of Millions to Hold us Back* – 1,896 murders

1989
The Central Park Jogger raped and beaten; black teenagers convicted of the crime are later exonerated by DNA evidence and the confession of serial rapist – 16-year-old Yusuf Hawkins is in Bensonhurst – *Seinfeld* debuts – David Dinkins elected the City's first black and, to date, last Democratic Mayor – Kool G. Rap & DJ Polo, *Road to Riches* – Beastie Boys, *Paul's Boutique* – Slick Rick, *The Great Adventures of Slick Rick* – De La Soul, *Three Feet High & Rising* – MTA declares victory in war on graffiti – Richard Condon named Police Commissioner – Michael Milken pleads guilty to a variety of securities violations – German director Uli Edel's film version of Hubert Selby's *Last Exit To Brooklyn* – 1,905 murders

1990
Arson at the Happyland Social Club in the East Tremont section of the Bronx kills 87 – US Supreme Court declares Board of Estimate unconstitutional – Brian Watkins, a tourist from Utah, is stabbed to death defending his family from muggers while awaiting a D train at 50th Street – Lee Brown named Police Commissioner – Al Sharpton leads boycott of two Korean groceries in Brooklyn – graffiti artist Sane Smith dies – X-Clan, *To The East Backwards* – Leonard Bernstein dies – subway fare rises to $1.15 – 2,245 murders

	population		
		Manhattan	1,487,536
		Brooklyn	2,300,664
		Queens	1,951,598
		Bronx	1,203,789
		Staten	378,977
			7,322,564

1991
First Gavin Cato, then Yankel Rosenbaum killed in what would be called Crown Heights "Riots" – a number 4 train crashes just above 14th Street, killing 5 – African Burial Ground discovered during construction near Foley Square – Gang Starr, *Step Into the Arena* – A Tribe Called Quest, *The Low End Theory* – deaths of Miles Davis and Harry Smith – 2,154 murders

1992
City hosts Democratic National Convention without significant incident – John Gotti, the Teflon Don, sentenced to life in prison – Tragedy Khadafi debut album (under the name Intelligent Hoodlum) – Pete Rock & CL Smooth, *Mecca and The Soul Brother* – Showbiz & A.G., *Runaway Slave* – Diamond D, *Stunts, Blunts & Hip-Hop* – Raymond Kelly named Police Commissioner – subway fare rises to $1.25 – John Cage dies – 1,995 murders

1993
Truck bomb explodes in World Trade Center parking garage: 6 killed, others wounded – 65 percent of Staten Islanders vote to secede from New York City – *Golden Venture*, a freighter carrying hundreds of illegal Chinese immigrants, runs aground off the Rockaways – 28-acre Riverbank State Park opens atop a sewage treatment on the Hudson River from W. 137th Street to W. 145th. Wu Tang Clan, *Enter the 36th Chamber* – Héctor Lavoe dies – 1,946 murders

1994
Anthony Baez dies under police custody after being arrested – Nas, *Illmatic* – Notorious BIG, *Ready to Die* – Gravediggaz, *Six Feet Under*, originally titled *Niggamortis* – MOP, *To the Death* – Jeru The Damaja, *The Sun Rises In The East*; its cover shows the World Trade Center towers ablaze – Game Five of New York Knicks versus Houston Rockets for NBA Championship interrupted by O. J. Simpson's white Bronco highway chase – William Bratton named Police Commissioner – Joe Brainard dies of complications from AIDS – New York Rangers win the Stanley Cup (for first time since 1940) – 1,561 murders

1995
Smoking banned in most New York City restaurants – Mobb Deep, *The Infamous* – Big L, *Lifestylez Ov Da Poor & Dangerous* – Raekwon, *Only Built 4 Cuban Linx . . .* , Smif-N-Wessun, *Dah Shinin'* – Ol' Dirty Bastard, *Return to the 36 Chambers: The Dirty Version* – AZ, *Do or Die* – Brooklyn-born Tupac Shakur appears in court for sentencing in a sexual assault case, days after being shot outside a Manhattan recording studio – subway fare rises to $1.50 – 1,177 murders

1996
Lincoln Kirstein, co-founder of New York City ballet, dies – state approves closing of Fresh Kills landfill on Staten Island – trade publication *Silicon Alley Reporter* debuts – Ghostface Killah, *Ironman* – Jay-Z, *Reasonable Doubt* – Heltah Skeltah, *Nocturnal* – OGC, *Da Storm* – Howard Safir named the City's first Jewish Police Commissioner – 983 murders

1997
Metrocard introduced – Allen Ginsberg dies in his East Village apartment – subway bomb plot is broken up by cops in Park Slope, Brooklyn – Abner Louima tortured in the 70th Precinct – New York Mets lose the "Subway Series" to the Yankees – Mayor Giuliani declares war on jaywalkers – Capone-N-Noreaga, *The War Report* – Boot Camp Clik, *For The People* – Willem de Kooning dies – 770 murders

1998
Thousands of crickets released into 1 Police Plaza auction hall during protest over the sale of community gardens on the Lower East Side – *Sex and the City* debuts to the chagrin of many – Jerome Robbins dies – in the schlock-terror action movie *The Seige*, Bruce Willis declares martial law in Brooklyn – *Black Star* self-titled debut – Killah Priest, *Heavy Mental* – 633 murders

1999
Unarmed Amadou Diallo is shot to death at 1157 Wheeler Avenue in the Bronx by four undercover police officers; the City later pays $3 million to settle wrongful death lawsuit – Mayor Giuliani battles the Brooklyn Museum over the "Sensation" exhibit – Giuliani battles mosquitos, ordering parts of the City sprayed with airborne pesticides he insists cause no harm to humans or wildlife – fantastic protests follow by horticulturists dressed as plants – Mos Def, *Black on Both Sides* – 667 murders

2000
Bloomberg CEO Michael Bloomberg switches parties, from Democrat to Republican – 26-year-old Patrick Dorismond of Brooklyn shot to death by undercover police outside a Hell's Kitchen bar; the City later pays $2.25 million to settle wrongful death lawsuit – Thunderbolt rollercoaster at Coney Island razed by the City under highly suspicious circumstances – despite protest, parts of the City are again sprayed with pesticides – Bernard Kerik named Police Commissioner – Tito Puente dies – Brooklyn-native Darren Aronofsky's film version of Hubert Selby's *Requiem For A Dream* – 673 murders

population	Manhattan	1,537,195
	Brooklyn	2,465,326
	Queens	2,229,379
	Bronx	1,332,650
	Staten	443,728
		8,008,278

2001
Mayor Giuliani establishes a City "decency panel" following the appearance of a naked female Jesus at the Brooklyn Museum – September 11 – dot.com-bubble-icon analyst Henry Blodget leaves Merrill-

Lynch; two years later he's banned for life from the securities industry – Michael Bloomberg elected Mayor – Cormega, *The Realness* – 649 murders

2002
Following tax hikes on cigarettes, City Council passes smoking ban in bars, effective March 2003 – despite thousands of people reporting respiratory ailments in the wake of exposure to 9/11, US Environmental Protection Agency reports no serious health risks for those near Ground Zero – in a posthumous defeat to former Mayor Giuliani, Friends of the High Line win lawsuit against the City – plans to reopen Park Row to traffic announced; five years later it remains closed – 587 murders

2003
300–400,000 people participate in protests against the upcoming Iraq War – 57-year-old City worker Alberta Spruill dies of heart attack after her Harlem apartment is mistakenly raided by NYPD SWAT team – unarmed Ousmane Zongo shot to death by undercover police officer in a Chelsea warehouse; City later pays $3 million dollars to settle a wrongful death lawsuit – August 14 blackout passes without great incident – City Council member James E. Davis shot to death in City Hall chambers – Staten Island Ferry collides with a pier at the St George Ferry Terminal, killing 10 people – Raymond Kelly named Police Commissioner again – 50 Cent, *Get Rich or Die Tryin'* – subway fare rises to $2 and the token is finally phased out – 597 murders

2004
Unarmed 19-year-old Timothy Stansbury is shot to death by a police officer on the roof of Louis Armstrong Houses in Bed-Stuy – Russell Jones, aka Ol' Dirty Bastard, dies of an accidental drug overdose in Manhattan – Masta Killa, *No Said Date* – 570 murders

2005
New York 2012 leader and Deputy Mayor Dan Doctoroff lose Olympics bid to London – planned construction of football stadium over the West Side railyards in Manhattan is thwarted by local and state opposition – City passes Williamsburg and Greenoint rezoning plan to encourage high-end construction – Mayor Bloomberg re-elected – sweetheart Yankees and Mets stadium deals follow – Dave Chappelle's *Block Party*, largely filmed in Bed-Stuy – 539 murders

population		
	Brooklyn	2,486,235
	Queens	2,241,600
	Manhattan	1,593,200
	Bronx	1,357,589
	Staten	464,573
		8,143,197

2006
Bronx Terminal Market razed to make way for Gateway Center Mall – unarmed Sean Bell killed in hail of 50 bullets following undercover NYPD operation at Club Kahlua in South Jamaica, Queens – tens of thousands of people gather near the Apollo Theater in Harlem to pay their last respects to Mr Dynamite, James Brown – state approves Atlantic Yards proposal, despite ongoing lawsuits – former Police Commissioner Bernard Kerik pleads guilty to state charges of accepting hundreds of thousands of dollars worth of gifts while in office – Nas, *HipHop is Dead* – Gilbert Sorrentino dies in Brooklyn – 596 murders

2007
Former Mayor Giuliani campaigns for President – Bernard Kerik faces Federal indictments for numerous crimes – Prodigy, *Return of the Mac*

Contributors

Marshall Berman is Distinguished Professor of Political Science at City College of New York and CCNY Graduate Center, where he teaches political theory and urban studies. He is the author of *On The Town: One Hundred Years of Spectacle in Times Square*; *Adventures in Marxism* and *All That is Solid Melts into Air: The Experience of Modernity*.

Brian Berger is a poet, journalist, and photographer who remembers the view of Playland from the terrace of his grandparents' apartment in Rockaway Beach, Queens. He's written about music for *Forced Exposure*, the *Austin Chronicle* and *Geek Weekly*, while his verse has appeared at jargonbooks.com and elsewhere. His own dark hollow is whowalkinbrooklyn.com.

Joseph Anastasio is a writer, photographer, programmer, and capitalist bastard. Born on the Lower East Side, raised and refusing to leave Astoria, his fondness for all things underground and abandoned has yielded a vast repository of content scraped off the dirty underside of the city, some of which can be found at www.ltvsquad.com.

Meakin Armstrong is a freelance writer and editor who has lived in Manhattan since 1986. He is currently writing a novel (only briefly set in New York). He is also fiction editor of *Guernica Magazine* (www.guernicamag.com).

Robert Atkins is an art historian and activist. His latest book is *Censoring Culture: Contemporary Threats to Free Expression*. He lives in Pacifica and Palm Springs, California, and can be found online at www.robertatkins.net.

Edmund Berrigan is the author of two books of poetry: *Disarming Matter* and *Your Cheatin' Heart*; he is also the co-editor of the *Collected Poems of Ted Berrigan*. A CD of his music, *Once I Had an Earthquake*, was recently released under the label I Feel Tractor. He lives in Brooklyn.

Philip Dray is the author of *Stealing God's Thunder: Benjamin Franklin's Lightning Rod and the Invention of America* and *At the Hands of Persons Unknown: The Lynching of Black America*, which won the Robert F. Kennedy Book Award, the Southern Book Critics Circle Award for Nonfiction, and was a Finalist for the Pulitzer Prize. He has lived in New York City since 1977.

Leonard Greene, a Brooklyn native, has been a journalist for 20 years, writing about education, politics, and urban issues for newspapers in New Jersey, San Francisco, Boston and New York. He is currently a columnist and news reporter at the *New York Post*.

Anthony Haden-Guest is a writer, reporter, and cartoonist. He was born in Paris, grew up in London and now lives mostly in New York. He won a New York Emmy for writing and narrating a program about the coming of Eurotrash to Manhattan. His most recent books were *True Colours: The Real Life of the Art World*; *The Last Party: Studio 54, Disco and the Culture of the Night* and *The Chronicles of Now*, a book of cartoons. He publishes in many magazines and writes a weekly column about the art world for the *Financial Times*. He is finishing a book but won't say what it's about.

Jim Knipfel is the author of *Slackjaw*, *The Buzzing*, and several other books. He lives somewhere in Brooklyn.

Paul Kopasz is a Kentucky-based writer and musician. He reviews films and books for the *Louisville Eccentric Observer* and among his many records is *Wilderness of Mirrors*. His latest album is called *Panopticon*, which can be purchased at paulkweathermen.com.

Leonard Levitt wrote the column "One Police Plaza" for *Newsday* from 1995 to 2005. Before that he worked as a reporter for the Associated Press and the *Detroit News*, as a correspondent for *Time*, and as the investigations editor of the *New York Post*. His work has appeared in *Harper's*, *Esquire* and the *New York Times* magazine. He received an Edgar Award in 2005 for his book *Conviction: Solving the Moxley Murder*, and he can be found online at www.nypdconfidential.com.

Allen Lowe is a guitarist, saxophonist, and American music historian. He has a book and accompanying CD set on the history of jazz, 1900–1950, *That Devilin Tune*, and his latest recording is *Jews in Hell: Radical Jewish Acculturation*. He lives in South Portland, Maine.

Steve Maluk was born on the Lower East Side and moved to Staten Island in 1956 (before "The Bridge"). A graduate of Wagner College, he is a Vietnam Veteran who lives in Great Kills with wife Linda, son James, and daughter Sasha.

Tim McLoughlin's first novel, *Heart of the Old Country* (2001), won Italy's Premio Penne Award, and is the basis for the movie *The Narrows* from Serenade Films. He is the editor of the Brooklyn Noir anthology series, and his short fiction has been included in Best American Mystery Stories.

Richard Meltzer is the author of *Autumn Rhythm*, *A Whore Just Like The Rest*, *The Night (Alone)*, and numerous other books. He lives in Portland, Oregon.

Margaret Morton is photographer/author of *Glass House*, *Fragile Dwelling*, *The Tunnel: The Underground Homeless of New York City*, and *Transitory Gardens*, *Uprooted Lives* (co-authored with Diana Balmori). She is a professor in the School of Art at The Cooper Union and lives in Manhattan.

Tom Robbins has been a newspaper and magazine writer covering New York City issues for 30 years. He has written about politics, labor, crime, and other topics for the *Village Voice*, the *Daily News*, the *New York Observer*, and *City Limits* magazine.

Luc Sante is the author of *Low Life*, *Evidence*, *The Factory of Facts*, and, most recently, *Kill All Your Darlings: Pieces 1990–2005*, and the editor and translator of Félix Fénéon's *Novellas in Three Lines*. He lives somewhere in Ulster County, New York.

Kate Schmitz was born in New York City in 1967. In her past life she was a bartender, painter and film editor; now she's primarily a babystore owner. She lives in a rent stabilized railroad apartment in Williamsburg.

Robert Sietsema is restaurant critic for the *Village Voice*, a frequent contributor to *Gourmet* magazine, and author of *The Food Lover's Guide to the Best Ethnic Eating in New York City*. He was born in Michigan, moved to New York City in 1977, and currently lives in Greenwich Village.

Brandon Stosuy is a regular contributor to *Pitchfork*, *The Believer* and the *Village Voice* and the editor of *Up Is Up, But So Is Down*, an anthology of downtown New York literature. He lives in Williamsburg .

John Strausbaugh's books include *Black Like You: Blackface, Whiteface, Insult & Imitation in American Popular Culture*, and *Rock 'Til You Drop: The Decline From Rebellion to Nostalgia*. He has written for the *New York Times*, the *Washington Post* and elsewhere.

C. J. Sullivan was born and raised in the Bronx. A Senior Court Clerk at King's County Supreme, he's also crime reporter for the *New York Post* and had a long-running column in *New York Press* called "The Bronx Stroll." His first book, *1001 Greatest Things Ever Said About New York*, was published in 2006.

Jean Thilmany was born and raised in Dubuque, Iowa. She is an associate editor for *Mechanical Engineering* and has written about politics, culture, and technology for many publications. Currently at work on a novel, she now commutes monthly to New York from her home in St Paul, Minnesota.
Kevin Walsh grew up in Bay Ridge, Brooklyn, where he witnessed the construction of the Verrazano Bridge as a kid. He is the author of *Forgotten New York*, which grew out of a website began in 1998 and continues today at www.forgotten-ny.com.

Armond White is author of *The Resistance: Ten Years of Pop Culture That Shook the World* and *Rebel for the Hell of It: The Art-Life of Tupac Shakur*. He is currently at work on a survey of post-9/11 cinema.

John Yau is a poet, fiction writer, critic, and publisher of Black Square Editions. Among his recent books are *Paradiso Diasporo* and *The Passionate Spectator: Essays on Art on Poetry*. A frequent contributor to *The Brooklyn Rail*, he is also a Professor at the Mason Gross School of Arts at Rutgers University. He lives in Manhattan.

Daniel Young is author of *The Paris Café Cookbook*, *The Bistros, Brasseries & Wine Bars of Paris*, and a forthcoming book about coffees of the world. He is co-author, with Vivian Constantinopoulos, of *Frappé Nation* (2006). Formerly the food critic of *The Daily News*, he has written for *The New York Times* and *The Los Angeles Times*.

Select Bibliography

History/Non-Fiction
Abel, Allen, *Flatbush Odyssey* (Toronto, 1995)
Alleman, Richard, *The Movie Lover's Guide to New York* (New York, 1988)
Ashton, Dore, *The New York School* (New York, 1973)
Barnes, Djuna, *Djuna Barnes' New York* (Los Angeles, 1989)
Barrett, Wayne, *Rudy! An Investigative Biography of Rudolph Giuliani* (New York, 2001)
—, *Grand Illusion: The Untold Story of Rudy Giuliani and 9/11* (New York, 2006)
Berman, Marshall, *All That is Solid Melts Into Air: The Experience of Modernity* (New York, 1982)
—, *On the Town: One Hundred Years of Spectacle* (New York, 2006)
Breslin, Jimmy, *The Short Sweet Dream of Eduardo Gutierrez* (New York, 2002)
Caro, Robert, *The Power Broker: Robert Moses and the Fall of New York* (New York, 1974)
Cohen, Rich, *Tough Jews* (New York, 1998)
Cohn, Nik, *In The Heart of the World* (New York, 1992)
Colón, Jesús, *A Puerto Rican in New York and Other Sketches* (New York, 1961)
Darton, Eric, *Divided We Stand: A Biography of the World Trade Center* (New York, 1999)
Delaney, Samuel R., *Times Square Red, Times Square Blue* (New York, 1999)
Davidson, Bruce, *East 100th Street* (Cambridge, 1970)
—, *Subway* (New York, 1986)
—, *Central Park* (New York, 1995)
Denson, Charles, *Coney Island: Lost and Found* (Berkeley, 2002)
DeSantis, John, *For The Color of His Skin: The Murder of Yusuf Hawkins and The Trial of Bensonhurst* (New York, 1991)
DiPrima, Diane, *Memoirs of a Beatnik* (New York, 1968)
—, *Recollections of My Life as a Woman: The New York Years* (New York, 2001)
Donaldson, Greg, *The 'Ville: Cops & Kids in Urban America* (New York, 1993)
Dwyer, Jim, *Subway Lives* (New York, 1991)
Dylan, Bob, *Chronicles* (New York, 2005)
English, T. J., *The Westies* (New York, 1991)
Fried, Albert, *The Rise and Fall of the Jewish Gangster in America*, revd edn (New York, 1993)
Friedman, Josh Alan, *Tales of Times Square* (Los Angeles, 1993)
Frommer, Myrna and Harvey, *It Happened in Brooklyn* (New York, 1993)
Ginsberg, Allen, *Snapshot Poetics* (New York, 1993)
Goodman, James, *Blackout* (New York, 2003)
Graham, Brian, *Twilight of the Beats* (Lisbon, 2005)
Haden-Guest, Anthony, *The Last Party: Studio 54, Disco, and the Culture of the Night* (New York, 1997)
Homberger, Eric, *Historical Atlas of New York* (New York, 1994)
Jackson, Kenneth T., ed., *The Encyclopedia of New York City* (New Haven, 1995)
Jones, Hettie, *How I Became Hettie Jones* (New York, 1990)
Kahn, Roger, *The Boys of Summer* (New York, 1972)
Koolhaas, Rem, *Delirious New York: A Retrospective Manifesto for Manhattan* (Oxford, 1978)
Kugelmass, Jack, *The Miracle of Intervale Avenue: The Story of a Jewish Congregation in the South Bronx*, expanded edn (New York, 1996)

Leeds, Mark, *Ethnic New York* (New York, 1996)

Levere, Douglas, *New York Changing: Revisiting Berenice Abbott's New York* (Princeton, 2004)

Lyon, Danny, *The Destruction of Lower Manhattan* (New York, 1969)

Maas, Peter, *Serpico* (New York, 1973)

Mahler, Jonathan, *Ladies and Gentlemen, The Bronx Is Burning: 1977, Baseball, Politics, and the Battle for the Soul of a City* (New York, 2005)

McAuliffe, Kevin, *Sayings of Generalissimo Giuliani* (New York, 2000)

McCourt, James, *Queer Street: The Rise and Fall of an American Culture, 1947–1985* (New York, 2004)

McCullough, David, *Brooklyn and How It Got That Way* (New York, 1993)

Morrone, Francis, *An Architectural Guidebook to Brooklyn* (Layton, Utah, 2001)

Newfield, Jack, *The Full Rudy: The Man, The Myth, The Mania* (New York, 2003)

——, and Wayne Barrett, *City for Sale: Ed Koch and the Betrayal of New York* (New York, 1989)

Nobile, Philip, *Sixteen Acres: Architecture and the Outrageous Struggle for the Future of Ground Zero* (New York, 2004)

O'Brien, Geoffrey, *The Times Square Story* (New York, 1998)

Oppenheimer, Joel, *The Wrong Season* (Highlands, NC, 1973)

Pileggi, Nicholas, *Wiseguy* (New York, 1986)

Podair, Jerald, *The Strike That Changed New York: Blacks, Whites, and the Ocean Hill-Brownsville Crisis* (New Haven, 2003)

Pritchett, Wendell, *Brownsville, Brooklyn: Blacks, Jews and the Changing Face of the Ghetto* (Chicago, 2002)

Reider, Jonathan, *Canarsie: Jews and Italians Against Liberalism* (New York, 1985)

Richmond, John, *Brooklyn U.S.A.* (New York, 1946)

Rivera, Edward, *Family Installments: Memories of Growing Up Hispanic* (New York, 1982)

Rosenthal, Mel, *In The South Bronx of America* (Wilmantic, 2001)

Sante, Luc, *Lowlife: Lures and Snares of Old New York* (New York, 1991)

Schwartzman, Paul, and Rob Polner, *New York Notorious* (New York, 1992)

Shabazz, Jamel, *A Time Before Crack* (New York, 2005)

Shapiro, Michael, *The Last Good Season: Brooklyn, The Dodgers and Their Final Pennant Race Together* (New York, 2003)

Sietsema, Robert, *The Food Lover's Guide to the Best Ethnic Eating in New York City* (New York, 2004)

Silver, Nathan, *Lost New York* (New York, 1967)

Simon, Kate, *Bronx Primitive* (New York, 1982)

Sloman, Larry, *Thin Ice: A Season in Hell with the New York Rangers* (New York, 1983)

Stoller, Paul, *Money Has No Smell: The Africanization of New York City* (Chicago, 2002)

Sukenick, Ron, *Down and In: Life in the Underground* (New York, 1987)

Taylor, Clarence, *The Black Churches of Brooklyn* (New York, 1994)

Taylor, William R., ed., *Inventing Times Square: Commerce and Culture at the Crossroads of the World* (New York, 1990)

Thomson, Virgil, *Virgil Thomson Reader* (New York, 1984)

Tosches, Nick, *King of The Jews* (New York, 2005)

Trachtenberg, Alan, *Brooklyn Bridge: Fact and Symbol* (New York, 1965)

Van Rank, Dave, and Elijah Wald, *Mayor of Macdougal Street* (New York, 2005)

Vega, Marta Moreno, *When The Spirits Dance Mambo: Growing Up Nuyorican in El Barrio* (New York, 2004)

Whitehead, Colson, *The Colossus of New York: A City in Thirteen Parts* (New York, 2003)

Winogrand, Garry, *The Man in the Crowd: The Uneasy Streets of Garry Winogrand* (New York, 1999)

——, *Figments From The Real World* (New York, 2003)

Literature

Alfau, Felipe, *Chronos* (Normal, 1990)

Algarín, Miguel, *Mongo Affair* (New York, 1978)

——, *Time's Now / Ya es tiempo* (Houston, 1985)

——, and Miguel Pinero, eds, *Nuyorican Poetry: An Anthology of Puerto Rican Words and Feelings* (New York, 1975)

Asch, Sholem, *East River* (New York, 1946)

Ashbery, John, *Flowchart* (New York, 1998)
Babín, María Teresa, and Stan Steiner, eds, *Borinquen: An Anthology of Puerto Rican Literature* (New York, 1974)
Barnes, Djuna, *New York* (Los Angeles, 1989)
Barthelme, Donald, *Paradise* (New York, 1996)
Bellow, Saul, *Seize the Day* (New York, 1956)
—, *Herzog* (New York, 1964)
Berrigan, Ted, *So Going Around Cities: New and Selected Poems, 1958–1979* (Berkeley, 1980)
Brainard, Joe, *I Remember* (New York, 2001)
Brosnan, Meredith, *Mr Dynamite* (Normal, 2005)
Brossard, Chandler, *Who Walk In Darkness* (New York, 1952; restored edn 2000)
Brown, Rosellen, *Street Games* (New York, 1974)
Clowes, Daniel, *Caricature* (Seattle, 1998)
Deitch, Kim, *Beyond the Pale* (Seattle, 1989)
Denby, Edwin, *The Complete Poems* (New York, 1986)
Doucet, Julie, *My New York Diary* (Montreal, 1999)
Dowell, Coleman, *A Star Bright Lie* (Normal, 1993)
Drexler, Rosalyn, *Art Does (Not) Exist!* (Normal, 1989)
Eisner, Will, *A Contract with God and Other Tenement Stories* (New York, 1978)
Esteves, Sandra María, *Yerba buena* (Greenfield,1980)
—, *Bluestown Mockingbird Mambo* (Houston,1990)
Friedman, Drew, and Alan Josh, *Any Similarities Between Persons Living or Dead* (New York, 1985)
—, *Warts and All* (New York, 1990)
Fuchs, Daniel, *Summer in Williamsburg* (New York, 1934)
Gaddis, William, *The Recognitions* (New York, 1955)
Goodman, Paul, *The Empire City: A Novel of New York City* (1959; Santa Rosa, 2001)
Grogan, Emmett, *Ringolevio* (New York, 1973)
Isler, Alan, *The Prince of West End Avenue* (New York, 1995)
Katchor, Ben, *The Jew of New York* (New York, 1998)
—, *The Beauty Supply District* (New York, 2000)
Kaz, *Underworld Vol. 1: Cruel and Unusual Comics* (Seattle, 1997)
Lethem, Jonathan, *Motherless Brooklyn* (New York, 1999)
—, *Fortress of Solitude* (New York, 2003)
Lopate, Philip, ed., *Writing New York* (New York, 1998)
Lorca, Federico Garcia, *Poet in New York*, trans. Greg Simon and Steven F. White (New York, 1988)
Markfield, Wallace, *To An Early Grave* (New York, 1964)
—, *Teitelbaum's Window* (New York, 1970)
—, *You Can Live if They Let You* (New York, 1974)
Markson, David, *Springer's Progress* (New York, 1977)
—, *Reader's Block* (Normal, 1996)
—, *This Is Not a Novel* (New York, 2001)
Matthews, Harry, *Cigarettes* (New York, 1986)
—, *Twenty Lines a Day* (Normal, 1988)
Mayer, Bernadette, *Bernadette Mayer Reader* (New York, 1992)
McElroy, Joseph, *Smuggler's Bible* (New York, 1966)
Miller, Henry, *Black Spring* (Paris, 1936)
Mohr, Nicholosa, *El Bronx Remembered* (New York, 1975)
—, *In Nueva York* (New York, 1977)
Noel, Urayoan, *Kool Logic / Lógica Kool* (Tempe, 2005)
Notley, Alice, *Grave of Light: New and Selected Poems* (Wesleyan, 2005)
O'Hara, Frank, *Collected Poems* (New York, 1971)
Oppenheimer, Joel, *Names & Local Habitations, Selected Poems* (Highlands, NC, 1988)
Ozick, Cynthia, *Puttermesser Papers* (New York, 1997)
Paley, Grace, *Little Disturbances of Man* (New York, 1959)
—, *Later The Same Day* (New York, 1985)
Perez, Loida Maritza, *Geographies of Home* (New York, 1999)
Pietri, Pedro, *Puerto Rican Obituary* (New York, 1973)
—, *Traffic Violations* (Maplewood, 1983)
Pilcer, Sonia, *Teen Angel* (New York, 1978)

Piñero, Miguel, *La Bodega Sold Dreams* (Houston, 1980)
Prose, Francine, *Household Saints* (New York, 1981)
Pynchon, Thomas, *V* (New York, 1964)
——, *Against the Day* (New York, 2006)
Quinones, Ernesto, *Bodega Dreams* (New York, 2000)
Ramone, Dee Dee, *Chelsea Horror Hotel: A Novel* (New York, 2001)
Reznikoff, Charles *Poems 1937–1975*, vols 1 and 2 (Santa Rosa, 1977)
Rodqriguez, Edward Jr, *Spidertown* (New York, 1993)
Rose, Joel, *Kill The Poor* (New York, 1988)
Rosenthal, Irving, *Sheeper* (New York, 1967)
Ruta, Suzanne, *Stalin in the the Bronx and Other Stories* (New York, 1987)
Sanders, Ed, *Fame and Love in New York* (Berkeley, 1980)
——, *Tales of Beatnik Glory* (New York, 1995)
Schuyler, James, *Collected Poems* (New York, 1993)
Schwartz, Lynne Sharon, *Leaving Brooklyn* (New York, 1989)
Selby, Hubert, *Last Exit To Brooklyn* (New York, 1964)
——, *Requiem For a Dream* (New York, 1978)
Sorrentino, Gilbert, *Steelwork* (New York, 1970)
——, *Imaginative Qualities of Actual Things* (New York, 1971)
——, *Little Casino* (Minneapolis, 2002)
——, *A Moon In Its* Flight (Minneapolis, 2004)
——, *Lunar Follies* (Minneapolis, 2005)
——, *A Strange Commonplace* (Minneapolis, 2006)
Spiegelman, Art, *In The Shadow of No Towers* (New York, 2004)
Stephens, Michael, *The Brooklyn Book of the Dead* (Normal, 1994)
Stosuy, Brandon, ed., *Up is Up, But So is Down: New York's Downtown Literary Scene, 1974–1992*
        (New York, 2006)
Sukenick, Ronald, *Up!* (New York, 1968)
——, *Death of the Novel and Others Stories* (New York, 1969)
——, *Out* (Chicago, 1973)
Tobocman, Seth, *War in the Neighborhood* (New York, 2000)
Waldman, Anne, and Lewis Warsh, *The Angel Hair Anthology* (New York, 2001)
Welish, Marjorie, *The Annotated "Here" and Other Poems* (Minneapolis, 2000)
Whitehead, Colson, *The Intuitionist* (New York, 1998)
Wright, Charles Stephenson, *Absolutely Nothing To Get Alarmed About* (New York, 1973)
Zukofsky, Louis, *A* (Berkeley, 1978)

Acknowledgments

The editors would like to thank *New York Calling*'s writers and photographers, their agents, Georges and Anne Borchardt, and the staff at Reaktion Books, London. This work is dedicated to the people of New York City.

Marshall Berman: For my sweet family—Shellie, Eli and Danny; Didi, Mia & John; my mom, Betty, & her sister Idie, and for all my friends who helped me through all those years.

Brian Berger owes it mostly to coffee and Willie Nelson records, but Meredith Brosnan, Phong Bui, Jason Cohen, David Crowe, Robert Cushing, Christine De La Garza, Nicole Ducharme, Jason Denholm, Merle English, Celia Farber, Billy Gorta, Katti Gray, Libertad Guerra, Moses Gates, Peter Keane, Rose Kim, Adrian Lesher, Michael Krugman, Angel Lopez, Tom Meyer, Urayoán Noel, Geoffrey O'Brien, Ann Peters, Joshua Pulver, Seth Rabinowitz, Andy Schwartz, Rani Singh, Shin-Pei Tsay, Hillary Torrence, Elijah Wald, Jeff Weinstein, Jonathan Williams and Dave Zollo have my gratitude too. Special thanks to Beat Street Records, Brooklyn Public Library, Cuchifrito 2000, Fatima, Karam, Kosher Bagel Hole, Last Exit Books, M. Poggi Wholesale Confectionary, Red Hook, Rockaway Playland, Smith Union Market, Yemen Cafe and my parents. Whatever errors and omissions remain, as Flatt & Scruggs sang, "I'll Take The Blame."

Photo Key

The editors, contributors and publisher wish to express their thanks to the below sources of illustrative material and/or permission to reproduce it.

p. 5 Lower Manhattan from Brooklyn Bridge, c. 2004. To date, only one building has risen from Ground Zero, the 52-story 7 World Trade Center. Photo Rex Features / Yannick Yanoff (550858A). **p. 8** New Yorkers wait to use payphone during the 1977 blackout. Photo Rex Features / Archive Photos (64518B). **p. 10** Lower Manhattan from Brooklyn Bridge, winter 2007. Photo: Brian Berger. **p. 11** Mural by Tats Cru, looking northwest from 207th St subway platform, Inwood, northern Manhattan, winter 2007. Photo: Brian Berger. **p. 12** View east from Empire State Building, c. 2004; high rise waterfront Queens and Brooklyn are a few years off yet. Photo Rex Features (526216AJ). **p. 13** Magic David Pizza, Fort Hamilton Parkway, Brooklyn, summer 2006. Photo: Brian Berger. **p. 15** South Bronx fire, early 1980s. Photo © Martha Cooper. **p. 16** Brooklyn Navy Yard, not-so-dry dry dock; Williamsburg Bridge in distance. Photo: Joseph Anastasio. **p. 18** *Life On Dawson Street* installation by John Ahearn and Rigoberto Torres, c. 1982–83, Dawson St at Longwood Ave, Bronx; winter 2006. Photo: Brian Berger. **p. 21 top** 7th Ave, Times Square, c. 1977. Photo Rex Features / Denis Cameron (223328C). **p. 21 bottom** 1626 Broadway, near 50th St, Manhattan, c. 1980, probably during garbage strike. Photo Rex Features/David McEnery (65692B). **p. 22** E. 138th St & Rider Ave, Mott Haven, Bronx, c. fall 2006. Photo: Brian Berger. **p. 24** Unknown subway car, c. 1977. Photo Rex Features / Frank Monaco (63416A). **p. 27** 'Crack Is Wack' mural by Keith Haring, 1986; 2nd Ave & 128th St, Harlem (photo c. winter 2006). Photo: Brian Berger. **p. 30** Red Grooms and Mimi Gross (with Ruckus Construction Co.), *Ruckus Manhattan: Subway*, 1975. Courtesy Marlborough Gallery, New York/© 2007 Red Grooms/Artists Rights Society (ARS), New York. **p. 33** Vyse Ave & 178th St, June 1980–March 2001. Photos: Camilo José Vergara. **p. 34** Kids running in front of Salsa de Hoy Dance Studio, 46th St, Sunset Park, Brooklyn, summer 2006. Photo: Brian Berger. **p. 36 left** Carlton Ave between Dean & Pacific, Prospect Heights, Brooklyn, winter 2007. Photo: Brian Berger. **p. 36 right** Broadway & 96th St, Upper West Side, winter 2007. Photo: Brian Berger. **p. 37** James Brown memorial event, Apollo Theater, Harlem, December 28, 2006. Photo: Brian Berger. **p. 38** Surf Ave, Coney Island mermaid parade, 2002. Photo Rex Features / Erik C Pendzich (384452l). **p. 39** REVS / HOPE sculpture, 5th Ave near 25th St, Brooklyn, February 2007; stolen shortly after. Photo: Brian Berger. **p. 43 top** Anomie rides the F–train, winter 2006. Photo: Brian Berger. **p. 43 bottom** Homeless person, F-train, winter 2006. Photo: Brian Berger. **p. 45** Two scenes from Walter Hill's 1979 film *The Warriors*. **p. 46** Brook Ave & 138th St, Mott Haven, Bronx, winter 2007. Photo: Brian Berger. **p. 47** Jay St-Borough Hall platform, Brooklyn, fall 2006. Photo: Brian Berger. **p. 48** Take the A-train, Mott Ave, Far Rockaway, Queens, 2004. Photo Rex Features / Sipa Press (501686H). **p. 49** #4 train, unidentified location, July 7, 2005. Photo Rex Features / Sipa Press (535049A). **p. 51 top** #1 train arriving 207th St platform, Inwood, Manhattan, winter 2007. Photo: Brian Berger. **p. 51 bottom** L train on the way to Canarsie, Brownsville, Brooklyn, summer 2006. Photo: Brian Berger. **p. 54** Looking south on Mercer St towards Canal St, SoHo; Pearl Paint in distance, probably late 1980s. Photo Rex Features / Neil Emmerson / Robert Harding (637159A). **p. 55** People With Aids Plaza, looking south on Park Row, lower Manhattan, fall 2006. Photo: Brian Berger. **p. 57** Looking north Wooster St between Prince & Spring St, SoHo, winter 2007. Photo: Brian Berger. **p. 58** Chelsea houses, 10th Ave & 25th St, winter 2006. Photo: Brian Berger. **p. 59** Avenue C, Alphabet City, lower Manhattan, c. 1983. Photo Rex Features / Images (101154B). **p. 61** Looking northeast from Essex & Delancey St, Lower East Side; the building that ate Norfolk St; much loved music club Tonic was next door; winter 2006. Photo: Brian Berger. **p. 63 top** Seafoam St, New Dorp, winter 2006. Photo: Brian Berger. **p. 63 bottom** Arthur Kill, Staten Island, winter 2006. Photo: Brian Berger. **p. 64 top** South Beach boardwalk, Staten Island; Verrazano Narrows behind, winter 2006. Photo: Brian Berger. **p. 64 bottom** Rossville ship graveyard, Staten Island, winter 2006. Photo: Brian Berger. **p. 67 top** Recent construction in Huguenot, Staten Island, winter 2006. Photo: Steve Maluk. **p. 67 bottom** Steep stairwell, New Brighton, Staten Island, winter 2006. Photo: Brian Berger. **p. 68** Jerry's Diner, Bay St, Stapleton, Staten Island, fall 2006. Photo: Brian Berger. **p. 70** Fresh Kills, Staten Island, fall 2006. Photo: Brian Berger. **p. 73** Old Clifton, Staten Island; Grimes Hill rises behind; fall 2006. Photo: Brian Berger. **p. 75** 9/11 Memorial, St George, Staten Island, with, from left to right, Jersey City, lower Manhattan and Brooklyn skylines, winter 2006. Photo: Steve Maluk. **p. 78** Stairwell between Webster & Clay Ave, Bronx, spring 2005. Photo: Brian Berger. **p. 79** Marble Hill, Bronx, looking northeast from Amtrak right of way, fall 2006. Photo: Brian Berger. **p. 80 top** Housing jumble, looking east from Morris Ave & E. 156th St, Bronx, winter 2005. Photo: Brian Berger. **p. 80 bottom** Paradise night club, Courtlandt Ave & E. 163rd St, Morrisania, Bronx, winter 2004. Photo: Brian Berger. **p. 81 left** Poster for Club Tempio, a Jamaican nightclub, Southern Boulevard, Bronx, Christmas morning 2006. Photo: Brian Berger. **p. 81 right** 'Noche de Rock' on Westchester Ave, Bronx, elevated subway above, winter 2007. Photo: Brian Berger. **p. 84** Al Pacino *Scarface* mural, Courtlandt Ave & E. 150th St, Melrose, Bronx. Photo: Brian Berger. **p. 87** Bible Church of Christ, Morris Ave at E. 166th St, Bronx, fall 2004. Photo: Brian Berger. **p. 88** White Plains Road, Bronx, around 225th St, winter 2006; note K&C American West Indian grocery. Photo: Brian Berger. **p. 89** E. 167th St between Sheridan Ave and Grand Concourse, Bronx; African restaurant, barber and pawn shop, a Morrisania trifecta! fall 2005. Photo: Brian Berger. **p. 92** REVS / TRIP. Page 219 of REVS's tunnel diaries, 2004. Photo: Joseph Anastasio. **p. 93** 'That Nigga Oats', looking west from Williamsburg, c. 2006. Photo: Joseph Anastasio. **p. 94** SANE, 2003; circle V is sign of the vandal squad, who deface pieces to antagonize, and perhaps trap writers. Photo: Joseph Anastasio. **p. 98 top** 'Former power plant near 3rd St and 3rd Ave, Brooklyn. Known as 'The Bat Cave' to the squatters that lived here, this building was nothing short of an unapproved graffiti museum. ' Sensationalist media coverage led to the squat's closure in late 2006, around the time of this photo. Photo: Joseph Anastasio. **p. 98 bottom** 'Gen 2 rocks out on a Williamsburg rooftop', 2006. Photo: Joseph Anastasio. **p. 100** 'Photographing various tags in a filthy tunnel under Manhattan', 2002. Photo: Joseph Anastasio. **p. 103** Gretchen Van Dyk and Chris Nelson, 2nd Ave & 6th St, East Village, Night Birds bar behind them. early 1980s. Photo: Robert Sietsema. **p. 104 top** Konopny's Shoe Store business card, c. 1962, courtesy Luc Sante. **p. 104 bottom** Mofungo / Information c. 1981; flyer by Robert Sietsema; courtesy Luc Sante. **p. 105** Strand Bookworkers Strike, 1979, photo courtesy Luc Sante, who also made the flyer. **p. 109** E. 14th St between Avenues B & C, East Village, early 1980s. Photo: Robert Sietsema. **p. 110** The Late Show business card, courtesy Luc Sante. **p. 112** Stinky's, either 5th or 6th St between 1st & 2nd Ave, Manhattan. Starekits band member Angela Jaeger drinks Pabst for victory, early 1980s. Photo: Robert Sietsema. **p. 114** Looking south over Miller Ave from Highland Park, Queens, summer 2006. Photo: Brian Berger. **p. 117** De Bajan Bus Stop, Kingston Ave near Pacific St, Brooklyn, spring 2006. Photo: Brian Berger. **p. 119** Looking north onto Gowanus Canal terminus from Union St drawbridge, Brooklyn, spring 1999. Photo: Brian Berger. **p. 121** Al Salaam, genius Lebanese market and lunch counter, 5th Ave, Brooklyn, winter 2005. Photo: Brian Berger. **p. 122** Ecowas African Market, Coco's Spanish & American Restaurant, Dominican Style beauty salon, New Lots Ave, Brooklyn, summer 2006. Photo: Brian Berger. **p. 123** Poster for Elite Ark, East New York, El & John's Barber Shop mural behind; New Lots Ave, Brooklyn, winter 2007. Photo: Brian Berger. **p. 124** Looking east from backside of Coney Island, Brooklyn, winter 2005. Photo: Brian Berger. **p. 126** 'Jesus is the way, the truth and the life, ' Junius St & Glemmore Ave, East New York, Brooklyn, summer 2006. Photo: Brian Berger. **p. 128** 'The largest and most unbelievable' Kosher condos ever seen, Avenue M, Brooklyn, spring 2006. Photo: Brian Berger. **p. 129** Three Guys From Brooklyn, Fort Hamilton Parkway, Brooklyn, spring 2005. Photo: Brian Berger. **p. 130** 74th Ave, Jackson Heights, Queens, winter 2006. Photo: Brian Berger. **p. 132** Utopia Bagels, Utopia Parkway, Whitestone, Queens, winter 2007. Photo: Brian Berger. **p. 134** Looking west from 47th Road, Queens, Long Island City rising, fall 2006. Photo: Brian Berger. **p. 135** Looking west, under the BQE (Brooklyn-Queens Expressway), across Calvary Cemetery, Laurel Hill, Queens, fall 2006. Photo: Brian Berger. **p. 136 left** The mysterious Jamaica Hunting & Fishing Club, South Jamaica, Queens, fall 2006. Photo: Brian Berger. **p. 136 right** 'Live! Live! Cricket Cricket' 101st Ave near Lefferts Blvd, Richmond Hill, Queens, winter 2007. Photo: Brian Berger. **p. 137 top** Broad Chanel,

Queens, in the rain, fall 2006. Photo: Brian Berger. **p. 137 bottom** Arverne in the fog, the Rockaways, Queens, fall 2006. Photo: Brian Berger. **p. 139** Fishing tackle in four languages; Roosevelt Ave, Woodside, Queens, fall 2006. Photo: Brian Berger. **p. 141** Chrissy's laundry, East River, 1993. Photo © Margaret Morton. **p. 142** Mac's first house, East River, 1992. Photo © Margaret Morton. **p. 143** Cathy and her cats, The Tunnel, 1995. Photo © Margaret Morton. **p. 144** Ramón and Esteban, The Tunnel, 1994. Photo © Margaret Morton. **p. 145** Jimmy, Norfolk and Broome Streets, 1991. Photo © Margaret Morton. **p. 147** BK and his dog, Poochie, East River, 1994. Photo © Margaret Morton. **p. 149** Hudson River cruise, early 1980s. Photo: Robert Sietsema. **p. 153 top** Former site of Macombs Dam Park, Bronx; old Yankee Stadium in distance; fall 2006. Photo: Brian Berger. **p. 153 bottom** 'Salves nuestros parques!' (Save our parks!), Highbridge, Bronx; fall 2006. Photo: Brian Berger. **p. 154** New York City Hall, looking northwest from Park Row, lower Manhattan, spring 2006. Photo: Brian Berger. **p. 157** Mayor Koch and New York Mets manager Davey Johnson celebrate World Series victory, 1986. Photo Rex Features / Sipa Press (129025A). **p. 159** Mayor David Dinkins, left, and Rev. Al Sharpton, at microphones, late '80s. Photo: Clayton Patterson. **p. 161** Robert Lederman's portraits of Mayor Giuliani as Hitler, c. 2000; Lederman was often arrested for his colorful protests against Giuliani-era censorship. Photo: Clayton Patterson. **p. 162** Fernando—or Freddy—Ferrer, campaigns his way to defeat on the #4 train, 2005. Photo Rex Features / Sipa Press (514583A). **p. 164 top** Marc Anthony and his wife, Jennifer Lopez, with Mayor Bloomberg at the Puerto Rican Day Parade; June 11, 2006. Photo Rex Features / Bill Davila (592605D). **p. 164 bottom** Bronx, All-America City, looking north from just over the Willis Ave Bridge, spring 2006. Photo: Brian Berger. **p. 167** NYPD on horseback, looking southeast on 7th Ave, Times Square, winter 2007. Photo: Brian Berger. **p. 168** Cops make an arrest near the Port Authority, c. 1988. Photo Rex Features / Frank Monaco (152481C). **p. 171** Cops investigate mass murder above the Carnegie Deli, Manhattan, May 10, 2001. Photo Rex Features / Erik C Pendzich (336747A). **p. 173** Commissioner Kelly, left, and Mayor Bloomberg, right, in aftermath of another false bomb threat, June 2005. Photo Rex Features / John Chapple (521996A). **p. 174** NYPD guards the New York Stock Exchange, Manhattan, c. 2004. Photo Rex Features (464096A). **p. 176** Random man arrested and hauled off the steps of the public library during the Republican National Convention, August 31, 2004. Photo: Joseph Anastasio. **p. 177** Preparing to march against police brutality in wake of the November 2006 shooting of Sean Bell, 5th Ave near Central Park South, December 16, 2006. Photo: Brian Berger. **p. 181** Caffe Capri, Graham Ave, Williamsburg, Brooklyn, fall 2006. Photo: Brian Berger. **p. 182 top** Graham & Meeker Ave, Williamsburg, Brooklyn, with the Brooklyn-Queens Expressway above, spring 2006. Photo: Brian Berger. **p. 182 bottom** Bedford Ave & N. 12th St, Williamsburg, Brooklyn, May 2006. Photo: Brian Berger. **p. 183** Emily's Pork Store, Graham Ave, Williamsburg, Brooklyn, summer 2006. Photo: Brian Berger. **p. 185 top** Model T Meats, Graham Ave, Williamsburg, Brooklyn, fall 2006. Photo: Brian Berger. **p. 185 bottom** Latino delivery man pedals kosher tricycle, Bedford Ave by the BQE trench, South Williamsburg, Brooklyn. Photo: Brian Berger. **p. 187** Ainslie St looking towards Manhattan Ave, Williamsburg, spring 2006; on the corner, Fortunato Brothers, with the best cappuccino in Brooklyn. Photo: Brian Berger. **p. 189** Homeless man, Leshko's Coffee Shop, a Polish joint at Avenue A & E. 7th St, Manhattan, at corner; mid-1980s. Photo: Clayton Patterson. **p. 191** Spanish Grocery and Hell's Angels' headquarters, 77 E. 3rd St, Manhattan, 1980s. Photo Rex Features / Henryk T. Kaiser (6340680). **p. 192** Probably 9th Ave midtown, late 1980s. Photo Rex Features / Henryk T. Kaiser (634068N). **p. 195** Carmine Galante takes the hard way out, Knickerbocker Ave, Bushwick, July 12, 1979. Photo Rex Features / Robert Kalfus (438713A). **p. 196 top** 'Torched Cars Are My Wildflowers,' E. 174th St near Webster Ave, Bronx, fall 2006. Photo: Brian Berger. **p. 196 bottom** 'Car Stripping Will Bring Police,' Degraw St near 4th Ave, Brooklyn summer 2006. Photo: Brian Berger. **p. 197** Bernhard Goetz surrenders to police, 1985. Photo Rex Features / Globe Photos Inc. (119983A). **p. 199** Aftermath of the Happyland Social Club arson, Southern Blvd near E. Tremont Ave, Bronx, 1990. Photo Rex Features / Sipa Press (169660A). **p. 201** Victor Julio Torres RIP, Brownsville, Brooklyn, fall 2006. Photo: Brian Berger. **p. 202** September 11, 2001. Photo Rex Features / Sipa Press (342393D). **p. 205** Pacific St between Albany & Ralph Ave, Brooklyn; renamed Michael Griffith St in 1999 as a memorial. Photo: Brian Berger. **p. 208** Tawana Brawley and Al Sharpton, 1987. Photo Rex Features / Sipa Press (150571A). **p. 209** Yusef Hawkins lies wounded on a Bensonhurst street, Brooklyn, August 29, 1989. Photo Rex Features / Sipa Press (162522A). **p. 211** 'American Dream,' memorial to Amadou Diallo, Wheeler Ave, Soundview, Bronx, fall 2006. Note Lucumi witchcraft store next door. Photo: Brian Berger. **p. 212** Sean Bell memorial, Liverpool St near 94th St, South Jamaica, Queens, November 29, 2006. Photo: Brian Berger. **p. 216** Tracy Camilla Johns and Spike Lee in Lee's 1986 film *She's Gotta Have It*. Photo Rex Features / c. Island/Everett (502280B). **p. 218** West Indian Day parade, Crown Heights, Brooklyn, early 1980s. Photo: Robert Sietsema. **p. 219** Bill Nunn and Spike Lee in Lee's 1989 film *Do The Right Thing*. **p. 220**

Michael Stewart protest flyer, courtesy Luc Sante; Stewart was arrested September 15, 1983 and died thirteen days later. **p. 221** Hervey Keitel in Spike Lee's 1995 film *Clockers*. **p. 222** Vern's Happiness Lounge and The Truth, St John's Place, Bed-Stuy, Brooklyn. Photo: Brian Berger. **p. 224 top** The Village Vanguard, 7th Ave, Greenwich Village, c. 1976. Photo: Tom Marcello. **p. 224 bottom** X-Ray Spex at CBGB, back when The Bowery was still The Bowery, c. 1980. Photo: Robert Sietsema. **p. 225** Athena the cat, c. 1982, courtesy Phil Dray. **p. 227** Salvation Army Band, 20 E. 14th St, Greenwich Village, c. 1980. Photo: Robert Sietsema. **p. 229** Northside Williamsburg, the under construction— and much disputed—'finger building' awaiting court decisions as to how high it can rise, winter 2007. Photo: Brian Berger. **p. 232** Allen Ginsberg and Harry Smith in Allen's kitchen, E. 12th St, Manhattan, 1984. Photo: Brian Graham. **p. 234** Tompkins Square Park protests, Lower East Side, c. 1988. Photo: Clayton Patterson. **p. 236** St Mark's Place, 2nd & 3rd Ave, Lower East Side, early 1980s. Photo: Robert Sietsema. **p. 238** Puerto Rican mural on the Lower East Side, early 1980s. Photo Rex Features / Henryk T. Kaiser (634068J). **p. 239** Mexican religious parade, Myrtle Ave, Clinton Hill, Brooklyn, fall 2006. Photo: Brian Berger. **p. 243** Two scenes from William Friedkin's 1971 film *The French Connection*, starring Gene Hackman as Popeye Doyle and Roy Scheider as Buddy Russo. **p. 245** Fire-eater in Washington Square Park, Judson Church behind, mid-1980s. Photo Rex Features / Henryk T. Kaiser (634068S). **p. 247** Unidentified subway train, c. 1985. Photo Rex Features / Sipa Press (113327H). **p. 248** Avenue D & E. 7th St, Lower East Side, mid-1980s. Photo Rex Features / C. Lewerentz (101154A). **p. 250** Tantalizingly familiar yet unidentified street, probably West Harlem, c. 1982. (Surely *someone* remembers Sol's Record World and Sunny Wigs?) (92804B). **p. 254** Studio 54, Manhattan, late 70s/early 80s. Photo Rex Features (87710B). **p. 256** Bum Bum Bar, Roosevelt Avenue, Woodside, Queens, fall 2006. Photo: Brian Berger. **p. 258** Christopher St video store, Greenwich Village, winter 2007. Photo: Brian Berger. **p. 259** Marching for gay pride and against Anita Bryant, near Madison Square Park, Manhattan, c. 1980. Photo: Robert Sietsema. **p. 260** Lesbian marchers, gay pride parade, 1995. Photo Rex Features / Sipa Press (245598A). **p. 263** David Wojnarowicz memorial, 1992. Photo: Clayton Patterson. **p. 264** Sheridan Park, Christopher St, Greenwich Village; George Segal's 1980 sculpture, *Gay Liberation*, commemorates the1969 Stonewall riots; following years of controversy, it was finally installed in 1992 (photo winter 2007). Photo: Brian Berger. **p. 267** Times Square, probably 42nd St, c. 1983. Photo Rex Features / Robin Anderson (101617A). **p. 268** Crowds outside Studio 54, 254 W. 54th St, Manhattan, late 1970s. Photo Rex Features / Images (279080V). **p. 269** 'New York When We Could Still Afford Taxis', early-to-mid-1990s. Photo: Leslie Lyons. **p. 271** Peepland, 7th Avenue between 48th & 49th St, midtown Manhattan. Photo Rex Features / Rex USA Ltd (273507D). **p. 273** The good the bad and the ugly in old New York graffiti, on an unidentified subway station, c. 1985. Photo Rex Features / Sipa Press (113327E). **p. 275** Beer in a bag outside CBGB, The Bowery, almost certainly a Sunday hardcore matinee, late 1980s. Photo Rex Features / Henryk T. Kaiser (634068V). **p. 276** Sin City, Park Ave near E. 138th St, Mott Haven, Bronx, fall 2006. Photo: Brian Berger. **p. 278** Betty Cuningham Gallery, SoHo, Manhattan, 1976. Photo: Gordon Moore, courtesy Betty Cuningham Gallery. **p. 282** The Gracie Mansions Gallery, Upper East Side, 1982. **p. 283** Jean-Michael Basquiat in Edo Bertoglia's 1981 film *Downtown 81*. Photo Rex Features / c. Zeitgeist/Everett (640509A). **p. 284** 535 W. 22nd St between 10th & 11th Ave, Chelsea, winter 2007; art and condos, condos and art, who can choose? Photo: Brian Berger. **p. 285 top** Pierogi 2000, 167 N. 9th St, Williamsburg, Brooklyn, late 1990s. Photo courtesy Pierogi Brooklyn. **p. 285 bottom** Protest Space, gallery, 'America For Sale' exhibit, 511 W. 20th St, Chelsea, winter 2006. Photo: Brian Berger. **p. 288** Sonny Stitt, 52nd St Jazz Fair, midtown Manhattan, 1976. Photo: Tom Marcello. **p. 290** Charles Mingus at an outdoor concert, 1974. Photo: Tom Marcello. **p. 291** William Parker (bass) and Rashid Bakr (drums), Studio Rivbea, lower Manhattan, c. 1977. Photo: Tom Marcello. **p. 294** Anthony Braxton, Rochester, NY, c. 1979. Photo: Tom Marcello. **p. 295 top** Jemeel Moondoc Quintet album *Nostalgia In Times Square* (Soul Note, 1986). Courtesy of Brian Berger. **p. 295 bottom** Zoot Sims (tenor, standing) and Bob Cranshaw (electric bass, seated), 52nd St Jazz Festival, Chelsea, 1976. Photo: Tom Marcello. **p. 296** EZ's Woodshed, 7th Avenue between 131st & 132nd St, Harlem, winter 2006. Photo: Brian Berger. **p. 298** CBGB interior, late 1970s – Ramones t-shirts and leather jackets didn't get you in free. Photo: Robert Sietsema. **p. 299** New York Dolls c. 1974: Johnny Thunders in stripes, David Johansen 'Immaculate Conception' t-shirt; from Bob Gruen and Nadya Beck's *All Dolled Up* (2006). **p. 300** Lydia Lunch c. 1979. Photo Rex Features / Ray Stevenson (565188Y). **p. 301 top** Chain Gang's 1978 single 'My Fly' b / w 'Cannibal Him' (Kapitalist Records). **p. 301 bottom** A Tier 3 flyer from 1980, courtesty Luc Sante. **p. 302** James White and the Blacks (James Chance, saxophone; Pat Place, guitar; Anya Phillips vocals, keyboard player Kristian Hoffman on the floor); venue unknown, early 1980s. Photo: Robert Sietsema. **p. 304** Once again, Elisa Ambrogio of Magik Markers resurrects rock for those few who deserve it: East River Bandshell,

August 19, 2006. Photo: Toby Carroll. **p. 309** Christie's, Rockefeller Plaza. Photo courtesy Christies, New York. **p. 310** David Hockney and Andy Warhol c. 1981. Photo Rex Features / Richard Young (83946A). **p. 312** Reflections on the art business, and the business of art, Madison Avenue, winter 2007. Photo: Brian Berger. **p. 315** Feigen Contemporary gallery, 535 W. 20th St, winter 2006. Photo: Brian Berger. **p. 317** Larry Gagosian and Damien Hirst, February 2007. Photo Rex Features / Sipa Press (646962H). **p. 320** Smokers outside 1411 Broadway, Manhattan, 2007. Photo: Dan Young. **p. 321 top** No Smoking in bars, 2003. Photo Rex Features / Dan Callister (450365F). **p. 321 bottom** 41st St & Broadway, Manhattan, 2006. Photo: Dan Young. **p. 322** Coffee cups, unidentified Manhattan deli, 2007. Photo: Dan Young. **p. 323** E. 187th St & Hughes Ave, Belmont, Bronx, winter 2007. Photo: Brian Berger. **p. 324** Lincoln Bakery and coffee shop, 'desayuno para' (breakfast to go), Morris Ave between 148th & 149th St, Mott Haven, Bronx, fall 2006. Photo: Brian Berger. **p. 325** Hoy Wong, 90 year old bartender at the Algonquin Hotel, midtown, c. 2006. Photo Rex Features / David Howells (622444C). **p. 326** Cigar smoker outside Farrell's, Windsor Terrace, Brooklyn, winter 2007. Photo: Brian Berger. **p. 327** Mars Bar, 2nd Avenue & E. 1st St, East Village, fall 2006. Photo: Brian Berger. **p. 328** Bryant Park, Fashion Week, September 2004. Photo Rex Features / Sipa Press (496762D). **p. 331** The downtown Strand Book Store, Fulton St, lower Manhattan, winter 2007. Photo: Brian Berger. **p. 335 top** Russian bookstore, Coney Island Ave, Brighton Beach, Brooklyn, winter 2007. Photo: Brian Berger. **p. 335 bottom** Spanish bookstore, 207th St, Inwood, northern Manhattan, winter 2007. Photo: Brian Berger. **p. 337** Looking south on 7th Ave between 2nd & 3rd St, Park Slope, Brooklyn, winter 2007. Photo: Brian Berger. **p. 342** Cheap Chinese eats on 8th Ave, Sunset Park, Brooklyn, summer 2006; the congee, we recall, was outstanding. Photo: Brian Berger. **p. 343** After the snow, East Broadway, Manhattan, winter 2007. Photo: Brian Berger. **p. 344** Mott St, Little Italy, lower Manhattan, c. 1977. Photo Rex Features / FM (68918A). **p. 345** Dominic DiFara making pizza *his* way, DiFara's, Ave J & E. 13th St, Midwood, Brooklyn, summer 2006. Photo: Brian Berger. **p. 346** Joe's of Avenue U, Gravesend, Brooklyn, summer 2005. Photo: Brian Berger. **p. 347** West African grocery; note 'We acept WIC and foods stamp' at bottom sign. Off Fulton St, Bed-Stuy, Brooklyn, summer 2006. Photo: Brian Berger. **p. 348 top** Pique y Pase, Lefferts Boulevard, Richmond Hill, Queens, fall 2006. Photo: Brian Berger. **p. 348 bottom** La Casa de Los Tacos, 1st Ave & E. 117th St, East Harlem, winter 2007. Photo: Brian Berger. **p. 349** Jewish bakery, Coney Island Ave, Midwood, Brooklyn, winter 2006. Photo: Brian Berger.